The Storytime Handbook

The Storytime Handbook

A Full Year
of Themed Programs,
with Crafts and Snacks

NINA SCHATZKAMER MILLER

For Shae,
I miss our days at Borders, but writing this book brought it all back for me. There is so much joy for us in the world of books and I'm so glad we've kept in contact. I hope you enjoy the book, maybe make some of the snacks like I used to bring to Borders for storytime!

Fondly,
Nina

McFarland & Company, Inc., Publishers
Jefferson, North Carolina

All photographs are by the author

Library of Congress Cataloguing-in-Publication Data

Miller, Nina Schatzkamer, 1956–
The storytime handbook : a full year of themed programs,
with crafts and snacks / Nina Schatzkamer Miller.
p.   cm.
Includes bibliographical references and index.

ISBN 978-0-7864-6668-9

softcover : acid free paper ∞

1. Children's libraries—Activity programs—United States.
2. Storytelling—United States.   I. Title.
Z718.3.M55 2014   027.62'51—dc23   2013044233

British Library cataloguing data are available

On the cover: Reading to students (Purestock/Thinkstock);
background © iStockphoto/Thinkstock

Manufactured in the United States of America

McFarland & Company, Inc., Publishers
Box 611, Jefferson, North Carolina 28640
www.mcfarlandpub.com

"The more that you read, the more things you will know.
The more that you learn, the more places you'll go."
— Dr. Seuss, from *I Can Read with My Eyes Shut*

Dedication and Acknowledgments

This book is dedicated first and foremost to my parents Mary Bray and William Schatzkamer, both teachers who spent their lives enriching the lives of those they taught. To my sons Alexander, Andrew and Austin, on whom I experimented with my earliest storytelling, crafting and music and without whose love and patience I would not be the mother I am proud to be. To my husband Steve, whose support has allowed my creative side to flourish throughout our many years together. To my siblings Helena Bunnow, Kyriena Schatzkamer, Mark Schatzkamer and Laura Schatzkamer: I have seen each of you accomplish so much in such varied fields and your successes always inspire me to try harder. To James Schwentker and Thom Schaffner at Borders, your belief in me and the gift of freedom to explore storytime in my own way allowed me to have a wonderful work experience and ultimately to find a whole new career. Helen Miller, I hope you are proud of me, since you were an early inspiration. Your interest and support, Bernard Miller, meant a lot to me. Helen Lach, you kept pushing me to finish. Without your help at the end, Sheila Stegeman, I would never have gotten all the craft and snacks made and photographed. Tammy Goodsell, you are a great writer and you inspire me in so many different ways, mostly by getting so much done and by always being there for me, no matter what the issue. And to the children and parents with whom I have had the privilege of sharing my storytime, thank you for providing me with the inspiration to share my storytime with the world. You are the ones who made it all happen and make all the effort worthwhile.

Table of Contents

Preface

And a little child shall lead them

In the midst of writing this book, I found out that the Borders bookstore where I worked was closing. My store had wonderful employees who were close like family, and we were very upset when customers descended on us like locusts, tearing our store apart in search of bargains. We couldn't keep up with the mess. Even more painful was that the days we loved were over. No more taking the time to help someone find a book, offer a suggestion or, what I loved most, my weekly children's storytime. I had a big crowd at storytime the last week. After I announced it was the last one, the parents thanked me, then stood and applauded. My affection for those families made me even more determined to make this book the best it could be. A particular experience I had in my last week of working there inspired me further.

One day I discovered a young girl in the children's area — my beloved area of the store — carefully going through the children's chapter books and sorting them, alphabetizing them, trying to put them back in order. I watched her for a few minutes, not sure what she was doing at first. But when it was clear, I was truly touched. I had given up on that area and put the books on the shelves in any order, just to have them off the floor. I went to get some leftover giveaway books and a store employee lanyard for her. When I returned, the young girl's mother was sitting on the floor waiting patiently as her daughter continued to work. I told her how deeply moved I was by her efforts, and presented her with my small tokens. The girl put on the lanyard and continued working, eventually finishing that area and moving on to another.

I felt like I had witnessed a small miracle. I am not a particularly religious person, but I thought of the phrase "and a little child shall lead them." That little girl inspired me to take more care with the books I needed to shelve. From that moment on, whenever I was in the children's area I would remember her and smile.

For weeks after that, many of my storytime regulars visited me on what would have been our storytime day. When I realized that storytime was the number one thing I would miss, I found another location where I could offer it. Once again I could be Miss Nina, the storytime lady, and find myself surrounded by the bright and smiling faces of my little children.

I hope I will always remember the little girl who reminded me that small miracles can happen when you need them most. When preparing for my weekly storytime I searched for resources for books to read, games to play, poems to read, songs to sing, crafts to make and snacks to eat. There were many books that helped with one or maybe two of the areas, but none that had everything that I wanted to include in my storytime. So here you have my book, which I felt was needed because there must be others who would like to offer a more complete storytime experience. This book will be useful to librarians, teachers, bookstore storytellers and parents. I hope the ideas it offers will help make storytime a real event, whether in the library, at school, in the bookstore, or at home or at a party.

Introduction

Why This Book?

I have searched for several years for a complete storytime guide and could not find one. There were books about crafts, games, books to read ... but not one book in which all things essential to a complete storytime experience for preschoolers could be found.

The Audience for This Book

This book is for anyone who wants to provide a complete storytime experience for children. It can be done for your own child at home, for a group of children at the library, in a preschool, at a bookstore or for a party.

How This Book Is Organized

This book is organized into storytime themes by month and week, with an entire year's worth of themes plus holidays. Care has been taken to space out the snacks, crafts and games so that there is not immediate repetition but some attention to using similar craft or snack parts fairly close together for budgeting, purchasing and ease of preparation.

There is a template at the back of the book to help you plan each storytime. The template is designed to follow these steps:

- Begin with group gathering
- Sing the arrival time song, "The More We Get Together"
- Make circle introductions and assemble the felt board character "Friend"
- Introduce the theme
- Read longest book (book 1)
- Read a short or nonfiction book about the theme (book 2)
- Read medium length storybook (book 3)
- Sing song or do fingerplay
- Play a game
- Read a poem or a short book (book 4)

- Play a game
- Read a short storybook (book 5)
- Make craft (play theme-related song while assembling)
- Make snack
- Read another book (book 6) while children are eating their snack
- Close storytime

What You Can Expect

You can use the ideas in this book and know that you will provide a great learning experience for the children for whom you provide storytime. Or you can pick and choose from the ideas to suit your own taste and materials and still provide a wonderful time for those children. Choose a game, craft and snack for each theme that best suits your group, and remember there are alternatives for each theme that might be a better fit. With the various alternatives provided, the activities in this book can be used for more than the year it outlines — at least four years or more.

We want to provide children an opportunity to interact with others and their environment. We want them to experience art, music, literature, movement and food in an hour's time, in a noncompetitive setting. When the child has a parent present, they can also benefit from the exposure to these areas in order to further the child's home learning experience.

For convenience, throughout the book I refer to the person who accompanies the child at storytime as the parent, although it might in fact be a grandparent or other relative, nanny or babysitter. If these individuals are present, have them sit around the edges of the circle of children, and be sure to find creative ways to involve them so that they enjoy storytime too.

The Components of Storytime

The storytime is planned for approximately one hour of time, divided into circle time, discussion of the theme, music, literature, movement, craft and snack. All of the child's senses are stimulated in the space of just one hour.

Introduction

Choose a place that's a little bit separate from the action if you're in a library or bookstore. You'll need some open space for the games, but it's also nice to have some kind of containment, such as bookshelves or other furniture to act as boundaries to keep the children in the designated area. You can use a large vinyl felt-backed tablecloth on the floor and have the children sit around it with their parents (if present) behind them. Feel free to sit on a low stool at one end of the cloth, with a CD player to one side, and a chair with the song poster taped to it to the other side. Place the books on the floor next to you in the order you plan to read them. If the craft and snack supplies are placed on the same cloth, be sure to cover them with another cloth so that they don't distract the children. Have the game supplies in place in other parts of the storytime area, ready for when it's game time.

Set the scene for the theme with simple decorations placed around the area related to the theme of that week. Also wear something related to the theme, like a hat, headband, clothing, or jewelry. Point out to the children as they arrive what you're wearing so they will know the day's theme. These introductions give the group time to gather so that everyone will be present and seated when it's time to begin.

Group Gathering

Show any parents where the storytime calendar is kept, where you display upcoming events, book lists and storytime books. Once it's storytime and everyone is seated, show any extra materials that might relate to that week's storytime, like books for adults or older children, CDs, DVDs, educational toys, stuffed animals or gifts.

Circle Time

This is the time to sing the group arrival song. Sing the same song every week so that the children and parents learn the words and recognize that this is the beginning of storytime. One of my favorites is the song "The More We Get Together":

> The more we get together, together, together
> The more we get together, the happier we'll be.
> For your friends are my friends,
> and my friends are your friends
> The more we get together, the happier we'll be.

Next, do name introductions, and if you've created a felt board character as part of your welcome, the children can help you assemble it. I call my felt board character "Friend." He (or she) is a large piece of cardboard covered with felt and cut out body parts made from familiar shapes. A circle for the head, stars for the eyes, a circle for the nose, a semicircle for the mouth, hearts for the ears, small triangles for the hair. A square for the torso, rectangles for the arms and legs, mitten shapes for hands, and rectangles rounded on one end for feet. Some children might want to help assemble Friend, but some may choose to watch. During this time there is minimal time required for the children to actively listen.

Felt pieces of Friend.

Circle Introductions

Introduce yourself first and then go around the circle. Say "I am _____," then point to the child on your left and say "This is my good friend__" and ask the child to say his/her name (or the parent may say it if the child is shy) and then repeat the child's name, both to make sure that all can hear it and also to help you remember the name. Keep going around the circle for introductions. If everyone there has been there before, you might ask the children to say your name instead of introducing yourself.

Assemble Friend

After the introductions, tell the children that you'd like to introduce them to a special friend, but "Friend" is a little shy and we'll all have to help him come to meet us. Have the cardboard felt-covered board next to you with the felt cut out pieces and invite each child to come up to place a piece of Friend on the board. Once Friend is complete, introduce the day's storytime theme.

Introduction to Theme

Give a short explanation of the week's theme, using pictures or props or the other items you are wearing or brought in to illustrate if helpful. Ask questions and allow the children to talk.

Literature

When you choose your books, make sure

Friend fully assembled.

that the material is appropriate to your audience and that the artwork is visually interesting. Be sure to structure your time so that reading and activities are intermingled, in order to minimize sitting still for long periods of time. Preschoolers need some practice to learn to sit still, but getting up to move around at intervals will help increase their ability to pay attention while seated. Select at least six books to bring to story time each week. Each theme has a list of suggested books that provides the book title, author's name, number of pages, year published, publisher and a brief description. Choose carefully and read your selections all the way through before storytime to be sure they're appropriate for your audience. Look for anything that you might need to check for pronunciation or definition. Not all children's books are simple with small words. Read them carefully in advance so that when you are reading to the children, you can hold the book out to your side and still be able to look up and around at the children while you're reading. Say the title and author of the book before you read it. This will help the children (or any parents present) remember the book or the author when they are out looking for books to read on their own.

Reading the books is my favorite part of storytime. I become an actress. The lights in the theater have dimmed, I've put on my costume and make up and as the curtain rises I am on stage, ready to give my best performance for the audience. I speak loudly and clearly, and enunciate every word. My facial expressions are broad and exaggerated so that the people in the last row can see my emotion. I give voice and life to the characters in the book as though I am playing those characters on stage. This is an important event. You might be the first person to read to that child. You might be the only person to read to that child that week.

Make your performance memorable. You're more than an entertainer; you are also an educator. You can spark children's interest in books and bring the world to them, if only for an hour each week. Change your tone when reading dialogue and try to talk in the way the characters might actually talk to each other. Practice in front of a mirror. Practice in front of an audience. If you have children of your own, you've probably enjoyed reading to them. Your nieces and nephews, grandchildren, neighbors ... try out your reading on them before you meet your storytime audience. And when you step on that stage, don't be nervous. Children are the most forgiving audience. Even if you are a little bit shy, remember that children will be delighted by the effort that you put into bringing storytime to them. This audience wants to love you. And with some effort on your part, they will. If you miss a word, keep going unless it changes the meaning of the story. If you need to make a correction, do it quickly and move on. The less fuss made about it the better. Watch some children's television with live actors to see how they talk to their audience. Listen to some audio books to get an idea of how professionals sound when reading stories. Record yourself to know how you sound. When you practice on your family, ask for feedback.

While reading, try to look out and make eye contact with each child at some point in the book without losing your place. If the children seem restless, pause and ask a question or two to reengage them. Sit close to your audience but make sure everyone can see the book as you hold it. Read the longest of your books first while the children are fresh. Read something short next, perhaps a nonfiction book that has photographs. If you still have their complete attention, read one more book before taking a break to do something else.

Always have more books than you plan to read, and don't worry if you don't get through them all. Provide a list of the book titles and authors to the children or their parents at the end of storytime. You don't have to include only the books you read that day, although you might want to highlight those, but feel free to use all the books in the lists provided in this book and add any others you have found on your own that go with the theme. Remember that new books come out every day. Libraries and bookstores will always have the tried and true classics, and libraries might have more of the older books on hand, but bookstores are great places to look to see what's new and fresh.

Music

Each week find either a short song that goes with the theme or make something up that goes to the tune of a popular children's song, like "Twinkle, Twinkle, Little Star" or "Frère Jacques." Print the lyrics to the song on the computer, using a graphics program like Print Shop or Print Artist, so that you can enlarge it to several sheets, poster-sized, that you tape together. Find some clip art to illustrate and print along with the lyrics. At storytime post this next to you where everyone can see it and help you sing. Never worry about your voice. Sing loudly and proudly and the children will be happy to hear it and any parents present will be supportive of your efforts. If you don't have a computer on which to print the lyrics, simply get a big marker and hand write your lyrics on poster board.

Movement

Small children can only sit still for so long. You've had them sitting while the group gathered, while you sang your welcome song, read one or two books and sang a song that goes with your theme. That's probably taken about fifteen minutes. It's time to get up and move around a bit. Try to have your first game be an active game where no one has to wait for a turn. Games should be fun. They shouldn't be competitive, and they should never involve exclusion. It's okay to sometimes have games that involve taking turns, but for the most part avoid activities here where the children have to wait.

Try to have a space that's clear of obstacles for movement games. Keep games short, about five minutes or less. Games should be simple and not involve much equipment. Goals for games should be to provide some movement in order to contrast with the sitting required for other parts of storytime but also something to learn that goes along with the theme. Some games need props but many do not. Some involve music. The most important feature of the game is to make it fun.

Crafts

Choose a craft that goes with the theme in some way. It could come from one of the books that you're reading or just the general theme. Make a sample of the craft ahead of time and do as much advance preparation of the materials as possible so that only a minimum amount of time is needed for assembly during storytime. The crafts in this book have been designed to be mostly assembled by the children with a little guidance and assistance.

Put the craft materials together in individual groupings so that it's easier to hand them out at storytime. If you have a separate craft area, you could put the materials out in advance. It's fun to do the crafts on the floor on a felt backed tablecloth with the children. Buy these cloths whenever you see them on sale so that you have a supply of them. Have a supply of basic craft materials, such as construction paper in different colors, glue sticks, craft sticks, large and small white paper plates, paper lunch bags in different colors, poster board, chenille stems, google eyes, fiberfill, colored tissue paper, white glue, cotton swabs, straws, sheet foam and yarn. Some tools you will use often will be children's scissors, a hole punch, and craft punches of varying sizes of circles, along with some other craft punch shapes, such as ovals and squares. These can be bought gradually, often with a coupon or when on sale. Having the craft punches will save you a lot of time rather than having to cut out many individual shapes. Save cardboard boxes, paper towel and toilet paper rolls, as well as quart sized plastic milk bottles. Some of these are used for crafts and some for games. Keep the supplies in labeled boxes so that you can easily find what you need each week. Buy supplies that will be used frequently, like glue sticks, paper plates and construction paper, whenever you see them on sale. While you're out in craft, discount, grocery or art stores always be looking for things that might be used in crafts or snacks.

In this book, I have tried to organize the crafts for the themes so that you might use some of the same materials again within a few storytimes. Each craft will be different, but this helps save you time while organizing and also makes it more economical if you have a limited budget. Play background music while the children are putting together the craft. I have suggested a song that goes with each theme. Buy these songs as Mp3 downloads on Amazon.com or iTunes for about a dollar each, then save them to iTunes. From there create a playlist for each month's music, whatever you'll need for games and craft and snack time, and then burn it onto a disk or create a playlist on your Mp3 player. Or you could buy children's music CDs and once you have a collection play songs from those disks. I have a Lego block CD player that the children love to look at, and I can put a song on repeat if I choose so that it plays until I turn it off.

Snack

Choose a snack that goes with the theme or a book in some way. View storytime snack as a treat, and since most children attend no more than once per week, most of the parents agree that cookies and cupcakes are an acceptable snack. If you bake your own cupcakes and cookies from mixes that you buy on sale at discount stores, stocking up when you find them, you can offer a snack on a limited budget. Use canned icing for ease. Invest in a set of gel colors so that you can make white icing into any color you need. Buy food markers. Stock up on the candies that are used for decorations, and any other items that you might need in the next month or two, such as marshmallows, pretzel sticks, cereals and crackers.

Try to have four different treat types each month, like a cupcake, a cookie, a fruit and vegetable or a pudding. Plan the treats like the crafts, with some ingredients repeated within a short time in case you have leftovers or can benefit from buying in bulk, yet keep the actual snack that's made different. Most of the snacks are meant to also be assembled by the children, similar to the craft. Children often take more interest in trying an unfamiliar food if they also take part in creating it, and this is especially helpful with fruits and vegetables. Don't assemble the sample snack ahead of time, but instead put it together right before you hand out the snack materials. Some snacks involve more assembly than others, and on the holidays you might present a treat that you made yourself, like a Christmas tree cake, or an Easter Bunny cake. Instructions for baking and assembling special cakes like these are easily found on the Internet. Once you distribute the snack ingredients, again play the song that you recorded for that week's theme while the children assemble their snacks. Once they're actually eating, stop the music and read one final book.

Closing Storytime

When you've finished the last book and the children have finished their snacks, have them help you clean up. Have a trash bag ready and bins in which to place leftover craft supplies. Start to clean up the snack trash with the trash bag. Encourage the children to return craft materials to their bins.

Offer and distribute the list of books with this week's theme for additional reading and exploration. Announce the theme for next week's storytime and any other upcoming events you might be planning. Have a monthly calendar to hand out that you've printed on your computer (Print Shop is useful for this), showing the month's dates, times and themes. Post this calendar every week on a chalk or dry erase board, updating it to start with the current week and go for the next four. Show everyone where you keep your monthly calendar, book lists and the display area for your storytime theme.

Thank everyone for coming. If you're in a bookstore, ask the manager ahead of time if you can offer a small discount that day. Many bookstores are very happy to offer a discount to storytime families. When I worked at Borders, we offered 10 percent off the entire purchase, just that day's one-time purchase, and the purchases that the families made, encouraged by that discount, helped to defray the store's craft and snack expenses. If you're in a library, encourage everyone to check out a book (perhaps from your list, so you want to make sure some of those are available prior to storytime) to take home.

Final Thoughts

When you are planning storytime think of objectives — what do you want the children to learn? What skill? Afterwards think about how it went. What worked well? What did the children really like? How can you repeat that? What didn't work that you won't repeat or could change? Listen to your audience — is there a theme or a particular book that they want you to read? Try to incorporate it into a storytime. Think things through, imagine how long each part will take. Have both quiet and active games. Start quiet, get active, then settle down with quiet again.

It takes some time to prepare for a weekly storytime. A template at the end of the book will help you plan for each session. You can choose to do all of the things that I include in each storytime theme or pick what you like or what suits your group. You might have only a half hour for storytime. In a half hour you could still include reading, music, a game, craft and snack. You might have different materials available to you. Improvise! Many crafts can use substitutes and many snacks can be made a multitude of ways. Don't be dismayed if it seems like a lot of work. If you sit in front of the television one evening with your craft materials you can get them ready pretty effortlessly. I usually prepare for more children than I expect, but in truth I never know how many will be there from week to week. If you are lucky enough to be in a setting where you can have the families sign up in advance for storytime, it will help you to know how many children to plan for. I did storytime and children's events at a Borders bookstore for several years, and while I had a core group of regulars, there were anywhere from five to 25 children on any given week.

I always felt most comfortable when I was well prepared. Have an extra activity or book in case there's time to fill. Keep things short, keep them moving, keep them simple. Write down your plan. You need materials to set the scene, the felt Friend, song poster, CD player and CD, books, craft supplies, cloth, snack supplies, game supplies, trash bags. And most important of all, a great attitude because you know that you are doing something wonderful with these children and you are all going to have fun!

January

Snow

Advance planning: To plan for this storytime, find a theme-related song to play during craft and snack times, like "Let It Snow," by Frank Sinatra. You will also want to select a poem, such as "Snowball," by Shel Silverstein (found at www.poemhunter.com, or in Silverstein's *Falling Up*), along with the books you plan to read. Decorate your space with polyester fiberfill snowballs, sheets of fiberfill quilt batting to look like snow, a snow shovel, winter hats, mittens and boots.

Introduction to the theme: What is snow? It's a special kind of precipitation — do you know what that means? Precipitation is when any kind of water or watery product falls from the sky. Snow is a frozen kind of precipitation made of ice crystals. For snow to fall the air has to be cold and there has to be moisture or water in the air. There have to be clouds to hold that moisture or water. What happens to the snow when it reaches the ground? If it's cold enough, it'll stay on the ground until it gets warmer and melts. Have you ever played in the snow? Made a snowball? Or a snowman? Today we'll read about snow and snowmen, play a snow game, make a snowman craft and eat a snowman snack.

Song: "Frosty the Snowman." Find the lyrics at www.metrolyrics.org, or sing "I'm a Little Snowman," to the tune of "I'm a Little Teapot":

> I'm a little snowman
> Short and fat.
> Here is my broom (pretend to hold broom handle)
> and here is my hat (touch head)
> When it's cold and icy,
> I will stay.
> When it's hot,
> I will melt away (shrink down to the floor).

Game: Inside snowball fight

Materials needed: White tissue paper, cut or torn in half, tables. At storytime: Have the children scrunch up pieces of white tissue paper to make snowballs. Make two forts by laying tables on their sides and throw snowballs back and forth.

Alternative Games

Snowball twirl. Have each child hold a cut snowflake (or the snowflake they make as their craft). They should twirl around with it and recite the poem below. At the end of the poem, they will drop their snowflakes as they also fall to the ground.

> Snowflakes whirling all around,
> all around, all around
> Snowflakes whirling all around
> Until they cover all the ground

Snowball relay race. Materials needed: cotton balls, tissue paper balls or Styrofoam balls. Place a bucket for each team about 20 feet away. Pile the same number of snowballs on the floor in front of each team. Each child walks with a snowball, drops it in the bucket and walks back. Then the next child in line takes a turn and so on until all the snowballs are in the bucket and everyone has carried a snowball.

Snowball pass. Pass around a snowball — either a real one or a pretend one made of rolled up tissue paper or styrofoam.

Pass the snowflake. Make a paper snowflake. Pass it around the circle of children and ask each child to say something about snow, like what they like to do in it, whether it's cold or hot, wet or dry, if they think it looks pretty, or simply make up a sentence that includes the word snow.

Craft: Paper plate snowman

Materials needed: Large paper plates, small paper plates, black, orange, red, brown construction paper, glue sticks, ribbon, stapler, google eyes or crayons. Advance preparation: Cut hats, mittens, arms, buttons and nose out of construction paper. Cut 24-inch lengths of ribbon. Staple a large plate to a small plate. At storytime: Have the children glue the hat, arms, nose, mittens and buttons to the snowman. If using google eyes, have them glue those on or they can draw on the rest of the face features with crayons. Drape the ribbon around the snowman's neck and staple down to look like a scarf.

Alternative Crafts

Paper bag snowman puppet. Use white paper bags and cut small black construction paper circles or squares for the children to glue on as the eyes, mouth and buttons. Cut orange construction paper carrot shaped nose and black construction paper hats to be glued on as well.

Paper plate snowman pieces.

Paper plate snowman.

Craft stick snowflakes. Drill holes in the center of three different colored craft sticks, large enough for a brass brad to fit through. Drill a small hole in the end of one of the craft sticks that an ornament hanger can fit through. Fasten the sticks together using the brass brad and attach the ornament hanger. Use glitter glue (either by dipping using a Q-tip or glitter glue applicator) to decorate the snowflake.

Cut paper snowflakes. Cut white paper into 8.5-inch squares. Fold in half diagonally. Fold in half again. Then fold over each side point toward the middle to make a triangle and cut off the dangling points. Then cut small shapes into both sides. Unfold and it will look like a snowflake.

Chenille stem snowflake. Cut a white chenille stem into thirds and bend one piece around another in the middle to make a cross. Add the third piece bent around the middle to make a star. Cut another chenille stem into six pieces. Bend each short piece around the end of the six points of the star to look like a snowflake tip.

Snack: Banana snowman

Materials needed: Skewers, bananas, apples, grapes, pretzel sticks, chocolate chips or raisins, orange Starburst candies, paper plates. Advance preparation: Cut bananas into thick slices. Slice apples in eighths, then in half lengthwise. Cut orange starburst into carrot like pieces. At storytime: Have children place three slices of banana on skewer, then top with apple piece and grape to look like hat. Lay the snowman down on the paper plate, place two pretzel sticks on sides to look like arms, add chocolate chips or raisins as eyes, mouth and buttons and small piece of orange starburst as nose.

Banana snowman.

Alternative Snacks

Snowman cupcake. Ice cupcakes with white icing, add large marshmallow and decorate side of marshmallow with food marker to look like snowman face. Place thin chocolate wafer cookie and either Junior Mint or peanut butter cup candy on top of wafer to look like hat. Place strip of Fruit by the Foot around neck to look like scarf. Put pretzel sticks in cupcake under marshmallow to look like arms.

Doughnut snowman. Put three powdered sugar doughnut holes on a skewer to look like snowman. Decorate your face with chocolate chips for eyes and pretzel sticks for arms.

SUGGESTED BOOKS

Brett, Jan. *The Three Snow Bears*. 32 pages. 2007. Penguin Group. The story of the Three Bears retold as an Alaskan Eskimo tale.

Bridwell, Norman. *Clifford's First Snow Day*. 32 pages. 1998. Cartwheel. Clifford plays in the snow for the very first time.

Briggs, Raymond. *The Snowman*. 32 pages. 1978. Random House Books for Young Readers. A wordless book that describes the friendship between a young boy and a snowman that ends with the snowman melting away.

Brunelle, Nicholas. *Snow Moon*. 31 pages. 2005. Viking. A child is awakened on a wintry night by a mysterious owl.

Buehner, Caralyn. *Snowmen All Year*. 32 pages. 2010. Dial. The narrator imagines a snowman who could accompany him to all sorts of events taking place all year.

Buehner, Caralyn. *Snowmen at Night.* A young boy imagines the games his snowman must be up to during the night when he appears to be a different shape the next day.

Burton, Virginia Lee. *Katie and the Big Snow.* 40 pages. 1974. Houghton Mifflin Harcourt Trade & Reference Publishers. Katie the bulldozer saves the day when she plows out the city of Geoppolis.

Butler, M. Christina. *The Smiley Snowman.* 32 pages. 2010. Good Books. A heartwarming tale of friendship involving a snowman built by several animal friends.

Carlstrom, Nancy White. *Mama Will It Snow Tonight?* 32 pages. 2009. Boyds Mill. A tale of three mothers whose young ones are anxious for winter to come.

Child, Lauren. *Snow Is My Favorite and My Best.* 32 pages. 2006. Dial. Lola wishes it would be winter all the time.

Colandro, Lucille. *There Was a Cold Lady Who Swallowed Some Snow.* 32 pages. 2003. Scholastic. The familiar song about the old lady who swallowed things retold as a winter tale.

Collins, Peggy. *In the Snow.* 38 pages. 2009. Applesauce Press. A little boy and his dad go out to play in the snow.

Cuyler, Margery. *The Biggest, Best Snowman.* 2004. Scholastic. Her friends encourage little Nell to build a snowman and it helps build her confidence.

Ehlert, Lois. *Snowballs.* 32 pages. 1995. Harcourt Books. Some children create a family out of snow. Plus information about what makes it snow.

Gay, Julie Louise. *Stella Queen of the Snow.* 32 pages. 2010. Groundwood Books. Stella and Sam discover a beautiful landscape in a world covered with snow.

Gibbons, Gail. *It's Snowing!* 32 pages. 2011. Holiday House. Lots of good factual information about snow.

Harper, Lee. *Snow Snow Snow.* 40 pages. 2009. Simon & Schuster Children's Publishing. The joy of the first snow of winter.

Iwamura, Kazuo. *Hooray for Snow!* 24 pages. 2009. North-South Books. Three little squirrels try to convince their dad to come out to play in the snow.

Keats, Ezra Jack. *The Snowy Day.* 48 pages. 1963. Viking Juvenile. A boy wakes up to discover that snow has fallen during the night.

Kroll, Steven. *The Biggest Snowman Ever.* 32 pages. 2005. Cartwheel. Clayton and Desmond join forces to make the biggest snowman ever.

Lakin, Patricia. *Snow Day.* 30 pages. Friends enjoy a snow day and sledding. It turns out they're adults who are happy school is closed.

Matsuoka, Mei. *Footprints in the Snow.* 32 pages. 2008. Henry Holt and Company. Wolf decides to write a story about a nice wolf, since so many stories depict wolves as mean.

Mayer, Mercer. *Just a Snowman.* 24 pages. 2004. Harper Festival. It's a snow day and Little Critter wants to build a snowman, but first he has to help his dad and his little sister.

Mayer, Mercer. *Just a Snowy Day.* 16 pages. 2006. Harper Festival. Scratch and sniff and pop ups fill this book about the wonders of a snowy day.

McDougle, Farrah. *Olivia and the Snow Day.* 24 pages. 2010. Simon Spotlight. A Ready-to-Read book. Olivia has the day off because of the snow and there's a lot to do.

McKie, Roy. *Snow.* 61 pages. 1962. Random House Children's Books. From the Dr. Seuss library comes this book of joyful verse relating to snow.

Moulton, Mark Kimball. *A Snowman Named Just Bob.* 26 pages. 1999. Ideals Children's Books. Bob the Snowman is the embodiment of sweet friendship.

Regan, Dian Curtis. *The Snow Blew Inn.* 32 pages. 2011. Holiday House. Emma is awaiting her cousin for a sleepover but a big snowstorm brings many other visitors. When her cousin finally arrives, they have their sleepover as a campout in the parlor since Emma gave up her room.

Reid, Barbara. *Perfect Snow.* 32 pages. 2011. Albert Whitman & Company. When the first snow of winter falls, two boys build a snow fort.

Rey, Margret, and H.A. Rey. *Curious George in the Snow.* 24 pages. 1998. Houghton Mifflin Harcourt Trade & Reference Publishers. George and the Man with the Yellow Hat enjoy the winter sports competition.

Rollins, Jack, and Steve Nelson. *Frosty the Snowman.* 32 pages. 2009. Odyssey Books. Thumpetty thump thump here comes Frosty.

Sams, Carl. R., II. *First Snow in the Woods.* 46 pages. 2007. Carl R. Sams II Photography. A tale of changing seasons and animals getting ready for winter.

Shulevitz, Uri. *Snow.* 32 pages. 2004. Farrar, Straus & Giroux. No one thinks one or two snowflakes will amount to anything.

Stringer, Lauren. *Winter Is the Warmest Season.* 30 pages. 2006. Harcourt Books. A child describes ways to keep warm during the winter.

Watt, Fiona. *That's Not My Snowman.* 10 pages. 2011. Usborne Books. Bright pictures and interesting textures make up this book that's part of the touch and feel series.

White, Kathryn. *When Will It Snow?* 32 pages. 2011. Good Books. Little Bear is wondering when it will be time to hibernate.

Wright, Maureen. *Sneezy the Snowman.* 32 pages. 2010. Marshall Cavendish Children's Books. Sneezy the Snowman is cold and has to try many things to warm himself up.

Ziefert, Harriet. *Snow Party.* 40 pages. 2008. Blue Apple Books. The snow men, women and children come out for a party if the first snow of the year happens on the first day of winter.

Community Workers

Advance planning: To plan for this storytime, find a theme-related song to play during craft and snack times, like "Holding Out for a Hero," by Bonnie Tyler. You will also want to select a poem, such as "Five Strong Police Officers" (found at www.canteach.ca), along with the books you plan to read. Decorate your space with a fireman helmet, construction hard hat, policeman badge, chef hat, and stethoscope—anything that a community worker might wear or carry. If you can get a policeman to come read *Officer Buckle and Gloria* or a fireman to read one of the firefighter books it would be very special for your storytime children.

Introduction to the theme: Who are the people who work in our community? Firemen, policemen, doctors, lawyers, nurses, construction workers, chefs, teachers, mail carriers. Can you think of more kinds of workers? It takes a lot of people who work very hard to keep our community going. There are people who work in offices, stores, hair salons, mechanics, carpenters, painters, artists, writers, dentists, bakers. Sometimes parents stay home from work to take care of their children. That's an important job too! Today we'll read about workers in our community, play a worker game, make a worker craft and eat a worker snack.

Song: "Community Workers" to the tune of "My Darling Clementine":

> Community Workers
> There are lots of them around.
> There are doctors, there are teachers,
> Firefighters in our town.
> Community Workers
> Community Workers
> They are helpful, kind and good,
> There are policemen, there are bakers
> And nurses in our neighborhood.

Game: Who's who

Materials needed: Pictures or photographs of people in uniform or workers doing various jobs. Advance preparation: Find the pictures on the Internet and print them or cut them out of magazines. You may want to glue them onto construction paper or cardstock so that they are readable and don't flop over when you hold them up. At storytime: Show pictures or photographs of people in uniform or doing the various jobs and ask the children to identify who they are and what their jobs are.

Alternative Games

Red light, green light. You are the "stop light" and the children try to tag you. At the start, all the children form a line about 15 feet away from you. You face away from the line of children and say "green light." At this point the children are allowed to move toward you. At any time you may say "red light!" and turn around. If any of the children are moving after this has occurred, they have to take three steps backwards. Play resumes when you turn back around and say "green light." When a child reaches you they win the game. If the child would like to be the stop light he or she can take a turn, otherwise you keep doing it and do more rounds of the game.

Bean bag toss. Bean bag toss on stoplight made of construction paper.

Worker concentration. Make a set of cards with two matching photos of each occupation. Let the children take turns turning over two cards to see if they can make a match.

Tool match. Match the tool to the worker. Print photos of different kinds of workers and the tools they might use in their jobs. Hold up a picture of a worker and then some of the tools and ask if that worker might use that particular tool.

Occupational musical chairs. Tape photos of different occupations to a row of chairs set up as for musical chairs. Play music and have the children walk around the row of chairs (one chair per child). When the music stops each child takes a seat. Ask one or two children to tell you what occupation the person on their seat does. Play the music and have the children walk again. Ask different children each time until each child has had a turn to tell you an occupation.

Craft: Police badge

Materials needed: Silver cardstock, glue dots or glue stick, silver permanent marker. Advance preparation: Cut badge shapes out of the silver cardstock. At storytime: Have the children glue the badge parts together and either the child or the parent can write the child's name on the badge in silver marker.

Alternative Crafts

Worker collage. Let the children cut pictures of different kinds of workers out of magazines and glue them to a background piece of construction paper into a collage.

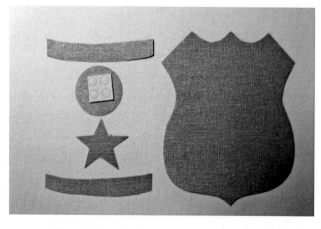

Above: Police badge pieces. *Right*: Police badge.

Self portraits. Each child could draw a portrait of themselves doing whatever occupation they'd like to be when they grow up.

Firetruck. Cut out squares and rectangles that put together will make a firetruck. Have each child glue the pieces to a background piece of construction paper.

Snack: Traffic light cupcake

Materials needed: Yellow cake cupcakes, white icing, red, green, yellow Skittles or M & Ms, small paper plates, plastic knives. At storytime: Give each child a cupcake on a plate along with a dollop of icing and a plastic knife and a red, green and yellow candy. They spread the icing and then place the candies on top to look like a traffic light.

Alternative Snacks

Traffic light cookies. Round sugar cookies topped with white icing and a red, green and yellow candy like Skittles or M & Ms.

Doughnut or doughnut holes.

Anything cut into a star shape, like cookies, sandwiches, etc. Anything from or with apples emphasizing that old adage that teachers love apples. Any kind of healthy snack, telling the children community workers all want to eat healthy snacks so that they can be strong and healthy to serve the community.

Traffic light cupcake.

SUGGESTED BOOKS

Ahlberg, Janet, and Allan Ahlberg. *The Jolly Postman*. 32 pages. 1986. Little, Brown & Co. A collection of letters sent from one fairy tale or Mother Goose character to another.

Allard, Harry. *Miss Nelson Is Missing*. 32 pages. 1985. Houghton Mifflin Harcourt. The kids take advantage of their teacher until she disappears and a mean substitute takes her place. But just who is this mean substitute really?

Allen, Julia. *My First Doctor Visit*. 23 pages. 1997. Aro Books Inc. Using limited vocabulary, children are taken through their first doctor visit.

Askew, Amanda. *Chef*. 24 pages. 2010. QEB Publishing Inc. Part of the People Who Help Us Series — this one explains the life of a chef.

Askew, Amanda. *Doctor*. 24 pages. 2010. QEB Publishing Inc. Part of the People Who Help Us Series — this one explains the life of a doctor.

Askew, Amanda. *Firefighter*. 24 pages. 2010. QEB Publishing Inc. Part of the People Who Help Us Series — this one explains the life of a firefighter.

Askew, Amanda. *Police Officer*. 24 pages. 2010. QEB Publishing Inc. Part of the People Who Help Us Series — this one explains the life of a police officer.

Askew, Amanda. *Vet*. 24 pages. 2010. QEB Publishing Inc. Part of the People Who Help Us Series — this one explains the life of a veterinarian.

Barton, Byron. *Building a House*. 32 pages. 1990. HarperCollins Publishers. Brief text and illustrations describe the steps in building a house.

Beaty, Andrea. *Doctor Ted*. 32 pages. 2008. Simon & Schuster Children's Publishing. Ted the Bear becomes a doctor.

Beaty, Andrea. *Firefighter Ted*. 32 pages. 2009. Simon & Schuster Children's Publishing. Ted the Bear becomes a firefighter.

Bourgeois, Paulette. *Postal Workers*. 32 pages. 2005. Kids Can Press, Limited. Children join letter carriers on their daily route in this Level 3 Reader.

Bowman-Kruhn, Mary. *A Day in the Life of a Police*

Officer. 24 pages. 2004. Rosen Publishing Group. From the Kids Career Library.

Carle, Eric. *Walter the Baker*. 40 pages. 1998. Aladdin. By order of the Duke, Walter must invent a roll through which the sun can shine three times.

Caviezel, Giovanni. *Fireman's Safety Hints*. 10 pages. 2004. Barron's Educational Series. Part of the Little People Shape Series. Illustrated board book shows the inside of a house and how to avoid safety hazards.

Caviezel, Giovanni. *Nurse*. 10 pages. 2008. Barron's Educational Series. Part of the Little People Shape Series that explains what nurses do.

Cousins, Lucy. *Doctor Maisy*. 24 pages. 2001. Candlewick Press. Tallulah and Maisy play hospital with Maisy as the doctor.

Dorling Kindersley Staff. *Emergency Vehicles*. 20 pages. 2009. A good book to use for photographs of emergency vehicles.

Dorling Kindersley Staff. *Firetruck*. 20 pages. 2009. A good book to use for photographs of fire trucks.

Florian, Douglas. *An Auto Mechanic*. 24 pages. 1991. HarperCollins Publishers. Routine garage activities are depicted in watercolor paintings.

Freeman, Don. *Mop Top*. 48 pages. 1978. Penguin Group. A six year old with floppy red hair tries to postpone his trip to the barber shop.

Gaspard, Helen. *Doctor Dan the Bandage Man*. 24 pages. 2004. Random House Children's Books. Little Golden Book classic that tells the story of Dan, who stops crying about his scratch when his mother puts a bandage on him.

Gergely, Tibor. *The Fire Engine Book*. 24 pages. 2001. Random House Children's Books, Little Golden Book. Classic book that has been reissued. Firefighters go to a fire and save the day.

Greenberg, Melanie Hope. *My Father's Luncheonette*. 24 pages. 1991. Penguin Group. A little girl eats and then helps her father at his luncheonette.

Hautzig, David. *At the Supermarket*. 32 pages. 1994. Scholastic. Takes us through a day at the supermarket.

Hayward, Linda. *A Day in the Life of a Police Officer*. 32 pages. 2001. Dorling Kindersley Publishing. Learn to read book that explains the duties of a police officer.

Jackson, Kathryn. *Nurse Nancy*. 24 pages. 2005. Random House Children's Books. Little Golden Book classic that tells the story of little Nancy, whose brothers are too busy to play with her until one of them needs her medical help.

Keats, Ezra Jack. *A Letter to Amy*. 32 pages. 1992. Penguin Group. Peter wants to invite Amy to his birthday party but wants it to be a surprise.

Lindeen, Carol K. *Fire Trucks*. 24 pages. 2005. Capstone Press. Introduces fire trucks and all their parts with photographs.

Lloyd, Sam R. *Doctor Meow's Big Emergency*. 32 pages. 2008. Holt, Henry & Co. Tom Cat is hurt and Doctor Meow needs to help him.

Maury, Inez. *My Mother the Mail Carrier*. 32 pages. 2004. Feminist Press at the City University of New York. Five year old Lupita's mother loves her and also loves her job as a mail carrier.

Mayer, Mercer. *When I Grow Up*. 24 pages. 2003. Random House Children's Books. Little Critter thinks about being different occupations when he grows up.

McMahon, Kara. *Police Officers*. 12 pages. 2006. Random House Children's Books. Elmo from Sesame Street explains what police officers do.

Merriam, Eve. *Daddies at Work*. 32 pages. 1991. Little Simon. Daddies work at all kinds of jobs.

Merriam, Eve. *Mommies at Work*. 32 pages. 1996. Aladdin Paperbacks. Examines many jobs performed by working mothers.

Miller, Margaret. *Guess Who*. 40 pages. 1994. HarperCollins Publishers. A simple question is posed about who does what with pictures offering different answers, some of which are silly.

Mitton, Tony. *Flashing Fire Engines*. 24 pages. 2000. Roaring Book Press. Rhyming book with action and adventure of animal fire fighters.

Munsch, Robert. *The Fire Station*. 24 pages. 1982. Annick Press Limited. Michael and Sheila visit a fire station and much adventure ensues.

Owen, Ann. *Keeping You Safe: A Book About Police Officers*. 24 pages. 2003. Picture Window Books. Describes things police officers do to keep us safe.

Oxenbury, Helen. *The Checkup*. 24 pages. 1983. Penguin Group. A young boy causes turmoil in the doctor's office while there for a checkup.

Pearson, Tracey Campbell. *Storekeeper*. 32 pages. 1991. Penguin Group. A busy day in the life of a general store.

Pellowski, Michael J. *What's It Like to Be a ... Police Officer*. 32 pages. 1997. Troll Communications. Describes how police officers are selected and trained and the tasks that they perform.

Poskazer, Susan. *What's It Like to Be a ... Chef*. 32

pages. 1990. Troll Communications. Describes the work of a chef as he goes about his job of cooking meals in a big restaurant.

Rathmann, Peggy. *Officer Buckle and Gloria.* 32 pages. 1995. Penguin Group Inc. Officer Buckle knows a lot about safety, but his speeches are boring until his dog Gloria comes along.

Rockwell, Anne. *At the Supermarket.* 32 pages. 2010. Henry Holt & Co. A young boy helps his mom buy what they need at the supermarket.

Rockwell, Anne. *Career Day.* 40 pages. 2000. HarperCollins Publishers. On Career Day the children in class introduce special visitors who represent a variety of different occupations.

Rockwell, Harlow. *My Doctor.* 24 pages. 1985. HarperCollins Publishers. Describes a young child's visit to the doctor's office.

Rogers, Fred. *Going to the Doctor.* 32 pages. 1986. Penguin Group. Explains the procedures in a routine checkup.

Shelby, Anne. *We Keep a Store.* 32 pages. 1990. Scholastic Inc. A family keeps a general store in a small rural town.

Staake, Bob. *Donut Chef.* 40 pages. 2008. Random House Children's Books. Donut bakers compete and get so fancy that they forget that sometimes people just want the simple things.

Stamper, Judith Bauer. *What's It Like to Be a ... Doctor.* 32 pages. 1990. Troll Communications. Describes the work done by a doctor.

Stamper, Judith Bauer. *What's It Like to Be a ... Nurse.* 32 pages. 1997. Troll Communications. Describes the work done by a nurse.

Stieg, William. *Doctor De Soto.* 32 pages. 1982. Farrar, Strauss & Giroux. Dr. De Soto is a mouse who is a dentist and treats the teeth of other animals.

Wilks, Shelley. *What's It Like to Be a ... Grocer.* 32 pages. 1997. Troll Communications. Describes the work done by a grocer.

Wilson, Sarah. *Garage Song.* 40 pages. 1991. Simon & Schuster Books for Young Readers. Describes the sights and sounds of a service station.

Yankovic, Weird Al. *When I Grow Up.* 32 pages. 2011. Harper Collins. Popular singer takes a fresh look at what readers might want to be when they grow up.

Yee, Wong Herbert. *Fireman Small.* 32 pages. 1996. Houghton Mifflin Harcourt Trade & Reference. Rhyming verse describes how Fireman Small is frequently called out of bed to rescue animals.

Yee, Wong Herbert. *Fireman Small: Fire Down Below.* 32 pages. 2004. Houghton Mifflin Harcourt Trade & Reference. Rhyming verse describes how Fireman Small leaves the fire station because of a leaky roof, goes to a hotel, where he gets called out to help with a fire in the hotel.

Dogs

Advance planning: To plan for this storytime, find a theme-related song to play during craft and snack times, like "Who Let the Dogs Out," by Baha Men. You will also want to select a poem, such as "My Dog Fred," by Kenn Nesbitt (found at www.poetry4kids.com), along with the books you plan to read. Decorate your space with a real dog if possible, or stuffed dogs, a leash, dog biscuits, dog toys.

Introduction to the theme: Dogs are four legged furry animals that originally were related to wolves. Over time people have turned them into pets and have bred them selectively so that there are lots and lots of different kinds of dogs now. Do you have a dog? Is it a big dog or a little dog? What's your dog's name? What do you like about your dog? Do you know what a baby dog is called? (puppy). Some dogs are working dogs and help us by aiding disabled people or the police. Today we'll read about dogs in many different ways, we'll sing a song about dogs, make a dog puppet and have a special snack that looks like puppy chow.

Song: "Bingo":

There was a farmer had a dog,
And Bingo was his name-o.
B-I-N-G-O!
B-I-N-G-O!
B-I-N-G-O!
And Bingo was his name-o!
There was a farmer had a dog,
And Bingo was his name-o.
(Clap)-I-N-G-O!
(Clap)-I-N-G-O!
(Clap)-I-N-G-O!
And Bingo was his name-o!
There was a farmer had a dog,
And Bingo was his name-o.
(Clap, clap)-N-G-O!
(Clap, clap)-N-G-O!
(Clap, clap)-N-G-O!
And Bingo was his name-o!
There was a farmer had a dog,
And Bingo was his name-o.
(Clap, clap, clap)-G-O!
(Clap, clap, clap)-G-O!
(Clap, clap, clap)-G-O!
And Bingo was his name-o!
There was a farmer had a dog,
And Bingo was his name-o.
(Clap, clap, clap, clap)-O!
(Clap, clap, clap, clap)-O!
(Clap, clap, clap, clap)-O!
And Bingo was his name-o!
There was a farmer had a dog,
And Bingo was his name-o.
(Clap, clap, clap, clap, clap)
(Clap, clap, clap, clap, clap)
(Clap, clap, clap, clap, clap)
And Bingo was his name-o!

Game: "Where has my little dog gone?"

Oh where oh where has my little dog gone? (look all around)
Oh where oh where can he be? (keep looking)
With his ears cut short (hands on ears)
and his tail cut long (wave hand behind like a tail)
oh where or where can he be (look around)
Here oh here is my little lost dog (clap hands)
he's right here behind me (point behind you)
with his ears cut short (hands on ears)
and his tail cut long (wave hand behind like tail)
he's right here behind me (point behind you)

Alternative Games

Dog puppet play. Introduce a dog puppet with the name Bingo. Have the puppet act
excited, jumping up and down. Try to calm the puppet down but when he won't calm down

tell the children that only by singing the song B-I-N-G-O will the dog calm down so you must sing the song.

Where's the biscuit? Have a small dog biscuit and secretly give it to one child seated in the circle and then ask the children to guess who has the biscuit. Give them three guesses and if they don't guess then show them who has it. Make them all close their eyes and then hide the biscuit with someone else. Repeat.

Feed the puppy. Make a large picture of a dog's face and cut an opening for the mouth. Place over a bowl and let the children toss biscuits at it. If children have a dog at home let them take home the leftover biscuits or donate them to a shelter.

In the doghouse. Create a doghouse by draping a sheet over a table with an opening at each end and putting a sign on it in a dogbone shape saying doghouse. Tell the children they are all going to pretend to be dogs so they must crawl on all fours in a circle that goes through the doghouse while you play the song "Who Let the Dogs Out." Stop the music occasionally and whoever is inside the doghouse needs to make sounds like a dog, such as barking, whining, yapping. Try to give everyone a chance at making dog sounds.

Craft: Paper bag dog puppet

Materials needed: White paper bags, google eyes, one white ear, one black ear, black nose, black whiskers, red tongue, black spots, glue sticks. Advance preparation: Cut paper pieces, assemble one puppet. At storytime: Show sample puppet and explain how to put it together. Attach the ears, eyes, nose and whiskers to the bottom flap of the bag, the spots to the body of the bag and the tongue under the flap.

Alternative Crafts

Dog puppet on a stick. Use precut paper or card stock shapes to make the head and ears. Glue to a craft stick. Add google eyes and a pom pom nose or draw on the facial features.

Standing dog card. Print a simple dog outline on the bottom half of pieces of cardstock, leaving the back of the dog long on the fold. Fold over the cardstock and let the children decorate the dog. The dog will stand with the cardstock slightly open.

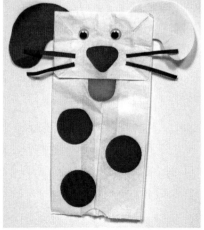

Left: **Paper bag dog puppet pieces.** *Right:* **Paper bag dog puppet.**

Snack: Puppy chow

Materials needed: For 36 servings: 9 cups crispy rice square cereal; ½ cup peanut butter; 1 cup semi-sweet chocolate chips; 1½ cups confectioners sugar; small cups or paper plates. Advance preparation: Melt the chocolate chips in a very large bowl in the microwave. Add the peanut butter and stir until smooth. Stir in the rice cereal. Pour powdered sugar into a large zip plastic bag. Add cereal and shake. Might have to do in batches until all cereal is coated. Store tightly covered. At storytime: Serve puppy chow in cups or on plates.

Puppy chow.

Alternative Snacks

Make biscuits or cookies shaped like dog biscuits, or serve any kind of cereal and call it puppy chow.

Suggested Books

Bansch, Helga. *I Want a Dog.* 32 pages. 2009. North-South Books. A little girl figures how to get what she wants, which is a dog.

Bedford, David. *The Way I Love You.* 24 pages. 2011. Little Hare Books. A little girl with her big personality and her much loved dog.

Benjamin, A.H. *Sausages: A Pop-Up Book.* 16 pages. 2012. Tango Books. A dog needs someplace safe to store his favorite food.

Bliss, Harry. *Bailey.* 32 pages. 2011. Scholastic. Bailey the dog surprises his humans with his antics.

Bryan, Sean. *The Juggling Pug.* 32 pages. 2011. Skyhorse Publishing. A town becomes famous when a pug learns to juggle.

Carnesi, Monica. *Little Dog Lost: The True Story of a Brave Dog Named Baltic.* 32 pages. 2012. Penguin Group. A curious dog wanders onto a sheet of ice that breaks free and travels down a river.

Crimi, Carolyn. *Pugs in a Bug.* 32 pages. 2012. Penguin Group. Pugs in a bug in a canine counting book.

Davis, Anne. *No Dogs Allowed.* 32 pages. 2011. HarperCollins Publishers. Two cats disagree over whether or not they should allow the dog in the house.

Fox, Dorothea Warren. *Miss Twiggley's Tree.* 44 pages. 2002. Purple House Press. Miss Twiggley lives in a tree with her dog.

Goodrich, Carter. *Say Hello to Zorro.* 48 pages. 2011. Simon & Schuster Children's Publishing. Mr. Bud the dog enjoys his routine and when a new dog enters the family it throws everything off.

Gormley, Greg. *Dog in Boots.* 32 pages. 2011. Holiday House. Dog heads to the shoe store and comes out with some splendid boots.

Graham, Bob. *"Let's Get a Pup" Said Kate.* 32 pages. 2003. Candlewick Press. Kate and her parents visit the animal shelter to pick out a dog.

Graham, Bob. *"The Trouble with Dogs."..Said Dad.* 32 pages. 2010. Candlewick Press. A sequel to *Let's Get a Pup*, where the family learns what's really important about having a dog.

Gravett, Emily. *Dogs.* 32 pages. 2010. Simon & Schuster Children's Publishing. Exploring the world of dogs with a twist ending.

Grogan, John. *Bad Dog, Marley!* 40 pages. 2007. HarperCollins Publishers. The puppy Marley enters the family's life with all his energy and antics.

Hernandez, Leeza. *Dog Gone.* 40 pages. 2012. Penguin Group. A pup runs away but misses his owner.

Hill, Eric. *Where's Spot?* 24 pages. 1980. Penguin Group. A lift the flap book. Spot's mother is looking for him.

Hills, Tad. *How Rocket Learned to Read.* 40 pages. 2010. Random House Children's Books. Rocket the dog learns to read with the help of a little yellow bird.

Inkpen, Mick. *Kipper.* 28 pages. 1999. Sandpiper. Kipper's basket is old and worn but can he find a better place to sleep?

Keats, Ezra Jack. *Whistle for Willie.* 40 pages. 1964. Penguin Group. Peter wants so much to be able to whistle for his dog.

Kerby, Johanna. *Little Pink Pup.* 32 pages. 2010. Penguin Group. The true story of Pink, the runt of the pig litter who was brought into the house to be with Tink, the dachshund mom. She adopted him and nursed him to health.

Koontz, Dean. *I, Trixie Who Is Dog.* 32 pages. 2009. Penguin Group. A glimpse into the imagination of Trixie, a Golden Retriever.

Kotzwinkle, William. *Walter, the Farting Dog.* 32 pages. 2001. North Atlantic Books. Walter's bad gas almost costs him his family, but when he saves the day they realize that they want to keep him after all.

Krupinski, Loretta. *The Snow Dog's Journey.* 32 pages. 2010. Penguin Group. In the spirit of the Velveteen Rabbit, a heartwarming tale about the transformative powers of love.

Marciano, John Bemelmans. *Madeline and Her Dog.* 32 pages. 2011. Penguin Books, Limited. A Level 2 Reader written in rhyme about Madeline's puppy Genevieve.

Marcus, Kimberly. *Scritch-Scratch a Perfect Match.* 32 pages. 2011. Penguin Group. A flea jumps on a dog. How can something so tiny cause so much trouble?

Mayer, Mercer. *A Boy, a Dog and a Frog.* 32 pages. 2003. Penguin Group. A boy and his dog go walking in the swamp.

McCue, Lisa. *Quiet Bunny and Noisy Puppy.* 32 pages. 2011. Sterling Children's Books. A heartwarming tale of friendship on a cold winter's night.

McFarland, Lyn Rossiter. *Widget and the Puppy.* 32 pages. 2004. Farrar, Straus & Giroux. Widget the dog lives comfortably until a puppy arrives who disrupts everything.

Meddaugh, Susan. *Martha Speaks.* 32 pages. 1995. Houghton Mifflin Harcourt. Martha the talking dog wins a call-in radio contest.

Pinkwater, Daniel. *I Am the Dog.* 32 pages. 2010. HarperCollins Publishers. A boy and his dog change places.

Rodrigue, George. *Why Is Blue Dog Blue?* 40 pages. 2002. Stewart, Tabori & Chang. An artist takes you on a tour of the color palette in order to find out why blue dog is blue.

Rylant, Cynthia. *The Bookshop Dog.* 40 pages. 1996. Scholastic. People in the town argue over who will look after the bookshop owner's dog when she goes into the hospital.

Schachner, Judith. *Skippyjon in the Doghouse.* 32 pages. 2010. Penguin Group. Skippyjon the Siamese Cat who thinks he's a Chihuahua is hiding out with his dog friends who are afraid of the bad Bobble-ito who has taken over their doghouse.

Shannon, David. *Good Boy, Fergus.* 40 pages. 2006. Scholastic. Fergus the dog is always getting into trouble.

Singer, Marilyn. *Every Day's a Dog's Day.* 32 pages. 2012. Penguin Group. Dog poems for a whole year.

Singer, Marilyn. *What Is Your Dog Doing?* 32 pages. 2011. Simon & Schuster Children's Publishing. Rhyming text about all the things dogs can do.

Soman, David. *Ladybug Girl and Bingo.* 40 pages. 2012. Penguin Group. Lulu and Bingo are camping for the first time.

Stevens, Janet. *My Big Dog.* A cat's life is disturbed when his family brings home a Golden Retriever puppy.

Thayer, Jane. *The Puppy Who Wanted a Boy.* 32 pages. 2003. HarperCollins Publishers. Petey the puppy has only one wish for Christmas — to have a boy of his very own.

Van Fleet, Matthew. *Dog.* 20 pages. 2007. Simon & Schuster. Twenty breeds of dog demonstrate action words, antonyms and synonyms.

Wells, Rosemary. *Bingo.* 18 pages. 1999. Scholastic. An illustrated version of the children's song.

Wells, Rosemary. *McDuff and the Baby.* 32 pages. 2006. Hyperion Books for Children. McDuff enjoys his life but it changes when they bring home a baby.

Willems, Mo. *City Dog, Country Frog.* 64 pages. 2010. Hyperion Press. A dog befriends a frog throughout all the seasons until sadly the frog is no longer there and the dog makes a new friend.

Willis, Jeanne. *Old Dog.* 32 pages. 2010. Andersen Press Limited. The young pups don't want to visit Grandpa so he sets out to show them that there's life in the old dog yet.

Yates, Louise. *Dog Loves Books.* 32 pages. 2010. Alfred A. Knopf. Dog loves books so much he opens his own bookstore.

Zion, Gene. *Harry the Dirty Dog.* 32 pages. 1976. HarperCollins Publishers. Harry hates baths and after running away one day he gets so dirty his own family doesn't recognize him.

Homes

Advance planning: To plan for this storytime, find a theme-related song to play during craft and snack times, like "Home," by Michael Bublé. You will also want to select a poem, such as "A House Is a House for Me," by Mary Ann Hoberman (found in her book of the same title), along with the books you plan to read. Decorate your space with toy houses and a poster showing different kinds of homes.

Introduction to the theme: What is home? It can mean the building that your family lives in, which could be a house or an apartment. It could even mean the city that you grew up in. Home is usually where you feel comfortable and safe, where you spend your time when your family's not at school or work. What's your home like? Who lives there with you? Today we'll read about homes, play a sounds of home game, make a home craft and have a snack that looks like a home.

Song: "Home on the Range":

> Oh, give me a home, where the buffalo roam,
> Where the deer and the antelope play,
> Where seldom is heard a discouraging word,
> And the skies are not cloudy all day.
> Home, home on the range,
> Where the deer and the antelope play,
> Where seldom is heard a discouraging word,
> And the skies are not cloudy all day.

Game: Sounds of home

Record sounds from the computer at www.findsounds.com that are heard at home. Burn them on a disk. Play them and ask the children to guess what the sounds are. Suggested sounds: door slam; baby crying; clock ticking; water running; telephone ring; laughing child; footsteps; dog barking; lawn mower; car horn; electric can opener; soda can opening; vacuum cleaner; doorbell; cat meow; thunder; rain; snoring; keyboard; door knock.

Materials needed: Blank CD, CD player. Advance preparation: Find and record sounds. At storytime: Play the prerecorded CD with the sounds and have the children guess what the sounds are.

Alternative Games

Make an igloo. Using a fabric parachute or a large tablecloth, have the children hold all around the sides and bring it up in the air and down again quickly trapping air under it, trying to make it look like an igloo or a tent. Explain that you're making a kind of house out of the cloth. Let the children have turns going under the cloth into the house.

Matching game. Make a matching game of people and animals and their homes.

Cardboard box homes. Have a big selection of very large cardboard boxes and let the children play in them making their own "homes." Ask them if they've ever enjoyed playing with cardboard boxes at home and what they might have made with them, or pretended that they were.

Spider homes. Provide lots of balls of yarn and encourage the children to unroll it and wind it around chairs and tables and make giant spider webs.

Craft: Craft stick house

Materials needed: Red, brown, green, yellow construction paper, craft sticks, glue sticks. Advance preparation: Cut red construction paper roof in triangle shape, door in brown rectangle shape, two windows in yellow squares. Cut some triangle shaped green trees with brown rectangle trunks. At storytime: Glue eight craft sticks into a square shape on background construction paper. Top with the red triangle roof. Place the brown rectangle door and the yellow square windows on top of the craft sticks and glue. Glue the green triangle trees with brown rectangle trunks next to the house.

Craft stick house pieces.

Alternative Crafts

Simple shapes house. Cut out squares, rectangles and triangles and let the children glue the different shapes down on a background piece of paper to look like a house.

Bookmark house. Make a bookmark that looks like a house with a triangular roof on top of a rectangle.

Box house. Have a box of some kind for each child. Let them decorate the box with construction paper and glue, crayons, markers and turn it into a house.

Craft stick house.

Snack: Gingerbread house

Materials needed: Graham crackers, white icing, gumdrops, Twizzlers twisted licorice or marshmallow twisted rope candy, paper plates, plastic knives. Advance preparation: Cut Twizzlers in lengths to make doors and windows on top of graham cracker. At storytime: Place one large graham cracker on each child's paper plate, Give them a dollop of white icing and a plastic knife, along with several pieces of Twizzler or rope candy and some gumdrops. The gumdrops can be either decorations or shrubbery; the Twizzler pieces can make doors and windows.

Alternative Snacks

Cheese sandwich house. Cut slices of cheese in half diagonally. Place a triangle

Gingerbread house.

cheese on top of a square piece of bread. Place two small square cheese windows and a rectangular cheese door on the bread.

Cracker house. Make a house out of large square wheat crackers and cream cheese "glue." Decorate with sliced fruits and vegetables.

SUGGESTED BOOKS

Adams, Stacey. *A Home for Brooks*. Tate Publishing & Enterprising. Brooks the dog waits patiently to be adopted.

Beake, Lesley. *Home Now*. 32 pages. 2007. Charlesbridge Publishing. A little girl can remember where she used to live, but learns about living in a new place from an orphaned baby elephant.

Bolam, Emily. *Happy Home*. 8 pages. 2011. Macmillan U.K. A board book where the animals scamper all over the house.

Brown, Margaret Wise. *Home for a Bunny*. 32 pages. 2003. Random House Children's Books. A little bunny tries to find a home.

Bunting, Eve. *Fly Away Home*. 32 pages. 1993. Houghton Mifflin Harcourt Trade & Reference Publishers. A homeless boy living in the airport learns from a bird that gains its freedom.

Bunting, Eve. *Sunflower House*. 32 pages. 1999. Houghton Mifflin Harcourt. A little boy creates a summer playhouse by planting sunflowers.

Burton, Virginia Lee. *The Little House*. 44 pages. 2012. Houghton Mifflin Harcourt. A country house is unhappy when a city grows up around her.

Child, Lauren. *I Slightly Want to Go Home*. 24 pages. 2011. Penguin Group. Lola goes for her first sleepover but misses home.

Deacon, Alexis. *A Place to Call Home*. 40 pages. 2011. Candlewick Press. A band of brothers outgrows their home and sets out on an adventure to find a new place to live.

Dewdney, Anna. *Llama Llama Home with Mama*. 32 pages. 2011. Penguin Group. Llama Llama is staying home because he doesn't feel well.

Dussling, Jennifer. *In a Dark, Dark House*. 48 pages. 1995. Penguin Group. A Learn to Read Book story of a little boy in a haunted house.

Edwards, Pamela Duncan. *The Old House*. 32 pages. 2009. Penguin Group. An old house gets a new lease on life when the right family comes along.

Gaydos, Nora. *Where Is My Home?* Read Write Level 2. 32 pages. 2009. Innovative Kids. Baby Chick is lost and trying to find his way home.

Grant, Donald. *Homes*. 38 pages. 2012. Moonlight Publishing. Visit homes all over the world.

Hoban, Tana. *Construction Zone*. 40 pages. 1997. HarperCollins Publishers. Photographs illustrate the kind of equipment found at construction sites. You could talk about how houses are built and these machines help to prepare the house site.

Hoberman, Mary Ann. *A House Is a House for Me*. 48 pages. 1978. Penguin Group. Rhyming text that lists houses for many different animals.

Kleven, Elisa. *Welcome Home, Mouse*. 32 pages. 2010. Ten Speed Press. Clumsy Stanley the elephant accidentally crushes Mouse's house but wants to help build a new one.

Joosse, Barbara M. *Sleepover at Gramma's House*. 40 pages. 2010. Penguin Group. Going to Gramma's takes lots of preparation for an excited little girl elephant.

Keats, Ezra Jack. *Over in the Meadow*. 32 pages. 1999. Penguin Group. An old nursery poem introduces animals, their young and their habitats.

Krauss, Ruth. *A Very Special House*. 32 pages. 2001. HarperCollins Publishers. A boy imagines a house to bring home a turtle, a little dead mouse, a very old lion and where nobody ever says stop.

Lionni, Leo. *The Biggest House in the World*. 32 pages. 1973. Random House Children's Books. A young snail dreams of having the biggest house in the world.

Lobel, Arnold. *Owl at Home* I Can Read 2. 64 pages. 1982. HarperCollins Publishers. Five stories about Owl, who is quite the homebody.

London, Jonathan. *Froggy Builds a Treehouse*. Froggy and his pals decide to build a treehouse but things don't go as planned.

Mayer, Mercer. *This Is My House*. 40 pages. 1988. Random House Children's Books. Little Critter introduces us to his house and family.

McClung, Robert. *Animals That Build Their Homes*. 26 pages. 1976. National Geographic Society. Text and photographs describing animals that build their own homes, like beavers, crayfish and bees.

Moore, Inga. *A House in the Woods*. 48 pages. 2011. Candlewick Press. It can be nice to have your friends move in, but it can also lead to some problems.

Morris, Ann. *Houses and Homes.* 32 pages. 1995. HarperCollins Publishers. The world is full of many different types of houses and homes.

Nelson, Robin. *Where Is My Home?* 23 pages. 2001. Lerner Publications. Simple text and photos show different kinds of homes.

Rey, H.A. *Anybody at Home?* 32 pages. 1998. Houghton Mifflin Harcourt. Short verses ask children to identify various homes and the animals that live there.

Rey, H.A. *Curious George Builds a Home.* 24 pages. 2011. Houghton Mifflin Harcourt Trade & Reference Publishers. Curious George meets a homing pigeon and decides his house needs some improvements in order to be a good home for the pigeon.

Rylant, Cynthia. *Let's Go Home.* 32 pages. 2002. Simon & Schuster Children's Publishing. A room by room tour of a cozy house.

Schachner, Judith. *Skippyjon Jones in the Doghouse.* 32 pages. 2005. Penguin Group. In his room for a time out, Skippyjon lets his imagination take him elsewhere.

Seuss, Dr. *In a People House.* 36 pages. 1995. Random House Children's Books. A mouse invites a bird to see what's inside a people house.

Shook, Babs. *A House for Mouse.* 32 pages. 2000. Reader's Digest Children's Publishing. An All Star reader where a little mouse goes off to find a new house.

Siegel, Mark. *Moving House.* 32 pages. 2011. Roaring Brook Press. The fog comes in and the family decides to move, but they love their house and so they decide to take it with them.

Smith, Alex. *Home.* 32 pages. 2010. ME Media LEC. Four best friends all live together happily until they decide they want their house to be different things.

Teague, Mark. *Firehouse!* 32 pages. 2010. Scholastic. Edward and his cousin Judy spend a hilarious day learning how to be firefighters.

Thompson, Colin. *Pictures of Home.* 32 pages. 2011. Random House Australia. An illustrated collection of quotations by children about the meaning of home.

Thompson, Lauren. *Leap Back Home to Me.* 32 pages. 2011. Simon & Schuster Children's Publishing. A little frog is scared to leave home, but knowing that his mother is there and ready to catch him inspires confidence.

Wildsmith, Brian. *Animal Homes.* 24 pages. 1991. Oxford University Press. Explains the answers to the questions where do animals live and why do they live there.

Wilson, Karma. *Where Is Home, Little Pip?* 40 pages. 2008. Simon & Schuster Children's Publishing. Pip gets lost and can't find her way home.

Wood, Audrey. *The Napping House.* 32 pages. 2009. Houghton Mifflin Harcourt. Rhyming text that culminates in the consequences of too many people and animals piling up in a bed.

Sheep

Advance planning: To plan for this storytime, find a theme-related song to play during craft and snack times, like "Counting Sheep," by Collin Raye. You will also want to select a poem, such as "Baa Baa Black Sheep" or "Little Bo Peep," along with the books you plan to read. Decorate your space with stuffed sheep and lambs, posters of different kinds of sheep, anything related to a farm, like a toy barn or toy farm animals, maybe a straw hat or overalls.

Introduction to the theme: Sheep are usually raised on farms and they're covered in fleece, or wool. Their wool can be shaved off without hurting them and turned into yarn, which can then be made into clothes or blankets. Their milk can be made into cheese. Baby sheep are called lambs. Sheep say "baa." Can you make a sound like a sheep? Say "baa." They're easily frightened and will run away from danger. Today we'll read about sheep, play some sheepish games, make a sheep craft and eat a sheep snack.

Song: "Mary Had a Little Lamb":

> Mary had a little lamb, little lamb, little lamb,
> Mary had a little lamb, whose fleece was white as snow.
> It followed her to school one day, school one day, school one day,
> It followed her to school one day which was against the rules.
> It made the children laugh and play, laugh and play, laugh and play,
> It made the children laugh and play to see a lamb at school.
> And so the teacher turned it out, turned it out, turned it out,
> And so the teacher turned it out, but still it lingered near.
> And waited patiently about, patiently about, patiently about,
> And waited patiently about till Mary did appear.
> Why does the lamb love Mary so? Mary so? Mary so?
> Why does the lamb love Mary so? The eager children cry.
> Why, Mary loves the lamb, you know, lamb you know, lamb you know
> Why, Mary loves the lamb, you know, the teacher did reply.

Game: Sheep herding

Materials needed: White balloons, black permanent marker, black curling ribbon, newspapers, scotch tape, hula hoop or masking tape. Advance preparation: Blow up balloons, draw sheeplike faces on them and tie a little piece of black curling ribbon to look like a tail. Roll the newspapers widthwise into a small baton like shape and tape so it will stay rolled. Either place the hula hoop on the floor or make a circle shape with masking tape. At storytime: Give each child a balloon sheep and a rolled up newspaper. Have them "herd" their sheep around the room with the newspaper to get it to the "barn," which is the hula hoop or taped area on the floor. Take some time to make a walk with the balloons.

Alternative Games

Sheep in the pen. Designate an area to be the sheep pen (mark it on the floor with masking tape or set some chairs as the border). Have the children start from the pen and then play music and lead the children as they pretend to be sheep leaving the pen and running around to play. Make lots of baa noises and romp and play, then have the music stop and become the sheepdog who rounds up the sheep and leads them back to the pen, where they are tired and lie down to take a nap.

Feed the sheep. Glue or tape pictures of sheep to paper plates. Have tongs or tweezers and fresh grass that was mown or picked from the lawn. Ask the children to pick up the grass with the tongs or tweezers and put it on the plate in order to "feed the sheep."

Find the sheep. Place a bunch of small construction paper sheep around the storytime area and place a basket for their collection. Read Little Bo Peep poem (just the first stanza) and then have the children go in search of her sheep. Tell them after they find one to return it to the basket, which is their pen, and then sit down. This gives everyone a chance to find a sheep. If there are many more sheep than there are children, let them find more than one.

Craft: Handprint sheep

Materials needed: White and black sheet foam or cardstock, google eyes, cotton balls or white pom poms, scissors, glue sticks or white glue, white crayons or pencils, paper plates and cotton swabs if using white glue. Advance preparation: Cut white cardstock or foam into a cloud like shape, big enough to cover a child's hand part (not including fingers) of a handprint. At storytime: Have parents trace around child's hand on the black cardstock or sheet foam with the white crayon or pencil. Cut out. Have child glue the white cloud shape to the hand part of the handprint. Glue the google eye at the end of the thumb on the black handprint. Cover the white cloud shape with glue and stick cotton balls or pom poms to it. If using white glue, pour into a paper plate and use cotton swabs to paint the glue onto the cloud shape.

Alternative Crafts

Sheep stick puppet. Cut out pictures of sheep (just an outline). Have the children glue cotton balls and google eyes to the sheep and then glue them to wooden sticks.

Sheep paper bag puppet. Use white paper bags as the base. Cut out cloud shaped white card stock to glue to the bottom flap as the sheep face and then black circles for the ears, eyes, muzzle and nose. Top the black eye circles with either smaller white circles or large google eyes. Could add a black curling ribbon tail to the back of the bag opening if desired.

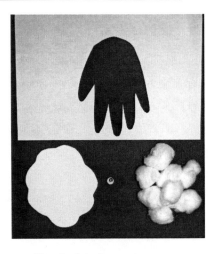

Handprint sheep pieces.

Snack: Sheep cupcake

Materials needed: Yellow cake mix, white icing, large marshmallows, food marker, mini marshmallows, clean scissors, small paper plates, plastic knives. Advance preparation: Bake cupcakes. Draw face on flat side of large marshmallows with food marker. Cut some of the mini marshmallows in half right before story time to be used as sheep ears. At storytime: Give each child a cupcake, a dollop of icing, a plastic knife, one large marshmallow, two of the cut mini marshmallows and a handful of mini marshmallows. Have them cover the cupcake in icing, place the large marshmallow in the center, stick the two cut mini marshmallows on it as ears and surround it with mini marshmallows.

Handprint sheep.

Alternative Snacks

Sheep cookies. Use the flower cookie cutter shape with sugar cookies and then make cookies just as the cupcakes above with the marshmallows. Or use just the white icing and some candies to make a face, such as chocolate chips, brown M & Ms, Skittles, etc.

Rice cake banana sheep. Place sliced bananas on top of a rice cake and add chocolate chips or raisins for eyes, mouth and nose. Or cover rice cake with cream cheese.

Sheep cupcake.

SUGGESTED BOOKS

Bauer, Jutta. *Selma*. 51 pages. 2003. Kane/Miller Books. For Selma the sheep, the answer to the question "what is happiness?" is simple: eating grass and playing with her children.

Beaty, Andrea. *Hide and Sheep*. 32 pages. 2011. Margaret K. McElderry Books. The mischievous sheep have escaped—who would want to stay on the farm when there are such great adventures to be had?

Beaumont, Karen. *No Sleep for the Sheep!* 32 pages. 2011. Harcourt Children's Books. One tired sheep wants nothing more than a good night's sleep.

Blanco, Josette. *On the Farm*. 20 pages. 1975. Child's Play. Illustrations without text showing life on the farm.

Brown, Margaret Wise. *The Big Red Barn*. 32 pages. 1989. HarperCollins Publishers. Rhythmic text about life on the farm.

Cordell, Matthew. *Another Brother*. 40 pages. 2012. Feiwel & Friends. Davy the sheep doesn't like it when his family keeps getting bigger and bigger.

Cousins, Lucy. *Maisy's Morning on the Farm*. 20 pages. 2001. Demco Media. Morning is a busy time on the farm.

de Seve, Randall. *Mathilda and the Orange Balloon*. 32 pages. 2010. HarperCollins Publishers. How can a small sheep become a big orange balloon?

Dunn, Judy. *The Little Lamb*. 32 pages. 2008. Random House. Photographs illustrate this story of a little girl and a lamb.

Fox, Mem. *Time for Bed*. 32 pages. 1997. Sandpiper. Darkness is falling and little ones are getting sleepy.

Fox, Mem. *Where Is the Green Sheep?* 32 pages. 2004. Harcourt Children's Books. There are red sheep and blue sheep but where is the green sheep?

Franklin, Kristine L. *The Shepherd Boy*. 32 pages. 1994. Atheneum Books for Young Readers. A simple prose poem describes how a Navajo boy cares for his family's sheep.

Harper, Piers. *Little Lamb*. 32 pages. 2007. Scholastic. Little Lamb loves to play hide and seek.

Helakoski, Leslie. *Woolbur*. 32 pages. 2008. HarperCollins Publishers. Woolbur is not like other sheep. He hangs out with wild dogs and cards his own wool among other things.

Helweg, Hans. *Farm Animals*. 32 pages. 1980. Random House Children's Books. Identifies and explains the usefulness of animals found on farms.

Hill, Susanna Leonard. *Can't Sleep Without Sheep*. 40 pages. 2010. Walker Childrens. When Ava can't sleep she counts sheep. But she takes so long to fall asleep that the sheep are getting tired.

Imai, Ayano. *108th Sheep*. 32 pages. 2006. ME Media. Emma can't sleep so she tries counting sheep.

Inkpen, Mick. *If I Had a Sheep*. 32 pages. 1992. Random House Children's Books. What would you do if you had a sheep as a pet?

Kemp, Moira. *Baa Baa Black Sheep*. 10 pages. 2000. Penguin Young Readers Group. Board book with four nursery rhyme favorites including the title poem.

Kitamura, Satoshi. *When Sheep Cannot Sleep: The Counting Book*. 32 pages. 1988. Farrar, Straus & Giroux. Wooly the sheep suffers from insomnia so goes for a walk and gets into just about everything.

Kutner, Merrily. *Down on the Farm*. 36 pages. 2004. Holiday House. Rhyming texts describes the sounds and activities of animals on the farm.

Lewis, Rob. *Friska, the Sheep That Was Too Small*. 32 pages. 1988. Farrar, Straus & Giroux. Laughed at because of her small size, Friska proves her worth when she stands up to a wolf and protects the flock.

Martin, Bill, Jr., John Archambault and Ted Rand. *Barn Dance!* An ordinary evening becomes a festival when neighbors gather in the barn for a dance.

McCue, Lisa. *Fuzzytail Lamb*. 22 pages. 1992. Random House Children's Books. A little lamb does a lot of things around the farm but his favorite is to snuggle up to mom.

Miller, Jane. *Farm Alphabet Book*. 32 pages. 1987. Scholastic Inc. Photographs of farm animals and objects.

Monroe, Chris. *Sneaky Sheep*. 32 pages. 2010. Carolrhoda Books. Rocky and Blossom are very sneaky sheep who are not good decision makers.

Nodset, Joan L. *Who Took the Farmer's Hat?* 32 pages. 1963. HarperCollins Publishers. The wind blows away the farmer's hat and the animals see some very strange things happen with it.

Palatini, Margie. *Bad Boys*. 40 pages. 2006. Katherine Tegen Books. Wally and Willy Wolf think they can fool the sheep by dressing as women wolves.

Pearson, Tracey Campbell. *Little Bo Peep*. 14 pages. 2004. Farrar, Straus & Giroux. A board book with the nursery rhyme illustrated by a baby in a crib and her stuffed sheep.

Pearson, Tracey C. *Old MacDonald Had a Farm*. 32 pages. 1987. Picture Lions. The inhabitants of Old MacDonald's farm are described, verse by verse.

Peet, Bill. *Buford the Little Bighorn*. 48 pages. 1983. Sandpiper. Buford's giant horns cause him all kinds of problems.

Rae, Philippa. *Count the Sheep to Sleep*. 28 pages. 2012. Skyhorse Publishing. A little girl decides she must count sheep in order to fall asleep.

Rivers-Moore, Debbie. *Sally Sheep's New Nibbles*. 14 pages. 2003. Sterling. Sally Sheep thinks she'd like a change of diet but changes her mind after she samples the food of her friends.

Royston, Angela. *Sheep*. 1993. 23 pages. Random House Value Publishing. Traces the life of a sheep on a farm in simple story form.

Runnells, Treesha. *Ten Wishing Stars: A Countdown to Bedtime*. 18 pages. 2003. Intervisual Books. Follows ten little sheep at bedtime as they gaze up at the night sky.

Schubert, Leda. *Feeding the Sheep*. 32 pages. 2010. Farrar, Straus & Giroux. Mom tends the family's flock of sheep as her daughter keeps asking "what are you doing?"

Scotton, Rob. *Russell and the Lost Treasure*. 32 pages. 2006. HarperCollins Publishers. Russell the Sheep is determined to find the lost treasure of Frogsbottom.

Scotton, Rob. *Russell the Sheep*. 32 pages. 2009. HarperCollins Publishers. Russell the Sheep is a little out of step with the rest of the sheep.

Shaw, Nancy L. *Sheep in a Jeep*. 32 pages. 1986. Houghton Mifflin Harcourt. About the misadventures of a flock of sheep driving through the country in a jeep.

Shaw, Nancy L. *Sheep on a Ship*. 32 pages. 1992. Houghton Mifflin Harcourt. The rhyming misadventures of a group of zany sheep on a pirate ship.

Shaw, Nancy L. *Sheep Out to Eat*. 32 pages. 1995. Sandpiper. The sheep are back, and this time they're hungry and venture into a tea shop.

Stohner, Anu. *Brave Charlotte*. 32 pages. 2005. Bloomsbury USA. Charlotte is different from the other sheep — she likes to explore.

Stohner, Anu. *Brave Charlotte and the Wolves*. 32 pages. 2009. Bloomsbury USA. Charlotte knows she has to do something about the sheep bullies. And about the other danger lurking in the woods.

Sundgaard, Arnold. *The Lamb and the Butterfly*. 32 pages. 2013. Scholastic. A butterfly doesn't understand why the lamb needs to stay close to her mother and the lamb doesn't understand the butterfly's free spirited ways.

Symes, Ruth Louise. *Sheep Fairy: When Wishes Have Wings*. 32 pages. 2003. Scholastic. Wendy is a sheep with a dream.

Tafuri, Nancy. *Early Morning in the Barn*. 24 pages. 1983. HarperCollins Publishers. A group of chicks visits all their barnyard buddies and hears the sounds they make.

Trapani, Iza. *Baa Baa Black Sheep*. 32 pages. 2001. Charlesbridge Publishing. Trapani takes an old rhyme and adds her own spin to it.

Trapani, Iza. *Mary Had a Little Lamb*. 32 pages. 2003. Whispering Coyote. A board book of the favorite nursery rhyme.

Weare, Tim. *I'm a Little Sheep*. An interactive puppet board book that allows the reader to act out a story about a little sheep who is trying to fall asleep on a noisy farm.

Williams, Sue. *I Went Walking*. 32 pages. 1990. Houghton Mifflin Harcourt. A young child goes for a walk and identifies animals of different colors.

February

Senses

Advance planning: To plan for this storytime, find a theme-related song to play during craft and snack times, like "I've Got Five Senses," by Shawn Brown. You will also want to select a poem, such as "Forgotten Language," by Shel Silverstein, which can be found at www.famouspoetsandpoems.com or in *Where the Sidewalk Ends*, along with the books you plan to read. Decorate your space with fabrics with different and interesting textures (touch), bells or whistles that make interesting noises (hearing), bright and colorful things (sight), herbs or flowers with a strong scent (smell) and foods with familiar flavors (taste).

Introduction to theme: We have five senses: Sight (point to your eyes), hearing (point to your ears), smell (point to your nose, taste (point to your mouth and tongue) and touch (rub your fingers together). Ask the children to repeat with you and point along with you as you show some of the items you brought that give good examples of how you use your senses. Pass around some of the items that you brought so that they can smell, or touch, etc. Today we'll read about our senses, play a game where we use our senses, make a craft using our senses and eat a snack that will use our senses. (After you read each book this week, ask the children which sense is involved in the book.)

Song: "With My Senses" (to the tune of "This Old Man" and adapted from a version originally found on www.mrsjonesroom.com):

> With my eyes, I can see
> I can see a great big tree
> I see and hear and feel and taste and touch
> With my senses I can do so much.
>
> With my ears, I can hear
> I can hear my mother dear
> I see and hear and feel and taste and touch
> With my senses I can do so much.
>
> With my hands, I can touch
> Love my puppy's fur so much
> I see and hear and feel and taste and touch
> With my senses I can do so much.

With my mouth, I can taste
Delicious donuts with chocolate glaze
I see and hear and feel and taste and touch
With my senses I can do so much.

With my nose, I can smell
Flowers that are really swell
I see and hear and feel and taste and touch
With my senses I can do so much.

Game: Guess what's in the boxes

Materials needed: The book *A Dark, Dark Tale* by Ruth Brown, a flashlight, small containers, different items that make noise, such as pebbles, rice, buttons, nails, water. Advance preparation: Fill the containers with the items. The contents must be hidden and well secured inside the container. At storytime: Turn out the lights and use the flashlight to read the book. Read *A Dark, Dark Tale* and then tell the children that you will pass around several containers and you will ask them to guess what's inside. Have them use their sense of hearing to shake the containers and listen to the noise the contents make when shaken. After all the children have had a chance to shake and guess, open each container to show them what's inside.

Alternative Games

Name that sound. Have a box of items that make noises or sounds. Have the children close their eyes while you pull something out and make a sound. Put it away, tell them they can open their eyes and then ask them to guess what made the sound. Show them after they've all had a chance to guess.

Textile touch. Glue some fabric swatches of particularly tactile fabrics to small cards. Wool, corduroy, velvet, knit, velour, cotton, satin, vinyl and fur are all good choices. Pass the cards around and let the children touch them, telling them that they are using their sense of touch to feel them. Could put the swatches in a box and let the children feel them without being able to see them, explaining that they can use just one sense at a time.

Body parts bingo. Prepare bingo cards on the Internet or make by hand using pictures of the body parts that are involved in the senses, such as eyes, ears, mouth, nose, hands.

Count with your ears. Show the children ten pennies and count them out. Then have them close their eyes and tell them that they can still count the pennies with just their ears. Drop each penny one at a time into a glass or metal container making noise and counting that way.

Twister. Use the traditional game with the mat and spinner or make up your own.

Loud dancing. Give each child some kind of musical instrument, or a few jingle bells attached to a piece of string or cardboard. Play some fast music for them to move to and see how loud they can jingle their bells, using their sense of hearing to hear them

How does it smell? Place a cotton ball inside a film canister or other small container. Put a drop of some kind of extract on the cotton ball, such as vanilla, almond, peppermint, and/or vinegar, lemon juice, evergreen needles, chocolate, soap. Pass each canister around and ask the children if they recognize the smell. After they've all smelled it and had a chance to guess tell them what each is.

Pick up. Dump out a lot of small different items on the cloth in the middle of the circle of children. Give each child a cup or bowl and ask them to pick up items one at a time, and to try to get as many different items as possible. Include things with different textures, such as pom poms, paper clips, marbles, small pieces of sandpaper, cotton balls. After the items are picked up, ask the children to each describe one of the items that they picked up. See if they can describe it using different senses, such as how it feels and how it looks.

Sound canisters. Put items that make sounds inside small containers, such as bells, paper clips, sand, rice, beans. Make enough so that each child can hold at least one and play a rhythm game where you shake out a rhythm and have the children try to match yours.

Sight. Place a variety of items on a tray and show it to the children. Have them close their eyes (or cover the tray with a towel) and remove one of the items without them seeing what you removed. Then show them the tray again and see if they know which item is missing. Show them the item, put it back, then repeat with another item.

Craft: My senses book

Materials needed: Computer or copy paper, stapler, crayons. Advance preparation: Create small booklets by cutting paper in half on the shorter side. Fold and staple two of

My senses book.

those pages together. At storytime: Have each child illustrate each of their senses on one page of the booklet. Tell them to draw something they can see on one page, something they can hear, something they can taste, something they can touch and something they can smell. Ask them as they're drawing to tell you about what senses are involved in each of their drawings.

Alternative Crafts

Touch. Have the parent trace the child's hand on a piece of cardstock, cut it out and glue it to a background piece of paper. Have small pieces of different textured things available to glue down to the fingers. Some ideas are: sandpaper, cotton balls, fur, vinyl, corduroy, small tiles or other items that have interesting textures and can be glued down.

Hearing. Make maracas using paper plates and beans. Let the children decorate the outside of a large white paper plate, then fold it over and staple it almost all the way closed. Put a small amount of dried beans (like navy beans) inside and staple the opening closed. You might also want to duct tape around the edge to keep the beans in and protect the children's hands from the staples. Let the children shake their maracas to some music.

Sight. Make pretend binoculars out of two toilet paper rolls decorated with crayons and then taped together.

Touch. Have small pieces of fabric in interesting textures. Let the children glue them down to a piece of cardstock to make a touching quilt.

Snack: Fruit face

Materials needed: Fruits that can be used to make facial parts, such as apples, oranges, grapes, bananas, large paper plates. Advance preparation: Slice the fruit. At storytime: Place two of most of the fruits on the paper plate. Two for eyebrows, ears, eyes. Then one for nose and a few for mouth. Orange and apple slices make good ears and eyebrows and mouth. Grapes sliced in half make good eyes, nose or mouth. Banana slices make good eyes or nose. Talk about the different senses that are associated with the different facial features.

Fruit face.

Alternative Snacks

Carrot sticks and dip. Explain that carrots are good for one's eyes, or the sense of sight.

Noisy foods. Have foods such as pretzels, carrots, celery. Foods that can be heard when they are eaten.

Eye cookies. Spread white icing on large round sugar cookies. Top with an M & M for the iris and a mini chocolate chip for the pupil. Could also do with a cracker, cream cheese and an olive slice.

Salty and sweet. Offer two snacks: one that's salty and one that's sweet, such as dill pickles and sugar cookies, or potato chips and M&Ms. Ask the children to compare the two tastes and explain that we have taste buds on our tongues that help us tell the difference between salty and sweet tastes.

SUGGESTED BOOKS

Aliki. *My Feet.* 32 pages. 1991. HarperCollins Publishers. Describes feet and all the things they help us do.

Aliki. *My Five Senses.* 32 pages. 1989. HarperCollins Publishers. A simple presentation of the five senses and how we use them.

Aliki. *My Hands.* 32 pages. 1991. HarperCollins Publishers. Describes the parts of the hand and all the things hands help us do.

Baer, Gene. *Thump, Thump, Rat-a-tat-tat.* 32 pages. 1996. HarperCollins Publishers. A distant marching band grows louder and larger as it nears and smaller and quieter as it goes away again.

Bonsall, Crosby. *Who's Afraid of the Dark?* 32 pages. 1985. HarperCollins Publishers. A small boy projects his fear of the dark onto his dog.

Bridwell, Norman. *Clifford and the Big Parade.* 32 pages. 2011. Turtle Books. The town is celebrating its 100th birthday and there's a big parade.

Brown, Marc. *Arthur's Eyes.* 32 pages. 1983. Little, Brown & Co. Arthur stops wearing his glasses when he's teased and then mistakes the girl's bathroom for the boy's.

Brown, Marc. *Arthur's Nose.* 32 pages. 1986. Little, Brown & Co. Arthur decides he doesn't like his nose.

Brown, Margaret Wise. *Country Noisy Book.* 48 pages. 1994. HarperCollins Publishers. Little city dog Muffin goes to the country and hears lots of different noises.

Brown, Margaret Wise. *Indoor Noisy Book.* 48 pages. 1994. HarperCollins Publishers. When Muffin the dog has to stay indoors he hears all sorts of sounds.

Brown, Ruth. *A Dark, Dark Tale.* 32 pages. 1992. Penguin Group. Going through a dark house, a black cat surprises the only inhabitant.

Brown, Tom. *Tom Brown's Guide to Wild Edible and Medicinal Plants.* 256 pages. 1986. Penguin Group. How to use every part of the plant and where to find useful plants. A resource guide for plants and herbs.

Bunnett, Rochelle. *Friends in the Park.* 33 pages. 1993. Checkerboard Press. A multi-ethnic group of children, some with disabilities, play together in the park.

Burns, Marilyn. *The Greedy Triangle.* 40 pages. 1994. Heinemann. Dissatisfied with its shape, a triangle asks to have more lines and angles added.

Caviezel, Giovanni. *My Own Five Senses.* 10 pages. 2005. Barron's Educational Series. The little girl in this board book is about to discover her own five senses.

Charles, Veronica Martenova. *Hey! What's That Sound?* 32 pages. 1996. Stoddart Kids. If it's a ring, a ding, a crash or a splash it must have something to do with Aunt Minnie's visit.

Ciboul, Adele. *The Five Senses.* 28 pages. 2006. Firefly Books, Ltd. This book features engaging ways to explain how the senses send information to the brain.

Crews, Donald. *Parade.* 32 pages. 1986. Mulberry. Presents the various elements of a parade.

dePaola, Tomie. *The Popcorn Book.* 32 pages. 1989. Holiday House. Some interesting popcorn stories.

Ehlert, Lois. *Fish Eyes.* 1990. Houghton Mifflin Harcourt. A Book You Can Count On. A counting book that depicts a child as the fish he'd like to be.

Falk, Laine. *Let's Explore the Five Senses with City Dog and Country Dog.* 24 pages. 2007. Scholastic Library Publishing. A story where you follow the dogs to see what they see, smell, etc.

Feldman, Jean. *Five Senses.* 12 pages. 2010. Rourke Publishing,. Sing along with Dr. Jean to learn about your five senses.

Freeman, Don. *Corduroy.* 28 pages. 2009. Baker & Taylor. A toy bear is anxious to have a home with a little girl who wants to buy him.

Haddon, Jean. *Make Sense!* 32 pages. 2006. Lerner Publishing Group. Try to figure out which sense you would use for each activity.

Hoban, Tana. *Look Book.* 40 pages. 1997. Greenwillow Books. Nature photos are first viewed through a cut out hole and then in their entirety.

Hoban, Tana. *Take Another Look.* 40 pages. 1981. Greenwillow Books. By viewing things through die cut holes and in full pages, the viewer learns that things may be perceived differently.

Howard, Ken. *Little Bunny Follows His Nose.* 32 pages. 2004. Random House Children's Books. Using scratch and sniff the reader can follow the same smells as Little Bunny.

Ichikawa, Satoma, and Elizabeth Laird. *Rosy's Garden: A Child's Keepsake of Flowers.* Rosy spends the summer learning about flowers, their folklore and their uses.

IKids. *The Five Senses.* 20 pages. 2009. Innovative Kids. We feel, taste, see, hear and smell nature's beauty every day.

Jayne, Lisa. *How Do You Know? A Book About the Five Senses.* 24 pages. 2007. Tate Publishing and Enterprises. The author captures the characteristics of the five senses.

Johnson, Jinny. *Discover Science Senses.* 56 pages. 2010. Kingfisher. Explains the senses in an accessible way.

Kuskin, Karla. *City Noise.* 32 pages. 1994. HarperCollins Publishers. An old tin can becomes an urban conch shell in this poem.

Litchfield, Ada B. *A Button in Her Ear.* 32 pages. 1976. Albert Whitman & Co. A little girl relates how her hearing deficiency is corrected with a hearing aid.

MacLachlan, Patricia. *Through Grandpa's Eyes.* 40 pages. 1983. HarperCollins Publishers. Through his blind grandfather's unique way of seeing, John makes discoveries about the world around him.

Martin, Bill, Jr., and Eric Carle. *Brown Bear, Brown Bear, What Do You See?* 28 pages. 2012. Henry Holt & Co. Eric Carle's paper collage artwork shows everything that the brown bear sees.

Martin, Bill, Jr., John Archambault and Ted Rand. *Here Are My Hands.* 32 pages. 1998. Henry Holt & Co. A board book that explains all the parts of the body including eyes, ears & nose.

Martin, Bill, Jr., and Eric Carle. *Panda Bear, Panda Bear, What Do You See?* 40 pages. 2011. Henry Holt & Co. A beginner reader version featuring endangered animals.

Martin, Bill, Jr., and Eric Carle. *Polar Bear, Polar Bear, What Do You Hear?* 32 pages. 2011.

Henry Holt & Co. Eric Carle's paper collage artwork shows everything that the polar bear hears.

Matthews, Derek. *Snappy Sounds, Moo!* 10 pages. 2004. Advantage Publishers Group. A pop up book with five farm animal sounds.

Matthews, Derek. *Snappy Sounds, Woof!* 10 pages. 2005. Silver Dolphin Books. A pop up book with five pet animal sounds.

McGovern, Ann. *Too Much Noise.* 48 pages. 1992. Houghton Mifflin Harcourt. Peter goes to the village wise man to find out what to do about his noisy house.

McMillan, Bruce. *Sense Suspense.* 40 pages. 1994. Scholastic. Two young islanders use their senses to explore different things.

McPhail, David. *Something Special.* 32 pages. 1992. Little, Brown & Company. All the animal characters have a special talent. Sam doesn't think he has one until one day he discovers what it is.

Miller, Amanda. *Let's Play a Five Senses Guessing Game.* 24 pages. 2007. Scholastic Library Publishing. A young boy talks about the things he perceived and gives the reader a chance to guess what they are.

Miller, Margaret. *My Five Senses.* 24 pages. 1998. Aladdin. A simple introduction to the five senses.

Molter, Carey. *The Five Senses.* 24 pages. 2001. ABDO Publishing. Pictures and simple text showing activities involving the five senses.

O'Brien-Palmer, Michelle. *Sense-Abilities: Fun Ways to Explore the Senses.* 176 pages. 1998. Chicago Review Press. A book of science activities to help teach children about their senses.

Otto, Carolyn. *I Can Tell by Touching.* 32 pages. 1994. HarperCollins Publishers. Explains how the sense of touch helps one identify everyday objects.

Perkins, Al. *The Ear Book.* 24 pages. 2008. Random House Children's Books. Pleasant sounds are described in simple words.

Perkins, Al. *Hand, Hand, Fingers, Thumb.* 36 pages. 1969. Random House Children's Books. A band of prancing monkeys explains hands, fingers and thumbs.

Perkins, Al. *The Nose Book.* 24 pages. 2003. Random House Children's Books. Noses are interesting and serve many purposes.

Peterson, J. *I Have a Sister, My Sister Is Deaf.* 32 pages. 1977. HarperCollins Publishers. A young, deaf child is affectionately described by her older sister.

Reber, Deborah. *Blues Clues: Magenta Gets Glasses.* 24 pages. 2002. Turtleback Books. Magenta can't see but a trip to the eye doctor gets things sorted out for her.

Royston, Angela. *Senses.* 32 pages. 2011. Sea to Sea Publications. Identifies the five senses and explains how they work.

Rius, Maria. *The Five Senses: Hearing.* 32 pages. 1985. Turtleback Books. An explanation of the sense of hearing with a diagram of the ear.

Rius, Maria. *The Five Senses: Sight.* 32 pages. 1985. Barron's. An explanation of the sense of sight with a diagram of the eye.

Rius, Maria. *The Five Senses: Smell.* 29 pages. 1985. Barron's. A short scientific explanation of our sense of smell with a diagram of the nose.

Rius, Maria. *The Five Senses: Taste.* 32 pages. 1985. Turtleback Books. An explanation of the sense of taste.

Rius, Maria. *The Five Senses: Touch.* 32 pages. 1986. Barron's. A variety of things to be felt with the skin along with an explanation of the sense of touch.

Robinson, Fay. *Sound All Around.* 32 pages. 1994. Scholastic Library Publishing. The nature, properties and principles of sound.

Seuss, Dr. *The Eye Book.* 36 pages. 1999. Random House Children's Books. A boy and a rabbit both have two eyes that see all kinds of things.

Showers, Paul. *Ears Are for Hearing.* 80 pages. 1993. HarperCollins Publishers. Describes the process of hearing.

Showers, Paul. *Find Out by Touching.* 35 pages. 1975. HarperCollins Publishers. Encourages an awareness of the sense of touch.

Showers, Paul. *Follow Your Nose.* 40 pages. 1963. HarperCollins Publishers. Follow your nose and find out what things smell like.

Showers, Paul. *How You Talk.* 32 pages. 1992. HarperCollins Publishers. Explains the mechanics of speech.

Showers, Paul. *The Listening Walk.* 32 pages. 1993. HarperCollins Publishers. A little girl and her father take a quiet walk and try to identify the sounds around them.

Showers, Paul. *Look at Your Eyes.* 32 pages. 1992. HarperCollins Publishers. Describes the parts of the eye and how they work.

Smith, Kathy Billingslea. *Smelling.* 24 pages. 1998. Troll Communications. Basic information about the senses in a question and answer format.

Tekavec, Heather. *What's That Awful Smell?* 32 pages. 2006. Penguin Group. A group of animals discovers a little piglet while investigating an odor on their farm.

Underwood, Deborah. *The Loud Book.* 32 pages. 2011. Houghton Mifflin Harcourt. Simple text explores the many loud sounds one might hear during the day.

Underwood, Deborah. *The Quiet Book.* 32 pages. 2010. Houghton Mifflin Harcourt. A picture book about all different kinds of quiet.

Wells, Rosemary. *Noisy Nora.* 32 pages. 2000. Penguin Group. Feeling neglected, Nora makes more and more noise to try to get her parents' attention.

Wild, Margaret. *All the Better to See You With.* 32 pages. 1993. A. Whitman. Kate is quiet compared to her noisy siblings and her parents are slow to realize that she needs glasses.

Witte, Pat, and Eve Witte. *The Touch Me Book.* 20 pages. 1984. Random House Children's Books. Ten tactile activities with smooth, scratchy, stretchy, furry, etc.

Wong, Janet S. *Buzz.* 32 pages. 2002. Houghton Mifflin Harcourt. A child experiences the sights and sounds of morning, including a bee buzzing outside the window.

Ziefert, Harriet. *You Can't Taste a Pickle with Your Ear.* 40 pages. 2006. Blue Apple Books. Explores how each of the five senses is hard at work all day long.

Royalty

Advance planning: To plan for this storytime, find a theme-related song to play during craft and snack times, like "Someday My Prince Will Come," from *Snow White and the Seven Dwarfs* sung by Adriana Caselotti. You will also want to select a poem, such as "The Queen of Hearts" (an eighteenth-century poem by an anonymous author), along with the books you plan to read. Decorate your space with a cardboard castle that you make out of a large appliance box, or smaller toy castles, royal looking plastic swords, plastic knight shields and armor, tiaras, crowns, posters of or stuffed dragons.

Introduction to theme: What do we mean by royalty? Some countries have a queen, or a king. Does our country have a queen or king? In some places the queen or king might really be in charge of what goes on in the country, but in others, they aren't. Think about England for a moment. They have a queen — her name is Elizabeth. She has sons who are princes and a daughter who is a princess. Have you ever seen a movie or read a book about a princess? We're going to read some books about royalty today, but they might not be exactly what you've been thinking about. We'll also play some royal games, make a crown craft and eat a snack that looks like a crown.

Song: "Sing a Song of Sixpence":

> Sing a song of sixpence,
> A pocket full of rye;
> Four and twenty blackbirds
> Baked in a pie!
> When the pie was opened
> The birds began to sing;
> Was that not a dainty dish
> To set before the king?
>
> The king was in his counting-house
> Counting all his money;
> The queen was in the parlour,
> Eating bread and honey.
> The maid was in the garden,

Hanging out the clothes;
When down there came a blackbird
And bit her on the nose.

Game: Princess says (like Simon says)

Materials needed: A list of things that the princess says to do. Advance preparation: None. At storytime: Princess Says: stand up; sit down; turn around; raise one hand; lower your hand; hop on one foot; stop hopping; curtsy; bow; close your eyes; open your eyes; raise both hands; lower your hands; salute; wave.

Alternative Games

Royalty bingo. Bingo games can be printed off the Internet. Some websites have ready made games that fit a particular theme, or there are some sites that allow you to upload your own photos and descriptions to make custom cards. Hand out bingo cards, colored discs for markers. Hold up each call space for everyone to see. Play until someone has covered their whole card.

Knight bravery and skill tests. If you made a cardboard castle, you could play some games using it, such as tossing bean bags into it as a skill test. You could make a large poster of a dragon and pretend to go on an expedition to slay it, maybe using some cardboard swords.

Princess and the pea. Put a dried bean or pea under a pillow to see if the children can feel it there. This works best if you've read *The Very Smart Pea and the Princess* or the story of the Princess and the Pea. Have some other bigger objects to put under the pillow to see if the children can feel those.

The Princess and the Pea by Hans Christian Andersen (abridged version)

Once upon a time there was a prince who wanted to marry a princess; but she would have to be a real princess. He travelled all over the world to find one, but nowhere could he get what he wanted. There were princesses enough, but it was difficult to find out whether they were real ones. There was always something about them that was not as it should be. So he came home again and was sad, for he would have liked very much to have a real princess.

One evening a terrible storm came on; there was thunder and lightning, and the rain poured down in torrents. Suddenly a knocking was heard at the city gate, and the old king went to open it.

It was a princess standing out there in front of the gate. But, good gracious! what a sight the rain and the wind had made her look. The water ran down from her hair and clothes; it ran down into the toes of her shoes and out again at the heels. And yet she said that she was a real princess.

Well, we'll soon find that out, thought the old queen. But she said nothing, went into the bed-room, took all the bedding off the bedstead, and laid a pea on the bottom; then she took twenty mattresses and laid them on the pea, and then twenty eider-down beds on top of the mattresses.

On this the princess had to lie all night. In the morning she was asked how she had slept.

"Oh, very badly!" said she. "I have scarcely closed my eyes all night. Heaven only knows what was in the bed, but I was lying on something hard, so that I am black and blue all over my body. It's horrible!"

Now they knew that she was a real princess because she had felt the pea right through the twenty mattresses and the twenty eider-down beds.

Nobody but a real princess could be as sensitive as that.

So the prince took her for his wife, for now he knew that he had a real princess; and the pea was put in the museum, where it may still be seen, if no one has stolen it.

There, that is a true story.

The queen (or king) commands You. Have everyone in a circle and start the game by doing some kind of movement and say "The queen commands you to..." and demonstrate what you would like them to do, such as turn in a circle, or bow, or kneel — any kind of movement. Then take turns going around the circle and let everyone be either a queen or a king and command the others to do their choice of movement.

Foam crown pieces.

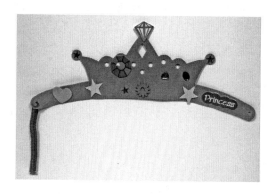

Foam crown.

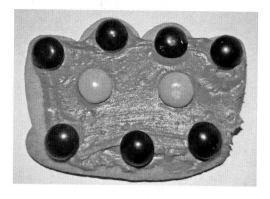

Crown cookie.

Craft: Foam crown

Materials needed: Foam crowns, foam royalty stickers and stick on jewels. Advance preparation: Order foam crowns, stickers and stick on jewels from Oriental Trading at www.orientaltrading.com. At storytime: Each child will decorate a foam crown with royalty stickers and stick on jewels.

Alternative Crafts

Boxes for royal jewels. Small papier mâché boxes painted gold or silver. Have children decorate with stick on jewels.

Aluminum foil crowns. You will need foil and tissue paper. Make cuffed strips of foil about 20 inches long. Fold 20-inch wide tissue paper into strips. At storytime, insert folded strips of tissue paper into foil cuff, trim tissue to points. Tape ends together to fit child's head.

Snack: Crown cookie

Materials needed: Cookie dough, crown-shaped cookie cutter, pink icing, candy decorations such as Skittles or M&Ms, small paper plates, plastic knives. Advance preparation: Bake cookies into crown shape. At storytime: Place a cookie on a paper plate along with a dollop of pink icing and some candy decorations. Have the children spread the icing and add the decorations.

Alternative Snacks

Princess cupcake. Cupcake iced in pink with chocolate chip eyes, licorice string mouth, red M & M cheeks with cut starburst crown on a toothpick.

Queen of hearts tarts. Flatten biscuits then indent with heart-shaped cookie cutter. Spread strawberry jam in the indentation and bake.

SUGGESTED BOOKS

Allen, Joy. *Princess Palooza*. 32 pages. 2011. Penguin Group. Six little girls have fun at a princess themed playground.

Andrews, Julie. *The Very Fairy Princess*. 32 pages. 2010. Little, Brown Books for Young Readers. Geraldine knows that she is a true fairy princess, even if her friends and family don't believe in fairies.

Auch, Mary Jane. *The Princess and the Pizza*. 32 pages. 2003. Holiday House. A princess competes with other princesses for the hand of a prince by cooking up food that turns out to be a pizza.

Coyle, Carmela Lavigna. *Do Princesses Have Best Friends Forever?* 32 pages. 2010. Taylor Trade Publishing. Two girls playing dress up celebrate friendship.

Coyle, Carmela Lavigna. *Do Princesses Scrape Their Knees?* 32 pages. 2006. Cooper Square Publishing. It's okay to scrape your knees when you're trying something new.

Coyle, Carmela Lavigna. *Do Princesses Wear Hiking Boots?* 32 pages. 2003. Cooper Square Publishing. It's okay to wear clothes that are appropriate for the activity you're doing, even if it's messy sometimes.

Deeble, Jason. *Sir Ryan's Quest*. 32 pages. 2009. Roaring Book Press. A knight must be brave to face everything on his quest.

dePaola, Tomie. *The Knight and the Dragon*. 32 pages. 1980. Penguin Group. A knight who has never fought a dragon and a dragon who has never fought a knight meet in battle.

Ferguson, Sarah. *Tea for Ruby*. 40 pages. 2008. Simon & Schuster. Ruby needs to learn good manners before she has tea with the Queen.

Freeman, Mylo. *Every Girl Is a Princess*. 30 pages. 2011. Clavis Publishing. Translated. Celebrates diversity among princesses of the world and what makes each one special.

Funke, Cornelia. *Princess Knight*. 32 pages. 2004. The Chicken House. The princess objects to being married off to a knight who will win her in a jousting contest.

Gardner, Carol. *Princess Zelda and the Frog*. 2011. 40 pages. Feiwel and Friends. Zelda the bulldog discovers one can't judge a castle by its moat, or a frog by its ribbets.

Grey, Mini. *The Very Smart Pea and the Princess to Be*. 32 pages. 2003. Random House Children's Books. The pea gives its own version of the story of the princess and the pea.

Gwynne, Fred. *The King Who Rained*. 48 pages. 1988. Aladdin. A little girl pictures the things her parents are talking about, including a king who rained (reigned) for 49 years.

Hargreaves, Adam. *Little Miss Princess*. 32 pages. 2011. Penguin Group. Little Miss Princess has always had people to take care of her. Would she be able to take care of herself on her own?

Heide, Florence Parry. *Princess Hyacinth: The Surprising Tale of a Girl Who Floated*. 48 pages. 2009. Random House Children's Books. How does one deal with a floating princess?

Hoffman, Mary. *Princess Grace*. 32 pages. 2008. Penguin Group. Grace hopes that she will be chosen as the parade princess and she asks her teacher to help her find the right costume.

Horowitz, Dave. *Twenty-Six Princesses*. 32 pages. 2011. Penguin Group. From Princess Alice through Princess Zaire, learn the alphabet with a frog at the palace.

Howland, Naomi. *Princess Says Goodnight*. 32 pages. 2010. HarperCollins Publishers. When the red-headed girl sees herself in the mirror, she becomes the princess she imagines herself to be.

Lewis, Jill. *Don't Read This Book!* 32 pages. 2010. ME Media. The king commands us to stop and go read something else, since his story isn't finished.

MacHale, D.J. *The Monster Princess*. 40 pages. 2010. Simon & Schuster. Deep in a cave there's a monster who wishes she was pretty, who wishes she could dance.

Mack, Todd. *Princess Penelope*. 32 pages. 2003. Scholastic Press. Penelope is absolutely certain that she's a princess.

Mayer, Mercer. *The Bravest Knight*. 32 pages. 2007. Penguin Group. The hero fights a dragon.

Melling, David. *The Kiss That Missed*. 32 pages. 2007. Barron's Educational Series. A king misfires his good night kiss and it goes right past his son and out the window.

Mortimer, Rachael. *Snoring Beauty*. 32 pages. 2011. RHCB. Everyone in the palace is being driven crazy by the princess's loud snoring. Who can save the day?

Munsch, Robert. *The Paper Bag Princess*. 32 pages. 1980. Annick Press Limited. A princess rescues her husband to be from a dragon with unexpected results.

Oppel, Kenneth. *The King's Taster*. 32 pages. 2009. HarperCollins Publishers. A six year old king is a very picky eater and so has a dog as his royal taster.

Read, Leon. *George the Knight*. 24 pages. 2011.

Crabtree Publishing Company. George wants to be a knight, but needs a sword, a shield and a horse.

Rogerson, Gillian. *You Can't Eat a Princess.* 32 pages. 2011. Penguin Group. How can a princess overtake a group of aliens? And what does chocolate have to do with it?

Ross, Tony. *I Want to Do It Myself: A Little Princess Story.* 32 pages. 2011. Lerner Publishing Group. The Little Princess is going camping and everyone wants to help but she wants to do things herself.

Spinelli, Eileen. *Princess Pig.* 40 pages. 2009. Alfred A. Knopf. When a sash blows in and lands on the pig, she thinks she must be a princess. But the other animals treat her differently and she's not sure that she wants to be a princess.

Thomas, Shelley Moore. *Get Well Good Knight.* Puffin Easy to Read Level 3. 48 pages. 2012. Puffin. The knight finds the dragons suffering

from colds and sets off to find something to cure them,

Wilson, Karma. *Princess Me.* 32 pages. 2007. Margaret K. McElderry Books. A child's bedroom is transformed into a princess' court in this bedtime story.

Wood, Audrey. *King Bidgood in the Bathtub.* 32 pages. 1985. Houghton Mifflin Harcourt Trade Reference Publishers. The king refuses to leave the bathtub and everyone in the kingdom tries to get him out.

Yolen, Jane. *Not All Princesses Dress in Pink.* 32 pages. 2010. Simon & Schuster Children's Publishing. Girls can do lots of things while wearing clothing that's not pink, but wearing their tiaras.

Ziefert, Harriet. *The Princess and the Pea.* 32 pages. 1996. Penguin Group. Level 2 Puffin Easy to Read. The queen has a plan to help the prince find a princess to marry.

Colors

Advance planning: To plan for this storytime, find a theme-related song to play during craft and snack times, like "De Colores," by Raffi. You will also want to select a poem, such as "A Box of Crayons," by Shane DeRolf (find it at www.kinderteacher.com), along with the books you plan to read. Decorate your space with posters showing the primary colors, objects in primary colors or other brightly colored every day objects.

Introduction to theme: You probably know that everything around you is has a color. But you might not have known that most colors we see come from just three colors that combine with each other to make other colors. (Hold up three objects, one at a time, that are red, blue and yellow) What color is this? (red) What color is this? (blue) What color is this? (yellow). What color are you wearing today? What color am I wearing? Do you have a favorite color? Today we'll read about colors, play a game with colors, make a colorful craft and eat a colorful snack.

Song: "I Can Sing a Rainbow," by Arthur Hamilton. Lyrics can be found at www.learning4Kids.net.

Game: I spy

Materials needed: List of items that you can see and their colors. Advance preparation: None. At storytime: Choose some things in the room that are clearly visible to all the children and make a list of them ahead of time. At storytime, say "I spy with my little eye, something that is blue" and have the children take turns guessing what is that you see. Do a few items of each color.

Alternative Games

Colored pictures. Show pictures that you've printed from the Internet or clipped from magazines of many different things that are one obvious color, like a green tractor, or red car, or different kinds of fruits and vegetables. Hold up a photo and have the children say what color it is.

Parachute play. If you have a multi colored parachute, could bounce a ball on it with the children standing all around and have them shout out the color the ball lands on with each bounce.

Bean bag toss. Place and tape circles of red, green, blue and yellow on the floor. Have the children take turns tossing bean bags at the circles after first saying the color they are trying to toss the bean bag on.

Red light, green light. Have the children line up side by side about 30 feet away from you across the room. Hold up a green circle and say "green light" and the children can start walking slowly toward you. Hold up a red circle and say "red light" and they stop. Have them start and stop often as they walk across the room.

Rainbow throw. Draw a large rainbow on a poster board. Have the children toss bean bags at the rainbow and say the color their bean bag landed on.

Color dance. You'll need one piece of colored construction paper per child, CD player, children's music. Play music and tell the children that when the music stops, they should stand on a piece of paper. Then ask each child to say what color paper they're standing on.

Sort by color. Before storytime, place circles of several different colors, like red, yellow and blue, all around the storytime area. Put out three buckets — one of each color and ask the children to go around the room and find the circles, bring them back and put them in the bucket that matches the color. Tell them they need to find each circle one at a time and bring it back, so that it will give all the children a chance to pick some up and take the game longer to play. You could also limit each child to one of each color.

Color circle pieces.

Craft: Color circle

Materials needed: Paper plates or cardstock, tissue papers, scissors, glue (liquid). Advance preparation: If using cardstock cut circles from cardstock with about a five-inch diameter. You could also do squares or triangles or could do multiple shapes and let the children choose. Cut many colors of tissue paper into small squares, about one to two inches square. At storytime: Pour white glue into paper plates and have the children spread glue on to their plate or cardstock shape in sections so that it doesn't all dry before they've attached the tissue paper. Have them

Color circle.

wad up the squares of tissue paper and then stick them in whatever manner they like onto the glue on their shape. Some children might choose to do the colors randomly; others might do their whole shape with one color or color in sections.

Alternative Crafts

Brown bear. Give each child an outline drawing of one of the animals in the *Brown Bear, Brown Bear, What Do You See?* book and have them color them in. Glue a popsicle stick to each animal and as you read the story, ask the child with the appropriate animal to hold it up (there may be multiples) and make the sound the animal makes.

Color caterpillar. Give each child eight different colored circles and have them glue them down to a sheet of paper in the shape of a caterpillar. They can add legs and eyes and antennae.

Color wreath. You will need paper plates, red, yellow and blue construction paper, yarn, ribbon, glue sticks. Cut out the middle of the paper plates to make wreath shapes. Cut circles of the different colors of construction paper with a big enough diameter to cover the paper plate wreath. Cut lengths of yarn for hanging in the back and ribbon to tie a bow on the front. Have the children glue the colored circles all around, covering the wreath. Tie the ribbon in a bow and glue to the top. Make a loop with the yarn and tape it to the back for a hanger.

Rainbow circle. Cut circles of different colors in different sizes, about an inch difference in diameter. Glue them in size order, with each smaller circle on top.

Snack: Fruits of many colors

Materials needed: Find a selection of fruits in different colors, such as oranges, blueberries, strawberries, grapes, pineapple or banana, paper plates or bowls, spoons.

Advance preparation: Wash and cut up the fruits. At storytime: Ask the children to identify the colors as they eat the pieces of fruit.

Alternative Snacks

Sprinkle cookies. Have round or rainbow-shaped cookies and let the children sprinkle sugars or other kinds of colored sprinkles. Could get multicolored sprinkles.

Colorful cookies. Have round cookies and color icing with blue, yellow and red, offering each child a choice of icing color or a little bit of each color to spread on their own cookie.

Multicolored jelly beans. Give each child at least one jelly bean of each color in the bag and ask them to identify the colors as they eat them.

Vegetables of many colors. Carrots, celery or green pepper, yellow and red pepper can be cut into small strips.

Colored applesauce. Turn applesauce into several different colors with food coloring or buy some different colors at the store.

Fruits of many colors.

SUGGESTED BOOKS

Baker, Alan. *White Rabbit's Color Book.* 24 pages. 1999. Kingfisher. White Rabbit jumps from one color paint bucket into another, learning about different colors.

Brown, Margaret Wise. *Color Kittens.* 24 pages. 2003. Random House Children's Books. Two kittens, with many cans of paint, make lots of colors.

Carle, Eric. *The Mixed-Up Chameleon.* 40 pages. 1984. HarperCollins Publishers. The chameleon's life got more exciting when he found he could change more than his color.

Crews, Donald. *Ten Black Dots.* 32 pages. 1986. HarperCollins Publishers. A counting book that shows what can be done with ten black dots.

Ehlert, Lois. *Color Zoo.* 40 pages. 1989. HarperCollins Publishers. Introduces colors and shapes that form animal faces.

Ehlert, Lois. *Planting A Rainbow.* 32 pages. 1988. Houghton Mifflin Harcourt. A mother and child plant a rainbow of flowers in the garden.

Fowler, Allan. *All the Colors of the Rainbow.* 32 pages. 1998. Scholastic Library Publishing. Explains how rainbows are formed.

Freeman, Don. *Rainbow of My Own.* 32 pages. 1981. Penguin Group. A little boy imagines what it would be like if he had his own rainbow.

Heller, Ruth. *Color.* 40 pages. 1999. Penguin Group. Transparencies and overlays show the world of color printing.

Hoban, Tana. *Colors Everywhere.* Wordless book that children will enjoy by naming the colors of the objects in the photos.

Hoban, Tana. *Is It Red? Is It Yellow? Is It Blue?* 32 pages. 1978. HarperCollins Publishers. Wordless book that teaches colors to very young children.

Hoban, Tana. *Of Colors and Things.* 24 pages. 1996. HarperCollins Publishers. Photographs of food, toys and other objects grouped by color.

Hoban, Tana. *Red, Blue, Yellow Shoe.* 12 pages. 1986. HarperCollins Publishers. A board book with photographs of common objects with the color written on each page.

Howard, Katherine. *Do You Know Colors?* 32 pages. 1979. Random House Children's Books. A parrot introduces colors and how they can be mixed to form new ones.

Hubbard, Patricia. *My Crayons Talk.* 32 pages. 1996. Henry Holt & Co. A story about talking crayons with colors and feelings explored.

Johnson, Crockett. *Harold and the Purple Crayon.* 64 pages. 1998. HarperCollins Publishers. Harold goes for a walk, drawing everything he needs as he goes.

Jonas, Ann. *Color Dance.* 40 pages. 1989. HarperCollins Publishers. Three dancers show how colors combine to make new colors.

Katz, Karen. *The Colors of Us.* 32 pages. 1999. Henry Holt & Co. A seven year old and her mother notice the variation in their and their friends' skin colors.

Kellogg, Steven. *The Mystery of the Flying Orange Pumpkin.* 32 pages. 1992. Puffin. A Halloween story that emphasizes the color orange in the drawings.

Kunhardt, Edith. *Red Day, Green Day.* 32 pages. 1992. HarperCollins Publishers. Takes the reader through all the colors of the rainbow in the story about Andrew and his class when they have a day to learn about each color.

Lamorisse, Albert. *The Red Balloon.* 48 pages. 1967. Random House Children's Books. The story of a young boy and his best friend, which is a red balloon.

Lionni, Leo. *A Color of His Own.* 30 pages. 2000. Random House Children's Books. All the animals except the chameleon have a color of their own.

Lionni, Leo. *Little Blue and Little Yellow.* 48 pages. 1995. HarperCollins Publishers. A little blue spot and a little yellow spot are best friends, and when they hug they turn green.

Martin, Bill, Jr., and Eric Carle. *Brown Bear, Brown Bear, What Do You See?* 32 pages. 1992. Henry Holt & Co. Children see a variety of animals, each one a different color, looking at them.

Mcmillan, Bruce. *Growing Colors.* 32 pages. 1998. HarperCollins Publishers. Photos of fruits and vegetables show the many colors found in nature.

Munsch, Robert. *Purple, Green and Yellow.* 32 pages. 1992. Annick Press Ltd. Brigid loves markers and when she draws on herself with permanent ink she must find a solution to stay out of trouble.

Onyefulu, Ifeoma. *Chidi Only Likes Blue.* 24 pages. 1997. Penguin Group. Chidi's older sister tries to teach him about the other colors found in their African village.

Peek, Merle. *Mary Wore Her Red Dress and Henry*

Wore His Green Sneakers. 32 pages. 2006. Sandpiper. All the animals come dressed in different colors on Katy's birthday.

Pinkwater, Daniel. *The Big Orange Splot.* 32 pages. 1977. Turtleback Books. When Mr. Plumbean's house gets splashed with orange paint he decides to make it a multi colored house.

Roger, Alan. *Green Bear.* 16 pages. 1997. World Book. Green Bear changes the color of his house to match the seasons.

Serfozo, Mary. *Who Said Red?* 32 pages. 1988. Margaret K. McElderry Books. A little girl and her brother introduce many colors as they wander about their farm.

Seuss, Dr. *Green Eggs and Ham.* 72 pages. 1960. Random House Children's Books. How do you know that you don't like green eggs and ham if you haven't tried them?

Seuss, Dr. *My Many Colored Days.* 40 pages. 1996. Random House Children's Books. An amusing look at how color affects children's lives and especially their behavior.

Stinson, Kathy. *Red Is Best.* 32 pages. 2006. Annick Press, Limited. One child has a stubborn preference for red.

Walsh, Ellen Stoll. *Mouse Magic.* 32 pages. 2000. Harcourt Children's Books. The wizard knows how to make colors jiggle and shake but the mouse discovers that the magic is in the colors, not the wizard.

Walsh, Ellen Stoll. *Mouse Paint.* 32 pages. 1995. Houghton Mifflin Harcourt. Three white mice discover jars of paint.

Westray, Kathleen. *A Color Sampler.* 32 pages. 1993. Houghton Mifflin Harcourt. Discusses primary and secondary colors and how to mix them to get new colors.

Whitman, Candace. *Red, Yellow, Blue and You.* 30 pages. 2008. Abbeville Press. Rhyming text celebrates primary colors.

Yolen, Jane. *How Do Dinosaurs Learn Their Colors?* 12 pages. 2006. Blue Sky Press. A board book that introduces different hues of color as the dinosaurs paint and play.

Alligators and Crocodiles

Advance planning: To plan for this storytime, find a theme-related song to play during craft and snack times, like "There's an Alligator in the Elevator," by the Peter Pan Kids. You will also want to select a poem, such as "How Doth the Little Crocodile," by Lewis Carroll (find it online or in the book *Alice's Adventures in Wonderland*), along with the books you plan to read. Decorate your space with green streamers, stuffed alligators, blue cloth or tarp to look like swamp with some greenery like a tropical houseplant or paper flowers like water lilies. You could play jungle sounds as arrival background and wear a pith helmet.

Introduction to theme: An alligator's mouth is shaped like the letter U. A crocodile's mouth is shaped like the letter V (show shapes with your hands or print a large U and V on paper to show the letters). When a crocodile closes its mouth you can still see almost all of its long sharp teeth. When an alligator closes its mouth you can only see the top teeth. Show some photos so that the children understand what you mean. Alligators keep growing their whole lives. The longer they live the bigger they get. Most grow to be about 10 feet long but the biggest alligator ever found was twice that long! Alligators like wet warm places like swamps, lakes, ponds and rivers. Most alligators live in South America. Most crocodiles live in Africa and prefer salty water. Today we'll read about alligators and crocodiles, play an alligator game, make an alligator craft and have a snack that even looks like an alligator.

Song: "Teasing Mr. Crocodile" (more of a poem than a song — no particular tune) author unknown.

Five little monkeys
Sitting in a tree
Teasing Mr. Crocodile,
"You can't catch me."
Along came Mr. Crocodile,
Quiet as can be
SNAP (make two hands motion of jaws snapping shut)
Four little monkeys
Sitting in a tree
Teasing Mr. Crocodile,
"You can't catch me."
Along came Mr. Crocodile,
Quiet as can be
SNAP (make two hands motion of jaws snapping shut)
Three little monkeys
Sitting in a tree
Teasing Mr. Crocodile,
"You can't catch me."
Along came Mr. Crocodile,
Quiet as can be
SNAP (make two hands motion of jaws snapping shut)
Two little monkeys
Sitting in a tree
Teasing Mr. Crocodile,
"You can't catch me."
Along came Mr. Crocodile,
Quiet as can be
SNAP (make two hands motion of jaws snapping shut)
One little monkey
Sitting in a tree
Teasing Mr. Crocodile,
"You can't catch me."
Along came Mr. Crocodile,
Quiet as can be
SNAP (make two hands motion of jaws snapping shut)
No more little monkeys
Sitting in a tree

Game: Rescue me!

Materials needed: Blue tarp, pictures of alligators. Advance preparation: Cut or print alligators. At storytime: Place a large blue plastic tarp or cloth on the floor. Place a bunch of alligator pictures (either cut from green construction paper or printed from the computer) on the floor all around the tarp. Line the children up to follow you across the swamp and say as you go: I'm walking, walking, walking across the big blue swamp. I hope those alligators don't go chomp (make a chomping gesture with your hands). Repeat going across saying other things, like I'm swimming, swimming, swimming or I'm tiptoeing, or skipping, or jumping, etc.

Alternative Games

Bigger Than, smaller than. Make up large cards with an alligator that has a wide open mouth that can face either left or right (use flip if using graphic software to print on your computer). Point the alligator's wide open mouth toward the larger of two objects, like shapes such as circles, squares, triangles and put a smaller shape on the other side of the alligator's mouth. Tell the children that the alligator is hungry and always wants to eat the bigger shape but ask them to tell you if the shape you're pointing to when you hold up the card is bigger or smaller. Make sure that the larger shape is sometimes on the left and sometimes on the right, and that the alligator's mouth is pointing toward it.

"The Crocodile Song." Do as a finger play. If you want to sing it, you can find the tune and lyrics at www.dltk-teach.com.

Frog toss. Use a big blue tarp as a swamp and place some construction paper or computer printed lily pads on it. Place several construction paper or computer printed alligators around the lily pads in the swamp. Have several green bean bags to be frogs (or use stuffed frogs if you have them, or make your own bean bag frogs from cut out felt and beans) and have the children try to toss the frogs onto the lily pads. They'll need to be careful not to let the frogs land in the swamp where the alligators might get them.

Alligator paper bag puppet pieces.

Alligator paper bag puppet.

Craft: Alligator paper bag puppet

Materials needed: Green paper bag, green, white, red, yellow, black construction paper, black crayons, glue sticks. Advance preparation: Cut face pieces and eye backgrounds from green construction paper. Cut eyes and nostrils from yellow paper and pupils from black paper. Cut teeth from white construction paper. Cut tongue from red construction paper. At storytime: Glue yellow eyes to green eye backgrounds. Glue black pupils to yellow eyes. Glue the completed eyes to the top face piece. Glue teeth to the bottom of the top face piece and the nostrils on the top face piece. Glue the bottom face piece under the flap of the bag and the red tongue on top of the bottom face piece where it will show under the teeth.

Alternative Crafts

Alligator puppet. Make an alligator stick puppet made from green card stock. Cut alligator body with top jaw and a separate piece of cardstock for the bottom jaw. Use hot glue to attach a craft stick to the bottom of the alligator belly so that it can be held with the stick and used as a puppet. Punch holes where bottom and top jaw meet and have children attach with a brass brad so it can move open and closed. Let the children hold their alligators with the stick with one hand and move the jaw with their other hand and go chomp chomp chomp.

Construction paper alligator. Fold a piece of green construction paper in half lengthwise. Draw a simple alligator shape on the side with the alligator's back at the top of the fold, and two legs at the bottom open edge. Mark several short diagonal lines on the alligator's back. Have the children cut out the shape and then cut the slits on the back. Open the paper, fold over the little triangles made by the slits and then fold it back. Tape the belly in three places to hold it together. Cut a jagged line at one end for teeth. Have the children make a dot for an eye on each side near the teeth.

Snack: Alligator cupcake

Materials needed: Cupcakes, green icing, green loop cereal, green mini marshmallows or chocolate chips, paper plates, plastic knives. Advance preparation: Bake cupcakes. Color icing green. At storytime: This is an alligator head. Cover the cupcake with green icing. Place two loop cereal pieces to look like eyes on one side and the two mini marshmallows or chocolate chips at the other side to look like the snout. If you want to make it look like an alligator head floating in water you could color some of the icing blue and make a triangular shape with the green and surround it with blue. Or you could get Nutter Butter cookies or circus peanuts to use as a shape for the head, cover it with green and then surround with blue.

Alligator cupcake.

Alternative Snacks

Alligator mouths. Make celery sticks or cucumber slices to look like alligator mouths. Cream cheese could be spread on the celery sticks to be teeth.

Snake cake. Bake a tube or bundt cake and cut it into pieces and link them up in a sort of snake shape. Ice with green icing and cover with green M&Ms. Put two white icing eyes and ice some white teeth.

SUGGESTED BOOKS

Beard, Alex. *Crocodile's Tears*. 48 pages. 2012. Abrams Books for Young Readers. Why is Crocodile crying? Everyone wants to know. It turns out that crocodile is sad because so many animals face extinction.

Berger, Melvin, and Gilda Berger. *Snap! A Book About Alligators and Crocodiles*. 37 pages. 2001. Scholastic Reader Level 3. Good source of facts and photos that could be shown.

Bergman, Mara. *Snip! Snap! What's That?* 32 pages. 2005. Greenwillow Books. An alligator comes into an apartment and threatens the children until they turn the tables on him.

Boekhoff, Carol. *Aunt Allie's Alligator*. 26 pages. 2005. BookSurge Publishing. When Aunt Allie comes to visit, she brings an alligator and the entire family shares quite an experience.

Bredeson, Carmen. *Fun Facts About Alligators*. 21 pages. 2008. Enslow Publishers. Good resource of facts about alligators.

Bryan, Sean. *A Girl and Her Gator*. 32 pages. 2011. Arcade Publishing. A girl wakes up with a gator in her hair and is worried about what everyone will think of it.

Charette, Rick. *Alligator in the Elevator*. 32 pages. 1998. Pine Point Record Co. Children don't know quite what to do when they come upon an alligator in the elevator. This books comes from the songwriter of the song by the same name that's suggested as the song to play during this storytime.

Child, Lauren. *But I Am an Alligator*. 24 pages. 2008. Grosset and Dunlap. Lola wants to wear her alligator costume everywhere, much to Charlie's embarrassment.

Clark, Emma Chichester. *Melrose and Croc Beside the Sea*. 32 pages. 2009. HarperCollins Publishers. Melrose the dog and his friend Croc keep each other's spirits up by taking a visit to the beach.

Croser, Josephine. *Crunch the Crocodile*. 32 pages. 1987. Scholastic. Crunch scares all the other animals in the river, but one day gets scared himself.

Donnio, Sylviane. *I'd Really Like to Eat a Child*. 32 pages. 2007. Random House Books for Young Readers. A little alligator gets nothing but bananas to eat and he wants to expand on that. His parents try to please him but he insists he wants to eat a child. He finally meets one but she outsmarts him.

Dorros, Arthur. *Alligator Shoes*. 24 pages. 1992. Puffin. An alligator spends the night in a shoe store.

Eastman, P.D. *Flap Your Wings*. 48 pages. 2000. Random House Books for Young Readers. A strange egg appears in their nest, but Mr. and Mrs. Bird go on to take care of it anyway. It hatches into an alligator, though, and this presents some problems.

Gibbons, Gail. *Alligators and Crocodiles*. 32 pages. 2010. Holiday House. A lot of good factual information about both alligators and crocodiles. Useful as a resource but some parts are too graphic to read or show to preschoolers.

Gralley, Jean. *Very Boring Alligator*. 32 pages. 2001. Henry Holt & Co. A very boring alligator comes to play one day and simply won't leave.

Heller, Ruth. *Chickens Aren't the Only Ones*. 48 pages. 1999. Penguin Group. An introduction to the animals that lay eggs.

Hoberman, Mary Ann. *The Lady with the Alligator Purse*. 28 pages. 1990. Little, Brown Books for Young Readers. The old jump rope nonsense rhyme.

Kubler, Annie. *See You Later Alligator*. 24 pages. 2004. Childs-Play International. Crocodile has lots of chores to do but Alligator is too busy to help.

Kvasnosky, Laura McGee. *See You Later, Alligator*. 24 pages. 1995. Houghton Mifflin Harcourt Publishers. Popular sayings relate to the first day of school.

Lionni, Leo. *An Extraordinary Egg*. 32 pages. 1998. Dragonfly Books. What kind of creature could it be inside that beautiful white egg?

Mayer, Mercer. *There's an Alligator Under My Bed*. 32 pages. 1987. Penguin Group. A nighttime adventure dealing with something under the bed.

Mozelle, Shirley. *Zack's Alligator*. 64 pages. 1995. HarperCollins Publishers. When Zack gets an alligator in the mail, much hilarity ensues.

Munsch, Robert. *Alligator Baby*. 32 pages. 2002. Cartwheel. There's a mix-up when parents bring home their baby. It seems they've brought home an alligator. It's up to the older daughter to return to the zoo and bring home the real baby.

Olson, Mary. *An Alligator Ate My Brother*. 32 pages. 2000. Boyds Mill Press. The parents don't believe one brother when he tells them an alligator is running loose in the house and is after his brother.

Paye, Won-Ldy. *Mrs. Chicken and the Hungry Alligator*. 32 pages. 2003. Holt, Henry & Company. A re-telling of an African tale about a vain chicken and an alligator.

Pringle, Laurence. *Alligators and Crocodiles*. 32 pages. 2009. Boyds Mill Press. Good lifelike drawings and facts. A resource for information, not a storybook to read.

Richardson, Adele. *Alligators*. 24 pages. 2005. Capstone Press. A brief introduction to alligators.

Rockwell, Anne. *Who Lives in an Alligator Hole?* 40 pages. 2006. HarperCollins Publishers. Describes the habitats of alligators.

Rylant, Cynthia. *Alligator Boy*. 32 pages. 2007. Houghton Mifflin Harcourt Publishers. Rhyming text about a boy who wants to be an alligator.

Sendak, Maurice. *Alligators All Around*. 32 pages. 1991. HarperCollins Publishers. An alligator jamboree with all the letters A through Z.

Sierra, Judy. *Counting Crocodiles*. 40 pages. 1997. Houghton Mifflin Harcourt Publishers. Monkey wants to get to the bananas on the neighboring island but the sea is full of crocodiles.

Stoops, Erik D., and Debbie Lynne Stone. *Alligators and Crocodiles*. 80 pages. 1996. Sterling. A resource for factual information and lots of photographs.

Swanson, Diane. *Alligators and Crocodiles*. 32 pages. 2010. Whitecap Books. A good resource for factual information and photographs. Not a storybook.

Waber, Bernard. *Lyle, Lyle Crocodile*. 48 pages. 1987. Houghton Mifflin Harcourt Publishers. A grouchy neighbor wants Lyle the Crocodile kept in the zoo but has a change of heart after Lyle saves the day.

Walton, Rick. *Suddenly Alligator: An Adverbial Tale*. 32 pages. 2004. Gibbs Smith. A boy decides to go to town for a pair of new socks but encounters many interesting things along the way.

Waring, Richard. *Alberto the Dancing Alligator*. 32 pages. 2002. Candlewick. When her alligator accidentally gets flushed down the toilet, Tina has to figure out how to save him.

Wells, Rosemary. *Hands Off Harry.* 40 pages. 2011. HarperCollins Children's Books. Kindergarteners work and play happily but Harry isn't being a good classmate.

Willems, Mo. *Hooray for Amanda and Her Alligator.* 72 pages. 2011. HarperCollins Publishers. Amanda has fun with her stuffed alligator, but when she gets a panda, her alligator has to learn to make friends.

Wilson, Karma. *A Frog in the Bog.* 32 pages. 2007. Margaret K. McElderry Books. A frog suddenly realizes that the log he's been sitting on is really an alligator.

Ziefert, Harriet. *Egad Alligator.* 40 pages. 2002. Houghton Mifflin Harcourt Publishers. An alligator goes for a walk and tries to be friendly to everyone he meets.

Holiday — Valentine's Day

Advance planning: To plan for this storytime, find a theme-related song to play during craft and snack times, like "You'll Be in My Heart," by Phil Collins. You will also want to select a poem, such as "A Valentine to Catherine" (find it at www.apples4theteacher.com), along with the books you plan to read. Decorate your space with lots of things in red, like big red hearts, a poster of cupid and his bow and arrow, the word love. Wear red clothes, red earrings — heart-shaped if possible.

Introduction to theme: Valentine's Day was once called Saint Valentine's Day and was considered to be a religious holiday by some. It's now known as a day when people who love each other give cards, candy or gifts to show their affection. Today we'll read about love and Valentine's Day, play a Valentine's Day game, make a Valentine's Day craft that you can give to someone you love and eat a Valentine's Day snack.

Song: "You're My Special Valentine" to the tune of "Mary Had a Little Lamb":

> You're my special Valentine, Valentine, Valentine
> You're my special Valentine
> Because I love you so.
> I'll follow you wherever you go, ever you go, ever you go
> I'll follow you wherever you go
> Because I love you so.

Game: Stacking hearts

Materials needed: Heart-shaped candies and paper plates. Advance preparation: None. At storytime: Give each child a handful of heart-shaped candies and a paper plate. Tell them to start stacking the hearts as tall as they can go when you start the time. Give them about 30 seconds to build and see how many they can stack in that time. Then they can knock the tower down and you can repeat the challenge to see if they can make it taller the second time.

Alternative Games

Heart bean bag toss. Cut a large heart "target" out of paper. Use a marker to make a large X in the center. Make three bean bags, heart-shaped in red if you like. To play: place the heart on the floor and place a piece of tape about six feet away. Have the children form a line and take turns standing at the tape. Toss the bean bags one at a time trying to hit the X.

Valentine's Day bingo. Make bingo cards online using the word HEART and finding either things to do with love or red things. Use conversation hearts as the markers and let the children keep them in a small plastic bag so that they can eat them later.

Find the hearts. Make or buy lots of red paper hearts and hide them throughout your storytime area. Send the children on a hunt for them.

Find Your match. Cut paper hearts in half with either unique designs or different decorative scissors. Hand each child half a heart and have them find the person with the other half.

Musical hearts. Place large paper hearts on the floor. Play music — ideally love songs. Stop the music and everyone needs to stand on a heart. When you start the music remove a heart. But no one is out if they are either touching a heart in some way when the music stops, like just the tip of a toe. Gradually remove the hearts until the group is quite crowded together.

Valentine card pieces.

Valentine card.

St. Valentine says (like Simon says). Sample things: stand on one foot, hop on one foot, wave your arms, put your hands on your hips, touch your toes, etc.

Craft: Valentine card

Materials needed: White card stock, foam or paper Valentine's Day stickers. Advance preparation: If you can run the cardstock through a computer printer, print "Happy Valentine's Day" on the inside of the card (assuming you will fold it in half width-wise). At storytime: Let the children decorate the outside front and inside of the card and then sign their names inside.

Alternative Crafts

Heart wreath. Cut a cardboard base circle about an inch or two wide from a paper plate. Cut or buy paper hearts of several different colors, including pink, red, purple, white. Have the children glue the hearts, overlapping them just slightly, around the circle.

Handprint wall hanging. Have each child make a fist with each hand, brush paint lightly on the pinky side of the hand and press it down on paper to make one side of a heart. Put paint on the other fist to make the other side of the heart and press down next to the first one. Write the child's name under the heart print, glue it to a background piece of paper and write Happy Valentine's Day across the top. Add string or yarn attached to punched holes at each side of the top paper to hang.

Tissue paper heart. Give each child a construction paper or cardstock heart, on which to glue small crumpled pieces of tissue paper. Use pinks, reds, purples. Could put magnet on back to use as a refrigerator magnet.

Heart ornament. Place small pieces of pink, purple, red tissue papers on clear contact paper places sticky side up. Cover with another piece of clear contact paper. Using a cardboard heart shape as a guide, cut around the contact paper to make it heart-shaped. Punch a hole in the top and attach yarn or string so that it can be hung.

Snack: Heart-shaped cupcake

Materials needed: Yellow or pink cake mix, pink icing, heart-shaped candies or pink heart-shaped marshmallows, foil, paper plates, plastic knives. Advance preparation: Bake the cupcakes making them heart-shaped by rolling a ball of foil and putting it in between the paper liner and the muffin tin. At storytime: Give each child a cupcake on a paper plate with a plastic knife and a dollop of icing. Have them spread the icing, then place the heart-shaped candy or marshmallow on top.

Heart shaped cupcake.

Alternative Snacks

Heart-shaped cookies with icing, heart-shaped Jell-O Jigglers, heart-shaped Rice Krispie treats, or cake pops with pink icing.

Large pretzels. Get pink meltable chocolate or pink icing and let the children cover large heart-shaped pretzels with the chocolate or icing and roll it in pink or red sprinkles.

Use a heart-shaped cookie cutter to cut pieces of bread. Spread with pink cream cheese.

SUGGESTED BOOKS

Albee, Sarah. *Elmo Loves You.* 24 pages. 2002. Random House Books for Young Readers. Elmo explains how each person is special in this board book.

Bond, Felicia. *The Day It Rained Hearts.* 36 pages. 2006. HarperCollins Publishers. Cornelia Augusta catches the hearts that rain one day, and she gives each one to just the right person.

Bottner, Barbara. *Miss Brooks Loves Books (and I Don't).* 32 pages. 2010. Random House Children's Books. Missy's classmates all find something they like to read, but can Miss Brooks help her find something she'll like?

Bunting, Eve. *The Valentine Bears.* 32 pages. 1985. Sandpiper. Mr. and Mrs. Bear have never celebrated Valentine's Day because they hibernate during the winter.

Cash, John Carter. *Daddy Loves His Little Girl.* 32 pages. 2010. Little Simon Inspirations. Narrator expresses his unconditional love for his daughter.

Cash, John Carter. *Momma Loves Her Little Son.* 32 pages. 2009. Little Simon Inspirations. The love of a mother for her son is boundless.

Charlip, Remy. *I Love You.* 32 pages. 1999. Cartwheel. A mother puts her child to bed saying endearments that get more and more outrageous and more serious.

Cocca-Leffler, Maryann. *Lots of Hearts.* 32 pages. 1997. Grosset & Dunlap. An early reader book about a little girl who makes Valentine's cards for her parents but they mysteriously disappear.

Colandro, Lucille. *There Was an Old Lady Who Swallowed a Rose!* 32 pages. 2012. Scholastic. She's swallowing items to make a gift for her valentine.

De Groat, Diane. *Roses Are Pink, Your Feet Really*

Stink. 2008. Live Oak Media. Gilbert writes two not very nice Valentines to classmates but there's time for a change of heart.

Di Angelo, N. *Happy Valentine's Day, Curious George!* 16 pages. 2011. Houghton Mifflin Harcourt. How much mischief can a little monkey get into on Valentine's Day?

Duksta, Laura. *I Love You More*. 34 pages. 2007. Sourcebooks. A mommy answers the question "Just how much do you love me?" in many ways.

Elliott, Laura Malone. *A String of Hearts*. 32 pages. 2010. HarperCollins Children's Books. Valentines come in all sorts of shapes and sizes.

Engelbreit, Mary. *Queen of Hearts*. 32 pages. 2008. HarperCollins Publishers. Ann Estelle is so busy making a valentines box she forgets to make valentines for her classmates.

Friedman, Laurie. *Ruby Valentine Saves the Day*. 32 pages. 2010. Lerner Publishing Group. An unexpected snowstorm threatens to ruin all of Ruby's plans for Valentine's Day.

Gantos, Jack. *Rotten Ralph's Rotten Romance*. 32 pages. 2005. Sandpiper. Misbehaving cat Rotten Ralph will do almost anything to avoid the Valentine's party and all the kisses he expects to get there.

Hallinan, P.K. *How Do I Love You?* 26 pages. 2002. Ideals Publications. A love poem from parent to child.

Harker, Jillian. *I Love You Daddy*. 32 pages. 2004. Parragon. Little Bear is getting old enough to try new adventures but will he be brave enough?

Harker, Jillian. *I Love You Mommy*. 32 pages. 2004. Parragon. Mommy Bear comes to Little Bear's rescue when he needs her.

Hector, Julian. *The Gentleman Bug*. 40 pages. 2010. Atheneum Books for Young Readers. Everything changes for the gentleman bug when the ladybug moves to town.

Holabird, Katharine. *Angelina Loves...* 24 pages. 2006. Grosset & Dunlap. Angelina loves dancing and being with her family. Find out what else she loves in this book.

Kann, Victoria. *Pinkalicious Pink of Hearts*. 24 pages. 2011. HarperFestival. Pinkalicious creates a wonderful card for someone in her class but worries that the one she receives won't be as nice.

Kroll, Steven. *The Biggest Valentine Ever*. 32 pages. 2006. Scholastic. Clayton and Desmond do better when they work together to make valentines.

London, Jonathan. *Froggy's First Kiss*. 32 pages. 1999. Puffin. Froggy is busy making an extra special Valentine for Frogilina.

Marley, Cedella. *One Love*. 32 pages. 2011. Chronicle Books. Based on the Bob Marley song, this is a testament to what we can do when we work together with love in our hearts.

McGuirk, Leslie. *Tucker's Valentine*. 28 pages. 2010. Candlewick. Tucker the Terrier loves his little girl.

McMullan, Kate. *Fluffy's Valentine's Day*. 40 pages. 2000. Cartwheel. An early reader about Fluffy the guinea pig, whose class wants to give him a bath and find him a girlfriend. Initially he doesn't like Valentine's Day but changes his mind.

Melmed, Laura Krause. *My Love Will Be with You*. 24 pages. 2009. HarperCollins Publishers. A lullaby of enduring devotion from a father to his child.

O'Connor, Jane. *Fancy Nancy Heart to Heart*. 24 pages. 2009. HarperFestival. Everything about Valentine's Day is fancy with Fancy Nancy.

Pallotta, Jerry. *Who Will Be My Valentine This Year?* 32 pages. 2011. Cartwheel Books. A Valentine's Day story about finding your own sweetheart.

Parish, Herman. *Amelia Bedelia's First Valentine*. 32 pages. 2011. HarperCollins Children's Books. Amelia Bedelia is sure she will love everything about Valentine's Day.

Parr, Todd. *The I Love You Book*. 32 pages. 2009. Little, Brown Books for Young Readers. Unconditional love explored in a heartfelt, playful way.

Petersen, David. *Snowy Valentine*. 32 pages. 2011. HarperCollins Publishers. Jasper the bunny searches the forest valley for a special gift for his loved one.

Pham, LeUyen. *All the Things I Love About You*. 40 pages. 2010. HarperCollins Publishers. Mama lists the reasons she loves her little boy.

Primavera, Elise. *Thumb Love*. 48 pages. 2010. Random House Children's Books. An unusual love story of a girl and her thumb and how she decides to give it up.

Roberts, Bethany. *Valentine Mice!* 32 pages. 2001. Sandpiper. The mice scamper across the wintry landscape to deliver Valentines to all their friends.

Rosenthal, Amy Krouse. *Plant a Kiss*. 40 pages. 2011. HarperCollins Publishers. One small act of love blooms into something bigger.

Rylant, Cynthia. *If You'll Be My Valentine*. 32 pages. 2005. HarperCollins Publishers. Loving wishes from a little boy to all the members of his family.

Sadler, Marilyn. *Honey Bunny's Honey Bear*. 32 pages. 2007. Random House Books for Young Readers. A learn to read book featuring Honey Bunny, who is trying to get Eddy Bear to notice her and she even makes him a Valentine, to no avail.

Scotton, Rob. *Love, Splat*. 40 pages. 2011. Harper-Collins Publishers. Splat has a crush on Kitten, but she doesn't seem to like him at all.

Scotton, Rob. *Splat the Cat Funny Valentine*. 16 pages. 2012. HarperFestival. A lift the flap book featuring Splat the Cat who wants to give something special to Mrs. Wimpydimple for Valentine's Day.

Spinelli, Eileen. *Somebody Loves You, Mr. Hatch*. 32 pages. 1996. Simon & Schuster Books for Young Readers. When Mr. Hatch gets a package from a secret admirer it really brightens up his life. Too bad it's a mistake, but by the time the mistake is discovered, his life has changed for the better.

Tillman, Nancy. *Wherever You Are My Love Will Find You*. 32 pages. 2010. Feiwel and Friends. Love is the one thing we can give our children that they can carry with them every day.

Weiss, Ellen. *I Love You, Little Monster*. 16 pages. 2012. Little Simon. Mama always loves her little monster, even when he's being a little monster.

Wilson, Karma. *The Cow Loves Cookies*. 40 pages. 2010. Margaret K. McElderry Books. Most of the animals on the farm eat what you'd expect, but not the cow.

Wing, Natasha. *The Night Before Valentine's Day*. 32 pages. 2000. Penguin Group. Another take off on the Night Before Christmas poem, kids dream of candy hearts.

March

March

Advance planning: To plan for this storytime, find a theme-related song to play during craft and snack times, like "Stars and Stripes Forever," march by John Philip Sousa. You will also want to select a poem, such as "In Like a Lion, Out Like a Lamb," by Lorie Hill (find it at www.scrapbook.com), along with the books you plan to read. Decorate your space with pictures of clouds and wind, stuffed lions and lambs.

Introduction to theme: Why are kids always so tired in April? The answer: Because they've just finished a long March! March is the name of a month, the month we're in right now. The name of the month comes from ancient Roman times and was named for the Roman God of War Mars, which is also the name of a planet. The first day of spring is in March, March 21st, and it can be a time of interesting weather, sometimes very nice, sometimes very stormy. There's a saying that if March comes in like a lion it will go out like a lamb. Talk about what the saying might mean, for example: If March starts out fierce, cold and "ferocious," like a lion, it will end up warm, mild and "gentle" like a lamb. Discuss what would make the weather "ferocious" like a lion? (rain, cold wind, storms, sleet, snow, etc.); What would make the weather "gentle" like a lamb? (sunshine, warm breezes, etc.) March can also mean a way of walking — a steady rhythmic walk in step with others, like soldiers might do. It's also a type of music, and we'll listen to a musical march today. Today we'll read about lions and lambs, play a marching game, make a lion and lamb craft and have a snack that looks like lions and lambs.

Song: The nursery rhyme "Rain, Rain, Go Away."

Game: March march
Materials needed: Recording of a march, such as John Phillip Sousa's Stars and Stripes Forever which can be downloaded from the Internet for about a dollar, CD player.
Advance preparation: Record a march on CD, or obtain a recording. At storytime: Have the children follow you around the storytime area using exaggerated marching motions, lifting knees high, moving arms up and down.

Alternative Games

Which lion? Which lamb? Print several different photos of lions and lambs from the Internet, such as a male lion with a big mane, a female lion, a lion cub and a few different lambs, such as a white one, a black one, a white one with a black face, a brown one. Show the children all of the photos, and then have them close their eyes. While their eyes are closed, hide one of the photos under something. Then when the children open their eyes again ask them which is missing — a lion or a lamb? And then which lion or lamb is missing.

Rain streamers. Give each child a crepe paper streamer about 2–3 feet long. Some should get pink — those are the flowers. Black is thunder, grey is lightning, blue is rain, yellow is the sun. Tell the children that in March there can sometimes be rain (the children with the blue streamers should wave their streamers whenever you say that it's raining and keep waving them until you say that the rain has stopped). Sometimes the rain turns into a thunderstorm, and there's thunder (the black streamers wave) and lightning (the grey streamers wave). Then as the weather calms down, the thunder stops. The lightning stops. And finally the rain stops. The sun comes out (the yellow streamers wave) and all that rain and now the sun makes the flowers bloom (the pink streamers wave). Let the flowers bloom for a moment and then take up all the streamers and end the game.

March weather. Show pictures of all of the different kinds of weather that can take place during March, such as sunny days, windy days, rain, snow, warm, cold (can show these by the clothes the people in the picture are wearing) and then ask the children what kind of weather is happening in each picture.

Lion and lamb meadow math. Using dried lima beans, which are white, spray paint one side of the beans yellow. The white side is the lamb; the yellow side is the lion. Place a bunch of beans on a green placemat, or piece of felt, to be the meadow. Start with some simple math, like one bean white side up, one bean yellow side up. Ask the children how many lions and how many lambs are in the meadow. Do harder combinations with more beans and have the children count how many lions and lambs.

Paper plate lion and lamb pieces.

Craft: Paper plate lion and lamb

Materials needed: Paper plates, glue sticks, cotton balls, crayons, yellow and white construction paper, black or brown construction paper. Advance preparation: Glue yellow construction

Paper plate lion and lamb.

paper to white construction paper. Cut ears. This way you have white on one side for sheep, yellow on other side for lion. Cut eyes and nose from black or brown construction paper. At storytime: Have children glue ears to plate. Yellow side will be lion, white side will be lamb. On side with yellow ears, draw lion's mane around the edge of the plate. Glue eyes and nose. Draw muzzle and dots where whiskers would be. Turn plate over and glue pieces of cotton ball (tear each cotton ball apart to get more pieces, make it easier to glue and fluffier). Glue eyes and nose. Draw muzzle.

Alternative Crafts

What March weather do you prefer? Have cut outs of clouds that make wind, snow and rain, the sun, lambs and lions. Let the children choose the kind of cloud that they would like in their picture, then have them glue the cloud on one side of their paper and the sun on the other. They can glue the lamb on the sun side and the lion on the cloud side since March bad weather comes like a lion and leaves like a lamb.

Lion and lamb paper bag puppet. Use white paper bags and draw black crayon facial features and glue cotton balls to one side as the lamb, and draw brown crayon facial features and glue brown cut yarn as the mane to the other side.

Windsock. Use large mailing envelopes, cutting off top and bottom to leave tube. Decorate with crayons on one side as the lion's face, and the other side as the lamb's face. Could also glue on yarn lion mane and cotton balls for lamb. Punch holes on each side of top of tube and attach length of yarn for hanging. Attach by tape, glue stick or staple some crepe paper streamers to bottom to move in the wind.

Snack: Lion and lamb cookie

Lion and lamb cookies.

Materials needed: Sugar cookie dough, flower cookie cutter, white icing, yellow food coloring, food marker, paper plates, and plastic knives. Advance preparation: Bake cookies using flower cookie cutter. Draw faces on the cookies with the food marker. Make some of the white icing yellow. At storytime: Let the children decide whether they'd like to have a lion or a lamb. Give them a dollop of white icing for the lambs or yellow icing for the lions and let them decorate around the outside edge of the cookies.

Alternative Snacks

Lion and lamb cupcakes. Give each child a cupcake and ask them if they'd like to make a lion or a lamb. For the lamb use white icing and mini marshmallows, two chocolate chips or M&Ms for the eyes and something pink for the nose, like a little piece of pink starburst candy. For the lion use chocolate icing, toasted coconut for the mane, two chocolate chips or M&Ms for eyes and nose, and black lace licorice pieces for whiskers.

Cracker lion and lamb. Surround a round cracker spread with cream cheese, topped with raisin eyes, nose and mouth with small carrot sticks as the mane. For lamb, surround the cracker with small cuts of celery so they look like curly fleece.

Cheese lion and lamb. Cut rounds of yellow cheese with a biscuit cutter and top with raisin eyes, nose and mouth and pretzel stick whiskers. Use white cheese for lambs and pretzel twists as the fleece.

SUGGESTED BOOKS

Abercrombie, Barbara. *The Show and Tell Lion.* 32 pages. 2006. Simon & Schuster Children's Publishing. Mathew tells his class during show and tell that he has a lion.

Asch, Frank. *Like a Windy Day.* 32 pages. 2008. Houghton Mifflin Harcourt. The wind is powerful and stormy.

Bauer, Marion Dane. *In Like a Lion, Out Like a Lamb.* 32 pages. 2011. Holiday House. March comes in as a lion to a little boy's world, and then leaves as a lamb in this rhythmic story.

Berger, Samantha. *It's Spring.* 30 pages. 2003. Scholastic. Rhyming story that tells the story of spring's arrival.

Brenner, Barbara. *Lion and Lamb.* 48 pages. 1999. Gareth Stevens Publishing. Three short stories relate the activities of two unlikely friends.

Brode, Robyn. *March.* 24 pages. 2002. Weekly Reader Early. Facts about the month of March.

Carr, Jan. *Splish, Splash, Spring.* 32 pages. 2002. Holiday House. Three children and a dog brave the wet weather and go outside.

Daugherty, James. *Andy and the Lion.* 72 pages. 1989. Puffin. A retelling of Androcles and the lion, where Andy meets a lion on his way to school and makes friends by removing a thorn from his paw.

Di Chiara, Francesca. *The Sun and the Wind.* 22 pages. 2008. Usborne Books. The classic fable where the moral is that sometimes the gentler one is actually the stronger one, told in simple text.

Dorros, Arthur. *Feel the Wind.* 32 pages. 1990. HarperCollins Publishers. A lot of facts about the movement of air.

Dylan, Bob. *Blowin' in the Wind.* 28 pages. 2011. Sterling Children's Books. The words to the famous song illustrated.

Fatio, Louise. *The Happy Lion.* 40 pages. 2010. Random House Children's Books. Everyone in the French zoo loves the lion and stops by to see him. One day he gets out and decides to visit his friends.

Fatio, Louise. *The Happy Lion Roars.* 40 pages. 2006. Random House Children's Books. A sequel to The Happy Lion.

Forest, Heather. *The Contest Between the Sun and the Wind.* 32 pages. 2007. August House. In this fable we find that being the most forceful does not make one the strongest.

Glaser, Linda. *It's Spring!* 32 pages. 2002. Lerner Publishing Group. When spring is here, there's a renewed energy.

Gomi, Taro. *Spring Is Here.* 40 pages. 2006. Chronicle Books. A playful tour of the four seasons.

Greenstein, Elaine. *One Little Lamb.* 32 pages. 2004. Viking Juvenile. Tells the story of how wool is obtained from sheep and ultimately made into mittens.

Hale, Sarah Josepha. *Mary Had a Little Lamb.* 24 pages. 2011. Marshall Cavendish Corp. Some touches of fantasy and humor update the traditional poem.

Hillenbrand, Will. *Spring Is Here.* 32 pages. 2011. Holiday House. Mole can smell spring in the air but Bear is still asleep. How will he wake him?

Hoberman, Mary Ann. *Mary Had a Little Lamb.* 32 pages. 2010. Little Brown Books. Mary brings her lamb to school, teaches it counting and the alphabet and even how to play baseball.

Hubbell, Patricia. *Hurray for Spring.* 32 pages. 2005. Cooper Square Publishing. Rhyming text provides a whimsical welcome to spring.

Hutchins, Pat. *The Wind Blew.* 32 pages. 1993. Aladdin. The wind blew and blew and blew.

Jackson, Ellen B. *March (It Happens in the Month of).* 32 pages. 2002. Charlesbridge Publishing. Gives a lot of factual information about the month of March.

Kesselring, Mary. *March (Months of the Year).* 24 pages. 2010. Looking Glass Library. This illustrated book tells readers what's special about March.

Knudsen, Michelle. *Library Lion.* 48 pages. 2009. Candlewick Press. Story of a lion that visits the library and breaks the rules for an important reason.

Kooser, Ted. *Bag in the Wind.* 48 pages. 2010. Candlewick. A bulldozer pushes a pile of garbage around a landfill and uncovers an empty bag that is carried away by the wind.

Mannis, Celeste. *One Leaf Rides the Wind.* 32 pages. 2005. Puffin. A book of Haiku poems about counting and the wind.

Pegram, Laura. *A Windy Day.* 18 pages. 1995. Writers and Readers Publishing. A board book that describes a windy day's outing to the park.

Pinkney, Jerry. *The Mouse and the Lion.* 40 pages. 2009. Little Brown Books for Young Readers. Wordless picture book showing the famous Aesop fable that explains how no act of kindness is ever wasted.

Rigo, L. *Little Lamb.* 10 pages. 2011. Barron's Educational Series. A board book that tells how the mother sheep looks after the little lamb.

Root, Phyllis. *One Windy Wednesday.* 24 pages. 1997. Candlewick. What happens when the wind blows and blows.

Sherman, Josepha. *Gusts and Gales: a Book about Wind.* 24 pages. 2006. Picture Window Books. Wind helps a kite fly and blows leaves from trees. Find out about wind in this book.

Singer, Marilyn. *On the Same Day in March: A Tour of the World's Weather.* 40 pages. 2001. Harper Festival. A trip around the world on the same day in March to see what the weather is like in many different places.

Sungaard, Arnold, and Eric Carle. *The Lamb and the Butterfly.* 32 pages. 1999. Scholastic. The lamb and butterfly meet out in the meadow and the lamb is astonished to find that the butterfly's life is very different from his.

Thompson, Lauren. *Wee Little Lamb.* 32 pages. 2009. Simon and Schuster Children's Publishing. A shy lamb finds a smaller and shyer animal to play with on the farm.

Tierney, Fiona. *Lion's Lunch.* 32 pages. 2010. Scholastic. A retelling of the classic Aesop's fable.

Trapani, Iza. *Mary Had a Little Lamb.* 32 pages. 2003. Charlesbridge Publishing. What happens when Mary's little lamb goes off to explore on his own?

Weeks, Sarah. *If I Were a Lion.* 40 pages. 2007. Atheneum Books for Young Readers. A young girl is sent to the time out chair and compares herself to wild animals.

Wolff, Ferida. *It Is the Wind.* 32 pages. 2005. HarperCollins Publishers. Lyrical prose invites readers to explore the magical world between dusk and dawn.

Wood, Jakki. *March of the Dinosaurs.* 30 pages. 2000. Frances Lincoln Children's Books. A prehistoric counting book.

Zolotow, Charlotte. *When the Wind Stops.* 32 pages. 1997. HarperCollins Publishers. Where does the wind go when it stops?

Ladybugs

Advance planning: To plan for this storytime, find a theme-related song to play during craft and snack times, like "Ladybug's Picnic," by Elizabeth Mitchell. You will also want to select a poem, such as "Five Little Ladybugs" (find it at www.canteach.ca), along with the books you plan to read. Decorate your space with stuffed or plastic ladybugs, red and black streamers, round red pillows.

Introduction to theme: Ladybugs are also called Lady Beetles, because they are a kind of beetle. They are sometimes called Ladybird Beetles. They're very small insects and probably the ones you've seen have been mostly red with black spots, but they can also be yellow or orange. They are very useful insects that mostly eat other insects that are harmful to our garden pants, our fruit trees and our field crops. Some people of the world consider seeing ladybugs to be very lucky. Today we'll read about ladybugs, play a ladybug game, make a ladybug craft and have a snack that looks like a ladybug.

Song: "LadyBug Picnic." Lyrics can be found at www.metrolyrics.com.

Game: Miss ladybug has lost her spots

Materials needed: Large picture of a ladybug with no spots, black bean bags. Advance preparation: Either print an enlarged clipart drawing of a ladybug with no spots from the computer and glue onto poster board or make a large ladybug on poster board by either drawing and coloring it in or cutting out colored paper and gluing it down. At storytime: Let the children take turns tossing the black bean bags onto the ladybug in order to give her spots.

Alternative Games

Fly away home. Play music and have the children pretend to be ladybugs flying around. Occasionally call out "hibernate!" and have the children huddle together in one area of the room. Then call out "springtime!" and the children can start flying around again.

"If I were a ladybug, I would..." Have the children finish the sentence.

Ladybug match. Make lots of ladybugs from red construction paper circles and place one to five dots on each side of a center line. Cut in half. Let the children match the ladybug halves.

Ladybug says (like Simon says). Try to incorporate actions that a ladybug might do, like fly around the room, flap a wing, etc.

Craft: Paper ladybugs

Materials needed: Red construction paper, black construction paper, google eyes, brass brads, glue sticks. Advance preparation: Cut black ladybug base shapes, cut small black circles, cut red construction paper wings, red semi circle mouth. At storytime: Have children glue base shapes together, glue black circles onto red wings, glue google eyes onto black ladybug base shape. Then place red wing where it's going to go and have parents use sharp scissors to punch holes through both the black base and the red wing and attach wings to base with brass brad. This allows the wing to move. Alternately glue wing down with gluestick.

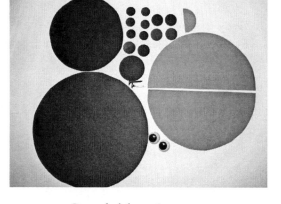

Paper ladybug pieces.

Alternative Crafts

Rock ladybug. Paint rocks red before storytime. Have children use black permanent markers to add line down middle and spots. Glue on small google eyes.

Paper plate ladybug. Give each child two paper plates, one white and one red. Cut the red one in half. Provide small black construction paper circles or black crayons to make black dots on the red halves. Attach a larger black construction paper circle to the uncut white paper plate as the head. Punch holes in the white plate on either side of the head and also in the corner of each of the red wing pieces and attach with brass brads. Draw a face on the black head circle if desired with a white crayon.

Paper ladybug.

Snack: Apple ladybug

Materials needed: Red apples, raisins, honey or peanut butter, pretzel sticks, grapes, paper plates, plastic knives. Advance preparation: Core apples and cut in half. At storytime: Place an apple half, a spoonful of honey or peanut butter, several raisins, two pretzel sticks and one grape on each child's plate. Have them place grape as head, pretzel sticks as antennae, and stick raisins as dots onto the apple with honey or peanut butter.

Alternative Snacks

Ladybug cookies. Make round cookies. Color icing red. Have children spread red icing on cookie, dot cookie with chocolate chips or brown M&Ms.

Grape ladybug cookies. Use dark grape halves and round cereal to be the spots and eyes on top of red iced cookies.

Ladybug Crackers. Spread red jam on a round cracker and top it with raisins for the spots.

Apple ladybug.

SUGGESTED BOOKS

Allen, Judy. *Are You a Ladybug?* 31 pages. 2003. Roaring Brook Press. Shows the life cycle of a ladybug in an entertaining way, comparing it to how it would be if humans were like ladybugs.

Ashley, Susan. *Ladybugs.* 24 pages. 2004. Stevens, Gareth Publishing. Photos showing the life cycle of the ladybug.

Berends, Polly Berrien. *Ladybug and Dog and the Night Walk.* 32 pages. 1980. Random House Children's Books. Ladybug and her friend Dog take her cousins on a night tour of the farm.

Bowers, Shallen. *The Ladybug and Me: Rainy Days.* 2010. Tate Publishing and Enterprises. Encouraging story with rhyming text about having fun even if it rains.

Carle, Eric. *The Grouchy Ladybug.* 48 pages. 1996. HarperCollins Publishers. The grouchy ladybug seems to be looking for a fight.

Cleland, JoAnn. *Ladybug, Ladybug What Are You Doing?* 16 pages. 2008. Ideal Publications. Colorful photos and bright text that shows different kinds of animals and fish.

Curry, Don L., and Johanna Kaufman. *More Bugs? Less Bugs?* 32 pages. 2000. Capstone Curriculum. Simple addition and subtraction that focuses on insects.

Donaldson, Julia. *What the Ladybug Heard.* 32 pages. 2010. Holt, Henry & Co. Thieves are planning to steal the farmer's prize cow but the ladybug will try to foil their plan.

Finn, Isobel. *The Very Lazy Ladybug.* 32 pages. 2003. ME Media. This ladybug is so lazy that she catches rides on other animals, not knowing she can fly.

Florie, Christine. *Lara Ladybug.* 32 pages. 2011. Scholastic Library Publishing. Lara Ladybug has lost her spots and goes searching for them.

Fowler, Richard. *Ladybug on the Move.* 20 pages. 1993. Houghton Mifflin Harcourt. Ladybug searches for a new home, but every place she goes is already occupied.

Gerth, Melanie. *Ten Little Ladybugs.* 22 pages. 2007. Piggy Toes Press. One by one, ten bugs disappear. Where did they go?

Gibbons, Gail. *Ladybugs.* 32 pages. 2012. Holiday House. An introduction to these beetles: life cycles, what they eat, how they protect themselves and more.

Hall, Margaret C. *Ladybugs.* 21 pages. 2005. Capstone Press. Describes the physical characteristics, behavior and habits of ladybugs.

Hartley, Karen. *Ladybug.* 32 pages. 2006. Heinemann-Raintree. A simple introduction to the characteristics, life cycle and habits of the ladybug.

Himmelman, John. *A Ladybug's Life.* 32 pages.

1998. Scholastic Library Publishing. Illustrations and simple text follow the activities of a ladybug.

Hopkins, Jeanette. *The Ladybug Waltz*. 32 pages. 2009. Ice Cube Press. A story told in the form of a waltz of lovely red gowns and antennae tiaras.

Jango-Cohen, Judith. *Hungry Ladybugs*. 32 pages. 2003. Lerner Publishing Group. Describes the physical characters and behavior of ladybugs.

Morgan, Sally. *Ladybugs and Beetles*. 32 pages. 2004. Black Rabbit Books. Photographs and illustrations of ladybugs, a kind of "minibeast."

Oblucki, Janusz. *Busy Bugs Board Books Little Ladybug*. 1999. Modern Publishing. Little Ladybug begins to worry when the rain starts to fall. Will her spots wash off?

Posada, Mia. *Ladybugs: Red, Fiery and Bright*. 32 pages. 2007. Lerner Publishing Group. Enter the magical realm of ladybugs to see how they grow.

Purcell, Larry. *Ladybug Picnic*. 32 pages. 2009. Tate Publishing and Enterprises. The two ladybugs in rhyming text on another journey.

Purcell, Larry. *Two Little Ladybugs*. 32 pages. 2008. Tate Publishing and Enterprises. Two ladybugs are used to illustrate a story about friends helping each other.

Riggs, Katie. *Ladybug (Grow with Me)*. 32 pages. 2012. Creative Education. Explore the life and growth of ladybugs with magnified photos and easy to follow text.

Robinson, Fay. *Creepy Beetles*. 32 pages. 2001. Scholastic. An introduction to all kinds of beetles, including ladybugs.

Sexton, Colleen. *The Life Cycle of a Ladybug*. 24 pages. 2010. Bellweather Media. Photo book showing ladybug life cycle.

Slade, Suzanne. *Ladybugs*. 24 pages. 2008. The Rosen Publishing Group. Describes the characteristics, diet, behavior, life cycle and enemies of ladybugs.

Smith, Sian. *Ladybugs (Creepy Critters)*. 24 pages. 2012. Heinemann-Raintree. Simple rhymes teach readers about ladybugs.

Soman, David, and Jacky Davis. *Ladybug Girl*. 40 pages. 2008. Penguin Group. Lulu's brother doesn't want her around and her parents are busy so she makes her own fun as her alter ego Ladybug Girl.

Soman, David, and Jacky Davis. *Ladybug Girl and Bingo*. 40 pages. 2012. Penguin Group. Lulu and Bingo the dog are camping for the first time.

Soman, David, and Jacky Davis. *Ladybug Girl and Bumblebee Boy*. 40 pages. 2009. Penguin Group. Lulu plays with a friend becoming a dynamic duo.

Soman, David, and Jacky Davis. *Ladybug Girl and Her Mama*. 14 pages. 2013. Dial. Ladybug Girl loves her Mama and can't wait to spend the day with her.

Soman, David, and Jacky Davis. *Ladybug Girl and the Bug Squad*. 40 pages. 2011. Penguin Group. Ladybug Girl's friends are going to come over to play but things don't go exactly as planned.

Thomas, Jan. *Can You Make a Scary Face?* 40 pages. 2009. Beach Lane Books. An interactive picture book that stars a bossy ladybug who asks such questions as "if a green bug were on your nose, could you make a scary face to frighten it away?"

Top That! Publishing Staff. *There's a Ladybug in My Book*. 10 pages. 2007. Top That! Publishing. Board book with a ladybug who's making her way through a maze.

Zoehfeld, Kathleen Weidner. *Ladybug at Orchard Avenue*. 32 pages. 1996. Soundprints. Ladybug goes up and down the rose stems in search of her favorite thing to eat: Aphids.

Spring

Advance planning: To plan for this storytime, find a theme-related song to play during craft and snack times, like Vivaldi's "Spring from the Four Seasons." You will also want to select a poem, such as "Spring," by Kaitlyn Guenther (find it at www.dltk-holidays.com), along with the books you plan to read. Decorate your space with flowers, plants, raincoats, umbrellas.

Introduction to theme: Spring is one of the four seasons and comes between winter and summer. March 21st is officially the first day of spring, but in some places it feels like spring sooner or later, depending on the weather and temperature. What are some signs that spring is coming? Warmer days, more hours of sunlight, grass turning green, flowers starting to bloom, seeing more animals outside... Sometimes the warm air meeting up with the cold air of winter can give us some stormy weather. But we also have wonderful warm sunny days where it just feels great to be outside after having been in so much of winter. Today we'll read about spring, play a springtime game, make a springtime craft and eat a springtime snack.

Fingerplay: "Flower." The poem and the instructions can be found at www.preschool express.com.

Game: Identify the season.

Materials needed: Pictures of different seasons. Advance preparation: Can find and print from the Internet. Summer: wheat field, sun, playing with sand toys on beach, reading on beach, swimming, sweating in hot sun. Autumn: rake, jack o'lantern, trees in color, autumn leaves, piles of leaves, pumpkins. Winter: snow, skier, snow shoveling, glove or mitten, winter coat, snowman. Spring: rain, flowers, umbrella, boots, spring shower. At storytime: Show pictures of different seasons and ask the children to identify the season.

Alternative Games

Signs of the seasons. Bring in actual items associated with the seasons, like plastic pumpkin, leaves, mittens, hats, umbrellas, flowers, swimsuit, sand toys. Show each one to the children and ask them to say which season they might use the item. Some items might be used in more than one season.

Memory game. Make a memory game using pairs of pictures of things associated with spring, like many different kinds of flowers, umbrellas, rainclouds. Place them face down and turn one over, then let each child take a turn to tell you which other card to turn over to see if a match can be made.

Kite flyers. Give each child a long piece of crepe paper streamer and tell them it's the tail of a kite. Let them run around the room holding their "kite" high in the air and pretend that the spring winds are blowing their kite tails.

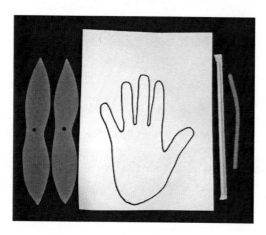

Handprint lily pieces.

Craft: Handprint lily

Materials needed: Green construction paper, white construction, cardstock or computer paper, yellow chenille stem, straw (green if possible), hole punch, scissors, pencil, tape. Advance preparation: Cut double leaf shapes from the green paper and punch hole in the middle. Cut yellow chenille stems in half with wire cutter. At storytime: Have parent trace child's hand onto the white paper and cut out the shape. Curl the white paper flower hands' fingers using the pencil to wrap them around it. Wrap the hand around the top of the straw and tape it. Slide the leaves onto the straw and tape in place. Fold the yellow chenille stem in half and curl the ends. Insert the folded end into the straw to look like a flower stamen.

Alternative Crafts

Pinecone bird feeder. Tie yarn around the pinecones so that they can hang from trees. Have the children spread peanut butter over a pinecone and then roll it in birdseed.

Cardboard boomerang. Cut thick cardboard X shape. Let children decorate with crayons or markers. Have them try tossing them to their parent holding it vertically, not like a flying disk. Explain that when they take it home they can try to use it outdoors and see if it will work like a boomerang and come back to them when they toss it. You need to flick the wrist to add spin as you toss it forward and slightly upward. It should start to turn and then flatten out as it coasts back to you. The easiest way to catch it is to clap it between both hands.

Spring collage. Cut out pictures from magazines of things that remind you of spring, like flowers, umbrellas, rainbows, raincoats, rain hats, watering cans, plants, clouds. Let the children glue the pictures to a background piece of paper as a collage. Alternately, give them pastel colors of tissue paper to tear and glue as a collage. Or combine the tissue paper with the magazine pictures.

Handprint lily.

Snack: Marshmallow flower cupcake

Materials needed: Yellow cake mix, green icing (or white icing and green sprinkles), large marshmallows, clean scissors, several colors of sugar sprinkles, small gumdrops, small paper plates, plastic knives. Advance preparation: Bake the cupcakes. Right before storytime snip the marshmallows in half and quickly cover the cut edges with different colored sprinkles. They will curl up and look like flower petals. At storytime: Give each child a cupcake and knife on a paper plate along with a dollop of green icing or white icing that they will cover with green sprinkles, one gumdrop and five marshmallow flower petals. Have them cover the cupcake in the green icing so that it looks like grass, then place the gumdrop in the center and surround it with the colored flower petals.

Marshmallow flower cupcake.

Alternative Snacks

Vegetable and fruit flower. Use several different kinds of fruits and vegetables to make flowers on paper plates. Orange or apple sections make good flower petals, surrounding a cracker or cucumber slice.

Have a spring "tea" with small cakes or sandwiches and cups of decaffeinated warm tea.

SUGGESTED BOOKS

Ackerman, Jill. *Welcome Spring.* 10 pages. 2009. Scholastic. A bright tactile board book that celebrates a first encounter with spring.

Berger, Samantha. *It's Spring!* A Hello Reader Level 2 book. 32 pages. 2001. Cartwheel Books. Animals spread the word that spring is here.

Bernard, Robin. *A Tree for All Seasons* (just the pages about spring). 16 pages. 2001. National Geographic Children's Books. Good photos show how the tree looks during each season.

Bunting, Eve. *Flower Garden.* 32 pages. 2000. Sandpiper. A little girl and her father get everything to bring home a window garden.

Butterfield, Moira. *Spring.* 32 pages. 2005. Franklin Watts. Explains what spring is, what happens in spring, how spring is different around the world.

Carle, Eric. *The Tiny Seed.* 36 pages. 2009. Little Simon. The life cycle of a flower is told through the adventures of a seed.

Carr, Jan. *Splish, Splash, Spring.* 32 pages. 2002. Holiday House. Spring is sloppy and rain-droppy.

Clifton, Lucille. *The Boy Who Didn't Believe in Spring.* 32 pages. 1992. Penguin Group. In the middle of the city, two young boys set out to find spring.

Day, Jennifer W. *What Is a Flower?* 24 pages. 1987. Random House Children's Books. Simple text and illustrations show the characteristics of various types of flowers.

Ehlert, Lois. *Planting a Rainbow.* 40 pages. 1992. Sandpiper. Shows how to plant seeds and nurture their growth.

Esbaum, Jill. *Everything Spring.* 16 pages. 2010. National Geographic Children's Books. Feel the warmth of spring seeing photos of baby animals.

Fogliano, Julie. *And Then It's Spring.* 32 pages. 2012. Roaring Book Press. A boy and his dog look forward to spring after a snow filled winter.

Fowler, Allan. *How Do You Know It's Spring?* 32 pages. 1992. Children's Press. A non-fiction book that discusses all the ways you can tell it's spring, from the flowers to the holidays, the baby animals, etc.

Glaser, Linda. *It's Spring!* 32 pages. 2002. Millbrook Press. A child observes the arrival of spring.

Good, Elaine W. *That's What Happens When It's Spring.* 32 pages. 1996. Good Books. The sights, sounds and special feelings of spring come alive.

Heller, Ruth. *The Reason for a Flower.* 48 pages. 1999. Penguin Group. Brief text and nice illustrations show the purpose of a flower.

Henkes, Kevin. *Little White Rabbit.* 40 pages. 2011. Greenwillow Books. A rabbit sets out for adventure on a spring day.

Hillenbrand, Will. *Spring Is Here!* 32 pages. 2011. Holiday House. Spring is in the air and Mole can smell it and tries to wake Bear.

Hirschi, Ron. *Spring.* 32 pages. 1996. Penguin Group. Spring is the time when many animals give birth to their young.

Hubbell, Patricia. *Hurray for Spring.* 32 pages. 2005. NorthWord Books for Young Readers. Rhyming text takes you through a spring day.

Iwamura, Kazuo. *Hooray for Spring!* 32 pages. 2009. North-South Books. What child doesn't love the first signs of spring?

Krauss, Ruth. *The Carrot Seed.* 32 pages. 1945. HarperCollins Publishers. Despite everyone's dire predictions, a little boy has faith in the carrot seed he plants.

Lach, William. *My Friends the Flowers.* 40 pages. 2010. Harry N. Abrams. A little bee loves to visit his friends, who happen to be flowers.

Latta, Sarah L. *What Happens in Spring.* 24 pages. 2006. Enslow Publishers. Each chapter begins with a question, such as what are the first signs of spring?

Lenski, Lois. *Spring Is Here.* 56 pages. 2005. Random House Children's Books. The children are playing outside because spring is here.

Lobel, Anita. *Hello, Day!* 40 pages. 2008. HarperCollins Publishers. It's a beautiful spring day and the animals all give a greeting.

Maass, Robert. *When Spring Comes.* 1997. Scholastic. A pictorial about the activities, sights and sounds of spring.

Macken, Joann Early. *Spring (Seasons of the Year).* 16 pages. 2006. Gareth Stevens Publishing. Photographs with simple sentences describing recognizable features of spring.

Manushkin, Fran. *How Mama Brought the Spring.* 32 pages. 2008. Penguin Group. Mama tells the story of how her mama could bring warm spring to their cold kitchen by making blintzes.

McCue, Lisa. *Quiet Bunny's Many Colors.* 32 pages. 2011. Sterling Publishing. Quiet Bunny loves the colors of spring.

Meddaugh, Susan. *Martha Says It with Flowers.* 24 pages. 2011. Houghton Mifflin Harcourt. Martha always seems to do the wrong thing around Grandma Lucille.

Na, Il Sung. *Snow Rabbit Spring Rabbit.* 24 pages. 2011. Random House Children's Books. What do the animals do when the snow falls to the ground and the trees are bare?

Pallotta, Jerry. *Flower Alphabet Book.* 32 pages. 1990. Charlesbridge Publishing. Describes a variety of flowers from A to Z.

Park, Linda Sue. *What Does Bunny See?* 32 pages. 2005. Houghton Mifflin Harcourt. A rabbit explores a garden.

Plourde, Lynn. *Spring's Sprung.* 32 pages. 2002. Simon & Schuster Books for Young Readers. Can Mother Earth soothe her daughters March, April and May?

Quellet, Debbie. *How Robin Saved Spring.* 32 pages. 2009. Henry Holt & Co. The animals, led by Robin, are determined to wake Sister Spring but Lady Winter would like the world to remain covered with snow.

Raczka, Bob. *Spring Things.* 32 pages. 2007. Albert Whitman and Co. Nature is busy budding and flowering.

Rawlinson, Julia. *Fletcher and the Springtime Blossoms.* 32 pages. 2009. Greenwillow Books. Fletcher loves everything about spring.

Roca, Nuria. *The Seasons.* 36 pages. 2004. Barron's Educational Series. Large color illustrations showing the activities of spring.

Thompson, Lauren. *Mouse's First Spring.* 32 pages. 2005. Simon & Schuster Books for Young Readers. Mouse and Momma head outside to play and start to see the first signs of spring.

Walker, Alice. *There Is a Flower at the Tip of My Nose Smelling Me.* 32 pages. 2006. Harper-Collins Publishers. Poetic text in this joyous celebration of self and nature.

Willems, Mo. *City Dog, Country Frog.* 64 pages. 2010. Hyperion. In Spring, City Dog meets Country Frog. Their friendship continues through the seasons until sadly one day, Country Frog isn't there any more.

Wilson, Karma. *Bear Wants More.* 40 pages. 2003. Margaret K. McElderry Books. When spring comes, Bear wakes and is ravenously hungry.

Worth, Bonnie. *Oh Say Can You Seed.* 45 pages. 2001. Random House Children's Books. All about flowering plants. From the Dr. Seuss library featuring the Cat in the Hat.

Farms

Advance planning: To plan for this storytime, find a theme-related song to play during craft and snack times, like "Down on Grandpa's Farm," by Raffi. You will also want to select a poem, such as "To the Farm" (find it at www.canteach.ca/elementary/songspoems.html), along with the books you plan to read. Decorate your space with toy barns, farm animals, straw. You might wear or bring some overalls, a straw hat.

Introduction to theme: A farm is a place where animals are raised or food is grown. Some farms have fruit trees, or orchards, some farms have cows and we get milk from them, and some farms grow grains that we use to make bread or vegetables for us to eat. Have you ever been to a farm? What did you see there? Are there foods that you eat that come from a farm? Do you know which ones? Today we'll read about farms, play a farm game, make a farm craft and eat a snack that comes from a farm.

Song: "The Farmer in the Dell":

> The farmer in the dell
> The farmer in the dell
> Hi-ho, the derry-o
> The farmer in the dell
> The farmer takes a wife
> The farmer takes a wife
> Hi-ho, the derry-o
> The farmer takes a wife
> The wife takes a child

The wife takes a child
Hi-ho, the derry-o
The wife takes a child
The child takes a nurse
The child takes a nurse
Hi-ho, the derry-o
The child takes a nurse
The nurse takes a dog
The nurse takes a dog
Hi-ho, the derry-o
The nurse takes a dog
The dog takes a cat
The dog takes a cat
Hi-ho, the derry-o
The dog takes a cat
The cat takes a rat
The cat takes a rat
Hi-ho, the derry-o
The cat takes a rat
The rat takes the cheese
The rat takes the cheese
Hi-ho the derry-o
The rat takes the cheese
The cheese stands alone
The cheese stands alone
Hi-ho, the derry-o
The cheese stands alone

Game: Farm animals

Materials needed: Pictures of many different farm animals. Recording of the sounds the animals make. Advance preparation: Cut out pictures of farm animals from magazines, gluing them to construction paper or card stock so that they remain vertical when you hold them up. Make a recording with various animal sounds using www.findsounds.com. At storytime: Hold up pictures of different farm animals and ask the children to identify them. Once they can identify all the animals, either play recordings of the sounds the animals make or make the sounds yourself while showing the pictures. Then make or play the sounds without showing the pictures to see if the children can identify which animal makes which sound.

Alternative Games

Animal pens. Mark off a few animal "pens" in the room either using masking tape or hula hoops on the floor. Designate them for certain kinds of animals by placing a toy of that animal in the pen, like cows in one, chickens in another, sheep, pigs. Choose several. Either let the children decide which animal they'd like to be or assign them to one of the pens to start. Play some lively farm-like music and tell them they've been let out of their pens and they're free to wander about the farm while the music plays. When the music stops, they return to their pen. Then rotate the animal figure so that the children get to be another kind of animal when you play the music again. Do this several times.

Apple toss. Provide a large bushel basket and either red apple bean bags or crumpled red tissue paper ball apples to toss into the basket.

Craft: Farm mini book

Materials needed: Paper, computer and graphic program such as Print Shop to print type, stapler, crayons. Advance preparation: Print the phrase "On my farm I have a" in large simple type in four places on the landscape oriented computer page. Top left, top right, middle left, middle right. Make sure the middle printings are below the midline because you are going to cut the pages in half lengthwise. Print the papers front and back, one sheet for each child. Cut the sheets lengthwise. Also cut one plain sheet for each child lengthwise to be the outer cover. Staple into booklets so that each booklet has eight pages inside with an outside cover. At storytime: Hand each child a booklet. Have the crayons available. Ask the children to think about what animals they would like to have if they had their own farm and draw a picture of each animal on each page of their booklet. If they have difficulty thinking of farm animals, show them some pictures from books or maybe have a poster made up of some photos of farm animals that you created from the Internet. If they don't finish their booklet at storytime, they can complete it at home.

Farm mini book pieces.

Farm mini book.

Alternative Crafts

Farm mobile. Have pictures of several farm animals, like cow, chicken and pig to cut out with holes punched to tie yarn and then tie to a paper towel roll.

Farm plate. Let the children cut out pictures of foods grown on farms from magazines or seed catalogs and packets. Have them glue those pictures to a white paper plate until they have a plate full of food grown on the farm.

Handprint sheep. Dip children's hands in paint and print on paper. The fingers make sheep legs, the thumb is the sheep's head. Cover the rest with cotton balls. Alternately, draw around hand and use glue to cover with cotton balls.

Snack: Farm fresh food

Materials needed: An assortment of fruits and/or vegetables, ideally fresh from a farm, paper plates. Advance preparation: Wash and cut up the fruits and

Farm fresh food.

vegetables. If you can get pictures of the farm the fruits and vegetables came from to show the children, that's great, too. At storytime: Put several bite sized pieces of fruits and vegetables on each plate, encouraging the children to try them all.

Alternative Snacks

Pig slop. Give each child a cup of pudding along with a choice of things to mix into it, like Chex cereal, mini marshmallows, chocolate chips, raisins, etc.

Milk and animal crackers. Try to get the children to identify the farm animals.

Churned butter. For each child, put 2 tablespoons of room temperature whipping cream into a baby food jar along with a pinch of salt. Have the children shake the jars until it turns into butter. Serve with crackers.

SUGGESTED BOOKS

Aliki. *Milk: From Cow to Carton.* 32 pages. 1999. Turtleback Books. Briefly describes how a cow produces milk and how it is processed.

Berger, Thomas [retold by]. *The Mouse and the Potato.* 30 pages. 1990. Floris Books. The farmer's daughter plants a potato that is so strong it takes a lot of people and animals to pull it out of the ground.

Blanco, Josette. *On the Farm.* 20 pages. 1975. Child's Play. Illustrations without text of life on the farm.

Bourgoing, Pascale De. *Vegetables in the Garden: A First Discovery Book.* 24 pages. 1994. Scholastic. Painted see-through pages that show children familiar fruits and vegetables and help them understand how they grow.

Brown, Margaret Wise. *Big Red Barn.* 32 pages. 1989. HarperCollins Publishers. Rhyming text illustrates a day in the life of a barnyard.

Carle, Eric. *Rooster's Off to See the World.* 32 pages. 1999. Aladdin. An introduction to numbers and sets as animals set off to see the world, led by the rooster.

Carle, Eric. *The Tiny Seed.* 36 pages. 2009. Little Simon. The tiny seed goes on an adventure to become a flower.

Casely, Judith. *Grandpa's Garden Lunch.* 32 pages. 1990. HarperCollins Publishers. Sarah's grandfather likes to garden and Sarah likes to help.

Cochran, Jean M. *Farmer Brown and His Little Red Truck.* 32 pages. 2009. Pleasant St. Press. Farmer Brown sets out on a journey, picking up animal after animal.

Cousins, Lucy. *Maisy's Morning on the Farm.* 24 pages. 2001. Candlewick Press. Morning on the farm is a busy time with lots of chores.

Cowley, Joy. *Mrs. Wishy-Washy's Farm.* 32 pages. 2006. Penguin Group. Mrs. Wishy-Washy is scrubbing all the animals on the farm.

Duffield, Katy S. *Farmer McPeepers and His Missing Milk Cows.* 32 pages. 2003. Cooper Square Publishing. A herd of cows borrows Farmer McPeepers' glasses so that they can have a day out on the town.

Ehlert, Lois. *Eating the Alphabet.* 40 pages. 1993. Houghton Mifflin Harcourt. Introduces upper and lower case letters while showing fruits and vegetables.

Ehlert, Lois. *Growing Vegetable Soup.* 32 pages. 1990. Houghton Mifflin Harcourt. A father and child share the joys of planting, watering and watching seeds grow.

Ehlert, Lois. *Planting a Rainbow.* 40 pages. 1992. Houghton Mifflin Harcourt. A mother and child plant a rainbow of flowers in the garden.

Fleischman, Sid. *The Scarebird.* 32 pages. 1994. HarperCollins Publishers. A lonely old farmer with only a scarecrow realizes the value of friendship when a young man comes to visit.

Florian, Douglas. *Vegetable Garden.* 32 pages. 1996. Houghton Mifflin Harcourt. Follow along with a family as they plant, tend and harvest their vegetable garden.

Fowler, Allan. *Quack and Honk.* 32 pages. 1993. Scholastic Library Publishing. A nonfiction book about ducks and geese.

Franklin, Kristine L. *The Shepherd Boy.* 32 pages. 1994. Atheneum Books for Young Readers. A poem that describes how a Navajo boy tends his family's sheep.

Gammell, Stephen. *Once Upon MacDonald's Farm.* 32 pages. 1990. Aladdin. Everyone's heard of Old MacDonald's farm, but according to this book, he wasn't really much of a farmer until he got some animals.

Geisert, Arthur. *Oink.* 32 pages. 1995. Houghton Mifflin Harcourt. Mama Pig and her eight piglets speak only one word, "oink," but there's adventure when the piglets run off and must be rescued.

Gibbons, Gail. *Farming*. 32 pages. 1990. Holiday House. An introduction to farming and the work done on the farm.

Gibbons, Gail. *The Milk Makers*. 32 pages. 1987. Aladdin. Beginning with the cow, and then progressing to how the milk is transported for delivery to stores.

Ginsburg, Mirra. *Good Morning, Chick*. 32 pages. 1989. HarperCollins Publishers. When he tries to imitate a rooster, a newly hatched chick falls in a puddle.

Harris, Trudy. *Wow, It's a Cow!* 16 pages. 2010. Scholastic. Kids love to guess the animal in this lift the flap book.

Helweg, Hans. *Farm Animals*. 32 pages. 1980. Random House Children's Books. Identifies and explains the usefulness of animals found on the farm.

Hutchins, Pat. *Titch*. 32 pages. 1993. Aladdin. Titch is so little that he feels left out until he has a seed that grows bigger than anything his brother and sister have.

Inkpen, Mick. *Everyone Hide from Wibbly Pig*. 24 pages. 2004. Penguin Young Readers Group. Wibbly Pig is playing hide and seek with other animals.

Jones, Carol. *Old MacDonald Had a Farm*. 32 pages. 1998. Houghton Mifflin Harcourt. Look through the peephole on each page to see which animal is to come.

Joosse, Barbara M. *Higgledy-Piggledy Chicks*. 34 pages. 2010. HarperCollins Publishers. Mama has seven new chicks and the barnyard is big.

Krauss, Ruth. *The Carrot Seed*. 32 pages. 1945. HarperCollins Publishers. Despite everyone's dire predictions, a little boy has faith in the carrot seed he plants.

Kroll, Steven. *The Biggest Pumpkin Ever*. 32 pages. 2007. Scholastic. Two mice help a pumpkin grow big but have different purposes in mind for the pumpkin.

Kutner, Merrily. *Down on the Farm*. 32 pages. 2005. Holiday House. Rhyming text describes what goes on during the day on a farm.

Lesser, Carolyn. *What a Wonderful Day to Be a Cow*. 32 pages. 1999. Random House Children's Books. Every month of the year the animals on the farm enjoy their way of life.

Martin, Bill, Jr., John Archambault and Ted Rand. *Barn Dance!* 32 pages. 1988. Henry Holt & Co. A little boy hears the music coming from the barn and goes to investigate.

McPhail, David. *Farm Morning*. 32 pages. 1991. Houghton Mifflin Harcourt. A father and his young daughter spend the morning feeding the animals on their farm.

McPhail, David. *Pigs Aplenty, Pigs Galore!* 32 pages. 1996. Penguin Group. Pigs galore invade a house and have a wonderful party.

Miller, Jane. *Farm Alphabet Book*. 32 pages. 1987. Scholastic. Letters of the alphabet illustrated by descriptions of animals and life on a farm.

Mitgutsch, Ali. *From Seed to Pear*. 24 pages. 1981. Lerner Publishing Group. Describes the cycle of a pear seed, which when planted, becomes a tree.

Modesitt, Jeanne. *Vegetable Soup*. 32 pages. 1991. Simon & Schuster. Two rabbits are reluctant to try foods they've never tasted before.

Most, Bernard. *The Cow That Went Oink*. 40 pages. 2003. Houghton Mifflin Harcourt. A cow that oinks and a pig that moos are ridiculed by the other animals.

Nodset, Joan L. *Who Took the Farmer's Hat?* 32 pages. 1988. HarperCollins Publishers. Although the farmer finds his hat after a long search, he decides to buy a new one anyway.

Pearson, Tracey C. *Old MacDonald Had a Farm*. 32 pages. 1984. Penguin Group. The folk song about Old MacDonald illustrated.

Pinkney, Jerry. *The Little Red Hen*. 32 pages. 2006. Penguin Group. The story of the hardworking hen and her lazy neighbors.

Politi, Leo. *Three Stalks of Corn*. 32 pages. 1994. Aladdin. The three stalks of corn in the garden take on new significance when Angelica's grandmother explains their uses and legends.

Potter, Beatrix. *The Tale of Peter Rabbit*. 70 pages (for the three tales in the book). 2009. Penguin Group. Peter disobeys his mother by going into Mr. McGregor's garden. A simplified adaptation for younger children.

Rockwell, Anne. *Apples and Pumpkins*. 24 pages. 2011. Aladdin. A little girl spends a fall day picking apples and searching for the perfect pumpkin.

Rylant, Cynthia. *This Year's Garden*. 32 pages. 1987. Atheneum Books for Young Readers. Follow the seasons of the year as reflected in the life of this garden of a large rural family.

Selsam, Millicent. *Egg to Chick*. An I Can Read Book Level 3. 64 pages. 1987. HarperCollins Publishers. How an egg develops from fertilization to hatching.

Shaw, Nancy L. *Sheep in a Jeep*. 32 pages. 1989. Houghton Mifflin Harcourt. The misadventures of a group of sheep that go riding in a jeep.

Stoeke, Janet Morgan. *Pip's Trip.* 32 pages. 2012. Penguin Group. The clueless hens wonder what it would be like to take a ride in the farmer's truck.

Tafuri, Nancy. *Early Morning in the Barn.* 24 pages. 1992. HarperCollins Publishers. All the barnyard animals wake up when the rooster crows.

Tafuri, Nancy. *This Is the Farmer.* 24 pages. 1994. HarperCollins Publishers. A farmer's kiss causes an amusing chain of events.

Thomas, Jan. *Is Everyone Ready for Fun?* 40 pages. 2011. Beach Lane Books. Chicken has some unexpected and exuberant cow visitors.

Waddell, Martin. *Farmer Duck.* 32 pages. 1996. Candlewick Press. Farmer Duck nearly collapses from overwork because the farm owner is lazy.

Williams, Sue. *I Went Walking.* 30 pages. 1992. Houghton Mifflin Harcourt. A young child goes for a walk and sees a colorful parade of animals along the way.

Wood, Jakki. *Moo, Moo Brown Cow.* 12 pages. 1996. Houghton Mifflin Harcourt. Readers learn about numbers and colors as a kitten visits a barnyard.

April

Rainbows

Advance planning: To plan for this storytime, find a theme-related song to play during craft and snack times, like Kermit the Frog's "Rainbow Connection" or "Somewhere Over the Rainbow," by Judy Garland. You will also want to select a poem, such as the extra poem that can be found on the Box of Crayons page at www.kinderart.com, along with the books you plan to read. Decorate your space with umbrellas, raincoats, ponchos, boots, streamers of all the colors of the rainbow.

Introduction to theme: Have you ever seen a rainbow in the sky? Did you notice that they appear when there's been rain? When the sun shines on the tiny drops of water that are still in the air after or during a rain it makes a rainbow appear in the sky. Sometimes you can see a rainbow near a waterfall or a water fountain. There are always seven colors in the rainbow: red, orange, yellow, green, blue, indigo and violet. Indigo is a very dark blue and violet is a shade of purple. Sometimes people think of the name ROY G BIV in order to remember the rainbow colors in order. Can you say all these colors with me? (Hold up a paper rainbow and point to the colors as everyone says them). Today we'll read about rainbows, play a rainbow game, make a rainbow craft and eat a rainbow snack.

Song: Sing the first verse of the "Rainbow Song," which can be found at www.metro lyrics.com.

Game: Balloon rainbow
    Materials needed: Balloons of as many different rainbow colors as possible and about one balloon or more per child. Advance preparation: Blow up the balloons. At storytime: Have the children try to get all the balloons up in the air and keep them there for a few minutes. Talk about the rainbow up in the sky.

Alternative Games

    Rainbow's end. Place small paper circles of all the different rainbow colors all around the storytime area. Send each child out to find a circle of each rainbow color. When they return with all the colors tell them they've found their rainbow and give them their craft supplies to make their own rainbow.

Paper rainbow. Give each child a sheet of construction paper in a color of the rainbow: red, orange, yellow, green, blue, indigo, violet. Tell them that they are going to make a human rainbow with their papers. Have them line up as you say the colors in order and hold up their pieces of paper so that they look like a rainbow.

Rainbow dance. Place sheets of paper in all of the colors of the rainbow on the floor. Play music. When the music stops, each child should stand on a sheet of paper. Ask each child to name the color of the paper he/she is standing on.

Rainbow streamers. Give each child a crepe paper streamer in one of the colors of the rainbow. Play music and let them move around the room holding their streamers high and waving them in the air. Periodically call out a color and ask the children holding that color to hold it high and wave it.

Missing rainbow color. Show the children a rainbow with a color missing and ask them to identify the missing color. Have many pictures of rainbows, each with one color missing.

Paper plate rainbow mobile pieces.

Craft: Paper plate rainbow mobile

Materials needed: Large white paper plates, crayons or markers, glue sticks, rolls of crepe paper streamer in as many colors of the rainbow as possible, such as red, orange, yellow, green, blue, purple. Hole punch, scissors, bright colored yarn, multicolored in rainbow colors would be ideal. Advance preparation: Cut paper plates in half. Punch hole in center of curved uncut side. Cut or tear 12 18-inch lengths of the colored crepe paper. Cut yarn in 18-inch lengths. At storytime: Have children color their paper plate piece in rainbow colors. Glue the colored crepe paper to the cut side of the plate, matching the colors if desired. Or alternately, glue crepe paper to plate following the arch of the plate. Tie the yarn to the hole that was punched in the curved side so that it can be hung.

Alternative Crafts

Cardstock lacing. Cut rainbow-shaped pieces of cardstock and punch holes in four arch shapes. Cut four pieces of yarn in rainbow colors and have children lace the colored yarn through the punched holes to make a rainbow.

Froot Loop rainbow. Cut rainbow-shaped pieces of cardstock. Have children use white glue that they spread with q-tips or paint brushes and glue the cereal pieces in rainbow arches of the same colors.

Rainbow windsock. For each windsock cut six two- to three-inch circles from construction paper. Cut tissue paper or crepe paper streamers same colors as circles. Glue a

Paper plate rainbow mobile.

streamer to each circle. Glue circles together overlapping slightly, then glue end circles together to make a circular windsock. Punch hole in top of a circle on each side and attach four 18-inch lengths of yarn so that the windsock can be hung.

Rainbow and clouds paper plate mobile. Cut large white paper plates in half. Have the children color them like rainbows then glue cotton balls to each rainbow end as clouds. Punch a hole in the top and hang with yarn or ribbon.

Snack: Rainbow cupcake

Materials needed: White cake mix, cupcake papers, white icing, food colors, small paper plates, plastic knives. Advance preparation: Divide cake batter into six equal portions and add food color to each batch using this instruction: Purple — 9 red and 6 blue drops; Blue —12 drops; Green —12 drops; Yellow —12 drops; Orange —12 yellow and 4 red drops; Red —18 drops. Put a spoonful of each color of batter gently into each cupcake paper liner in muffin tin in the order listed above (so purple will be on the bottom and red is on the top). Bake as directed on the box. At storytime: Give each child a cupcake on a paper plate with a plastic

Rainbow cupcake.

knife and a dollop of white icing. Tell them that the icing is like the cloud up in the sky with the rainbow and after they put their icing cloud on the cupcake they can taste their rainbow. Make sure they look at the inside of the cupcake after they take a bite. Talk about all the colors inside.

Alternative Snacks

Rainbow cookie. Using circle cookie or biscuit cutter, cut out cookies, then cut the circles in half and bake. Color white icing (paste or gel food color is best for icing) in several colors and let children apply several colors on their cookie with a plastic knife at storytime.

Get fruits and/or vegetables in many colors of the rainbow, such as cherry tomatoes or strawberries, orange peppers, carrots, oranges or cantaloupe, yellow peppers, bananas or pineapple, green peppers, celery, kiwi fruit, honeydew melon or green grapes, blueberries, purple or concord grapes.

Banana Jell-O rainbow. Banana pieces dipped into Jell-O powder — red, orange, yellow, green, blue, violet. You will need half a banana for each child and one package of red, orange, yellow, green, blue and purple Jell-O. There are seven colors in the rainbow red, orange, yellow, green, blue, indigo and violet. Blue and purple can be mixed to make indigo. Cut each banana half into seven pieces. Have the children dip each piece into the Jell-O. The longer the Jell-O sits on each piece of banana, the brighter the color becomes. After dipping the bananas in the Jell-O mix, ask the children to put them in the order of a rainbow. Might want to use toothpicks to keep the children from getting the Jell-O color on their hands.

Rainbow cookie. Cut cookies with circle cutter, then cut in half to make rainbow shape. At storytime let the children ice with white icing then give them several different colors of either Skittles or M & M candies to make a rainbow on the cookie. Could do this with cupcakes too.

SUGGESTED BOOKS

Arvetis, Chris. *What Is a Rainbow?* 1988. Checkerboard Press. This book explains how rainbows are made.

Baguley, Elizabeth. *Little Pip and the Rainbow Wish.* 28 pages. 2008. Good Books. Little Pip the mouse wants to play with friends but is shy until he sees a rainbow and tries to give it to his friends.

Collins, Judy. *Over the Rainbow.* 26 pages. 2010. Charlesbridge Publishing. Some lyrics that were never in the Wizard of Oz are added to the well known lyrics from the song, beautifully illustrated. The book comes with a CD of Judy Collins singing the song.

Cousins, Lucy. *Maisy's Rainbow Dream.* 32 pages. 2003. Walker Children's Hardbacks. Maisy's night time dream world has all the colors of the rainbow.

Ehlert, Lois. *Planting a Rainbow.* 40 pages. 1992. Houghton Mifflin Harcourt Trade & Reference Publishers. Colorful artwork that shows all the plants in the family garden.

Fielding, Beth. *Animal Colors: A Rainbow of Colors from Animals Around the World.* 32 pages. 2009. EarlyLight Books. Discover the world of animals in a kaleidoscope of color.

Fowler, Allan. *All the Colors of the Rainbow.* 32 pages. 1999. Children's Press. A good reference that shows the rainbow and gives an explanation for it.

Fox, Mem. *Whoever You Are.* The human rainbow, or children of all colors, are found all over the world.

Freeman, Don. *A Rainbow of My Own.* 32 pages. 1978. Penguin Group. A little boy imagines how it would be if he had a rainbow to play with.

Hallinan, P.K. *A Rainbow of Friends.* 32 pages. 2006. Ideals Children's Books. Friends come in all different colors and sizes.

Kalman, Bobbie. *I Eat a Rainbow.* 16 pages. 2010. Crabtree Publishing Company. Colorful pictures show many different kinds of foods children can eat from all the colors of the rainbow.

Karmel, Anabel. *I Can Eat a Rainbow.* 18 pages. 2009. Dorling Kindersley Publishing. Colorful photos that show how children can eat lots of very colorful healthy fruits and vegetables.

Katz, Karen. *The Colors of Us.* 32 pages. 2002. Holt Henry & Co. A little girl and her mother observe the differences in color of the skin of the people around them.

Lionni, Leo. *Little Blue and Little Yellow.* 48 pages. 1995. HarperCollins Publishers. A little blue spot and a little yellow spot are friends. When they hug, they become green.

Lyon, George Ella. *Weaving the Rainbow.* 40 pages. 2004. Simon & Schuster Children's Publishing. Shows how a tapestry is made, starting with shearing the sheep.

Mangieri, Catherine C. *What Is a Rainbow?* 12 pages. 2001. Rosen Publishing Group. An early reader book that describes rainbows.

Martin, Bill, Jr., John Archambault and James Endicott. *Listen to the Rain.* 32 pages. 1988. Henry Holt & Co. The beauty, the mystery and the sounds of the rain.

McKee, David. *Elmer and the Rainbow.* 32 pages. 2011. Lerner Publishing Group. Elmer the colorful patchwork elephant is sad that the rainbow has lost its colors.

Meadows, Daisy. *The Rainbow Fairies.* 32 pages. 2010. Scholastic. A learn to read book that introduces the Rainbow Fairies series, a popular children's chapter book series.

Morpugo, Michael. *The Rainbow Bear.* 32 pages. 2000. Trans World Publishers Limited. Snow Bear's wish to be colorful as the rainbow is granted.

Parton, Dolly. *I Am a Rainbow.* 32 pages. 2009. Penguin Group. Talks about feelings as described by colors, like tickled pink or green with envy.

Pfister, Marcus. *The Rainbow Fish.* 32 pages. 1992. North-South Books. The beautiful rainbow fish doesn't have any friends until he learns to share.

Rabe, Tish. *Chasing Rainbows.* 16 pages. 2012. Random House Books for Young Readers. Sally and Nick want to paint rainbows but they don't know what colors to use. And where do rainbows come from?

Romain, Trevor. *The Boy Who Swallowed a Rainbow.* 32 pages. 2001. Boyds Mill Press. Lucas accidentally swallows a rainbow and runs into trouble when thieves want to see if there's a pot of gold at the end of it.

Russell, Lyndsay. *The Rainbow Weaver.* 48 pages.

2008. Oldcastle Books Limited. The king of the hobgoblins is stealing the threads of color that make the rainbow and Tillie tries to stop him.

Salzano, Tammi. *One Rainy Day.* 24 pages. 2011. ME Media. A board book that shows all the things Duck can do on a rainy day, like wear boots and see a rainbow surprise.

Schwartz, Betty Ann. *What Makes a Rainbow?* 14 pages. 2000. Dalmatian Press. Ribbons going throughout the pages show a complete rainbow at the end of the book.

Shannon, David. *A Bad Case of Stripes.* 32 pages. 2004. Scholastic Paperbacks. Camilla Cream is very worried about what other people think of her. She's so worried that she breaks out in stripes.

Walsh, Ellen Stoll. *Mouse Magic.* 32 pages. 2001.

Houghton Mifflin Harcourt. A mouse discovers that there's magic in colors, not necessarily provided by a wizard.

Walsh, Ellen Stoll. *Mouse Paint.* 40 pages. 1989. Houghton Mifflin Harcourt Trade & Reference Publishers. Three white mice discover what can be done with paint in three colors.

Walsh, Melanie. *Ned's Rainbow.* 24 pages. 2000. DK Preschool. Ned loves rainbows but he's never seen a real one. Until one day a beautiful rainbow comes out and Ned can't wait to catch its beautiful colors.

Wyler, Rose. *Raindrops and Rainbows.* 32 pages. 1989. Silver Burdett. Simple text and experiments illustrate why it rains and how clouds and rainbows form.

Yolen, Jane. *Color Me a Rhyme.* 32 pages. 2000. Wordsong. What colors do you see in nature?

Horses

Advance planning: To plan for this storytime, find a theme-related song to play during craft and snack times, like "All the Pretty Little Horses," by Ingrid DuMosch. You will also want to select a poem, such as "The Old Brown Horse," by W.F. Holmes (find it at www.english-for-students.com), along with the books you plan to read. Decorate your space with stuffed horses, stick horses, posters of horses, western hats, even a saddle if one is available.

Introduction to theme: Have you ever seen a horse? They are big, beautiful animals with four legs and hard hooves as feet. They can run very fast and are sometimes ridden in races. Some horses work at pulling wagons or carts, some horses give rides to people for fun. Female horses are called mares, and they give birth to baby horses called foals. Some people think ponies are baby horses, but they're actually smaller versions of horses and never grow up to be as big. Have you ever ridden a pony or a horse? You usually sit on a leather saddle, put your feet in stirrups and hold on to the reins that tell the horse to turn or stop. Today we'll read about horses, play a horse game, make a horse puppet craft and eat a snack that horses might like to eat.

Song: "Yankee Doodle"

> Yankee Doodle went to town
> riding on a pony
> Stuck a feather in his cap
> and called it macaroni.

Game: Find the lost horses

Materials needed: Many small plastic horses. Advance preparation: Hide the horses around the storytime area before the children arrive. Draw a barn on a large piece of paper. At storytime: Have the children go looking for the lost horses and bring them back to the barn on the piece of paper.

Alternative Games

Horseshoes (rubber). Set up horseshoe game and let children take turns tossing rubber or plastic horseshoes.

Feedbag races. Get burlap or cloth sacks and have sack races calling them feedbags.

Stick horses. Make or borrow some stick horses and let the children ride them around.

Horse bingo. Make a bingo game online using horse and horse-related items.

Craft: Sock stick horse

Materials needed: Wooden dowels, small boys' white cotton crew socks, polyester fiberfill, black permanent markers, rubber bands, scissors, yarn. Advance preparation: Cut wooden dowels in twelve-inch lengths. At storytime: Have the children stuff the tube socks with fiberfill, tie off with a rubber band and use the same or another rubber band to attach the end of the tube sock to one end of the dowel rod. Draw eyes, nostrils and a mouth on the stuffed sock horse head. Tie yarn around the head like a bridle and make a long loop for the reins. Could make these horses before game time and ride them around the storytime area as the game.

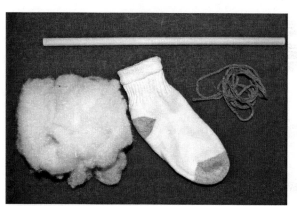

Sock stick horse pieces.

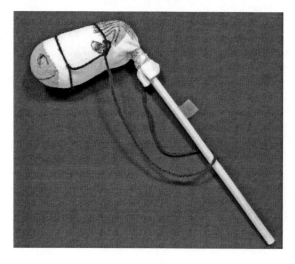

Sock stick horse.

Alternative Crafts

Paper bag horse puppet. Brown paper lunch bags, brown and tan construction paper, large google eyes, glue sticks, scissors, brown yarn, hole punch. Cut out dark brown construction paper horse heads and lower jaws. Cut out tan construction paper forelocks. Cut lengths of yarn for tails. Punch hole in rear bottom to attach yarn tail. Have children glue horse heads to flap of bag and lower jaw under flap. Glue forelock between ears. Glue on google eyes. Tie several lengths of yarn to back as tail.

How many hands? Provide large butcher paper and crayons and have the parents draw an outline of each child lying down on the paper. Explain that horses' heights are measured in hands, and they are measured at their withers, and show this spot (the bump at the bottom of the mane where the front of the saddle goes). The width of the hand is about four inches. Once the child's outline has been drawn on the paper, have the child and parent measure how many hands tall the child is. Ask for the information. Explain that an average horse is fifteen hands high (remember that's the withers, not the top of the head) and compare how tall the children are to that. Let the children color their outlines.

Snack: Apples and carrots

Materials needed: Apples, carrots, plates, knife, vegetable peeler. Advance preparation: Core and slice apples, peel and slice carrots. At storytime: Place a few carrot slices and an apple slice on each plate and explain that these are foods that horses like to eat as snacks too.

Apples and Carrots

Alternative Snacks

Horse cookie. Supplies needed: round cookies for body, sugar cookies for legs and neck, circus peanuts for heads, decorating icing for mane and eyes, licorice for tails.

Horseshoe-shaped biscuits. Supplies needed: biscuit dough, plates. Roll dough into 6-inch long "snakes," shape into a U like a horseshoe and bake.

Granola. Make your own or buy prepared granola and explain that horses love to eat grains, especially when they're sweetened like granola is sweetened.

SUGGESTED BOOKS:

Adams, Jean Ekman. *Clarence Goes Out West and Meets a Purple Horse.* 32 pages. 2000. Cooper Square Publishing. The story of a friendship between a boy and a horse.

Addy, Sharon Hart. *When Wishes Were Horses.* 32 pages. 2002. Houghton Mifflin Harcourt Trade & Reference Publishers. Zeb makes wishes that keep coming true.

Barnes, Laura T. *Twist and Ernest.* 32 pages. 1999. Barnesyard Books. Little Ernest is a lonely donkey but when the big show horse Twist arrives he doesn't seem to want to be friends.

Bradley, Kimberly Brubaker. *The Perfect Pony.* 32 pages. 2007. Penguin Group. A little girl surprisingly chooses a dirty, shaggy pony for her own.

Brett, Fritz. *Fritz and the Beautiful Horses.* 32 pages. 1987. Houghton Mifflin Harcourt Trade & Reference Publishers. Fritz the pony isn't one of the beautiful horses but he saves the day when he's the only one who can rescue the children.

Cantrell, Charlie. *A Friend for Einstein, the Smallest Stallion.* 40 pages. 2011. Hyperion Books for Children. Einstein is a miniature horse in search of a playmate.

Carle, Eric. *The Artist Who Painted a Blue Horse.* 32 pages. 2011. Penguin Group. All sorts of animals in imaginatively different colors.

Carle, Eric. *Mr. Seahorse.* 32 pages. 2004. Penguin Group Incorporate. Explains how differently some marine animals carry and care for their young. Another kind of horse.

Chandler, Edna Walker. *Pony Rider.* 48 pages. 1974. Benefic Press. Tom Logan and his family travel west in a covered wagon and see a pony express rider.

Dannenberg, Julie. *Cowboy Slim.* 32 pages. 2010. Charlesbridge Publishing. Slim gets sent to the rear of the herd because he can't seem to do anything right. Will he ever be a real cowboy?

Donovan, Jane Monroe. *Winter's Gift.* 32 pages. 2004. Sleeping Bear Press. A Christmas story about an old man who'd rather forget about Christmas but he has a surprise visitor.

Goble, Paul. *The Girl Who Loved Wild Horses.* 32 pages. 1993. Simon & Schuster Children's Publishing. A Native American girl loves horses so much that she becomes one of them in this folktale.

Gray, Rita. *The Wild Little Horse.* 32 pages. 2005. Penguin Group. Little Horse goes on an adventure but his parents are close behind.

Haas, Jessie. *Scamper and the Horse Show.* 32 pages. 2004. HarperCollins Publishers. Molly and Anna are going to the horse show with Scamper. Will he behave?

Hoban, Russell. *Rosie's Magic Horse.* 32 pages. 2013. Candlewick Press. An old ice-lolly stick is picked up by Rosie and placed in a box, where it comes to life later as a horse.

Hobbie, Holly. *Everything but the Horse: A Childhood Memory.* 32 pages. 2010. Little, Brown Books for Young Readers. Holly Hobbie's story of her own childhood and love of horses.

Hoff, Syd. *The Horse in Harry's Room.* 32 pages. 1985. HarperCollins Publishers. Although no one else can see it, Harry is very pleased to keep a horse in his room. An I Can Read book.

Janni, Rebecca. *Every Cowgirl Needs a Horse.* 32 pages. 2010. Penguin Group. Nelli Sue gets a bicycle for her birthday when she really wanted a horse.

Jeffers, Susan. *My Pony.* 32 pages. 2008. Hyperion Press. A little girl dreams about having her own pony.

Keith, Kody. *Horace the Horse Threw a Shoe.* 2010. Tate Publishing and Enterprises. Horace doesn't like vegetables and gets so mad he throws things.

Krauss, Ruth. *Charlotte and the White Horse.* 32 pages. 2001. HarperCollins Publishers. A reissue of the original Maurice Sendak story of a little girl and her love of a horse.

Kumin, Maxine. *Oh Harry!* 32 pages. 2011. Roaring Book Press. Harry calms new and excited horses but has a different challenge to face when a mischievous six year old boy shows up.

McDonnell, Flora. *Giddy-Up! Let's Ride* 32 pages. 2002. Candlewick Press. Describes ways people ride horses.

McGeorge, Constance W. *Chestnut.* 32 pages. 2004. Peachtree Publishers. A steadfast horse is brought to life with beautiful paintings that depict early 20th century city life.

Milbourne, Anna. *Little Pony.* 24 pages. 2009. EDC Publishing. Follows the life of a new foal to being a grown up pony.

Numeroff, Laura Joffe. *Ponyella.* 32 pages. 2011. Hyperion Press. The Cinderella story with a twist.

Ohi, Ruth. *Chicken, Pig, Cow Horse Around.* 32 pages. 2010. Annick Press, Limited. Chicken, Pig and Cow are happy together until Horse arrives.

Ongman, Gudrun Geibel. *The Sleep Ponies.* 32 pages. 2000. Mindcastle Books. Dreaming children ride ponies in their sleep.

Peck, Jan. *Way Out West on My Little Pony.* 2010. Pelican Publishing Company. A surprise ending to this story of a little girl out for a ride who encounters some interesting animals.

Rash, Andy. *Are You a Horse?* 32 pages. 2009. Scholastic. Roy's friends give him a saddle for his birthday but he doesn't know what a horse is.

Sewell, Anna. *The Story of Black Beauty* 24 pages. 2008. EDC Publishing. An English horse tells of his life with both cruel and kind masters.

Sharp, Thelma. *The Saturday Appaloosa.* 32 pages. 2002. Red Deer Press. Beautiful artwork in this book.

Stein, David Ezra. *Cowboy Ned & Andy.* 32 pages. 2006. Simon & Schuster Children's Books. Andy is Ned's horse. In this book they discover that friendship is a good birthday gift.

Stein, David Ezra. *Ned's New Friend.* 32 pages. 2007. Simon & Schuster Children's Books. Cowboy Ned meets someone he'd like to get to know better but his horse Andy is jealous.

Taylor-Butler, Christine. *A Pony to Love.* 32 pages. 2004. Sterling. With a little imagination, horse-loving boys and girls will be off on this magical adventure.

Turnbull, Ann. *The Sand Horse.* 32 pages. 2002. Andersen. The sand horse at the seashore wants to run with the white horses in the waves.

Yolen, Jane. *Hush, Little Horsie.* 32 pages. 2010. Random House. A soothing bedtime story with mama horses and their babies.

Rain

Advance planning: To plan for this storytime, find a theme-related song to play during craft and snack times, like "Singin' in the Rain," by Gene Kelly. You will also want to select a poem, such as the classic "Rain Rain Go Away," along with the books you plan to read. Decorate your space with umbrellas, rain sticks, rain coats, boots, ponchos, grey streamers.

Introduction to theme: Do you know why it rains? Where does the water come from?

There is water on the ground, in the rivers, lakes and oceans. The sun heats the water and some of it evaporates, or goes up into the air. There is water in the air around us all the time. Some of the water goes up to the clouds, which are full of water and when the clouds get too heavy and full of water they rain the water back down to the ground. Have you ever been out in the rain? Did you wear boots or a raincoat? Carry an umbrella? Have you ever seen a puddle made by the rain? Splashed in one? Today we're going to read some books about rain, sing some songs, play some games, make our own rainsticks and eat some clouds. We're also going to see if we can make it rain inside!

How: Fill a glass jar with very hot water. Turn the jar lid over and fill it with ice. Place the lid on top of the jar. Now, wait and watch from time to time while you read books. In about 15 minutes you will see "rain" fall inside the jar. The Explanation: Some of the hot water turns into steam and collects on the lid. The ice cools the steam and turns it back into liquid. When enough water collects on the lid it falls as "rain." This process is condensation.

Song and Fingerplay: "The Itsy Bitsy Spider"

The Itsy Bitsy Spider went up the water spout (use your fingers to pretend to climb)
Down came the rain and washed the spider out (move fingers down
wiggling like the rain and then move to the sides to wash the spider away)
Out came the sun and dried up all the rain (make a circle
with your hands and hold up to look like the sun)
And the Itsy Bitsy Spider went up the spout again (use fingers to climb)

Game: Make a rainstorm

Materials needed: None. Advance preparation: None. At storytime: Have the children stand in a circle, and explain the motions they'll be doing to simulate a rainstorm. Start with rubbing hands together. Have each child in turn follow you until you go around the circle and everyone is rubbing their hands together. Then switch to snapping your fingers. While the group continues to rub hands, first one child and then another will start snapping until, once again, everyone is doing the same thing. In the same way, move on to leg-slapping and lastly foot-stomping, before following the same steps in reverse. Tell the children to listen and they will they hear the sounds of a rain storm.

Alternative Games

Making it rain. Give each child several pieces of blue or grey tissue paper and have them crumple the paper, telling them that they're making raindrops. Open an umbrella and play some recorded rain sounds and have them walk around the room with you under the umbrella tossing their "raindrops" on the ground, picking them up again, and tossing them repeatedly. When you're ready to stop, turn the umbrella upside down and have the children toss their raindrops into the umbrella.

Rainstorm tag. Explain that you are the beginning of a storm, and you are going to get bigger and bigger by tagging a child, who will then hold your hand as you move about the room making storm sounds. That child then tags another child, who holds on to you, and that child tags another, etc. until everyone is holding someone else's hand and you are a very big storm.

Rain or sun? Bring in pictures that show either rain and rainy day activities and clothing or sun and sunny day activities and clothing. Hold up each picture and ask the children to identify if it's sunny or rainy.

Craft: Rain stick

Materials needed: Cardboard tube like paper towel rolls or poster tubes, silver paint, foil, dry rice, duct tape. Advance preparation: Paint the paper towel tubes silver. Cover one end of the tube with duct tape by placing one piece over the hole, then another piece crosswise and a third piece wrapped around the end of the tube covering the ends of the other pieces to seal. Cut foil into approximately 12-inch squares, two for each child. At storytime:

Rain stick pieces.

Rain stick.

Explain that the rain stick is a musical instrument from South America. Traditionally, rain sticks are made from the wood skeleton of a cactus. First, the thorns are pulled off and pushed back through the soft flesh of the cactus. Then the cactus is left in the sun to dry — with the thorns on the inside. Later, the hollow cactus is filled with small pebbles, and the ends are sealed with pieces of wood. We're going to make rainsticks from cardboard instead of cactus with foil inside instead of the thorns. Then we'll put in rice instead of the pebbles. How: Roll the foil squares like a snake. Make two. After they're rolled take the two and twist the tops together then twist it into a chain. Put inside of cardboard tube. Pour in about a quarter cup of rice. Tape the open end. Gently tip the rainstick over and listen to the rice fall from one end to the other. Tip over again and again.

Alternative Crafts

Rain cloud. Cut out white cloud shapes, two per child. Cut several lengths of grey crepe paper streamers. Place a little fiberfill stuffing on one of the cloud shapes, run a glue stick around the outside edge, place the grey streamers on the bottom edge of the glue and press the other cloud shape on top. Punch a hole in the top of the cloud; tie a piece of yarn to hang.

Cloud lace up. Cut out white cloud shapes. Punch holes around the outside edge, about an inch apart. Let each child take a length of yarn and run it around the edge.

Rainy day picture. Give each child a piece of construction paper. With crayons, encourage them to draw a picture of a rainy day. Suggest clouds, raindrops, a child wearing a raincoat and boots, carrying an umbrella.

Snack: Cloud cookie

Materials needed: Sugar cookies cut with a flower-shaped cookie cutter so that they look like clouds. White icing. Advance preparation: Make the cookies. At story-time: Give each child a cookie and a dollop of icing. Let them spread the icing on their "cloud."

Alternative Snacks

Fruit umbrella. Give each child an orange segment or apple slice and a pretzel stick to place on a plate to look like an umbrella.

Cookies in the shape of raindrops and blue tinted icing.

Fruit snacks in the shape of raindrops.

Cloud cookies.

SUGGESTED BOOKS

Barrett, Judi. *Cloudy with a Chance of Meatballs.* 32 pages. 1982. Atheneum Books for Young Readers. The weather brings large food three times a day, threatening the town of Chewandswallow.

Bauer, Marion Dane. *Clouds.* 32 pages. 2004. Simon Spotlight. Where do clouds come from?

Bauer, Marion Dane. *If Frogs Made the Weather.* 32 pages. 2005. Holiday House. What the weather would be like if different animals controlled it.

Bauer, Marion Dane. *Rain.* 32 pages. 2004. Simon Spotlight. Where does rain come from?

Branley, Franklyn M. *Down Comes the Rain.* 32 pages. 1997. HarperCollins Publishers. Explains how the water cycle leads to rain and different kinds of weather patterns.

Branley, Franklyn M. *Flash, Crash, Rumble and Roll.* 32 pages. 1999. Collins. Learn all about thunderstorms.

Brett, Jan. *The Umbrella.* 32 pages. 2004. Putnam Juvenile. A boy drops his umbrella and animals climb into it keeping the boy from seeing the animals in the rain forest.

Bright, Paul. *The Bears in the Bed and the Great Big Storm.* 32 pages. 2008. Good Books. Strange shadows appear in the night.

Burningham, John. *Mr. Grumpy's Motor Car.* 32 pages. 1976. HarperCollins Publishers. Everyone wants to ride in Mr. Grumpy's car, but it starts to rain and the car gets stuck in the mud.

dePaola, Tomie. *The Cloud Book.* 32 pages. 1985.

Holiday House. Introduces the ten most common types of clouds.

Eagle, Kin. *It's Raining It's Pouring.* 32 pages. 1997. Charlesbridge Publishing Inc. An expanded version of the traditional rhyme about what happens to the old man when it's raining and pouring.

Formby, Caroline. *Wild Weather Soup.* 32 pages. 1995. Child's Play International. Winnifred Weathervane takes a break from making the weather, with hilarious consequences.

Gliori, Debi. *Stormy Weather.* 32 pages. 2009. Walker & Co. A mama fox soothes her baby's fear of the storm outside.

Gorbachev, Valeri. *One Rainy Day.* 40 pages. 2002. Penguin Young Readers Group. A counting book where Goat tries to figure out why Pig is sopping wet.

Hesse, Karen. *Come on Rain.* 32 pages. 1999. Scholastic. A young girl eagerly awaits a coming rain storm because of the summer heat.

Hest, Amy. *In the Rain with Baby Duck.* 32 pages. 1995. Candlewick Press. Baby Duck hates rain so her grandparents give her boots and an umbrella.

Jango-Cohen, Judith. *Why Does It Rain?* 47 pages. 2006. Lerner Publishing Group. Explains the water cycle and how clouds, rain, snow and hail form.

Kalan, Robert. *Rain.* 32 pages. 1991. HarperCollins Publishers. Using graphics and very few words, explains rain storms.

Kotzwinkle, William. *Rough Weather Ahead for Walter the Farting Dog*. 32 pages. 2007. Penguin Group. Walter's digestive disorder ends up causing him to blow up like a balloon and float out the window.

Lichtenheld, Tom. *Cloudette*. 40 pages. 2011. Henry Holt & Co. How can such a little cloud do something big?

Lloyd, David. *Hello Goodbye*. 32 pages. 1995. Candlewick Press. A tree stands in the sun and a bear approaches it and says hello. Small voices answer. But what happens when it starts to rain?

London, Jonathan. *Puddles*. 32 pages. 1999. Penguin Group. Morning is magical after a night of rain and thunder.

Macken, JoAnn Early. *Waiting Out the Storm*. 32 pages. 2010. Candlewick Press. A gentle tale for children who are afraid of storms.

Martin, Bill, Jr., John Archambault and James Endicott. *Listen to the Rain*. 32 pages. 1988. Henry Holt & Co. The beauty, the mystery and the sounds of the rain.

McKinney, Barbara Shaw. *A Drop Around the World*. Follow a drop of water and learn about the water cycle.

McPhail, David. *The Puddle*. 32 pages. 2000. Farrar, Straus & Giroux. What better to do on a rainy day than sail a boat in a puddle?

Milbourne, Anna. *The Rainy Day*. 24 pages. 2005. EDC Publishing. Takes you through what happens on a rainy day.

Munsch, Robert. *Mud Puddle*. 32 pages. 1996. Annick Press, Limited. Whenever Jule Ann goes outside a mud puddle jumps on her and gets her all muddy.

Murphy, Mary. *Here Comes the Rain*. 24 pages. 2000. DK Publishing. Cat hates the rain and tries to run away from it but discovers it's not so bad after all.

Pomerantz, Charlotte. *The Piggy in the Puddle*. 32 pages. 1989. Aladdin. Verse about a young pig who refuses to leave her mud puddle.

Rockwell, Anne. *Clouds*. 40 pages. 2008. Collins. Look at the clouds to see if you can tell what the weather will be like.

Rockwell, Lizzy. *What's the Weather?* 24 pages. 2009. Scholastic Library Publishing. Four types of weather are explored: sunny, windy, rainy, snow.

Shannon, David. *The Rain Came Down*. 32 pages. 2000. Scholastic. Chaos follows an unexpected downpour.

Shaw, Charles G. *It Looked Like Spilt Milk*. 32 pages. 2009. HarperCollins Publishers. A cloud appears to be many different shapes.

Shulevitz, Uri. *Rain Rain Rivers*. 32 pages. 2000. Farrar, Straus & Giroux. As it rains, a child feels a nice coziness.

Spier, Peter. *Rain*. 40 pages. 1997. Random House Children's Books. Wordless picture book captures a brother and sister's fun in the rain.

Stojic, Manya. *Rain*. 32 pages. 2009. Random House Children's Books. Rain comes to the dry African savanna and the animals welcome it.

Tafuri, Nancy. *The Big Storm: A Very Soggy Counting Book*. 32 pages. 2009. Simon & Schuster Books for Young Readers. As the sky turns grey, the animals, counting from 1 to 10, start to run.

Thaler, Mike. *In the Middle of the Puddle*. 32 pages. 1992. HarperCollins Publishers. A frog and a turtle watch the rain turn their puddle into an ocean.

Yashima, Taro. *Umbrella*. 40 pages. 2004. Penguin Group. Momo eagerly awaits a rainy day so she can use her new umbrella.

Yee, Wong Herbert. *Who Likes Rain?* 32 pages. 2010. Henry Holt & Co. It's time to put on your rain gear for a rainy day romp.

Plants and Seeds

Advance planning: To plan for this storytime, find a theme-related song to play during craft and snack times, like "Little Seed," by Elizabeth Mitchell. You will also want to select a poem, such as "The Little Plant" and "My Garden" (find them at www.canteach.ca/elementary/songspoems), along with the books you plan to read. Decorate your space with plants, seeds, gardening tools.

Introduction to theme: What is a seed? A seed is actually like a baby plant inside a special kind of coat, called a seed coat, that's similar to a coat that you wear to keep warm.

Most plants come from seeds. How do seeds travel? Some blow in the wind, some are moved by insects or birds, some on water. What do seeds need to grow? Water, warmth and a good place to grow, like soil. Why do we need plants? Some plants make the air that we breathe, we eat some plants, and animals eat plants. Some plants are made into medicine or clothing, or our houses. Today we'll read about plants, play a plant game, make a plant craft and eat a snack that looks like the dirt in which we plant seeds.

Song: "The Gardener Plants the Seeds" (To the tune of "Farmer in the Dell") lyrics can be found at www.canteach.ca/elementary/songspoems. "Little Seed" (To the tune of "I'm a Little Teapot") lyrics can be found at www.macaronisoup.com/songs.

Game: Plant the seed

Materials needed: Large seeds (sunflower, green bean) or beans (navy beans), empty plastic gallon milk bottle. Advance preparation: None. At storytime: Give each child 10 seeds and have him/her stand in front of the milk bottle and try to drop as many seeds as possible in the bottle.

Alternative Games

Flower toss. Cut several flower patterns out of different colors of foam sheets. Cut out center circle. Clean an empty half-liter clear plastic soda bottle, removing the label. Fill bottle with water and 1–2 drops of green food coloring. Place the flower top over the open neck of the bottle, and then tightly screw on the bottle lid. Use large paper circles cut from paper plates with the center cut out to throw over the flowers.

Cooperative story. Start a story about a seed and then go around the circle and ask each child to add something to the story.

Grow Little seeds. Start with everyone squatting down low and pretending they are plant seeds. Play some quiet music. Turn the volume up slowly on the CD player and describe what is happening to the seeds. First they are planted in the ground where it's nice and warm. Now it's raining and the seeds are getting a drink. The sun comes out and is warming them and will help them grow. The seed is opening and roots are coming out. Oh! Now it's raining again. And now here comes the sun! Finally, the plants are coming out of the ground.

Craft: Planter pot

Materials needed: biodegradable peat starter plant cup, dirt, seeds, markers to decorate planter cups. Advance preparation: None. At storytime: Let the children decorate their planter with markers, then fill them with dirt and

Left: **Planter pot pieces.** *Right:* **Planter pot.**

plant several seeds under the surface. Give them instructions that suit the seed planted, such as how much to water, how much sun for planting, explain that the peat pot can be planted.

Alternative Crafts

Flower bookmark. Cut a flower from sheet foam. Cut a small hole in the middle of the flower and in the middle of a piece of ribbon. Fold the ribbon over and place the foam flower on top of the hole and put a brad through the flower and the ribbon to hold it together.

Flower bouquet. Put foam sheet flowers on the ends of pencils and arrange a few pencils in a small jar to look like a bouquet.

Snack: Dirt pudding cup

Materials needed: Chocolate pudding, gummy worms, spoons, clear plastic drink cups, crushed chocolate wafer cookie or Oreos. Advance preparation: Crush the wafer cookies or Oreos. Make pudding. At storytime: Give each child a cup in which to drop a gummy worm and cover it with chocolate pudding followed by crushed chocolate cookies.

Dirt pudding cup.

Alternative Snacks

Fruit and veggie flower. Make a flower out of various fruits and vegetables, like orange segments for the petals, cucumber or carrot slice for the face, and celery for the stem and lettuce leaves for the leaves. Let the children put the flower together on a paper plate.

Fruit kebabs. Give the children different small pieces of fruit and a bamboo skewer and let them make their own kebabs.

SUGGESTED BOOKS

Aliki. *Corn Is Maize: The Gift of the Indians.* 40 pages. 1986. Collins. Shows how corn is grown and its many uses.

Aston, Diana Hutts. *A Seed Is Sleepy.* 40 pages. 2007. Chronicle Books. Introduces children to plant and seed facts.

Bourgeois, Paulette. *Franklin Plants a Tree.* 32 pages. 2001. Kids Can Press. Franklin is disappointed with the small tree he is given on Earth Day.

Brisson, Pat. *Wanda's Rosebush.* 32 pages. 2000. Boyds Mill Press. Wanda discovers a rosebush growing in an empty lot.

Bunting, Eve. *Sunflower House.* 32 pages. 1999. Houghton Mifflin Harcourt. A young boy creates a playhouse by planting sunflowers.

Carle, Eric. *The Tiny Seed.* 40 pages. 2001. Simon & Schuster Children's Publishing. The wind blows flower seeds and carries them far, with only a few surviving to become plants.

Child, Lauren. *I Really Wonder What Plant I'm Growing.* 10 pages. 2009. Penguin Books, Ltd. Lola plants a seed and hopes it will grow into something amazing.

Cole, Henry. *Jack's Garden.* 32 pages. 1997. HarperCollins Publishers. Traces a little boy's flower garden from tilling the soil to blossoms.

Cooney, Barbara. *Miss Rumphius.* 32 pages. 1985. Puffin. Miss Rumphius fulfills her dream to have adventures in faraway places and then sets out to make the world more beautiful.

DeGroat, Diane. *Ants in Your Pants, Worms in Your*

Plants. 32 pages. 2011. HarperCollins Publishers. Gilbert seems to the be the only one in his class who can't think of an Earth Day project.

Ehlert, Lois. *Eating the Alphabet: Fruits and Vegetables from A to Z*. 40 pages. 1989. Houghton Mifflin Harcourt Publishers. Teaches upper and lower case letters while introducing fruits and vegetables from around the world.

Ehlert, Lois. *Growing Vegetable Soup*. 32 pages. 1991. Houghton Mifflin Harcourt. A father and child share in the planting and growing of vegetables for soup.

Ehlert, Lois. *Planting a Rainbow*. 40 pages. 1992. Sandpiper. A young child relates in simple sentences the yearly process of planning, planting and picking flowers in a garden.

Fleischman, Paul. *Weslandia*. 40 pages. 2002. Candlewick. Wesley needs a summer project and he decides to plant a garden. His crop grows strange fruit that will provide food, shelter, clothing and even recreation.

Fowler, Allan. *From Seed to Plant*. 32 pages. 2001. Childrens Press. Explains the parts of a plant accompanied by photos.

Galdone, Paul. *The Little Red Hen*. 48 pages. 2011. HMH Books. The little red hen asks for help in growing the wheat and making the bread, but no one wants to help her.

Gibbons, Gail. *From Seed to Plant*. 32 pages. 1993. Holiday House. Illustrated guide to the life cycles of different types of plants.

Jordan, Helene J. *How a Seed Grows*. 32 pages. 1992. HarperCollins Publishers. How does a tiny acorn grow into a big oak tree?

Kalman, Bobbie. *How a Plant Grows*. 32 pages. 1996. Crabtree Publishing Company. Introduces children to the amazing lives of plants.

Krauss, Ruth. *The Carrot Seed*. 32 pages. 2004. HarperCollins. A little boy tends his plant despite everyone telling him it won't grow.

Metzger, Steve. *Dinofours: My Seeds Won't Grow*. 2001. Scholastic Reference. Upset that the plants that he's growing are the smallest, Brendan switches the names on the containers, then regrets it.

Mitgutsch, Ali. *From Seed to Pear*. 24 pages. 1981. Lerner Publishing Group. Describes the cycle of a pear seed from planting to tree to seeds.

Moore, Sean. *Veggies, Smeggies*. 32 pages. 2007. Simply Read Books. The main character doesn't know why anyone would want to eat anything that comes out of the ground.

Palazeti, Toualla. *A Seed Was Planted*. 32 pages. 2009. Continental Sales. A giving cycle begins when pieces of a walnut tree are passed from person to person.

Patterson, Diane. *Stone Soup*. 32 pages. 1981. Troll Publications. Villagers have hidden their food from the soldiers, who try to make soup from water and stones.

Pattou, Edith. *Mrs. Spitzer's Garden*. 2001. Harcourt Children's Books. Mrs. Spitzer is a wise teacher who knows about children and knows about gardens, and how similarly they grow when tended well.

Polette, Keith. *Paco and the Giant Chile Plant*. 32 pages. 2008. Continental Sales. Based on the traditional story of Jack and the Beanstalk.

Powell, Patricia Ruby. *Zinnia: How the Corn Was Saved*. 32 pages. 2003. Salina Bookshelf. A Navajo Indian story of a little boy who searches for help to save the crops.

Rey, H.A. *Curious George Plants a Tree*. 24 pages. 2010. Houghton Mifflin Harcourt Publishers. The science museum plans a green day for recycling and planting trees and George wants to help.

Rey, H.A. *Elizabite: Adventures of a Carnivorous Plant*. 32 pages. 1999. Houghton Mifflin Harcourt Publishers. Elizabite is a carnivorous plant who eats insects and meat.

Rosenthal, Amy Krouse. *Plant a Kiss*. 40 pages. 2011. HarperCollins Publishers. One small act of love blooms into something bigger.

Schaefer, Lola M. *This Is the Sunflower*. 24 pages. 2000. HarperCollins Publishers. Gardeners discover how one sunflower gradually becomes a patch of sunflowers.

Siminovich, Irina. *I Like Vegetables*. 10 pages. 2011. Candlewick Press. Introduces difference vegetables and the concept of opposites.

Sollinger, Emily. *Olivia Plants a Garden*. A learn to read book. 24 pages. 2011. Simon & Schuster Children's Publishing. Olivia's class is given mystery seeds to plant and she can't wait to see what grows.

Wellington, Monica. *Zinnia's Flower Garden*. 32 pages. 2007. Penguin Group. Zinnia has quite an affinity for growing things.

Worth, Bonnie. *Oh Say Can You Seed? All About Flowering Plants*. 48 pages. 2001. Random House Books for Young Readers. The Cat in the Hat examines the various parts of plants, seeds and flowers.

Holiday — Easter

Advance planning: To plan for this storytime, find a theme-related song to play during craft and snack times, like "Easter Parade," by Judy Garland. You will also want to select a poem, such as "The Easter Bunny Song," by Jenny Wanderscheid (find it at www.childfun.com), along with the books you plan to read. Decorate your space with bunnies, pastel colors, eggs.

Introduction to theme: Easter is a Christian holiday that celebrates the Resurrection of Jesus Christ. Easter is a time to celebrate the renewal of life. The Easter Bunny and Easter egg hunts have become part of the Easter celebration as celebrated by many people. Today, we'll read about Easter, play an Easter game, make an Easter craft and eat an Easter snack.

Song: "If You Love the Easter Bunny" by Stephen Elkins, to the tune of "If You're Happy and You Know It." Can be found at www.wonderworkshopsongs.com.

Before playing the bunny hop game, make the bunny ears craft.

Craft: Bunny ears

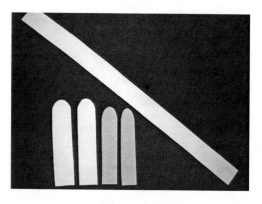

Bunny ears pieces.

Materials needed: White poster board, pink construction paper, stapler, Easter stickers. Advance preparation: Cut white poster board into 20 8 × 2-inch strips and eight and a half-inch ear shapes. Cut seven and a half-inch pink construction paper into ear shapes. At storytime: Glue the pink ears inside the white ears. Decorate the long white strip with stickers. Fit the band around the head and staple it in four places. Staple the ears inside the band at the back.

Alternative Crafts

Foam eggs. Egg-shaped foam sheets to decorate with small stickers. Put a magnet strip on the back.

Butterfly craft. To celebrate spring's arrival, make some butterflies. Needed: sticky backed butterflies, tissue paper pieces, glue sticks, scissors. Peel off paper from butterflies to reveal sticky side. Stick down individual small pieces of tissue paper for stained glass effect. Might need to use glue sticks. When done, trim around from opposite side with scissors.

Rabbit paper collage. Supplies needed: rabbit pieces cut out of papers, glue sticks, background cardstock.

Somebunny thinks you're special bookmarks. Make white cardstock bookmarks with

Bunny ears.

an outline of a bunny and the phrase "Somebunny thinks you're special!" and let the children color them.

Bunny. Have a cut out bunny shape for each child, markers or crayons to decorate it, glue sticks and cotton balls for the tail. Everyone can make their own version of the Easter Bunny.

Magic color scratch Easter egg ornaments. Can be ordered at www.orientaltrading.com.

Game: Bunny hop

Materials needed: CD player, CD with Bunny Hop music. Advance preparation: None. At storytime: After making the Bunny Ears craft, have everyone put on their ears and do the Bunny Hop. Children form a Conga line, behind you; play the recording of the Bunny Hop music and bunny hop around the story time area.

Alternative Games

Rabbit ring toss. But an inflatable rabbit ear ring toss game.

Barnyard sounds game. See if the children can tell what animals that you might see on a farm are making these sounds. Needed: disk with animal sounds, CD player. Make up disk with animal sounds and play them to have everyone guess what animal is making the sound — rooster; cow; turkey; cat; donkey; dog; chick; goat; duck; horse; lamb; goose; mouse; pig; sheep; chicken.

Chicken dance. supplies needed: disk with chicken dance music, CD player. Everybody on your feet — it's time for the Chicken Dance! Here's how you do it: fingers do beak four times; arms tucked flap wings four times; shake tail feathers four times; clap four times. Get everyone to try it, and then put music on.

Bunnies hopping. Place a bunch of stuffed bunnies on top of a cloth tablecloth or parachute. Have the children hold the sides of the parachute or cloth and see if they can bounce the bunnies off. Repeat if they do it too quickly. Or see how high they can bounce the bunnies without them falling off.

Bunny, bunny, rabbit (like Duck, duck, goose). Have children sit in a circle. One child is "it" and hops around the circle tapping each child on the head and saying, "bunny, bunny, bunny..." until he/she finally says, "RABBIT." Both children hop around the circle trying to reach the vacated spot first.

Barnyard. Supplies: Picture of animals — children must know what sound they make (two of each animal). Bucket. Have each child draw a picture out of the bucket. They must then find their partner by making the sound that the animal makes and listening to the other children for an animal making the same sound as they are. Make sure there are same number of pictures as there are children — have them paired ahead of time and then put correct number in bucket.

Easter egg blow. Put plastic Easter eggs on the floor and have children blow them across the room; as they make it across have they can open their eggs and find toy bunny finger puppets inside.

Snack: Bunny cake

Materials needed: Yellow cake mix, white icing, decorator colors of icing, small candies, small plates, forks, knife. Advance preparation: Make a bunny cake. Bake two nine-inch round cakes. Cut one of them into two ear shapes and a bow tie. Place the ears above the other round, the bow tie below. Ice in white. Draw on a bunny face and decorate the bow tie with either small candies or icing dots. At storytime: Serve the cake.

Alternative Snacks

Egg-shaped cookies. Give each child an egg-shaped cookie, some icing and small candies to decorate.

Dyed hard boiled eggs. Let the children peel and eat.

Bunny cupcakes. Ice with white, then place whole large marshmallow with face drawn on with food marker on top, then cut marshmallows and quickly cover cut sides with pink sugar sprinkles and stick those on top of the head marshmallow with some white icing.

Make a rabbit face on a plate using four apple slices as the ears, one apple slice as the mouth, three grapes as the eyes and nose, and thin strips of carrot as the whiskers.

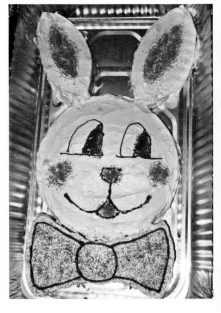

Bunny cake.

SUGGESTED BOOKS

On holidays with religious significance it's best to choose books to suit your audience. The toddler books will have more emphasis on the fun aspects of Easter, but some of the books will give an explanation of the crucifixion and resurrection.

Adams, Michelle Medlock. *What Is Easter?* 26 pages. 2006. Candy Cane Press. Explains in a gentle way what Easter is really about, along with the fun things.

Berenstain, Mike. *The Berenstain Bears and the Easter Story.* 32 pages. 2012. Zonderkidz. Papa tells the cubs about the resurrection and shows them that salvation is sweeter than candy.

Berenstain, Stan, and Jan Berenstain. *The Berenstain Bears and the Real Easter Eggs.* 32 pages. 2002. Random House Books for Young Readers. Mama worries that the true meaning of Easter is getting lost in the Easter egg hunt.

Berger, Samantha. *It's Spring.* 30 pages. 2003. Cartwheel. An illustrated rhyming story about spring.

Brett, Jan. *The Easter Egg.* 32 pages. 2010. Penguin Group. If Hoppi can make the best Easter egg, he'll get to help the Easter Bunny.

Bridwell, Norman. *Clifford's First Easter.* 14 pages. 2010. Scholastic. A lift the flap board book where Clifford looks for eggs.

Bridwell, Norman. *Clifford's Happy Easter.* 32 pages. 2011. Scholastic. Clifford loves to help Emily Elizabeth but his big paws keep breaking the eggs.

Brown, Margaret Wise. *The Golden Egg Book.* 32 pages. 2004. Random House Children's Books. The story of a lonely little rabbit who hatches a friend.

Brown, Margaret Wise. *Home for a Bunny.* 32 pages. 2003. Golden Books. Follow this bunny on his journey to find a home.

Capucilli, Alyssa Satin. *Happy Easter, Biscuit!* 20 pages. 2000. HarperFestival. Biscuit's first Easter egg hunt is going to be extra special.

Chaconas, Dori. *Looking for Easter.* 32 pages. 2011. Albert Whitman and Company. Little Bunny can sense something new in the air. It smells like Easter!

DeBoer, Jesslyn. *The First Easter.* 12 pages. 2005. Zondekidz. The story of Easter as told by a little lamb.

dePaola, Tomie. *My First Easter.* 12 pages. 2008. Grosset & Dunlap. The importance of both family and sharing in this board book.

Dunrea, Olivier. *Ollie's Easter Eggs*. 32 pages. 2010. Houghton Mifflin Books for Children. Gossie, Gertie, Boo Boo and Peedie are all dying Easter eggs.

Freeman, Don. *Corduroy's Easter Party*. 32 pages. 2000. Penguin Group. Corduroy wonders if the Easter Bunny is real.

Hill, Eric. *Spot's First Easter*. 12 pages. 2004. Penguin Group. A lift the flap board book where Spot searches for eggs.

Hillenbrand, Will. *Spring Is Here*. 32 pages. 2011. Holiday House. Spring is in the air. Mole can smell it but Bear is still asleep.

Hills, Tad. *Duck & Goose, Here Comes the Easter Bunny!* 22 pages. 2012. Schwartz and Wade. A board book featuring Duck and Goose, who have lots of ideas about the Easter Bunny.

Kleinberg, Naomi. *In Elmo's Easter Parade*. 12 pages. 2009. Random House Books for Young Readers. It's time to celebrate at the Bunny Hop and everyone is making their own Easter bonnet.

Knudsen, Michelle. *Happy Easter!* 14 pages. 2003. Little Simon. A shimmery Easter holiday treat of a book.

Kroll, Steven. *The Biggest Easter Basket Ever*. 32 pages. 2008. Cartwheel Books. Mice friends Clayton and Desmond further learn the benefits of working together.

Lionni, Leo. *Let's Make Rabbits*. 32 pages. 1993. Turtleback Books. Let's make rabbits, said the scissors to the pencil.

Lucado, Max. *The Easter Story for Children*. 32 pages. 2013. Zonderkidz. A retelling of the Easter story where Jesus' final days come to life.

Mayer, Mercer. *Happy Easter, Little Critter*. 24 pages. 2004. Random House Books for Young Readers. Little Critter and family celebrate Easter.

Mortimer, Anne. *Bunny's Easter Egg*. 32 pages. 2010. Bunny has spent a long night hiding eggs, but is having trouble getting to sleep.

Murphy, Chuck. *Easter Egg Hunt*. 12 pages. 1999. Little Simon. Easter eggs everywhere. Can you find them all?

Newberry, Clare Turlay. *Marshmallow*. 32 pages. 2008. HarperCollins. Marshmallow the bunny comes to live with Oliver the cat, and this is the story of how they learn to get along.

Numeroff, Laura. *Happy Easter Mouse!* 24 pages. 2010. HarperCollins Publishers. Mouse tries to figure out who's leaving Easter eggs all over his house.

O'Connor, Jane. *Fancy Nancy's Elegant Easter*. 16 pages. 2009. HarperFestival. Throwing a fabulous Easter party is a big job.

Ottersley, Martha T. *The Muppets: Easter Eggstravaganza!* 16 pages. 2013. LB Kids. Someone is leaving mysterious Easter eggs for the Muppets everywhere.

Paz, Veronica. *Dora's Easter Bunny Adventure*. 16 pages. 2012. Simon Spotlight. Dora and Boots are eagerly awaiting the Easter Bunny but have to watch out for Swiper.

Pingry, Patricia A. *The Easter Story*. 32 pages. 2006. Ideals Children's Books. Tells the story of Jesus and explains his death as the means of salvation for mankind.

Rey, H.A. *Happy Easter, Curious George!* 24 pages. 2010. Houghton Mifflin Harcourt. George and the man with the yellow hat head to the park on Easter morning.

Root, Phyllis. *Hop*. 16 pages. 2010. Candlewick Press. Non stop antics of five little bunnies.

Root, Phyllis. *Quack*. 24 pages. 2005. Walker Children's Hardbacks. Mama Duck calls quack quack quack!

Schulz, Charles M. *Peanuts: The Easter Beagle Egg Hunt*. 12 pages. 2009. Running Press Kids. It's Easter and Lucy can't wait to find all the eggs, but the Easter Beagle has another idea.

Scotton, Rob. *Splat the Cat, Where's the Easter Bunny?* 16 pages. 2011. HarperFestival. Easter is almost here, but where's the bunny?

Smath, Jerry. *The Best Easter Eggs Ever!* 32 pages. 2003. Cartwheel. The story of the Easter Bunny and his three helpers.

Smythe, Theresa. *Chester's Colorful Easter Eggs*. 24 pages. 2013. Henry Holt & Co. Chester decorates eggs in the colors of the rainbow.

Speirs, John. *The Best Easter Hunt Ever!* 32 pages. 1997. Cartwheel. Readers will have fun looking for Easter things.

Stileman, Kali. *Roly-Poly Egg*. 32 pages. 2011. Tiger Tales. Splotch is a small bird who lives in a tree. One day she lays an egg.

Tegen, Katherine. *The Story of the Easter Bunny*. 40 pages. 2005. HarperCollins Publishers. A little rabbit watches an old couple paint Easter eggs and then eventually takes over their tasks.

Tudor, Tasha. *The Easter Bunny's Assistant*. 40 pages. 2012. HarperCollins. A simple funny Easter book with a skunk helping the Easter Bunny.

Tudor, Tasha. *A Tale for Easter*. 32 pages. 2004. Aladdin. Springtime is special, and Easter is a magical day.

Wax, Wendy. *Easter Bunny on the Loose!* 32 pages. 2013. HarperCollins. The Easter Bunny can't wait to deliver the eggs but there aren't any.

Wells, Rosemary. *Max Counts His Chickens*. 32 pages. 2009. Puffin. Max and Ruby in a counting book about Easter things.

Wells, Rosemary. *Max's Chocolate Chicken*. 32 pages. 1999. Viking Juvenile. Max and his sister Ruby go on an egg hunt.

Wells, Rosemary. *Max's Easter Surprise*. 24 pages. 2008. Penguin Group. Max wants to take Easter eggs in the parade.

Wing, Natasha. *The Night Before Easter*. 32 pages. 1999. Penguin Group. In a take off on the Night Before Christmas, siblings witness the arrival of the Easter Bunny.

Young, Miriam. *Miss Suzy's Easter Surprise*. 41 pages. 1990. Aladdin. A family of orphaned squirrels gives Miss Suzy a special reason to celebrate.

Ziefert, Harriet. *I Need an Easter Egg!* 16 pages. 1999. Little Simon. A Lift the Flap book where Little Rabbit is looking for the perfect Easter egg for his grandma.

Zolotow, Charlotte. *The Bunny Who Found Easter*. 32 pages. 2001. HMH Books for Young Readers. A lonely rabbit searches for others of his kind and finds one special bunny.

May

Butterflies

Advance planning: To plan for this storytime, find a theme-related song to play during craft and snack times, like "Butterfly Wishes," by Sarah Pirtle. You will also want to select a poem, such as "The Butterfly Song" (find it at www.canteach.ca/elementary), along with the books you plan to read. Decorate your space wearing a butterfly headband, with posters or images of butterflies on other objects.

Introduction to theme: Butterflies are a kind of flying insect with large, colorful wings. The butterfly's life cycle consists of four parts: egg, larva, pupa (or chrysalis) and adult. Butterfly eggs are fixed to a leaf with a special glue and then hatch into larvae, or caterpillars, which eat plant leaves and spend practically all of their time in search of food. The larva changes into a pupa (or chrysalis) by attaching itself to a branch. The pupa then changes into a butterfly through a process called metamorphosis. Today we'll read about butterflies, play a butterfly game, make a butterfly craft and have a snack that looks like a butterfly.

Song: "Fly, Fly Butterfly" (sung to the tune of "Skip to My Lou").

> Fly in the sky my butterfly,
> Fly in the sky my butterfly,
> Fly in the sky my butterfly,
> Fly in the sky my friend.

Game: Flying butterflies

Materials needed: Green construction paper, scissors. Advance preparation: Cut large green leaf shapes (as many leaves or more as you have children) from construction paper or print on computer using images from Google or a graphics program like PrintShop and cut out. At storytime: Place paper leaves randomly on floor but spread out a little. Play butterfly song and have children fly around flapping their "wings" and landing on leaves.

Alternative Games

Caterpillar, butterfly. Crawl like a caterpillar, fly like a butterfly. Have the children alternate between being caterpillars and butterflies. Could play it like red light, green light with the children approaching you.

Caterpillar tag. You start as a caterpillar and all the children are butterflies. The children fly around the room flapping their wings. As you tag a child, he/she joins hands with you and becomes a caterpillar and stops flying, and helps you tag another child. Your group will get longer and longer as you tag the butterflies until you're a very long caterpillar and there are no butterflies left.

Butterfly collection time. Place paper or plastic butterflies all around the room. Have the children search for them, pick them up and place them in a "bug jar."

Coffee filter butterfly pieces.

Craft: Coffee filter butterfly

Materials needed: White basket style coffee filters, washable markers, black chenille stems, paper towels, spray bottle filled with water. Advance preparation: None. At storytime: Children color filter with markers then wrap chenille stem around middle, fan out the filter and bend the stem ends to look like antennae. Place the filters on paper towels to absorb water, then spray with water. Let dry.

Alternative Crafts

Clothespin butterfly treats. Decorate a clothespin with paints, markers and/or glitter glue. Fill a plastic Ziploc bag with some kind

Coffee filter butterfly.

of treat, like pretzels or candy. Pinch the bag in the middle to divide in half and attach the clothespin so it looks like the halves of the bag are the butterfly wings. Could attach small piece of chenille stem in the clothespin and bend to look like antennae.

Butterfly mobile. Make a paper chain for the butterfly body. Tape it to a wing-shaped piece of construction paper. Attach google eyes or draw eyes on the construction paper. Hang with a cord from the paper chain.

Tissue paper butterflies. Buy sticky butterfly chipboard shapes. Have the children peel off the paper covering the sticky side and attach small squares of colored tissue paper to cover all the sticky side.

Colorful butterfly mobile. Cut two pieces of clear contact paper. Have the children attach small pieces of colored tissue paper to one sheet of contact paper. Cover with the other piece. Cut a butterfly shape, punch a hole with a hole puncher and hang with cord.

Snack: Butterfly cookie

Materials needed: Sugar cookie dough, butterfly cookie cutter, canned vanilla frosting, M&Ms or other colored candy pieces, small gummy worms (regular or sugar covered), paper plates, plastic knives. Advance preparation: Bake sugar cookies using butterfly cookie cutter. At storytime: Let children ice the cookies with canned vanilla frosting and decorate with M&Ms or other colored candy pieces. Use small gummy worms as antennae.

Alternative Snacks

Butterfly cupcakes. After icing cupcakes, children place gummy worm body and two candy fruit slices (facing outward) as wings.

Choose the foods that the caterpillar ate in *The Very Hungry Caterpillar.*

Celery or carrot stick as the butterfly body. Oval crackers spread with cream cheese as the wings. Two pretzel sticks as the antennae.

Butterfly bags. Place any kind of snack in a small plastic sandwich bag. Clip it in the middle with a clothespin and fan out like butterfly wings. Could make this the craft and snack by decorating the clothespin with glitter and chenille stem antennae.

Butterfly cookie.

SUGGESTED BOOKS

Allen, Judy. *Are You a Butterfly?* 28 pages. 2003. Roaring Book Press. Cleverly tells the story of the butterfly's metamorphosis by posing it in human terms (like what a baby would weigh if it ate as much as a caterpillar).

Araki, Mie. *Kitten's Big Adventure.* 40 pages. Gulliver Books. A kitten starts out chasing a butterfly but the butterfly ends up chasing the kitten.

Bunting, Eve. *Butterfly House.* 32 pages. 1999. Scholastic. A little girl and her grandfather make a house for a butterfly larva, watch it grow and then set it free.

Cain, Sheridan. *The Crunching Munching Caterpillar.* 32 pages. 2006. ME Media. Caterpillar wishes he could fly.

Canizares, Susan. *Butterfly.* 16 pages. 1998. Scholastic. Shows the life cycle stages of the butterfly.

Carle, Eric. *The Very Hungry Caterpillar.* 32 pages. 1994. Penguin Group. A hungry caterpillar eats his way through a lot of food, then forms a chrysalis and becomes a butterfly. Colorful illustrations.

Collard, Sneed B. *Butterfly Count.* 32 pages. 2002. Holiday House. A girl and her mother search for a special butterfly at the annual butterfly count.

DK Publishing. *Butterfly: See How They Grow.* 24 pages. 2007. DK Publishing. Step by step photography showing a butterfly emerging from a cocoon.

Davol, Marguerite W. *Why Butterflies Go by on Silent Wings.* 32 pages. 2001. Orchard. When the world was new, butterflies were noisy until a storm changed and silenced them.

Delafosse, Claude. *Butterflies.* 24 pages. 2006. Scholastic. Interesting facts about butterflies with plastic overlays.

DeLuise, Dom. *Charlie the Caterpillar.* 40 pages. 1990. Simon & Schuster Children's Publishing. A caterpillar is rejected as a friend by other creatures until it becomes a butterfly, then it later befriends another caterpillar.

Edwards, Pamela Duncan. *Clara Caterpillar.* 40 pages. 2004. HarperCollins Publishers. Clara saves another caterpillar from a crow.

Elwell, Peter. *Adios, Oscar! A Butterfly Fable.* 32 pages. 2009. Scholastic. A feisty caterpillar realizes his fondest dream.

Faulkner, Keith. *Caterpillar's Dream.* 12 pages. 2003. Silver Dolphin Books. Caterpillar dreams of flying.

Foley, Greg. *Don't Worry Bear.* 32 pages. 2008. Penguin Group. Bear worries about his caterpillar friend as it makes a cocoon. Later it returns as a moth.

Ganeri, Anna. *Butterflies and Caterpillars.* 24 pages.

2011. QEB Publishing. The lifecycle of the butterfly in simple text.

Gibbons, Gail. *Monarch Butterfly*. 32 pages. 1991. Holiday House. Explains the life cycle of the Monarch butterfly.

Haskins, Lori. *Butterfly Fever*. 32 pages. 2009. Kane Press. A little girl misses her friends after she moves, but makes new ones as they study butterfly migration.

Heiligman, Deborah. *From Caterpillar to Butterfly*. 32 pages. 1996. HarperCollins Publishers. Where did the caterpillar go?

Himmelman, John. *A Monarch Butterfly's Life*. 32 pages. 2000. Children's Press. Realistic color paintings.

Horácek, Petr. *Butterfly Butterfly*. 16 pages. 2007. Candlewick Press. Beautiful color illustrations follow Lucy's search for a butterfly. Final page has gorgeous pop up butterfly.

Jeunesse, Gallimard. *Butterflies: Scholastic First Discoveries*. 24 pages. 2007. Scholastic. See through overlay pages that show the parts, life cycle and different kinds of butterflies.

Johnston, Tony. *Isabel's House of Butterflies*. 32 pages. 2005. Gibbs Smith, Publisher. A little girl in Mexico is worried about the trees on her land that are home to the migrating butterflies each year.

Lerner, Carol. *Butterflies in the Garden*. 32 pages. 2002. HarperCollins Publishers. Shows how to lure butterflies to your garden.

Lieshout, Maria van. *Bloom: A Little Book About Finding Love*. 48 pages. 2007. Feiwel and Friends. A pig learns about love, that it's more about what's on the inside than the outside.

Minarik, Else Holmelund. *Butterfly Garden*. 23 pages. 2004. Harper Festival. Little Bear finds caterpillars in the garden, sees them make cocoons and then become butterflies.

Moriuchi, Mique. *Butterfly Girl*. 32 pages. 2007. Hodder & Stoughton, Ltd. Butterfly Girl helps a sad little bird find his lost song.

O'Flatharta, Antoine. *Hurry and the Monarch*. 40 pages. 2009. Random House Children's Books. A monarch makes friends with a tortoise during migration.

Rabe, Tish. *My Oh My A Butterfly*. 48 pages. 2007. Random House Children's Books. Part of the Cat in the Hat Learning Library Series, the Cat explains the life cycle of butterflies, beginning with the egg, growing into the caterpillar, the chrysalis and finally the butterfly.

Rockwell, Anne. *Becoming Butterflies*. 28 pages. 2004. Walker & Company. Long detailed book about classroom that acquires caterpillars and studies their metamorphosis. Nice cut paper artwork.

Rodger, Elizabeth. *Caterpillar to Butterfly*. 12 pages. 1996. Scholastic. Pop-up book that details the metamorphosis of the caterpillar.

Ryder, Joanne. *Where Butterflies Grow*. 32 pages. 1996. Penguin Group. Describes how it feels to change from a caterpillar to a butterfly.

Sandved, Kjell B. *The Butterfly Alphabet*. 64 pages. 1999. Scholastic. Letters of the alphabet with rhyming text and letter like markings on the wings of butterflies.

Schapiro, Karen. *Butterflies* (Scholastic Reader Level 2). 32 pages. 2002. Scholastic. Rhyming text gives lesson in metamorphosis.

Shahan, Sherry. *Little Butterfly*. 24 pages. 1998. Random House Children's Books. Follows a newly hatched caterpillar through metamorphosis and migration.

Swinburne, Stephen. *A Butterfly Grows*. Level 2 Reader. 14 pages. 2009. Houghton Mifflin Harcourt Publishing. Short easy reader with nice photos of caterpillar through butterfly.

Willis, Jeanne. *Caterpillar Dreams*. 32 pages. 2011. Andersen Press, Limited. Two caterpillars dream of all the things they'll do when they become butterflies.

Zemlicka, Shannon and Knudsen, Shannon. *From Egg to Butterfly*. 24 pages. 2002. Lerner Publishing Group. Development of a butterfly.

Ziefert, Harriet. *Butterfly Birthday*. 40 pages. 2010. Blue Apple Books. On the first day of spring, dressed up bugs greet each other after a long winter.

Flowers

Advance planning: To plan for this storytime, find a theme-related song to play during craft and snack times, like "Waltz of the Flowers" from *The Nutcracker* by Tchaikovsky. You will also want to select a poem, such as the classic "Roses Are Red," along with the books you plan to read. Decorate your space with real or silk flowers, flowering plants. Wear clothing with flowers on it, a flower in your hair or a floral headband. Hang posters of flowers.

Introduction to theme: Flowers are blooms or blossoms of flowering plants. Flowers are often where seeds or fruits begin. Many flowers are quite colorful and beautiful and have a nice smell. Some flowers are important sources of food or medicine. Most of the time we think of flowers as a nice decoration for our homes or gardens and as a lovely gift for someone we care about. I brought some flowers today that we can look at and smell (if they're real). Show the flowers and pass a few of them around that have strong smells. Today we'll read about flowers, play a flower game, make a flower craft and have a snack that looks like a flower.

Song and Fingerplay: "Here We Go 'Round the Mulberry Bush"

> Here we go 'round the mulberry bush,
> The mulberry bush, the mulberry bush
> Here we go 'round the mulberry bush,
> So early in the morning.

Do the "Flower" fingerplay which can be found at www.preschoolexpress.com.

Game: Ring around the rosy

Materials needed: None. Advance preparation: None. At storytime: Have all the children stand in a circle and hold hands. Start moving clockwise and all say the nursery rhyme Ring Around the Rosy, which can be found on the Internet. When you get to the end of the rhyme everyone drop hands and sit down on the floor. Stand up and repeat going counter clockwise.

Alternative Games

Tiptoe through the tulips. You will need pictures of tulips printed on paper, the song "Tiptoe Through the Tulips," by Tiny Tim, recorded on CD and CD player. Find pictures of tulips on the Internet and print them, about four to a sheet of paper. Cut out. Have enough for each child to hold two pictures. Have the children all stand in a line. Play the music and have them place their tulip pictures on the floor, one at a time and step on each one as they cross the room. As they step on one, they pick up the one behind and put it down in front. Literally tiptoeing across the room on the tulips while the song is playing.

Flower relay. Have at least two flower pots and a bunch of silk flowers. Set the flower pots at one end of the storytime area and the flowers in equal bunches in front of two lines of children at the other end. Have each child pick up a flower and take it to the flower pot and "plant" it in the pot, then come back and go to the end of the line and sit down. When everyone has had a turn to plant a flower the relay is over. Alternately you could do this as a "watering" relay using watering cans filled with paper confetti and flowers already in the flowerpots, letting each child do a little "watering."

Flower pot toss. Have several flower pots lined up and some things to toss into them, like silk flowers or large seeds or ping pong balls or a mix of items. Let the children see how far away they can get from a pot and still get the items into the pots.

Musical flowers. Place large flower shapes on the floor and play musical chairs, except no one gets eliminated. Remove a flower shape each round but tell the children that as long as some part of them is either touching one of the flower shapes or touching someone else who is touching a flower shape they're still in the game. Eventually they will all get pretty close together!

Craft: Tissue paper flowers

Materials needed: Brightly colored tissue paper, green chenille stems, bamboo skewer sticks, green paint. Advance preparation: Cut enough tissue paper into approximately 6-inch squares for each child to have six sheets. Paint the bamboo skewers green. At storytime: Stack six different color sheets of tissue paper and then fold the stack accordion style with about

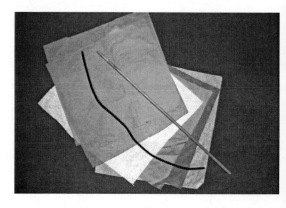

Tissue paper flower pieces.

a one-inch fold. Wrap the green chenille stem around the center of the folded tissue paper. Fan out the tissues paper stack and gently pull up one layer of paper at a time toward the chenille stem in the center. Wrap the chenille stem around the length of bamboo skewer stick.

Alternative Crafts

Handprint lily. You will need green construction paper, white construction, cardstock or computer paper, yellow chenille stem, straw (green if possible), hole punch, scissors, pencils and tape. Cut double leaf shapes from the green paper and punch hole in the middle. Cut yellow chenille stems in half with wire cutter. Have parent trace child's hand onto the white paper and cut out the shape. Curl the white paper flower hands' fingers using the pencil to wrap them around it. Wrap the hand around the top of the straw and tape it. Slide the leaves onto the straw and tape in place. Fold the yellow chenille stem in half and curl the ends. Insert the folded end into the straw to look like a flower stamen.

Tissue paper flower.

Heart and Flowers. Cut four heart shapes and two leaves from construction paper. Glue the heart shapes to one end of a craft stick with the points in the center as the bloom, and the two leaves lower on the stick.

Snack: Fruit and vegetable flower

Materials needed: Small oranges like Clementines, round crackers or cucumber slices, raisins, lettuce leaves, celery, paper plates. Advance preparation: Peel and separate orange segments, enough for each child to have six segments. Slice cucumbers if using. Cut celery into four-inch pieces. At storytime: Place cracker or cucumber slice in center of paper plate for face. Surround with orange

Fruit and vegetable flower.

segments to make flower. Place raisins on face to look like eyes. Put the celery piece under to look like a stem. Place the lettuce leaves next to the celery stem to look like flower leaves.

Alternative Snacks

Flower cupcake. Ice cupcakes in green or sprinkle with green sugar. Snip small marshmallows in half and immediately sprinkle the cut part with different colored sugars. They will curl and look like flower petals. Give each child a cupcake, icing and some marshmallow petals as well as a gumdrop to use as the center of the flower on their cupcake.

Flower sandwich. Using a flower or cloud-shaped cookie cutter, cut pieces of bread and cheese.

Flower crackers. Spread a round cracker, like Ritz, with cream cheese. Place several grape halves around a raspberry center to look like a flower. Could also be done with a cookie and icing.

SUGGESTED BOOKS

Barry, Frances. *Big Yellow Sunflower.* 22 pages. 2008. Candlewick Press. A seed is falling to the ground. What will it be?

Bauer, Linda. *Fruits and Flowers and Footprints OH MY!!!* 38 pages. 2007. Linda Bauer. Life in the country is good. Fresh air, flowers and a party.

Brisson, Pat. *Wanda's Roses.* 32 pages. 2000. Boyds Mill Press. Wanda mistakes a thorn bush for a rosebush but cares for it so tenderly that the neighbors don't want her to be disappointed.

Bunting, Eve. *Flower Garden.* 32 pages. 2000. Houghton Mifflin Harcourt Trade & Reference Publishers. A father and his little girl buy flowers to take home for the mother to make a window garden.

Carle, Eric. *The Tiny Seed.* 40 pages. 2001. Simon & Schuster Children's Publishing. The story of a seed that survives many perils in order to grow.

Davenport, Zoe. *Garden.* 16 pages. 1995. Houghton Mifflin Harcourt Publishing Company. Names the parts of a flower.

Day, Jennifer W. *What Is a Flower.* 31 pages. 1985. Goldencraft. A Little Golden Book that shows in simple text and illustrations all about flowers.

Dussling, Jennifer. *One Little Flower Girl.* 32 pages. 2009. Scholastic. The rhyming story of a little flower girl in a wedding.

Edwards, Pamela Duncan. *Rosie's Roses.* 32 pages. 2003. HarperCollins Publishers. Rosie has four roses for her aunt, but they seem to be disappearing.

Ehlert, Lois. *Planting a Rainbow.* 32 pages. 1988. Houghton Mifflin Harcourt Trade & Reference Publishers. Colorful artwork that shows the results of planting flower bulbs in the fall.

Gillingham, Sara. *In My Flower.* 12 pages. 2010. Chronicle Books. In this board book discover just what makes Butterfly's flower so cozy.

Greenstein, Elaine. *One Little Seed.* 32 pages. 2004. Penguin Group. Follows a seed from the time it's planted until it becomes a flower.

Hall, Zoe. *The Apple Pie Tree.* 32 pages. 1996. Scholastic. Two sisters watch their apple tree through the seasons, including spring when it's full of flower blossoms.

Heilbroner, Joan. *Robert the Rose Horse.* From the Dr. Seuss library. 72 pages. 1989. Random House Children's Books. Robert is allergic to roses and this causes him lots of problems in finding a job. Finally as a police horse his allergy actually saves the day.

Heller, Ruth. *The Reason for a Flower.* 48 pages. 1999. Penguin Group. A good resource that explains the different purposes that flowers serve.

Henkes, Kevin. *My Garden.* 40 pages. 2010. HarperCollins Publishers. A little girl who helps her mother in the garden imagines what her own garden would be like if it could be as she wishes.

Lach, William. *My Friends the Flowers.* 40 pages. 2010. Abrams. A bee likes to visit all of his friends, who are flowers.

Leaf, Munro. *The Story of Ferdinand.* 72 pages. 1936. Penguin Group. Ferdinand the bull would rather sit and smell the flowers than fight.

Lewison, Wendy Cheyette. *Princess Buttercup: A Flower Princess Story.* A learn to read book. 32

pages. 2001. Penguin Group. Princess Buttercup gets lost when she goes to gather flowers and follows a butterfly.

Lobel, Arnold. *The Rose in My Garden*. 40 pages. 1993. HarperCollins Publishers. Starting with a rose, a garden comes alive with the addition of many kinds of flowers.

Lodge, Jo. *Patch Grows Flowers*. 1997. Harcourt Children's Books. With pull tabs on the book, the reader is involved in planting a pot of flowers and growing them.

McKee, David. *Elmer and Rose*. 32 pages. 2010. Lerner Publishing Group. Elmer the patchwork elephant meets Rose, the pink elephant. Not really about flowers, but there is a lot of floral plant life in the book.

Meddaugh, Susan. *Martha Says It with Flowers*. 24 pages. 2011. Houghton Mifflin Harcourt Trade & Reference Publishers. Martha has a hard time choosing the right gift for Grandma Lucille.

Morine, Kristin. *From Dirt to Showers How Seeds Become Flowers*. 24 pages. 2007. Trafford Publishing. A learn to read book. Pretty cut paper and mosaic artwork with a worm that explains how seeds become flowers.

Nyeu, Tao. *Wonder Bear*. 48 pages. 2008. Penguin Group. Two children plant mysterious seeds, out of which grows a bear.

Park, Linda Sue. *What Does Bunny See?: A Book of Colors and Flowers*. 32 pages. 2005. Houghton Mifflin Harcourt Trade & Reference Publishers. A bunny wanders through a garden and sees lots of colorful flowers.

Porter, Matthew. *Flowers*. 20 pages. 2010. Simply Read Books. A board book featuring flowers in bright colors.

Ross, Mandy. *Hello Lily!* 14 pages. 2007. Child's Play International. Learn simple facts about a pond flower.

Schaefer, Lola M. *This Is the Sunflower*. 24 pages. 2000. HarperCollins Publishers. Rhythmic verses describing the sunflower's life cycle.

Tremblay, Carole. *Floop's Flowers*. 24 pages. 2009. The Rosen Publishing Group. The English version of a French character who gets distracted while searching for a centerpiece for a friend's visit.

Trimble, Marcia. *Flower Green: A Flower for All Seasons*. 32 pages. 2002. Images Press CA. Children meet Flower Green, a sprout growing in a magical garden.

Tuxworth, Nicola. *Let's Look at Flowers*. 20 pages. 1996. Lorenz Books. A colorful photographic book for preschoolers.

Whipple, Vicky. *The Little Weed Flower*. 32 pages. 2010. Continental Sales. A little flower in a weed patch longs to be in a real garden.

Wolf, Helmut. *Flowers of India*. 24 pages. 2010. Tara Publishing. A book of photos of flowers of India.

Worth, Bonnie. *Oh Say Can You Seed?* From the Dr. Seuss library. 48 pages. 2001. Random House Children's Books. A good resource for information about flowering plants.

Zion, Gene. *No Roses for Harry*. 32 pages. 1958. HarperCollins Publishers. Harry the dog doesn't want to wear the sweater with roses on it that Grandma gave him.

Baseball

Advance planning: To plan for this storytime, find a theme-related song to play during craft and snack times, like "Take Me Out to the Ballgame," by David Plummer. You will also want to select a poem, such as "If School Were More Like Baseball," by Kenn Nesbitt (find it at www.poetry4kids.com), along with the books you plan to read. Decorate your space with a baseball, a bat, baseball glove, maybe a jersey, hat or pennant.

Introduction to theme: Baseball is a sport that uses bats and balls and gloves. Players hit the ball with the bat and run around the bases that are set into a diamond shape in order to score points, which are called runs. There are nine players on each team. The teams take turns either hitting the ball and running or being in the field and throwing and catching the ball to each other. Have you ever seen a baseball game? Ever been to one or watched one on television? Today we'll read about baseball, play a game with baseballs, make a baseball craft and have a snack that looks like a baseball.

Song: "Take Me Out to the Ball Game."

Game: Baseball knock down

Materials needed: Six styrofoam cups, baseball team logos printed on paper from the Internet and glued or taped onto the cups, three soft baseballs. Advance preparation: Print the baseball team logos and tape or glue to the cups. At storytime: Stack the cups in a pyramid, three on the bottom, then two on top of those and one more on top. Have the children take turns throwing the three soft baseballs at the cup pyramid to knock them down.

Alternative Games

Catch. Have a large soft baseball or beachball that looks like a baseball and with the children in a circle try tossing the ball back and forth.

Home run. If you have room, set up four bases, line the children up at home plate and have them run the bases. You could let them toss a soft large baseball to you at the pitcher's mound as their hit before they take off to run the bases.

Find your team. Make a set of cards by printing images from the computer, using stamps, cutting pictures from magazines on index cards, one per child, of several different categories, such as animals, modes of transportation, community workers. Each of these categories could even have a subset, like pets vs. zoo animals, emergency vehicles vs. cars, medical workers vs. emergency personnel. Hand each child a card and have them find others with similar cards so that they can form a "team." You could start with the larger groups and move to the subsets so that the children have to reform their teams.

Tissue paper baseball pieces.

Craft: Tissue paper baseball

Materials needed: Square cardstock base with baseball pattern printed from computer on them, small squares of tissue paper (about 1 ½-inches square) in red, green and white, glue sticks. Advance preparation: Print baseball pattern cards, cut up tissue paper pieces. At storytime: Crumple tissue paper pieces and glue down to cardstock pattern.

Alternative Crafts

Stuffed baseball. Cut two circles of white paper. Decorate with red crayon or marker to look like stitching on a baseball. Use gluestick around the edge of the inside of one of the circles, place a bit of fiberfill in the middle, then stick the other circle on top.

Paper plate baseball. Decorate a paper plate with

Tissue paper baseball.

red crayon or marker to look like the stitching. Could use holepunch to make a hole and red string or yarn to hang like an ornament.

Baseball magnet. Cut white circles from sheet foam. Have the children draw the red stitching on the foam with permanent marker or special foam marker. Glue a magnet to the back with foam glue.

Snack: Baseball cupcake

Materials needed: Cupcakes, icing, plastic knives, paper plates, licorice laces or red candies such as M&Ms or Skittles. Advance preparation: Bake cupcakes, cut licorice laces to size needed. At storytime: Ice cupcakes, lay licorice pieces on top to look like baseballs. Alternately stick red candies on end in two curved arcs as on a baseball.

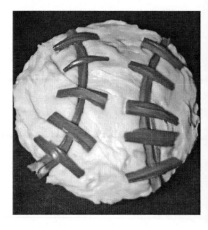

Baseball cupcake.

Alternative Snacks

Baseball cap cupcake. Place a cupcake upside down on a large cookie and decorate with icing to look like a baseball cap.

Ballpark snacks. Serve snacks that are typically found at the ballpark, like popcorn or pretzels.

SUGGESTED BOOKS

Abrahams, Peter. *Quacky Baseball*. 32 pages. 2011. HarperCollins. A funny story about baseball playing ducklings.

Behrens, Janet. *Let's Talk Baseball*. 24 pages. 2008. Children's Press. Helps children learn the basic terminology of baseball and experience what a game would be like.

Blackstone, Barbara. *This Is Baseball*. 32 pages. 1997. Henry Holt & Co. An introduction to baseball for young children.

Buckley, James. *Baseball 1-2-3*. 24 pages. 2001. DK Publishing. This book uses baseball equipment to teach counting.

Diehl, David. *Home Run! My Baseball Book*. 2008. Lark Books. A board book that is a good first book about baseball.

Dorling Kindersley. *My Baseball Book*. 18 pages. 2002. DK Publishing. Introduces the game of baseball to young children.

Driscoll, Laura. *Curious George at the Baseball Game*. 24 pages. 2006. Houghton Mifflin Harcourt Publishers. George goes to watch a baseball game but his curiosity once again gets him into trouble.

Dunrea, Oliver. *Peedie*. 32 pages. 2004. Houghton Mifflin Harcourt. Peedie the gosling never forgets to wear his favorite baseball cap.

Gibbons, Gail. *My Baseball Book*. 24 pages. 2000. HarperCollins Publishers. The game of baseball explained in a very thorough but simple to understand way.

Herzog, Brad. *H Is for Home Run*. 40 pages. 2004. Sleeping Bear Press. A baseball alphabet book that defines terms.

Herzog, Brad. *Little Baseball*. 20 pages. 2011. Sleeping Bear Press. A board book of rhyming riddles introduces the game of baseball.

Hoff, Syd. *The Littlest Leaguer*. I Can Read Level 1. 48 pages. 2008. HarperCollins. Harold is the littlest baseball player who doesn't play very well and sits on the bench until one day he gets a chance to play.

Isadora, Rachel. *Nick Plays Baseball*. 32 pages. 2003. Puffin. The championship game is coming and Nick can't wait to pitch for his team.

Joyce, William. *Baseball Bob*. 10 pages. 1999. HarperCollins Publishers. Baseball Bob, a big green dinosaur, is recruited by another team.

Keane, Dave. *Daddy Adventure Day*. 32 pages. 2011. Penguin Group. A child spends time with his dad at a baseball game.

Kessler, Leonard. *Here Comes the Strikeout*. 64 pages. 1992. I Can Read Level 2. HarperCollins. Bobby gets help to learn to hit.

Kinerk, Robert. *Clorinda Plays Baseball.* 40 pages. 2012. Simon & Schuster. Clorinda the Cow is a baseball player.

Kovalski, Maryann. *Take Me Out to the Ball Game.* 32 pages. 2006. Fitzhenry & Whiteside Limited. Grandma takes kids to a baseball game — set to the lyrics of the familiar song.

Lester, Helen. *Batter Up Wombat.* 32 pages. 2008. Houghton Mifflin Harcourt Publishers. The new kid is a wombat and he wants to fit in by joining the baseball team.

Lies, Brian. *Bats at the Ballgame.* 32 pages. 2010. Houghton Mifflin Harcourt Publishers. Teams of bats play a night baseball game.

London, Jonathan. *Froggy Plays T-Ball.* 32 pages. 2009. Penguin Group. Froggy has one last chance to prove he's a t-ball star.

McGrath, Barbara Barbieri. *The Baseball Counting Book.* 32 pages. 1999. Charlesbridge. Uses baseball to count from 1 to 20 in verse.

Murphy, Frank. *Babe Ruth Saves Baseball.* Step into Reading Level 3. 48 pages. 2005. Random House Children's Books. Babe Ruth needs to bring the fans back to baseball.

Newman, Jeff. *The Boys.* 40 pages. 2010. Simon & Schuster's Children's Publishing. Wordless book about a shy little boy's wish to join the other kids who are playing baseball in the park.

Parish, Peggy. *Play Ball, Amelia Bedelia.* I Can Read Level 2. 64 pages. 1995. HarperCollins Publishers. Amelia Bedelia fills in for a sick player.

Preller, James. *Mighty Casey.* 32 pages. 2009. Feiwel and Friends. Casey Jenkins tries to lead his losing team to their first win.

Rey, H.A., Margret Rey and Anna Grossnickle Hines. *Curious George at the Baseball Game.* 24 pages. 2006. Perfection Learning. George is going to watch a game and as usual he's curious.

Rodriguez, Alex. *Out of the Ballpark.* 32 pages. 2007. HarperCollins Publishers. Before he was a major league ballplayer, Alex Rodriguez was just a kid who wanted to play baseball.

Smith, Charles. *Let's Play Baseball!* 24 pages. 2006. Candlewick Press. A baseball asks a little boy to play with him.

Soto, Gary. *Lucky Luis.* 32 pages. 2012. Penguin Group. Luis' father helps him understand that practice is more important than superstition.

Spradlin, Michael. *Baseball from A to Z.* 32 pages. 2010. HarperCollins Publishers. An alphabet book that matches each letter to a simple baseball fact.

Teague, Mark. *The Field Beyond the Outfield.* 40 pages. 2006. Scholastic. Ludlow wants to play baseball to overcome his night fears but is placed so far into the outfield that he becomes part of another game in which some weird things happen.

Vernick, Audrey. *Brothers at Bat: The True Story of an Amazing All-Brother Baseball Team.* 40 pages. 2012. Houghton Mifflin Harcourt. The Acerras had 16 children, more than enough for a baseball team.

Wheeler, Lisa. *Dino-Baseball.* 2010. Carolrhoda Books. Meat eaters vs. veggie eating dinosaurs play baseball.

Family

Advance planning: To plan for this storytime, find a theme-related song to play during craft and snack times, like "We Are Family," by Sister Sledge. You will also want to select a poem, such as the first stanza of the poem "Biscuits of Love," by Mindy Carpenter (find it at www.netpoets.com), along with the books you plan to read. Decorate your space with family tree posters, dolls of all different kinds, pictures of many different kinds of families.

Introduction to theme: What is a family? Is it two parents and two children? Maybe a boy and a girl? Or is it like my family where there are two parents and three boys? Or my sister's family, where it's my sister and her son? Or my father's family, where he married my mother and had four children, then got divorced, got married again and had two more children? Or my friend Michelle, who has her mother living with her and her three sons? These are all families. Some are big with lots of people living together in the same place and some are small. What is the same about all families? (love each other) What's your family like? Today we'll read about families, play a family game, make a family craft and eat a snack that honors fathers and grandfathers.

Fingerplay: Do the fingerplay "My Family" which can be found at www.preschooleducation.com.

Song: "Mommy Is Her Name-O," to the tune of BINGO:

> I love my mom and she loves me
> And Mommy is her name-o
> M-O-M-M-Y M-O-M-M-Y M-O-M-M-Y
> And Mommy is her name-o.
> I love my dad and he loves me
> And Daddy is his name-o
> D-A-D-D-Y D-A-D-D-Y D-A-D-D-Y
> And Daddy is his name-o.

Game: Family chores

Materials needed: None if acting out, or pictures if using pictures. Advance preparation: Think of how you'll act out the chores or print pictures. At storytime: Act out the chores or show the pictures and have the children guess. Family Chores: wash and dry the dishes; sweep the floor; clean the windows; throw out the garbage; rakes leaves; mow the lawn; wash the car; vacuum the rug; put clothes in the dryer; get the mail from the mailbox; dust the furniture; ironing; set the table for a meal; put toys away in the toybox; feed the pet; water the plants.

Family tree pieces.

Alternative Games

"Five Little Ducks" fingerplay, which can be found online. Do as a fingerplay holding up the number of fingers as the number of ducks and making hand motions for hill and quacking.

What's missing? Make a tray of about eight baby related items. Show the children the items and name each one, explaining that they are things for the youngest members of families. Then ask them to close their eyes while you remove an item and cover it. Then have them open their eyes and tell you which item is missing.

Craft: Family tree

Materials needed: Brown, green, red construction paper and another color for background, crayons or markers, gluesticks. Advance preparation: Cut tree trunks from brown paper, big leafy top from green

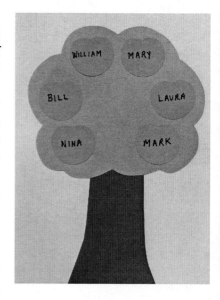

Family tree.

paper, apples from red paper. Cut the apples with a two-inch circle punch then shape the top to look like an apple. Use one shaped apple as a guide to cut the rest. Six apples per child should be enough. At storytime: Have parent write the names of family members on the apples. Glue tree trunk to background paper, green leafy top and apples to tree trunk.

Alternative Crafts

Family portraits. Provide paper and crayons and ask each child to draw a portrait of his/her family, including any pets.

Family handprints. Parent traces around both her own and child's hand on a piece of paper. Then ask child to say what's special about the parent and write on the hand and the parent writes something that's special about the child on the child's handprint. Could also cut out the handprints and glue them down to another color of paper.

Another family tree. For this one have some real leaves that the children can glue down to a tree that they draw on a piece of paper. Have pieces of paper that the parents can write the names of the family members and glue the names to the leaves.

Snack: Popcorn

Popcorn.

Materials needed: Popcorn, bowls or cups or special popcorn bags or boxes. Advance preparation: Make or buy popcorn. At storytime: In many families, the father or grandfather is often called Pop. Put some popcorn in bowl or cup. Ask them, "Do you know why popcorn pops?" Each kernel of popcorn contains a small drop of water stored inside a circle of soft starch. The soft starch is surrounded by the kernel's hard outer surface. As the kernel heats up, the water begins to expand. As the water turns into steam it changes the starch inside each kernel into a superhot gelatinous goop. The kernel continues to heat until the pressure inside finally bursts the hull open. As it explodes, steam inside the kernel is released. The soft starch inside the popcorn becomes inflated and spills out, cooling and forming the shape we know. A kernel swells 40 to 50 times its original size!

Alternative Snacks

Family pretzel trees. Pretzel rods, pretzel sticks, candies like M&Ms, large paper plates. Place one pretzel rod and several pretzel sticks and several small candies on a large paper plate. Have the children place the pretzel rod vertically and then branch off the small pretzel sticks. Place the candies next to the pretzel sticks to be leaves or fruit.

Leaf Cookies. Cookies cut with leaf shape cutters. Place the cookies on a piece of paper with a tree drawn on it.

SUGGESTED BOOKS

Amato, Mary. *The Chicken of the Family*. 32 pages. 2008. Penguin Group. A little girl runs off when her sisters tease her into believing she's actually a chicken.

Barden-Quallen, Sudipta. *Quackenstein Hatches a Family*. 32 pages. 2010. Abrams Books for Young Readers. Quackenstein is lonely until he finds an egg and hatches it.

Bennett, Kelly. *Your Daddy Was Just Like You*. 32 pages. 2002. Penguin Group. A little boy gets to hear how his daddy behaved when he was little (and sometimes misbehaved) as told to him by his grandma.

Blaine, Marge. *The Terrible Thing That Happened at Our House*. 30 pages. 1983. Scholastic. A little girl has to learn to adjust when her mother goes back to work.

Brown, Marc. *Arthur's Baby*. 32 pages. 1999. Bantam Doubleday. A good book for older children expecting a younger sibling.

Brunhoff, Laurent de. *Meet Babar and His Family*. 30 pages. 2002. Abrams. Introduces the famous French family of Babar the elephant as well as discusses the seasons.

Carlson, Nancy. *Louanne Pig in the Perfect Family*. 32 pages. 2004. Lerner Publishing Group. Louanne Pig would like to be part of a bigger family, as she is an only child.

Cole, Joanna. *I'm a Big Brother*. 32 pages. 2010. Harper Festival. A good book to prepare little boys for having younger siblings.

Cole, Joanna. *I'm a Big Sister*. 32 pages. 2010. Harper Festival. A good book to prepare little girls for having younger siblings.

Conrad, Pam. *The Tub People*. 32 pages. 1995. HarperCollins. Toys come to life and there is drama involving the toy child and the drain.

Cooney, Barbara. *Miss Rumphius*. 32 pages. 1985. Puffin. Miss Rumphius seeks adventure in far away places.

Crum, Shutta. *A Family for Old Mill Farm*. 32 pages. 2007. Houghton Mifflin Harcourt Trade & Reference Publishers. An animal real estate agent and a human real estate agent are both showing families a farm at the same time.

Curtis, Jamie Lee. *Mommy Hung the Moon*. 40 pages. 2010. HarperCollins. A story of unconditional love between a mother and child.

Curtis, Jamie Lee. *When I Was Little: A Four Year Old's Memoir of Her Youth*. 32 pages. 1995. HarperCollins. A little girl is growing up and can do many more things than she used to be able to do.

Cusimano, Maryann K. *You Are My I Love You*. 32 pages. 2001. Philomel. A day in the life of a parent and child with lots of love.

dePaola, Tomie. *Nana Upstairs and Nana Downstairs*. 32 pages. 2000. Puffin. A little boy has a grandmother who is active and downstairs and a great grandmother who is old (and who ultimately dies) and stays in her room upstairs.

Eastman, P.D. *Are You My Mother?* 72 pages. 1960. Random House Children's Books. A newly hatched little bird who doesn't know what his mother looks like, goes searching for her.

Guarino, Deborah. *Is Your Mama a Llama?* 32 pages. 2004. Scholastic. Lloyd the llama finds out what kind of animal his mama really is.

Hoban, Russell. *A Baby Sister for Frances*. 32 pages. 1993. HarperCollins Publishers. Frances finds a way to feel important when her baby sister arrives.

Hoberman, Mary Ann. *All Kinds of Families*. 40 pages. 2009. Little Brown & Company. Rhyming text celebrates belonging to all kinds of families.

Hoberman, Mary Ann. *A House Is a House for Me*. 48 pages. 1978. Penguin Group Inc. In a rhyme, the author introduces us to all kinds of homes, for both people and animals.

Hoberman, Mary Ann. *The Seven Silly Eaters*. 40 pages. 2000. Houghton Mifflin Harcourt Trade & Reference Publishers. A family of picky eaters.

Holt, Kimberly Willis. *The Adventures of Granny Clearwater and Little Critter*. Granny and Little Critter are accidentally thrown from the covered wagon and go in search of their family, having many adventures.

Johnston, Tony. *The Quilt Story*. 32 pages. 1996. Puffin. A long time ago a little girl put a quilt in an attic where it's found by another little girl.

Keats, Ezra Jack. *Peter's Chair*. 40 pages. 1998. Penguin Group. Peter learns to accept his new baby sister.

Keillor, Garrison. *Daddy's Girl*. 40 pages. 2005. Hyperion. Ordinary life events are turned into celebrations with a dad and his little girl.

Kraus, Robert. *Whose Mouse Are You?* 40 pages. 2000. Simon & Schuster Books for Young Readers. "Nobody's" mouse becomes the hero of his family, including his new baby sister.

Levinson, Rikki. *I Go with My Family to Grandma's*. 32 pages. 1992. Puffin. Cousins and their families arrive at Grandma's house.

London, Jonathan. *Froggy's Baby Sister*. Froggy was hoping for a baby brother but gets a sister instead.

Manning, Peyton. *Family Huddle*. 32 pages. 2009. Scholastic. The NFL star writes a story about his childhood with brother Eli and dad Archie, also NFL stars.

Mayer, Mercer. *Grandma, Grandpa and Me*. 24 pages. 2007. Harper Festival. Little Critter is having a sleepover at his grandparents' house.

Mayer, Mercer. *Just Grandma and Me.* 24 pages. 2001. Random House Books for Young Readers. Little Critter spends the day at the beach with his grandmother.

Mayer, Mercer. *Just Grandpa and Me.* 24 pages. 2001. Random House Books for Young Readers. Little Critter goes to the department store with his grandfather.

Mayer, Mercer. *Just Me and My Dad.* 24 pages. 2001. Random House Books for Young Readers. The story of a camping trip with Little Critter and his dad.

Mayer, Mercer. *Just Me and My Mom.* 24 pages. 2001. Random House Books for Young Readers. Little Critter spends a day in the city with his mom.

Mayer, Mercer. *The New Baby.* 24 pages. 2001. Random House Books for Young Readers. Helps prospective big brothers and sisters to know what to expect.

McCloskey, Robert. *Blueberries for Sal.* 64 pages. 1976. Puffin. A little girl goes blueberry picking with her mother at the same time as a bear and her cub.

McGhee, Allison. *Someday.* 40 pages. 2007. Atheneum Books for Young Readers. A mother's love and her dream for her child.

Munsch, Robert. *Love You Forever.* 32 pages. 1986. Firefly Books. The classic story of the mother who will love her baby forever, even after he's a grown up man with a baby of his own.

Murphy, Jill. *All in One Piece.* 32 pages. 2006. Walker Children's Paperbacks. Mr. and Mrs. Large are trying to get ready to go out. Can Mrs. Large make it all in one piece?

Muth, Jon J. *Zen Shorts.* 40 pages. 2008. Scholastic Press. Stillwater the panda tells ancient Zen tales.

Parr, Todd. *The Family Book.* 32 pages. 2003. Little, Brown Books for Young Readers. Celebrating all different kinds of families.

Polacco, Patricia. *My Rotten Redheaded Older Brother.* 32 pages. 1998. Aladdin. Patricia's brother can do everything better than she can.

Relf, Patricia. *That New Baby!* 20 pages. 1984. Golden Books. Elizabeth decides she doesn't want to be a big sister.

Rylant, Cynthia. *The Relatives Came.* 32 pages. 2003. Live Oak Media. Two sides of a family come together.

Schaefer, Lola M. *Grandmothers.* 24 pages. 2008. Capstone Press. Explains all about grandmothers with lots of photos of them.

Schaefer, Lola M. *Grandfathers.* 24 pages. 2008. Capstone Press. Explains all about grandfathers with lots of photos of them.

Sicks, Linda. *Nick the Wise Old Cat: How I Found My Family.* 40 pages. 2010. Nick the Cat learns the importance of caring for all family members.

Sicks, Linda. *Nick the Wise Old Cat: How My Family Changed.* 40 pages. 2010. Nick the Cat learns about how to handle change.

Sicks, Linda. *Nick the Wise Old Cat: How My Family Grew Overnight.* 40 pages. 2010. Nick the Cat. Nick the Cat shares what he learns about family after he meets the Nice Lady caregiver.

Simon, Norma. *All Kinds of Families.* 40 pages. 1976. Albert Whitman and Company. Explores what a family is and how they vary.

Tillman, Nancy. *Wherever You Are: My Love Will Find You.* 32 pages. 2010. Feiwel and Friends. A book about the love of a mother for her child.

Velasquez, Eric. *Grandma's Gift.* 40 pages. 2010. Walker Childrens. Eric spends his winter break with his grandmother.

Willems, Mo. *Knuffle Bunny: A Cautionary Tale.* 36 pages. 2004. Hyperion Press. The bunny gets left behind at the laundromat.

Willems, Mo. *Knuffle Bunny Free: An Unexpected Diversion.* 52 pages. 2010. HarperCollins Publishers. The family is going to visit grandparents in Holland but is the bunny going too?

Willems, Mo. *Knuffle Bunny Too: A Case of Mistaken Identity.* 48 pages. 2007. Hyperion Press. Trixie takes the bunny to school but there's an awful surprise in store.

Williams, Vera. *More More More Said the Baby.* 40 pages. 1996. Greenwillow Books. 3 babies play with their grownups and always want more of whatever activity they're doing.

Wood, Don, and Audrey Wood. *The Napping House.* 32 pages. 2009. Harcourt Children's Books. The piling up of too many sleepy people and animals.

Ziefert, Harriett. *Families Have Together.* 40 pages. 2005. Blue Apple Books. A rhyming description of the ins and outs of families.

Feathered Friends

Advance planning: To plan for this storytime, find a theme-related song to play during craft and snack times, like "Chicken Dance" (the original version). You will also want to select a poem, such as the first stanza of the poem "Weird-Bird," by Shel Silverstein, which can be found at www.poems.writers-network.com, or in *Falling Up*, along with the books you plan to read. Decorate your space with stuffed birds, perhaps perched in a large plant or tree, feathers, a poster of a colorful bird like a parrot or macaw.

Introduction to theme: This week we're going to read stories about some of our feathered friends. What kind of animals have feathers? Do you have feathers? Would you like to have feathers? What's special about most animals with feathers? Do you wish you could fly? Birds have feathers, a beak with no teeth, they lay eggs, and they have a lightweight but strong skeleton. Do you know what a skeleton is? All birds alive today have wings. Wings are special forelimbs, and most birds can fly. Can you think of a kind of bird that can't fly? (penguins) Birds also have unique insides that work well for flying. Today we'll read about birds, play a feathered friend game, make a bird puppet and have a snack that looks like food that birds might eat.

Song: "The Bird Song," by Phil Rosenthal which can be found at www.songsforteaching. com.

Game: Birds fly.

Make a list of creatures, some that fly, some that don't. Have children stand and let them know that this is sort of like Simon Says, but you're going to say the name of an animal that either flies or does not fly but you're going to say that it flies. If it's an animal that does really fly, they should flap their arms like wings. If it doesn't fly, they shouldn't flap. You can start out by doing the correct motion when you say the animal, but if they're good at the game you might try to fool them by doing the flapping even when it's something that doesn't fly. Here are some ideas for animals: Elephants (don't) fly; Bluebirds fly; Cardinals fly; Pigs (don't) fly; Horses (don't) fly; Eagles fly; Pigeons fly; Cows (don't) fly; Crows fly; Dogs (don't) fly; Robins fly; Butterflies fly; Cats (don't) fly; Dragonflies fly; People (don't) fly; Fish (don't) fly; Hummingbirds fly. When you've run out of animals, ask them: Can you name something that flies? Something that doesn't fly? Give each child a turn if they can think of something.

What's that bird? Find bird sounds at: www.findsounds.com, and record them on a disk. Print pictures of those birds from the Internet. Play each sound, see if anyone can guess what bird it is, then show the picture of the bird. Suggested birds to find: owl, rooster, chick, turkey, goose, duck, chicken, peacock, parrot, dove, flamingo, penguin, cardinal, canary, eagle, and robin.

Flying feathers. Place a bowl on the floor and let the children try to drop feathers into it. They'll discover how feathers move on the air currents. Experiment with holding the feathers higher or lower and seeing how it makes it easier or harder to get them into the bowl.

Fly like a bird. Give each child two large paper plates and play some music. Show them how to flap their "wings" and fly around the room.

Bird watching. If you have a window with a tree nearby, hang a bird feeder in the tree a day or two before your storytime to see if you can attract some birds. Then look out the window during storytime.

Alternative Games

Chicken dance. Materials needed: Chicken Dance music on CD, CD player. Advance preparation: Learn the motions for the dance: Beak quacking—squeeze thumb toward hand four times; Wings—flap arms four times; Tail feathers—shake rear end four times; Clap four times. At storytime: Introduce the moves and practice first, and then play music. Have children stand and go over the four dance motions with them before playing the music. Explain that the chicken is squawking, flapping its wings, shaking its tail feathers and then you clap before starting the motions again. Then play the song and do the dance.

Craft: Paper bag bird puppet

Materials needed: Colorful paper bags, either all one color or multiple colors. Yellow, orange, green, blue, purple and red construction paper, glue sticks, google eyes or black and white circles, feathers, tape. Advance preparation: Cut eye background circles out of yellow construction paper. Cut beak top and beak bottom from orange construction paper. Cut cheek circles from red construction paper. Cut wings from remaining colors of construction paper. At storytime: Have children glue background eye circles down, then google eyes on top. Glue cheek circles and beak pieces on top and under flap. Tape several feathers to the back of the bottom of the bag as if on top of the bird's head. Glue wings to back of bag.

Paper bag bird puppet pieces.

Alternative Crafts

Pine cone bird feeders. Pine cones rolled in peanut butter then in bird seed. Tie a string around it to hang from a tree as a bird feeder.

Brown bag nest. Crumple a brown paper lunch bag up to make it look like a nest. Place some twigs or floral moss in it to line it and then place a few plastic eggs inside. If desired, glue everything down.

Snack: Bird snack cake

Materials needed: Rice cakes, cream cheese, assortment of nuts, seeds, chips, raisins, along

Paper bag bird puppet.

with paper plates and spoons. Advance preparation: None. At storytime: Give each child a rice cake, a dollop of cream cheese and a few spoonfuls of toppings. Let them spread the cream cheese and add the toppings. Tell them: Birds love suet cakes and you can make a snack that looks like one by taking a rice cake, spreading cream cheese on top and then sprinkling a mixture of sunflower seeds, chocolate chips, raisins and rolled oats.

Bird snack cake.

Alternative Snacks

Duck feed. Made from Chex cereal, mini pretzels, candy corn or other snacks.

Chicken cupcakes. Cupcakes with yellow icing, candy corn beaks, and short pieces of licorice for crest and chocolate chip eyes.

Bird food. Provide sunflower seeds, berries or other foods that birds like to eat.

Nest eggs. If making the brown paper lunch bag nest for the craft (as described above), place some kind of edible eggs inside, such as hard boiled or chocolate.

SUGGESTED BOOKS

Bernard, Robin. *Penguins Through the Year.* 16 pages. 1995. Scholastic. From the I Can Read About Science Library. A lot of factual information, detailing what happens to penguins all year long, discussing by the season.

Black, Sonia. *Plenty of Penguins.* 32 pages. 2000. Scholastic. From the Hello! Reader Science Series. A book for beginning readers. An introduction to penguins, their living and eating habits and the excitement of newly hatched penguins.

Boring, Mel. *Birds, Nests and Eggs.* 48 pages. 1998. Cooper Square Publishing. An informative take along guide that illustrates fifteen birds.

Brett, Jan illustrator. *The Owl and the Pussycat.* 32 pages. 1991. Penguin Group. Edward Lear's poem illustrated.

Bruel, Nick. *Little Red Bird.* 32 pages. 2008. Roaring Brook Press. When the cage door is left open the little bird wanders out and explores. When she returns to the cage, will she go back in?

Chessin, Betsey. *Counting Penguins.* 14 pages. 2000. Scholastic. A Science Emergent Reader. Photos and simple text invite the reader to count penguins.

Cronin, Doreen. *Duck for President.* 40 pages. 2004. Atheneum Books for Young Readers. If he walks like a duck and talks like a duck he'll be the next president.

Cronin, Doreen. *Giggle, Giggle, Quack.* 32 pages. 2002. Atheneum Books for Young Readers. Duck makes trouble for Farmer Brown's brother Bob, who has come to take over while Farmer Brown goes on vacation.

Eastman, P.D. *Are You My Mother?* 72 pages. 1960. Random House Children's Books. From the Dr. Seuss library, an endearing story about a baby bird who hatches while his mother is off in search of food for him.

Eastman, P.D. *The Best Nest.* 72 pages. 1968. Random House Children's Books. From the Dr. Seuss library, Mr. and Mrs. Bird search for a place to build a nest and they find some peculiar spots.

Eastman, P.D. *Flap Your Wings.* 48 pages. 2000. Random House Books for Young Readers. A strange egg appears in their nest, but Mr. and Mrs. Bird go on to take care of it anyway. It hatches into an alligator, though, and this presents some problems.

Eastman, P.D. *My Nest Is Best.* 14 pages. 2005. Random House Children's Books. Mr. Bird thinks his nest is best until Mrs. Bird tells him it's not.

Foley, Greg. *Purple Little Bird.* 32 pages. 2011. HarperCollins Publishers. Little bird can't find any place as nice as his little purple home.

Franco, Betsy. *Birdsongs: A Backwards Counting Book.* 40 pages. 2007. Margaret K. McElderry

Books. Celebrate neighborhood birds and count their sounds backwards.

Henkes, Kevin. *Birds*. 32 pages. 2009. Harper-Collins Publishers. Simple text with pretty paintings. The narrator imagines what it would be like to be a bird, and thinks about where birds go when you can't see them.

Hills, Tad. *Duck and Goose*. 40 pages. 2006. Random House Children's Books. Both Duck and Goose want the egg that they found.

Hills, Tad. *How Rocket Learned to Read*. 40 pages. 2010. Random House Children's Books. A little bird teaches Rocket the dog how to read.

Jenkins, Martin. *The Emperor's Egg*. 32 pages. 2002. Candlewick Press. Facts about nature's most devoted dad.

Johnston, Tony. *The Barn Owls*. 32 pages. 2001. Charlesbridge Publishing. Poetry book that describes the lives of generations of owls.

Kaczman, James. *A Bird and His Worm*. 32 pages. 2002. Houghton Mifflin Harcourt Publishers. A bird who doesn't like to fly becomes friends with a worm.

Lester, Helen. *Tacky the Penguin*. 32 pages. 1990. Houghton Mifflin Harcourt. Tacky's an odd bird who ends up saving the day.

Lionni, Leo. *Inch by Inch*. 32 pages. 1995. Harper-Collins Publishers. To keep from being eaten an inchworm volunteers to measure different body parts for various birds, like necks, tails, etc.

Lionni, Leo. *Nicolas, Where Have You Been?* 32 pages. 2010. Random House Children's Books. Nicolas the mouse is taken by a crow when he wanders off in search of berries. He ultimately needs to trust the birds who he thought were his enemies.

Long, Ethan. *Bird and Birdie in a Fine Day*. 48 pages. 2010. Ten Speed Press. Bird and Birdie spend all day together in this tale of friendship.

Massie, Diane Redfield. *The Baby Beebee Bird*. 32 pages. 2000. HarperCollins Publishers. Originally published in 1963, this is the story of a baby bird in the zoo who makes noise all night long.

Peters, Andrew Fusek. *The No-No Bird*. 32 pages. 2009. Lincoln Frances Limited. Rhyming text about a bird who says no to everything for so long that he becomes known as the No-No Bird.

Pfister, Marcus. *Penguin Pete and Pat*. 25 pages. 1989. North-South Books. Penguin Pete is back and all the penguins come out to greet him.

Rabe, Tish. *Fine Feathered Friends: All About Birds*. 48 pages. 1998. Random House Children's Books. From the Dr. Seuss Library, introduces Sally and Dick to a variety of birds.

Rayner, Catherine. *Sylvia and Bird*. 32 pages. 2009. Good Books. Sylvia the dragon wonders if she and her bird friend are too different to remain friends.

Reed, Lynn Rowe. *Basil's Birds*. 32 pages. 2010. Marshall Cavendish Corporation. The school custodian has a nest of birds in his hair.

Ruddell, Deborah. *Today at the Bluebird Cafe: A Branchful of Birds*. 40 pages. 2007. Margaret K. McElderry Books. A world of birds unfolds in twenty-two poems.

Sayre, April Pulley. *Bird, Bird, Bird!: A Chirping Chant*. 32 pages. 2007. Cooper Square Publishing. Real bird names are inserted into the rhyming chants throughout this book.

Schindel, John. *Busy Penguins*. 10 pages. 2000. Random House Children's Books. A board book where there's so much to do when you're a penguin.

Sierra, Judy. *Antarctic Antics: A Book of Penguin Poems*. 32 pages. 2003. Houghton Mifflin Harcourt. A collection of poems celebrating Emperor Penguins.

Sill, Catherine. *About Birds: A Guide for Children*. 40 pages. 1993. Peachtree Publishers, Ltd. Describes various species of North American birds.

Springman, I.C. *More*. 40 pages. 2012. Houghton Mifflin Harcourt. One magpie, lots of stuff and a few friendly mice show us less is more.

Tankard, Jeremy. *Boo Hoo Bird*. 32 pages. 2009. Scholastic. Bird gets bonked on the head and needs comforting.

Tankard, Jeremy. *Grumpy Bird*. 32 pages. 2007. Scholastic. Bird wakes up feeling grumpy.

Vase, Catherine. *The Penguin Who Wanted to Fly*. 32 pages. 2007. Scholastic. The penguin wants desperately to fly and tries to do so in many different ways.

Waddell, Martin. *Owl Babies*. 32 pages. 2002. Candlewick Press. Three baby owls awake to find their mother gone and wonder where she went.

Watkins, Greg. *A Big Beaked, Big Bellied Bird Named Bill*. 30 pages. 2004. Cute and Cuddly Productions. Bill is the new bird in town and the other birds aren't friendly so he makes some other friends.

Willems, Mo. *Don't Let the Pigeon Drive the Bus*. 36 pages. 2003. Hyperion Press. The pigeon whines and begs to be allowed to drive the bus.

Willems, Mo. *Don't Let the Pigeon Stay Up Late.* 40 pages. 2006. Hyperion Books for Children. Toddlers don't want to go to bed, and neither does the pigeon.

Willems, Mo. *The Duckling Gets a Cookie.* 40 pages. 2012. Disney Press. The duckling asks for a cookie, and gets one. Is the pigeon happy about that?

Willems, Mo. *The Pigeon Finds a Hot Dog.* 40 pages. 2004. Hyperion Books for Children. When the pigeon finds a hot dog, he can't wait to eat it.

Willems, Mo. *The Pigeon Wants a Puppy.* 40 pages. 2008. Hyperion Press. The pigeon begs and whines to be allowed to get a puppy.

Willems, Mo. *There Is a Bird on Your Head.* 64 pages. 2007. Hyperion Press. Piggie wants to help her friend Gerald the Elephant who has birds on his head.

Zoehfeld, Kathleen Weidner. *Penguins.* 32 pages. 2002. Scholastic. Scholastic Science Reader Series. Provides information about penguins, discussing the different types, how they move, where they live, what they look like, what they eat, and how baby penguins are born.

June

Bathtime and Bedtime

Advance planning: To plan for this storytime, find a theme-related song to play during craft and snack times, like "Rubber Ducky You're the One," by Ernie of *Sesame Street*, "The Lion Sleeps Tonight," by Adrian Baker or "Stay Awake" from *Mary Poppins*. You could also find some lullabies, like "Brahms' Lullaby." You will also want to select a poem, such as "Splish Splash," by Francine Pucillo (find it at www.wrensworld.com/bathtime.htm), along with the books you plan to read. Decorate your space with blankets, pillows, towels, bath toys, stuffed animals. Encourage the children to bring "bedtime buddies" with them by announcing the theme the week before.

Introduction to theme: Bathtime can be a quick wash in the tub to get clean, or a long soak with some toys to have fun. Do you like taking baths? My boys were always funny about bathtime — it was hard to get them into the tub, and then once they were in, it was hard to get them out! Do you have toys to play with in the bath? What's your favorite toy? Do you usually take a bath at night before you go to bed? What else do you do when you're getting ready for bed? Have a snack? Brush your teeth? Read some books? Today we'll read about bathtime and bedtime, play some bath and bedtime games, make a bathtime craft and eat a bedtime snack.

Song: "This Is the Way We Wash Our Hair"

> This is the way we wash our hair,
> Wash our hair,
> Wash our hair.
> This is the way we wash our hair
> So early in the morning.

Since this is a short song, could also do "Twinkle Twinkle Little Star," so there's a song for bathtime and a song for bedtime.

> Twinkle twinkle little star,
> How I wonder what you are.
> Up above the world so high,
> Like a diamond in the sky.
> Twinkle twinkle little star,
> How I wonder what you are.

Alternative Song

"Rubber Ducky," which can be found online.

Game: Duck dance

Materials needed: Duck dance music recording, CD player. Advance preparation: None. At storytime: Demonstrate the motions of the Duck dance: Beak quacking—squeeze thumb toward hand four times; Wings—flap arms four times; Tail feathers—shake rear end four times; Clap four times. Have children stand and go over the four dance motions with them before playing the music. Explain that the duck is quacking, flapping its wings, shaking its tail feathers and then you clap before starting the motions again. Then play the song and do the dance.

Alternative Games

Daytime-nighttime activities. Find from magazines or print from the Internet pictures to show activities that normally happen in daytime or nighttime (eating, sleeping, etc.). Hold up a picture and ask the children to tell you whether it's a daytime or nighttime activity.

Hand shadow puppets. You'll need a sheet, flashlight, table. Hang a sheet over a table so that you can get down behind it or from the ceiling. Place flashlight on a raised surface like a box about a foot away from the sheet. At storytime, put your hands between the light and the sheet, but close to the sheet and do some simple hand shadows, like a swan, dog, rabbit and bird in flight. See Internet websites for instructions by googling hand shadow puppets.

Pillowcase hop—like a sack race but using pillowcases. Set up lanes using cones to mark the course for the race.

Freeze dance—but instead of freezing pretend to sleep and snore when the music stops and then stretch and wake up when the music starts.

Pop the ducky bath bubbles. Decorate a large plastic storage tub with pictures of rubber ducks, or get some small rubber ducks from a party store and fill it with bubble wrap so that it looked like a big bathtub full of bubbles. Announce that it's "bathtime," and pull the bubble wrap out and let the kids jump all over the bubble wrap to pop the bubbles. Play the song "Splish Splash I was Taking a Bath" while they jump around. Check out different sizes of bubble wrap to find some that are easiest for children to make popping sounds when jumping on.

Sailboat pieces.

Share. If the children brought their "bedtime buddies" to storytime, let them have turns telling the name and what's special about their buddy.

Craft: Sailboat

Materials needed: Rectangular sponges, straws, foam sheets. Advance preparation: Cut sponges in half. Cut a slit through the sponge toward one of the shorter ends of the rectangle. Cut foam sheets into small triangles to use as the sail for the boat. Cut two slits in the foam sheet sail. At storytime: Insert straw through two slits in the foam sail. Insert sail into the slit in the sponge. After making boats, sing "Row, Row, Row Your Boat":

> Row, row, row your boat
> Gently down the stream,
> Merrily merrily, merrily, merrily
> Life is but a dream

If possible, have a small tub of water so that the children can try out their boats in the water. If you did the bubble wrap game, you could have a container of water set aside to fill the same tub that you used for the bubble wrap.

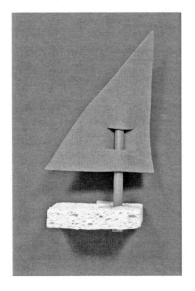

Sailboat.

Alternative Crafts

Construction paper rubber duck. Cut large yellow oval for duck body, trace around child's hands to make wings out of yellow construction paper. Orange construction paper for diamond-shaped beak and webbed feet. White construction paper ovals for eye backgrounds, black construction paper ovals (smaller than white) for eye pupils. Glue wings hanging off on sides of large oval, feet hanging off on bottom, and eyes and beak in upper half of oval.

Fleece tied fiber filled pillows. Cut two squares of fleece. Cut off corner squares. Cut each side into 1-inch strips. Tie the strips together making knots. Do three sides and half of fourth side. Then stuff with fiberfill. When filled, tie last half side.

Pillowcases decorated with fabric markers. Buy plain white cotton pillowcases. Let the children decorate with fabric markers. Could plan a theme design, like moon and stars, or let them make their own design.

Snack: Rubber ducky cookie

Materials needed: Sugar cookie, either round or duck-shaped, yellow icing, chocolate chip eyes, orange icing or orange candies like Skittles or M&Ms for cheeks and forehead, candy corn for beak, small paper plates, plastic knives. Advance preparation: Bake cookies. Mix yellow and orange icing (more yellow than orange). At storytime: Give each child a cookie, a dollop of each color icing on their plate with a plastic knife. Have them spread the yellow all over the cookie. Dab the orange on the cheeks and the forehead or add the orange candies. Add two chocolate chips for eyes, one candy corn for beak.

Alternative Snacks

Hot milk or cocoa and cookies, as you might have at bedtime.

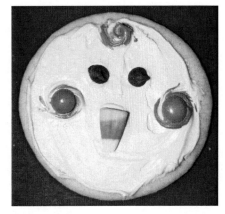

Rubber ducky cookie.

Rubber ducky snacks. Get rubber ducky paper cups and place any kind of small snack in them, like cereal or candies. Could make ice cream balls and roll them in rubber ducky sprinkles.

SUGGESTED BOOKS

Allen, Jonathan. *I'm Not Sleepy.* 32 pages. 2010. Hyperion Press. Baby Owl is definitely not ready for bedtime.

Andres, Kristina. *The Elephant in the Bathtub.* 32 pages. 2010. North-South Books. There's plenty of room in Elephant's bathtub, so many other animals come and join him.

Arnold, Tedd. *No More Water in the Tub.* 32 pages. 1998. Penguin Group. After filling his bathtub one night, William goes sailing through his apartment building, collecting his neighbors as he goes.

Becker, Bonnie. *A Bedtime for Bear.* 48 pages. 2010. Candlewick Press. Bear is very fussy about his bedtime, quite different from his friend Mouse. But surprisingly it's Bear who turns out to be afraid of the dark.

Bedford, David. *Bedtime for Little Bears!* 28 pages. 2007. Good Books. Little Bear and Mother Bear take a walk to try to get Little Bear sleepy.

Bedford, David. *Bouncy Bouncy Bedtime.* 32 pages. 2011. Egmont Books, Limited. Rhythmic text has animals filling a bed getting ready for bedtime.

Boynton, Sandra. *Barnyard Bath.* 10 pages. 2008. Workman Publishing Company. A waterproof book that's a cousin to Barnyard Dance.

Boynton, Sandra. *Bath Time!* 10 pages. 2007. Workman Publishing Company. This is a very short plastic covered book. Good to show parents that they can get books that can be read in the bathtub.

Boynton, Sandra. *Night Night Little Pookie.* 15 pages. 2009. Random House Children's Books. A board book about little Pookie the Pig getting ready for bed.

Boynton, Sandra. *Pajama Time!* 24 pages. 2000. Workman Publishing Company. All the animals are wearing pajamas and getting ready for bed.

Bridwell, Norman. *Clifford's Bathtime.* 24 pages. 1991. Scholastic. A board book that shows how Clifford doesn't want to take a bath but then learns how much fun it can be.

Brown, Margaret Wise. *Goodnight Moon.* 32 pages. 1991. HarperCollins Publishers. The classic story of the little rabbit bidding everything in his room goodnight.

Brown, Margaret Wise. *Sleepy ABC.* 40 pages. 2009. HarperCollins Publishers. Tender rhymes illustrating every letter of the alphabet, geared especially to bedtime.

Capucilli, Alyssa Satin. *Bathtime for Biscuit.* 32 pages. 1998. HarperCollins Publishers. A learn to read book about trying to get Biscuit the puppy out of the mud and into the bath.

Carlson, Nancy. *It's Bedtime Wibbly Pig.* 32 pages. 2004. Penguin Group. Wibbly goes through all the typical delaying tactics of going to bed.

Casler, Kristie S. *Have You Ever Seen a Llama in Pajamas?* 24 pages. 2008. PublishAmerica. Silly situations with funny pictures and rhyming phrases.

Child, Lauren. *I Am Not Sleepy and I Will Not Go to Bed.* 32 pages. 2001. Candlewick Press. Charlie helps Lola get ready for bed, despite many obstacles.

Conrad, Pam. *Tub People.* 32 pages. 1999. HarperCollins Publishers. A wooden toy family ride on floating soap but after the toy child nearly goes down the drain they adjourn to the bed, where they climb the mountain ridges of the covers.

Conway, David. *Bedtime Hullabaloo.* 32 pages. 2010. Walker and Company. Alliterative romp with animals all about a little animal whose snores are keeping everyone awake.

Cousins, Lucy. *Maisy Takes a Bath.* 24 pages. 2000. Candlewick Press. Maisy is taking a bath when Tallulah comes to visit. Tallulah wants to play tennis but ends up joining Maisy in the bathtime where they find out that bathtime can be playtime as well.

Crow, Kristyn. *Bedtime at the Swamp.* 29 pages. 2008. HarperCollins Children's Books. Everyone ends up in a tree in a swamp when they're afraid of the swamp monster at bedtime. Rhythmic text is almost musical.

Dewdney, Anna. *Llama Llama Red Pajama.* 40 pages. 2005. Penguin Group. In this rhyming book, the baby llama turns bedtime into quite a drama.

Dreidemy, Joelle. *Bath Time, Beth!* 24 pages. 2006. Child's Play International. It's Beth's bath time, but she has other ideas. Has a felt character that you push through as she makes her escapes.

Elgar, Rebecca. *Time for Bed.* 14 pages. 2004. Egmont Books, Limited. Lift the flap book with a pop up surprise at the end.

Goss, Sheila M. *Once Upon a Bathtime.* 32 pages. 2011. Tradewind Books. Fairy tales for the tub as a little girl gets ready for bed.

Helquist, Brett. *Bedtime for Bear.* 32 pages. 2010. HarperCollins Publishers. It's wintertime and that means bedtime for Bear, but his friends don't want him to go to bed.

Jacobs, Parker. *Only in Dreams: A Bedtime Story.* 36 pages. 2008. Chronicle Books. Paul Frank's monkey character Julius goes on an adventure in dreamland.

Jarman, Julia. *Big Red Tub.* 32 pages. 2004. Scholastic. When it's time for Stan and Stella to take their bath, they're joined by a lot of animals.

Langreuter, Julia. *Little Bear Won't Go to Bed.* 32 pages. 2000. Lerner Publishing Group. Little Bear doesn't want to go to bed and his parents are very tolerant.

Lum, Kate. *What! Cried Granny: An Almost Bedtime Story.* 32 pages. 2002. Penguin Group. A little boy is spending the night at his grandmother's and when he is missing something, she goes to great lengths to supply substitutes.

Lyon, George Ella. *Sleepsong.* 26 pages. 2009. Atheneum Books for Young Readers. Rhythmic text about getting ready for bed is an actual song. The book provides the music as well as the lyrics.

Malam, John. *The Very Sleepy Pig.* 22 pages. 2010. Hinkler Books. About the pig who can't get up in the morning.

Numeroff, Laura. *If You Give a Pig a Party.* 32 pages. 2005. HarperCollins Publishers. The circular story of what happens when you give a pig a party, then she'll want to decorate with balloons, then invite her friends for a slumber party, and so on.

Ottolenghi, Carol. *Tip the Mouse Can't Sleep.* 24 pages. 2005. Gingham Dog Press. Tip the Mouse worries that someone is going to take his teddy bear. When he finally falls asleep he has good dreams.

Palmer, Helen. *A Fish Out of Water.* 64 pages. 1961. Random House Children's Books. From the Dr. Seuss library, it shows how the rapidly growing fish quickly outgrows all the containers (including the bathtub) he's put in.

Paul, Cinco. *Sleepy Kittens.* 10 pages. 2010. Hachette Book Group. A Despicable Me board book featuring a soothing story and soft kitten finger puppets.

Perl, Erica S. *Chicken Bedtime Is Really Early.* 32 pages. 2005. Abrams. Rhyming story that follows along with all the usual things done to get ready for bed, but it's all being done by farm animals.

Pfister, Marcus. *Bertie at Bedtime.* 32 pages. 2008. North-South Books. Bertie the hippo is not ready for bed and might wear his dad out before he's ready to go to sleep.

Pfister, Marcus. *The Rainbow Fish Bath Book.* The abridged version of the story about the fish that learns to share. This version is for reading in the bathtub.

Plourde, Lynne. *Pajama Day.* 40 pages. 2005. Penguin Group. One person in class forgot to wear his pajamas on pajama day but comes up with some ingenious ways to join in.

Priddy, Roger. *Bathtime.* 12 pages. 2010. St. Martin's Press. A simple touch and feel board book.

Rathmann, Peggy. *Goodnight, Gorilla.* 40 pages. 2000. Penguin Group. The zookeeper thinks it's bedtime for all the animals but surprisingly finds them in his bed after the gorilla gets hold of his keys.

Rathmann, Peggy. *10 Minutes Till Bedtime.* 48 pages. 1998. Penguin Group. Countdown to bedtime with a family of hamsters in numbered jerseys.

Rosenthal, Amy Krouse. *Bedtime for Mommy.* 32 pages. 2010. Bloomsbury Publishing. In this family's night time ritual, it's all about who's putting Mommy to bed.

Segal, John. *Pirates Don't Take Baths.* 32 pages. 2011. Penguin Group. The pirate pig refuses to take a bath.

Seuss, Dr. *Dr. Seuss's Sleep Book.* 64 pages. 1962. Random House Children's Books. No one can resist all these sleepy creatures.

Shea, Bob. *Dinosaur Vs. Bedtime.* 40 pages. 2008. Hyperion Press. Nothing can stop the little dinosaur — not grown ups nor bathtime. But what happens when he comes up against bedtime?

Sierra, Judy. *The Sleepy Little Alphabet: A Bedtime Story from Alphabet Town.* 40 pages. 2009. Alfred A. Knopf. All the members of the alphabet have something they need or want that keeps them from going to bed.

Stewart, Amber. *Bedtime for Button.* 32 pages. 2009. Scholastic. Button is afraid he's going to have a bad dream when he falls asleep.

Thomas, Shelly Moore. *A Good Knight's Rest.* 30 pages. 2011. Dutton Children's Books. All the Good Knight wants is a little rest and relaxation but the dragons take a while to understand.

Thompson, Lauren. *Little Quack's Bedtime*. 32 pages. 2005. Simon & Schuster Children's Publishing. Little Quack is keeping everyone awake and Mama would like everyone to go to sleep.

Watson, Wendy. *Bedtime Bunnies*. 32 pages. 2010. Houghton Mifflin Harcourt Trade. It's always bedtime for someone, and in this book it's bedtime for bunnies.

Wolfe, Myra. *Charlotte Jane Battles Bedtime*. 32 pages. 2011. Houghton Mifflin Harcourt Trade. Charlotte's a pirate girl whose day is too full for bedtime.

Wood, Audrey. *King Bidgood in the Bathtub*. 32 pages. 1985. Houghton Mifflin Harcourt Trade Reference Publishers. The king refuses to leave the bathtub and everyone in the kingdom tries to get him out.

Wood, Audrey. *The Napping House*. 32 pages. 1984. Houghton Mifflin Harcourt Trade. Sleepy people and animals are all napping quietly in bed until the flea disturbs them all.

Yolen, Jane. *How Do Dinosaurs Say Goodnight?* 40 pages. 2000. Scholastic. Rhyming text that has dinosaur children challenging bedtime, but finally give in to sleep.

Zion, Gene. *Harry the Dirty Dog*. 32 pages. 1956. HarperCollins Publishers. Harry doesn't want to take a bath and he gets so dirty his family doesn't recognize him. He finally has to clean up so that they'll know who he is again.

Magic

Advance planning: To plan for this storytime, find a theme-related song to play during craft and snack times, like "Magic," by Pilot. You will also want to select a poem, such as "My Magic Hat Is Marvelous," by Kenn Nesbitt (find it at www.poetry4kids.com), along with the books you plan to read. Decorate your space with a magician's cape, hat, magic wand, and stuffed rabbit.

Introduction to theme: What is magic? Have you ever seen someone perform a magic trick? That person is called a magician. Some magicians do tricks with cards; some use a hat or a wand. A magician can make amazing things look real when they're not. We know that we shouldn't believe it when we see a magician do a trick, but if the magician's good, we forget that we don't really believe in magic, and things seem real. Today we'll read about magic, play a magic game, make a magician's craft and eat a magical snack.

If you are in a bookstore that has puppets, perhaps you have the hat with rabbit puppet. Try to learn some kind of simple magic trick. Here's one that you can call "sawing a lady in half." You will insert a paper doll into a paper tube. The children can see the doll's head and feet sticking out of both ends of the tube. You will then cut the tube in half. When the doll is removed, it's fully intact. To perform this trick, you will need paper, a pen, an envelope and scissors. Seal the envelope and cut off the ends. You'll want a tube that's about four inches long. You'll also need a paper doll, which is simply a strip of paper with a person drawn on it. Use a strip of colored paper that is cut about 8.5 inches long × 1.5 inches wide. You have to flatten the tube and cut two slits into what will become the bottom of the tube. Basically, you'll separate the tube into thirds with the two slits. Make sure that the slits are wide enough so the paper doll can slide through them. This is the secret. Now you're ready to perform the trick.

Slide the paper doll into the paper tube. However, once the doll enters the tube, you need to slip the end of the doll through the first slit and out of the back of the envelope. And as you further work the doll into the tube, you'll need to slip the doll back into the tube through the second slit. In the middle part of the tube, the doll is actually under the tube. Although from the front, everything will appear normal. Begin to cut the envelope, however, be sure that the scissors are cutting under the envelope, but above the paper doll. After you're done cutting, hold the two pieces of the envelope together and pull out the paper doll. It will appear that the paper doll has survived the cutting. You can allow spectators to examine the doll, but quietly crumple-up and discard the paper tube before they ask to see it.

Or you can do a water trick. Have a deep light colored bowl of slightly tinted water and a glass that will go entirely under the depth of the water. Before storytime, tilt the glass and fill it with the water in the bowl and then place it upside down in the bowl. For the trick, draw up the glass and it will remain filled with water if you keep the rim just slightly under the water. The tint in the water makes it easier to see that the water has remained inside the glass. You can say the glass is a water magnet.

Fingerplay: "Finger Magic." Now let's do some magic with our fingers. Have the children do the hand motions with you:

> A little boy lives in this house (right thumb tucked inside right fist)
> A little girl lives in this house (left thumb tucked inside left fist)
> One day the little boy came out of his house (release right thumb)
> He looked up and down the street (move thumb slowly)
> He didn't see anyone, so he went back into his house (tuck thumb back in)
> One day the little girl came out of her house (release left thumb)
> She looked up and down the street (move thumb slowly)
> She didn't see anyone, so she went back into her house (tuck thumb back in)
> The next day the little boy came out of his house and looked all around
> (release right thumb and move it around)
> The little girl came out of her house and looked all around
> (release left thumb and move it around)
> They saw each other (point thumbs toward each other)
> They walked across the street and shook hands
> (move thumbs toward each other until they meet)
> The decided to stay outside together and play (move thumbs up and down and all around)
> When it got dark, the little girl went back inside her house (tuck left thumb in)
> and the little boy went back inside his house (tuck right thumb in)
> but they had promised to come out to play again tomorrow.

Game: Magic mirror

Materials needed: None. Advance preparation: None. At storytime: Have the children stand and tell them that they're going to pretend they're looking into a magic mirror when they're looking at you. Whatever movement you do they do too: raise arms; raise hands; raise legs; wiggle legs; wave arms; turn around; bend knees; bend down; jump; make different faces. Then tell them the magic mirror has changed and give each child a turn to make a movement and the rest of you will copy.

Alternative Games

Juggling. Provide a variety of soft foam balls and let the children try to juggle them.

Magic tricks. Learn some simple magic tricks to demonstrate for the children. These can be found online, and there are instructional videos on YouTube.

Print some pictures of real and make believe objects. Show them to the children to let them decide which things are real and which things are make believe.

Magic wand pieces.

Magic wand.

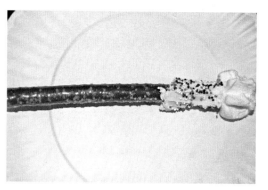

Magic wand snack.

Magical tale. Start a story with one sentence saying something magical. Let each child add a sentence to the story, making up a fantasy tale.

Craft: Magic wand

Materials needed: Wooden dowels, black paint, ribbon, black cardstock, tape, small shiny star confetti and glue sticks or star stickers, or glitter or jewels. Advance preparation: Cut dowels to twelve-inch lengths. Paint black. Cut cardstock stars. Cut ribbon to eighteen-inch lengths, two per child. At storytime: Tie ribbon pieces to one end of dowel. Tape over to hold in place. Glue or stick shiny stars to cardstock stars. Put glue on back side of one star. Lay ribbon end of the dowel down on it, and then glue other star over it.

Alternative Crafts

Glitter wands. Make magic wands from other materials, such as paper towel tubes, the cardboard tubes from pants hangers, poster tubes. Let the children paint them and apply glitter. Punch a hole in one end with a hole punch and tie a ribbon to the hole.

Magical hat. Cut black top hat shapes from black cardstock. Cut a slit inside the rim. Cut out white rabbit shapes that will fit through that slit. Let the children decorate their rabbits, then show them how they can make the rabbit appear out of the hat by placing it behind the hat and moving it up through the slit.

Snack: Magic wand

Materials needed: Pretzel rods, frosting, sprinkles, marshmallows (star-shaped if possible), paper plates, plastic knives. Advance preparation: None. At storytime: Give each child a pretzel rod, a dollop of frosting, a marshmallow, a plastic knife and some sprinkles on a paper plate. Have the children spread the frosting on one end of the pretzel rod and roll it in the sprinkles, then attach the marshmallow.

Alternative Snacks

Licorice twist magic wands. Melt candy coating and let children dip the ends of licorice twists into the candy coating and then roll in sprinkles or candy confetti.

Rabbit cookies. Cookies cut with a rabbit-shaped cutter, like the rabbit that the magician pulls out of his hat. Ice with white icing.

SUGGESTED BOOKS

Agee, Jon. *Milo's Hat Trick*. 32 pages. 2001. Michael Di Capua Books. Milo's magic is a mess until he teams up with a bear.

Ahlberg, Allan. *The Pencil*. 48 pages. 2008. Candlewick. One day a pencil magically begins to draw and creates its own world.

Ahlberg, Janet, and Allan Ahlberg. *The Jolly Postman*. 32 pages. 2001. LB Kids. Amusing correspondence from one fairy tale character to another.

Ashman, Linda. *Maxwell's Magic Mix-up*. 32 pages. 2001. Simon & Schuster. When Maxwell the magician entertains, everything gets mixed up and someone else has to save the day.

Base, Graeme. *Enigma: A Magical Mystery*. 48 pages. 2008. Abrams Books for Young Readers. Bertie Badger visits the retirement home for elderly magicians.

Baum, L. Frank. *The Wonderful Wizard of Oz: A Commemorative Pop-Up*. 16 pages. 2000. Little Simon. A shimmering homage to a classic.

Baynton, Martin. *Jane and the Magician*. 32 pages. 2007. Candlewick. Jane learns about the consequences of acting in anger.

Berger, Barbara. *Grandfather Twilight*. 32 pages. 1984. Philomel. When day is done, it's time for Grandfather Twilight to put on his jacket and go for a walk.

Bissett, Josie. *Tickle Monster*. 36 pages. 2008. Compendium. A lovable monster comes from Planet Tickle with his mission to bring joy and laughter.

Buehner, Caroline. *Snowmen at Night*. 32 pages. 2005. Harcourt School Publishers. A child wonders why the snowman looks droopy in the morning.

Bulloch, Ivan. *I Want to Be a Magician*. 32 pages. 1997. World Book Inc. A how-to book on magic with detailed illustrations for a variety of simple tricks.

Carroll, Lewis and Sabuda, Robert. *Alice's Adventures in Wonderland: a Pop-Up Adaptation*. 12 pages. 2003. Little Simon. With text faithful to the original story and foil and multi-faceted special effects pop-ups, this is a beautiful book to show.

Cate, Annette. *The Magic Rabbit*. 32 pages. 2009. Candlewick. Ray the magician loses his bunny.

Chwast, Seymour. *Mr. Merlin and the Turtle*. 24 pages. 1996. Greenwillow. A pet turtle can be boring until turned into a progression of other animals.

Clemlinson, Katie. *Magic Box*. 32 pages. 2009. Hyperion Book. Eva finds a lot of things in her magic box.

dePaola, Tomie. *Strega Nona*. 40 pages. 2011. Little Simon. Strega Nona helps everyone and one of her workers disobeys her and gets into her magical pasta pot.

Donaldson, Julia. *Room on the Broom*. 32 pages. 2003. Puffin. The witch picks up a lot of passengers on her broom.

Faller, Regis. *Polo and the Magician*. 32 pages. 2009. Roaring Book Press. Polo's life is never boring.

Fox, Mem. *The Magic Hat*. 32 pages. 2002. Harcourt Children's Books. A magic hat appears in the sky and makes magic wherever it lands.

Freeman, Don. *The Paper Party*. 40 pages. 1977. Puffin. A boy goes through his television screen for a party with puppets.

Galdone, Paul. *The Magic Porridge Pot*. 32 pages. 1979. Clarion Books. The porridge pot always makes food for the little girl but everything goes wrong when her mother tries to use it.

Higginson, Sheila Sweeny. *Olivia the Magnificent*. 16 pages. 2009. Simon Spotlight. Olivia wants to become a great magician.

Hoban, Russell. *Rosie's Magic Horse*. 32 pages. 2013. Candlewick. A discarded ice pop stick becomes a horse.

Johnson, Crockett. *Harold and the Purple Crayon*. 64 pages. 1998. HarperCollins. Harold creates his own world with a crayon and his imagination.

Johnson, Crockett. *Harold's Fairy Tale*. 64 pages. 1994. HarperCollins. Harold uses his crayon to create his own bedtime fairy tale.

Johnston, Tony. *The Witch's Hat*. 32 pages. 1984. Putnam Juvenile. The witch's hat causes some mayhem.

Kent, Jack. *There's No Such Thing as a Dragon*. 40 pages. 2001. Golden Books. When Billy finds a dragon in his room, his mother tells him there's no such thing. That only makes the dragon bigger.

Konnecke, Ole. *Anton Can Do Magic*. 32 pages. 2011. 21st Century. Anton wants to make things disappear.

Many, Paul. *The Great Pancake Escape*. 32 pages. 2002. Walker Books for Young Readers. The magician Dad's pancakes magically take flight.

McKee, David. *Melric: The Magician Who Lost His Magic*. 32 pages. 2012. Andersen Press. Melric sets out to find his lost magic but the kingdom is under attack — will he find his magic in time?

Munsch, Robert. *The Paper Bag Princess.* 32 pages. 1992. Annick Press, Ltd. A humorous and irreverent tale about a princess about to be married who rescues her prince from a dragon.

Palmer, Helen. *A Fish Out of Water.* 72 pages. 1961. Random House Books for Young Readers. A fish outgrows every container it's put in.

Reed, Neil. *The Midnight Unicorn.* 36 pages. 2006. Sterling. A little girl who loves unicorns and a statue comes to life in this shimmering book.

Reynolds, Peter H. *The Dot.* 32 pages. 2003. Candlewick. A little girl makes one little dot on her paper and that begins her journey into artful surprise and self-discovery.

Seeger, Pete. *Abiyoyo.* 48 pages. 2001. Simon & Schuster Books for Young Readers. A little boy and his father help save their town from a giant, after the townspeople turn them out.

Sendak, Maurice. *Where the Wild Things Are.* 48 pages. 1988. HarperCollins Publishers. Max goes looking for mischief and ends up being sent to bed without his supper. Fortunately, a forest grows in his room and he's able to continue his adventures.

Stieg, William. *Sylvester and the Magic Pebble.* 42 pages. 2005. Simon & Schuster Books for Young Readers. Sylvester the donkey finds a magic pebble but it has unforeseen consequences.

Thompson, Colin. *The Great Montefiasco.* 40 pages. 2005. Starbright Books. The magician does bad tricks and has a bad assistant.

Tullet, Herve. *Press Here.* 56 pages. 2011. Chronicle Books. Press the yellow dot on the cover, and then follow the instructions inside the book to go on a magical journey.

Van Allsburg, Chris. *The Polar Express.* 32 pages. 2009. Houghton Mifflin. A magical train ride takes a boy to the North Pole on Christmas Eve.

Van Dam, M. Nicole. *Inca Dink: The Great Houndini (Magician in Training).* 32 pages. 2010. CreateSpace. Inca Dink causes some mishaps for his friend Hilary Mouse.

Vivian, Bart. *Imagine.* 32 pages. 2013. Aladdin. This book invites the reader to imagine ordinary events as wonderful and magical occurrences.

Watson, Richard Jesse. *The Magic Rabbit.* 42 pages. 2005. Blue Sky Press. A rabbit finds many treasures inside his hat.

Wiesner, David. *Tuesday.* 32 pages. 1991. Clarion Books. An almost wordless book about the unpredictable events of a particular Tuesday.

Yarrow, Peter, Lipton, Lenny and Puybaret, Eric. *Puff the Magic Dragon.* 32 pages. 2010. Sterling. The famous song about Jackie Paper and his friend Puff is brought to life in this book.

Wong, Herbert Yee. *Abracadabra: A Mole and Mouse Story.* 48 pages. 2010. Sandpiper. Mouse and Mole are excited about Minkus the Magnificent coming to town.

Mice

Advance planning: To plan for this storytime, find a theme-related song to play during craft and snack times, like "Mouse Jamboree," by Mary Kaye. You will also want to select a poem, such as the classic "Hickory Dickory Dock," along with the books you plan to read. Decorate your space with stuffed mice, cats and pictures of cheese.

Introduction to theme: Mice are small mammals in the animal family of rodents. Some people think of them as pets. Some people think of them as pests. They don't see very well, but they can hear and smell extremely well. Sometimes mice try to get into houses to get warm and to find food, but it's not so good to have mice in your house because they can do damage and spread disease. The mice in books, in movies and on television are usually pretty nice mice. Can you think of a mouse you might have seen on TV or in a movie? Today we'll read about mice, play a cat and mouse game, make a mouse craft and eat a snack that looks like a mouse.

Song: "The Mouse in the House" to the tune of "The Wheels on the Bus":

The mouse in the house goes squeak, squeak, squeak,
squeak, squeak, squeak,
squeak, squeak, squeak,
The mouse in the house goes squeak, squeak, squeak
All through the day.

Game: Cat and mouse

Materials needed: Stuffed mouse and stuffed cat. Advance preparation: None. At storytime: Children and adults in a circle. Start the mouse being passed around, then the cat. The object is to see if the cat can catch the mouse so everyone needs to pass them quickly.

Alternative Games

Cat and mouse bounce. You'll need a stuffed cat, stuffed mouse, parachute or large tablecloth. At storytime, use the parachute or large cloth tablecloth to bounce a stuffed cat and mouse on it, trying to bounce them off.

Find the mice. Cut mouse shapes from colored construction paper and hide them in children's area. Have the children be cats and go find the mice and bring them back to you. Or at Halloween time buy packages of small toy mice that are often sold as party favors.

What does the mouse whisper? Whisper a phrase such as "The mouse loves green cheese" to the adult or child next to you. Then that person whispers it to the person next to him/her. Include the adults and have the phrase go around the circle until the last person announces what they think the phrase was.

Craft: Mouse shapes

Materials needed: Black construction paper sheets for background, red, blue, yellow, green, orange construction paper, glue sticks. Advance preparation: Cut shapes from construction paper. Squares and circles for bodies, triangles for heads, circles for ears and eyes, rectangles for arms, hands, legs, feet, triangles for tails. At storytime: Have children glue down shapes to make mice such as those in *Mouse Shapes* by Walsh.

Mouse shapes pieces.

Alternative Crafts

Mouse finger puppet. Cut grey, white or brown construction paper nine by twelve sheets into four pieces, then fold lengthwise and cut curve on open side to look like mouse. Punch holes in top rear of curve. Cut pink circles about one-inch diameter. Cut yarn in six-inch lengths. Cut tiny circles of black construction paper. Glue open back seam together. Grey, white or brown construction paper, pink construction paper, black construction paper, brown or black yarn, small google eyes, hole punch, scissors,

Mouse shapes.

glue sticks. Glue on google eyes and pink circles to form ears. Tie on yarn piece to look like tail. Glue on tiny black circle for nose.

Mouse and cheese. Cut yellow construction paper rectangles and punch out circles to look like Swiss cheese. Cut egg-shaped mouse body, two circles for ears and tail from brown or grey construction paper. Cut small black circle for nose. Have children glue mouse pieces together, add google eyes, then glue mouse to cheese piece. Could add cord tied to cheese in order to hang.

Foam mouse stick puppet. Cut an oval and two smaller circles out of sheet foam. Glue the oval to a craft stick as the body and the two smaller circles to the oval as ears. Glue on google eyes and a mini pom pom as the nose, as well as a piece of yarn for the tail.

Heart mouse. Cut heart shape from construction paper and use that as the mouse's head. Draw two eyes, a nose and mouth and attach a yarn tail at the heart point by punching a hole.

Snack: Strawberry mouse

Materials needed: Fresh strawberries, mini chocolate chips, slivered almonds, paper plates, red licorice laces, cheese such as Swiss. Advance preparation: Cut small slice off one side of strawberries so they will sit flat when on their sides. Poke a hole in the back of each strawberry to make it easier to insert the licorice tail. Cut licorice into three-inch long lengths. Cut cheese into small wedges. At storytime: Place a strawberry, three mini chocolate chips, one licorice lace, two slivered almonds and one cheese wedge on a plate.

Strawberry mouse.

Have the children place one chip as the nose and two as eyes. The almonds are ears and the licorice is the tail. Place the cheese in front of the mouse.

Alternative Snacks

White mice cupcakes. Cupcake iced in white. Add pink jellybean or red M&Ms or red Skittle for nose, two chocolate chips or brown M&Ms for eyes. Necco wafers for ears or flattened marshmallows. Add licorice lace for tail.

Mouse nibbles. Any kind of small crackers, small vegetables, small fruit pieces. Mice will eat just about anything, but will nibble at it. Have the children pretend to be mice when they eat the snack and take little nibbles.

Mouse cookies. Bake round sugar cookies with two small cookies attached as ears. Decorate at storytime with white icing, red candy nose, brown candy eyes, and licorice string whiskers.

Cracker mouse. Using a large round cracker for the mouse head, spread with cream cheese, use small twisted pretzels as two ears, pretzel sticks as whiskers and raisins as eyes, nose and mouth.

SUGGESTED BOOKS

Anderson, Heidi. *Goodnight Tiny Mouse.* 28 pages. 2009. Tate Publishing & Enterprises. The tiny mouse has a hard time finding a quiet place in the forest to sleep.

Barbey, Beatrice. *Meow Said the Mouse*. 40 pages. 2005. Parallax Press. A circular book that begins with a thirsty mouse who turns into a cat after drinking the cat's milk.

Becker, Bonny. *A Bedtime for Bear*. 48 pages. 2010. Candlewick Press. Very funny story about Bear trying to get to sleep with his bubbly overnight guest Mouse.

Becker, Bonny. *A Birthday for Bear*. 56 pages. 2009. Candlewick Press. Bear doesn't want to celebrate his birthday but Mouse wants to have a party.

Becker, Bonny. *The Sniffles for Bear*. 32 pages. 2011. Candlewick Press. Bear doesn't feel well and doesn't want Mouse to cheer him up.

Becker, Bonny. *Visitor for Bear*. 56 pages. 2008. Candlewick Press. Bear doesn't want any visitors, but Mouse comes over and insists on hanging around.

Brett, Jan. *Town Mouse Country Mouse*. 32 pages. 2002. Penguin Group. After trading houses, the town mouse and the country mouse discover that there's no place like home.

Burkert, Rand. *Mouse and Lion*. 32 pages. 2011. A telling of the Aesop's fable where the mouse helps the lion and later the lion returns the favor.

Chaconas, Dori. *One Little Mouse*. 32 pages. 2002. Penguin Group. A counting and rhyming story about a little mouse who goes looking for another home.

Dachman, Adam. *The Player Piano Mouse*. 32 pages. 2008. Player Piano Mouse Productions. A talented mouse discovers a musical gift by chewing holes.

Fleming, Denise. *Lunch*. 32 pages. 1996. Henry Holt & Co. The hungry mouse keeps on eating until his belly won't hold another bite.

George, Lindsay Barrett. *Inside Mouse, Outside Mouse*. 40 pages. 2006. HarperCollins Publishers. The mice go on a trip going up and down, inside and out and finally meet in the middle.

Gravett, Emily. *Little Mouse's Big Book of Fears*. 32 pages. 2008. Simon & Schuster Children's Publishing. Little Mouse, who's afraid of everything, records her fears in this notebook.

Henkes, Kevin. *Chrysanthemum*. 32 pages. 1991. HarperCollins Publishers. When Chrysanthemum starts school, the other children make fun of her name.

Henkes, Kevin. *Wemberley Worried*. 32 pages. 2000. HarperCollins Publishers. Wemberley the mouse worries about everything, especially the first day of school.

King-Smith, Dick. *A Mouse Called Wolf*. 96 pages. 1999. Random House Children's Books. Wolfgang Amadeus Mouse shares his musical gift with a widowed concert pianist.

Kirk, Daniel. *Library Mouse*. 32 pages. 2007. Abrams. Sam the library mouse writes stories and leaves them for the library patrons, who want to know who the mysterious writer is.

Kirk, Daniel. *Library Mouse: A Friend's Tale*. 32 pages. 2009. Abrams. The second in the series about Sam the library mouse, this time dealing with a little boy who needs a partner for a book making assignment.

Kirk, Daniel. *Library Mouse: A World to Explore*. 32 pages. 2010. Abrams. The third in a series about Sam the library mouse, this time exploring how to research a subject and overcome fears.

Kleven, Elisa. *Welcome Home Mouse*. 32 pages. 2010. Ten Speed Press. Stanley the elephant clumsily knocks down Mouse's house but tries to make amends.

Lionni, Leo. *Alexander and the Wind-Up Mouse*. 40 pages. 1991. Random House Children's Books. Collage artwork showing a real mouse that envies a mechanical mouse.

Lionni, Leo. *Frederick*. 32 pages. 1990. Random House Children's Books. Frederick daydreams while the other mice are gathering food for the winter. But when winter comes he entertains them to get them through the dreary months.

Lionni, Leo. *Geraldine, the Music Mouse*. 32 pages. 2009. Random House Children's Books. Geraldine the mouse finds a statue made of cheese that plays music. What can she do when her friends want to eat the cheese?

Low, Alice. *Blueberry Mouse*. 24 pages. 2004. Mondo Publishing. Everything is blue, including the house made of blueberries, which Blueberry Mouse causes some trouble for herself by starting to nibble on. Rhyming text.

McFarland, Lyn Rossiter. *Mouse Went Out to Get a Snack*. 32 pages. 2005. Farrar, Straus & Giroux. While searching for a snack, Mouse finds a big feast but has difficulty getting it back to his mouse hole.

Monks, Lydia. *Eeeek, Mouse!* 32 pages. 2010. Egmont USA. Full of mouse holes and surprises.

Numeroff, Laura Joffe. *If You Give a Mouse a Cookie*. 32 pages. 1985. HarperCollins Publishers. If you give a mouse a cookie, he'll want some milk. If you give him some milk, he'll want something else, and on and on in a circle until you come back to the cookie.

Numeroff, Laura Joffe. *If You Take a Mouse to School.* 32 pages. 2002. HarperCollins Publishers. If you take a mouse to school, he'll want your lunchbox, then he'll want a sandwich, and on and on in a circle until you come back to the school. A story that starts and ends with taking a mouse to school.

Numeroff, Laura Joffe. *If You Take a Mouse to the Movies.* 40 pages. 2000. HarperCollins Publishers. If you take a mouse to the movies, he'll want some popcorn, then he'll want to string it, and on and on in a circle until you come back to the movie. A Christmas time story that starts and ends with taking a mouse to the movies.

Riley, Linnea. *Mouse Mess.* 32 pages. 1997. Scholastic. Cut paper artwork depicts a story of a mouse who makes a mess in the kitchen when getting snacks.

Schoenherr, Ian. *Cat and Mouse.* 40 pages. 2008. HarperCollins Publishers. Cat and Mouse are friends, but they still like to play chase.

Smith, Jeff. *Little Mouse Gets Ready.* 32 pages. 2009. Raw, Junior. Mouse has a lot to do before he's ready to go visit the barn.

Thompson, Lauren. *Mouse's First Fall.* 32 pages. 2006. Simon & Schuster Children's Publishing. Mouse learns all about the fall season.

Thompson, Lauren. *Mouse's First Snow.* 32 pages. 2005. Simon & Schuster Children's Publishing. Mouse loves the snow and winter season.

Thompson, Lauren. *Mouse's First Spring.* 32 pages. 2005. Simon & Schuster Children's Publishing. Mouse is enchanted by the beauty of spring.

Thompson, Lauren. *Mouse's First Summer.* 32 pages. 2004. Simon & Schuster Children's Publishing. The Fourth of July in summer is brought to life in this book about Mouse.

Urban, Linda. *Mouse Was Mad.* 40 pages. 2009. Houghton Mifflin Harcourt Trade & Reference Publishers. Which animal knows the best way to be mad? The bear that stomps? The bobcat that screams? Or the quiet and still mouse?

Vandine, JoAnn. *Little Mouse's Trail Tale.* 24 pages. 1995. Mondo Publishing. One dark night a little mouse follows a trail to a trap.

Waber, Bernard. *Do You See A Mouse?* 32 pages. 1996. Houghton Mifflin Harcourt Trade & Reference Publishers. Everyone at the Park Snoot Hotel denies that there is a mouse, but he appears in every picture on every page of the book.

Waber, Bernard. *The Mouse That Snored.* 32 pages. 2004. Houghton Mifflin Harcourt Trade & Reference Publishers. Rhyming text about a very quiet family with a very noisy mouse.

Walsh, Ellen Stoll. *Mouse Count.* 32 pages. 2010. Houghton Mifflin Harcourt Trade & Reference Publishers. Learn about counting with the mice.

Walsh, Ellen Stoll *Mouse Paint.* 32 pages. 1995. Houghton Mifflin Harcourt Trade & Reference Publishers. A lesson about colors told by mice getting into the paint.

Walsh, Ellen Stoll *Mouse Shapes.* 32 pages. 2011. Houghton Mifflin Harcourt Trade & Reference Publishers. Learn about shapes, creativity and cooperation with the mice.

Williams. Rozanne Lanczak. *City Mouse and Country Mouse.* 16 pages. 1998. Creative Teaching Press. City Mouse and Country Mouse decide to change places to see if they'd like to live differently.

Wood, Audrey. *The Little Mouse, the Red Ripe Strawberry and the Big Hungry Bear.* 32 pages. 1984. Child's Play International Limited. The mouse and the bear like strawberries.

Yee, Wong Herbert. *Eek! There's a Mouse in the House.* 32 pages. 1995. Houghton Mifflin Harcourt Trade & Reference Publishers. It starts with a mouse but escalates with each animal being sent in to catch the mouse, making more and more trouble.

Young, Ed. *Seven Blind Mice.* 36 pages. 2012. Penguin Group. Seven blind mice discover different parts of an elephant and argue about its appearance.

Foods

Advance planning: To plan for this storytime, find a theme-related song to play during craft and snack times, like "Food Glorious Food" from the musical *Oliver.* You will also want to select a poem, such as "A Pizza the Size of the Sun," by Jack Prelutsky (find it at www.lifeinaskillet.com), along with the books you plan to read. Decorate your space with a poster of My Plate, the new government food pyramid replacement, some fake or real fruit or a toy fruit assortment.

Introduction to theme: There are many different kinds of foods. Everyone needs food to live and grow. It's important to eat lots of healthy foods. Some different kinds of healthy foods are foods that are made from plants like wheat, corn and oats — things like bread and cereal, vegetables — can someone name a kind of vegetable? Fruits — how about naming your favorite fruit? Milk, yogurt, cheese — those are dairy foods, and protein foods like meat and beans. It's also important to get some exercise every day. What do you do for exercise? Do you have a favorite food? what is it? Someone made up a good way for us to plan good amounts of all the kinds of foods we should eat every day and they called it "My Plate," which is a special plate that shows the different types of foods we should eat and how much of our plate those types of foods should cover (print a large image of My Plate from www.choosemyplate.gov and show the children the big picture). The vegetable and grain portions of the plate are the biggest and then fruits and protein next bigger and dairy a little smaller. In general, good food advice that the government gives us is: enjoy food but eat less; avoid oversized portions; make half your plate fruits and vegetables; drink water instead of sugary drinks; switch to fat-free or low-fat (1 percent) milk; compare sodium in foods; make at least half your grains whole grains. Today we'll read about food, play a food game, make a food craft and eat a snack.

Song: Sing and do the hand motions for "I'm a Little Teapot," which can be found at www.lyrics007.com.

Game: Name the fruits and vegetables

Materials needed: Pictures of many different kinds of fruits and vegetables. Advance preparation: Find pictures of fruits and vegetables on the Internet and print them and cut them into individual pictures. Suggested foods: Fruits — strawberry, pear, apple, cherry, lemon, watermelon, peach, grape, orange, banana pineapple; Vegetables — broccoli, carrots, sweet potato, onion, cauliflower, corn, mushroom, celery, peas, cucumber, potato. At storytime: Hold up each individual picture and let the children name the fruits and vegetables.

Alternative Games

Match game. You will need poster board, matching pairs of pictures of foods printed from Internet, paper. Make a rectangular grid on poster board. Glue down pictures of matching pairs of foods in a random order. Cover each space with a small piece of paper and let the children take turns trying to match them by lifting the pieces of paper.

Popcorn counting. Give each child a large paper plate full of popcorn. Have them separate them into piles of 1, 2, 3, 4, 5. Then direct them to eat the popcorn from different piles, but not in counting order. For instance, have them eat the pile of 3 first, then 1, then 4, 2, 5.

Food bingo. Make up bingo cards with pictures of different foods. Could use some kind of food as markers if desired, such as Smarties candies, then let the children eat their markers when the game is over.

Craft: My Plate food plan

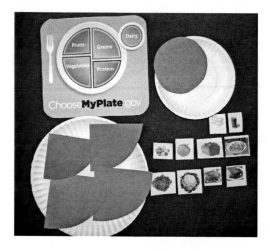

My plate food plan pieces.

My plate food plan.

Peas and carrots cupcake.

Materials needed: Large white paper plates, small white paper plates, glue sticks, red, orange, green, purple and blue construction paper, photos printed from Internet of different kinds of food that fit the plate: fruits, grains, vegetables, protein and dairy.

Advance preparation: Cut the partial circles and circle for the plates from the construction paper, print and cut out photos of the different types of food. At storytime: Have the children create a copy of the new My Plate government food plan. Start with a large white paper plate and have partial circles in the same colors and sizes as the real My Plate. Have a small white paper plate and blue circle for dairy. They could draw on those colored parts an example of a type of food that they like that's in that category, or you could have sample photos printed from the Internet or cut from magazines from which they could choose and glue.

Alternative Crafts

Construction paper watermelon slice. Need red construction paper, green tissue paper, black construction paper, glue sticks. Cut 6-inch circles from the red construction paper and cut the circles in half. Cut 2-inch squares of green tissue paper. Snip tiny pieces of black construction paper. Have the children crumple the pieces of green tissue paper and glue them to the outside of the circle to look like watermelon rind. Glue small pieces of black pieces to red to look like seeds.

Sheet foam watermelon Slice. Could use sheet foam for the red and black and put a magnet piece on the back to turn it into a refrigerator magnet. If using sheet foam will need to use foam glue. It's easiest to apply it with cotton swab after pouring the glue into a paper plate.

Chenille stem flowers. Give each child three different colored pieces of chenille stems plus three green stems. Have them wind the three stems into bloom shapes, like a cloverleaf, and then attach the green stems.

Snack: Peas and carrots cupcake

Materials needed: Cupcakes, icing, plastic knives, paper plates, green Skittles candies, orange Starburst candies, sharp knife. Advance preparation: Bake cupcakes. Cut Starburst candies into four pieces to look like carrots. At storytime: Place cupcake on paper plate with plastic knife. Put a dollop of icing on top of the cupcake. Place about 12 green Skittles on the plate and about five pieces of orange Starburst. Have the children ice the cupcakes and then place the Skittles and Starburst on top to look like peas and carrots.

Alternative Snacks

Cereal necklace. Froot Loop cereal or other colorful ring cereal, string, masking tape, scissors. Cut 24-inch lengths of string. Wrap small piece of masking tape around one end to make it stiff and easier to thread through the cereal. Have the children thread cereal on the string. Once the necklace is long enough, tie it off and cut off the masking tape.

Burger cupcakes. Bake yellow and chocolate cupcakes, twice as many yellow as chocolate since you'll need two yellow pieces for every chocolate piece. Slice them horizontally in thirds. Tint white icing yellow, green and red. Place one yellow cupcake piece, top it with one chocolate cupcake piece, let the children decorate with yellow "mustard," red "ketchup," green "lettuce." Top with another yellow cupcake piece.

SUGGESTED BOOKS

Benjamin, Alan. *Let's Eat*. 26 pages. 1992. Simon & Schuster Children's Publishing. A simple text baby book that shows eating words in both English and Spanish.

Berenstain, Jan, and Mike Berenstain. *The Berenstain Bears Go Out to Eat*. 32 pages. 2009. HarperCollins Publishers. The bear family goes out to eat, and even that is an adventure.

Berenstain, Stan, and Jan Berenstain. *The Bears' Picnic*. 72 pages. 1966. Random House Children's Books. Rhyming text has Papa taking the family out for a picnic.

Berenstain, Stan, and Jan Berenstain. *The Berenstain Bears and Too Much Junk Food*. 32 pages. 1985. Random House Children's Books. Papa and the cubs are getting chubby so Mama helps them cut down on the junk food they eat.

Block, Serge. *You Are What You Eat*. 32 pages. 2010. Sterling Publishing Co. A boy who doesn't like to try new foods gets some confusing words of advice.

Brown, Marcia. *Stone Soup: An Old Tale*. 48 pages. 1987. Simon & Schuster Children's Publishing. Soldiers get villagers to make soup by making them think that they can make it from stones.

Butler, M. Christina. *Who's Been Eating My Porridge?* 32 pages. 2004. ME Media. Because Little Bear hates porridge, his parents set out his bowl for "Scary Bear," and someone always comes along and eats it, convincing Little Bear that there really is a Scary Bear.

Carle, Eric. *Today Is Monday*. 32 pages. 1997. Penguin Group. Each day of the week brings a new food, until on Sunday all the children of the world can come and eat.

Carle, Eric. *The Very Hungry Caterpillar*. 22 pages. 1969. Philomel Books. Follows a caterpillar as he eats his way through a lot of food.

Child, Lauren. *I Will Never Not Ever Eat a Tomato*. 32 pages. 2000. Candlewick Press. A fussy eater tries different foods after her brother convinces her they are from outer space.

dePaola, Tomie. *Pancakes for Breakfast*. 32 pages. 1978. Houghton Mifflin Harcourt Trade & Reference Publishers. Wordless picture book about the difficulty a woman has making pancakes.

dePaola, Tomie. *The Popcorn Book*. 32 pages. 1984. Holiday House. Information about popcorn.

Ehlert, Lois. *Eating the Alphabet: Fruits and Vegetables from A to Z*. 40 pages. 1989. Houghton Mifflin Harcourt Trade & Reference Publishers. Teaches upper and lower case letters while showing many different fruits and vegetables.

Ehlert, Lois. *Growing Vegetable Soup*. 30 pages. 1987. Harcourt Inc. Simple text and illustrations feature a father and child growing vegetables and making soup.

Frederick, Heather Vogel. *Babyberry Pie*. 29 pages. 2010. Harcourt Children's Books. A recipe for making a "babyberry" pie from picking him to putting him in pie crust covers in bed.

Freymann, Saxton. *Fast Food*. 32 pages. 2006. Scholastic. Photos of real fruits and vegetables in clever sculptures.

Freymann, Saxton. *How Are You Peeling? Foods with Moods.* 48 pages. 2004. Scholastic. Photos of real food depicting different moods.

Harley, Bill. *Sitting Down to Eat.* 32 pages. 2000. August House Publishers. A young boy's snack time is disturbed by a parade of different animals.

Hicks, Barbara Jean. *Monsters Don't Eat Broccoli.* 40 pages. 2009. Alfred A. Knopf. Monsters insist that they don't like broccoli.

Hoban, Russell. *Bread and Jam for Frances.* 32 pages. 1993. HarperCollins Publishers. Frances wants to only eat bread and jam for all her meals.

Hoberman, Mary Ann. *The Seven Silly Eaters.* 40 pages. 2000. Houghton Mifflin Harcourt Trade & Reference Publishers. A mother gives in to her picky eating children until one day they surprise her with something on her birthday that solves her problem.

Hornsey, Chris. *Why Do I Have to Eat Off the Floor?* 24 pages. 2005. Little Hare Publishers. The dog asks many questions including why he has to eat his food off the floor.

Hutchins, Pat. *The Doorbell Rang.* 24 pages. 1989. HarperCollins Publishers. Ma has made a dozen delicious cookies. It should be enough, except the doorbell keeps ringing and more and more friends come to eat them.

Jenkins, Emily. *Sugar Would Not Eat It.* 40 pages. 2009. Random House Children's Books. A little boy finds a kitten and brings it home but the kitten is a very picky eater.

Kann, Victoria. *Pinkalicious.* 40 pages. 2006. HarperCollins Publishers. When Pinkalicious eats too many pink cupcakes, she turns pink.

Landry, Leo. *Eat Your Peas, Ivy Louise!* 32 pages. 2005. Houghton Mifflin Harcourt Trade & Reference Publishers. Louise imagines her peas are a circus.

Lipson, Eden Ross. *Applesauce Season.* 28 pages. 2009. Roaring Book Press. A family makes applesauce with many different types of apples.

Litchfield, Jo. *Sam the Chef.* 21 pages. 2004. Usborne Publishing. Fimo clay models in this book about a chef cooking a meal for a famous rock star.

Lloyd, Sam R. *Yummy Yummy Food for My Tummy.* 32 pages. 2009. ME Media. Sharks in the water are keeping chimps that live on nearby islands apart when they'd like to get together to share food.

Lobel, Arnold. *Mouse Soup.* An I Can Read Book. 64 pages. 1983. HarperCollins Publishers. Weasel is ready for dinner, and poor Mouse is it. Can he stop Weasel from eating him for dinner?

Numeroff, Laura. *If You Give a Cat a Cupcake.* 32 pages. 2008. HarperCollins Publishers. If you give a cat a cupcake, he'll want some sprinkles. If you give him some sprinkles, he'll want something else, and on and on in a circle until you come back to the cupcake.

Numeroff, Laura. *If You Give a Moose a Muffin.* 32 pages. 1991. HarperCollins Publishers. If you give a moose a muffin, he'll want some jam. If you give him some jam, he'll want something else, and on and on in a circle until you come back to the muffin.

Numeroff, Laura. *If You Give a Mouse a Cookie.* 40 pages. 1985. HarperCollins Publishers. If you give a mouse a cookie, he'll want some milk. If you give him some milk, he'll want something else, and on and on in a circle until you come back to the cookie.

Numeroff, Laura. *If You Give a Pig a Pancake.* 32 pages. 1998. HarperCollins Publishers. If you give a pig a pancake, she'll want some syrup. If you give her some syrup, she'll want something else, and on and on in a circle until you come back to the pancake.

Oud, Pauline. *Eating with Lily and Milo.* 28 pages. 2010. Clavis Publishing. Lily and Milo go off to a picnic but something happens to the food before they get there.

Rosenthal, Amy Krouse. *Little Pea.* 36 pages. 2005. Chronicle Books. If Little Pea doesn't eat his sweets, he'll get no vegetables for dessert!

Rubin, Adam. *Dragons Love Tacos.* 40 pages. 2012. Penguin Group. Dragons love all kinds of tacos. But when they eat hot salsa, watch out.

Scheer, Julian. *Rain Makes Applesauce.* 32 pages. 1964. Holiday House. A book of silly talk.

Schoenherr, Ian. *Read It Don't Eat It.* 32 pages. 2009. HarperCollins Publishers. If you're holding a book, you should open it and find out what's inside it.

Seuss, Dr. *Green Eggs and Ham.* 72 pages. 1960. Random House Children's Books. Sam-I-Am wants to get another creature to try some green eggs and ham.

Sharmat, Mitchell. *Gregory the Terrible Eater.* 32 pages. 1980. Simon & Schuster Children's Publishing. Gregory is a goat who wants to eat eggs and juice for breakfast, unlike the other goats.

Shaw, Nancy E. *Sheep Out to Eat.* 32 pages. 1995. Houghton Mifflin Harcourt Trade & Reference Publishers. The sheep go to a tea shop, wreak havoc and are asked to leave.

Shields, Carole Diggory. *Food Fight.* 32 pages. 2002. Chronicle Books,. Late at night the food in the fridge comes alive.

Souhami, Jessica. *Piglet's Picnic: A Story About Food and Counting.* 28 pages. 2010. Lincoln, Frances Limited. Piglet invites her friends to a picnic and asks them to bring their favorite foods.

Swain, Gwenyth. *Eating.* 24 pages. 1999. Lerner Publishing Group. A simple board book that shows toddlers eating.

Urbanovic, Jackie. *Duck Soup.* 29 pages. 2008. HarperCollins Children's Books. Duck tries to make soup but his friends are too helpful.

Willems, Mo. *The Pigeon Finds a Hot Dog.* 32 pages. 2004. Hyperion Books for Children. Pigeon finds a hot dog but someone else wants to share it.

Wilson, Karma. *Whopper Cake.* 31 pages. 2007. Margaret K. McElderry Books. Grandfather makes a whopper of a cake for grandmother.

Wright, Al. *Do Mice Eat Rice?* 32 pages. 2005. Tuttle Publishing. Rhymes that help to teach children how to read.

Yolen, Jane. *How Do Dinosaurs Eat Their Food?* 40 pages. 2005. Scholastic. Young dinosaurs need to learn how to behave at the table.

July

Beach Vacation

Advance planning: To plan for this storytime, find a theme-related song to play during craft and snack times, like "Surfin' Safari," by the Beach Boys, or "Hot Hot Hot," by Buster Poindexter. You will also need "Limbo Rock," by Chubby Checker for the limbo game. You will also want to select a poem, such as "Seaside," by Shirley Hughes (find it at www.k12.hi.us/~shasincl/poems_ocean.html), along with the books you plan to read. Decorate your space with beach towels, beach balls, sand toys, a big umbrella, flip flops, sunglasses.

Introduction to theme: Show the beach towels and sand toys. Have you ever seen the ocean? Or a big lake? Or even a river that has a sandy beach? Lots of people like to take vacations at the beach. There's fun to be had there, building sandcastles, swimming, maybe having a picnic. Some people surf on surfboards in the waves, walk along the beach to collect shells, go on boats. It can be fun to spend time in the sun, but remember to wear sunscreen so you don't get a sunburn! Today we'll read about fun on the beach, play a game that you might play there, make a flower lei craft like people on the beaches of Hawaii might wear and have a snack that looks like the beach.

Song: "I'm a Little Fishy," to the tune of "I'm a Little Teapot":

> I'm a little fishy (put hands together in front and move like swimming)
> See me swim
> Look at my fish tail (put hands behind rear end and wiggle like a tail)
> Look at my fin (put hands behind head and move like a fin)
> When I'm in the ocean
> I have fun (go back to hands together in front and move like swimming)
> I swim and swim
> All day in the sun. (put head back and close eyes like basking in the sun)

Game: Beach party limbo

Materials needed: Pool noodle or broomstick, music like "Limbo Rock," which can be downloaded from the Internet. Advance preparation: None. At storytime: Have two parents hold the pool noodle, play the music and lead the kids under it. Have the noodle lowered and go back and forth as long as you want to play.

Alternative Games

Beach volleyball. Need a pool noodle or broomstick. Have two parents hold the pool noodle and have the children hit the beach ball over it back and forth.

Story shell. Have a large shell and pass it from child to child while chanting, "Story shell, story shell, what is the story you want us to tell?" and ask each child to add a sentence to the story that you started about a trip to the beach.

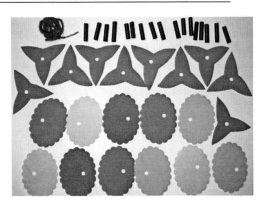

Construction paper lei pieces.

Craft: Construction paper lei

Materials needed: Construction paper, straws, yarn, hole puncher, tape, scissors, large scalloped oval punch. Advance preparation: Cut lots of construction paper flowers using the large scalloped oval punch in many colors. Cut lots of leaves in various shades of green. Punch holes in center of leaves and flowers. Cut yarn in 24-inch lengths and tape one end so that it's easier to thread through the paper. Tie a knot in the other end of the yarn. Cut straws into one-inch pieces. At storytime: Thread leaves and flowers alternating with straw pieces until long enough to go around a child's neck. Tie ends together, cut off taped end.

Alternative Crafts

Beach collage. Supplies needed: sand, construction paper, white glue, cotton swabs, small shells. Buy package of small shells at craft store. Let children use swabs to spread white glue on construction paper. Could use blue construction paper to look like the ocean. Give them a small cup of sand to sprinkle onto the glue and smooth it down with fingers. Glue small shells onto the sand.

Construction paper lei.

Ocean mural. Have large butcher paper and let everyone draw an ocean mural with crayons or markers. Display it in the storytime area.

Seaweed scene. Have crepe paper streamers and let the children tear and crumple lengths of it and then glue it down to blue construction paper and draw some sea creatures hiding in the seaweed.

Snack: Pudding beach scene

Materials needed: Vanilla pudding, clear plastic cups, graham crackers, vanilla wafers or oatmeal cookies (something that looks like sand when crushed), Teddy Grahams or Gummy Bears, Fruit by the Foot or Fruit Rollups, cocktail umbrellas, spoons, paper plates. Advance preparation:

Pudding beach scene.

Crush cookies or wafers to look like sand. Cut Fruit by the Foot or Rollups in 1 ½-inch lengths (to look like beach towels for the Teddy Grahams or Gummy Bears). At storytime: Put the vanilla pudding in the cups. Place some crushed vanilla wafers or cookies on top of the pudding. Put the pudding cup on a paper plate along with the fruit piece and the bear. Have the children place the piece of Fruit by the Foot or Fruit Rollup on top of the "sand," lay the Teddy Graham or Gummy Bear on top of the sand, place the umbrella over the bear like a beach umbrella.

Alternative Snacks

Beach scene cupcake. Supplies needed: cupcakes, icing, Teddy Graham or Gummy Bears, Fruit by the Foot. Make icing blue. Let children spread blue icing on cupcake, then put piece of Fruit by the Foot to look like beach towel and lay bear on top.

Ocean and sand. Blue Jell-O topped with graham cracker crumbs.

SUGGESTED BOOKS

Apperley, Dawn. *In the Sand*. 14 pages. 1996. Little, Brown & Co. A beginning book that reveals things that happen in the sand.

Ashman, Linda. *To the Beach*. 32 pages. 2005. Houghton Mifflin Harcourt Trade & Reference Publishers. Rhyming text tells of a family's attempts to get to the beach that's delayed by repeated trips to get forgotten items.

Berry, Lynne. *Duck Dunks*. 32 pages. 2008. Henry Holt & Co. Five little ducks are having a day in the sand and the sun.

Bond, Michael. *Paddington at the Beach*. 32 pages. 2009. HarperCollins. Paddington Bear has a counting adventure with seagulls at the beach.

Briant, Ed. *Day at the Beach*. 32 pages. 2006. HarperCollins Publishers. A perfect day at the beach except Alice and Baxter don't have their swimsuits.

Cooper, Elisha. *Beach*. 40 pages. 2006. Scholastic. Building sandcastles and collecting seashells on the beach is described in poetic text.

Docherty, Thomas. *To the Beach*. 40 pages. 2009. Candlewick Press. A little boy looks out his window on a rainy day and imagines going to the beach.

Ehrlich, H.M. *Gotcha, Louie!* 32 pages. 2002. Houghton Mifflin Harcourt Trade & Reference Publishers. Louie plays a game with his parents where they chase him.

Gamble, Adam. *Goodnight Beach*. 20 pages. 2007. Our World of Books. Shows what's going on at the beach during the day. Designed as a bedtime book.

Hennessey, B.G. *Corduroy Goes to the Beach*. Based on the books by Don Freeman. 20 pages. 2006. Penguin Group. Corduroy and his friends head to the beach in this lift the flap book.

Huneck, Stephen. *Sally Goes to the Beach*. 38 pages. 2008. Abrams. Sally the Labrador Retriever goes to the beach.

Keller, Holly. *Miranda's Beach Day*. 32 pages. 2009. HarperCollins Publishers. Miranda has a great day at the beach building a sand castle but is sad when the tide comes in.

Kotzwinkle, William. *Walter the Farting Dog Banned from the Beach*. 32 pages. 2009. Penguin Group. Walter's gas problem once again saves the day after annoying some of the guests on the beach.

Lester, Alison. *Magic Beach*. 32 pages. 2006. Allen and Unwin. Rhymes and make believe stories of adventures on the beach.

Lies, Brian. *Bats at the Beach*. 32 pages. 2006. Houghton Mifflin Harcourt Trade & Reference Publishers. Bats have a great time on a moonlit night at the beach.

Lionni, Leo. *On My Beach There Are Many Pebbles*. 32 pages. 1995. HarperCollins Publishers. This book challenges the reader to look more closely at ordinary things.

Mathers, Petra. *Lottie's New Beach Towel*. 32 pages. 2001. Simon & Schuster Children's Publishing. Lottie doesn't realize how useful her new beach towel will be.

Morgan, Sally. *Me and My Dad*. 24 pages. 2011. Little Hare Books. While spending a day on the beach, a child learns his dad isn't afraid of much of anything.

Oud, Pauline. *Going to the Beach with Lily and Milo*. 28 pages. 2011. Clavis Publishing. Lily the rabbit and her mischievous mouse friend

Milo have so many decisions about what to take to the beach that they might not ever get there.

Oxenbury, Helen. *Beach Day.* 14 pages. 1981. Penguin Group. An event filled day at the beach with a spirited child.

Oxenbury, Helen. *Tom and Pippo on the Beach.* 24 pages. 1997. Candlewick Press. Daddy makes sure Tom wears his sun hat but Tom wants Pippo to have a sun hat too.

Paratore, Coleen Murtagh. *Catching the Sun.* 32 pages. 2008. Charlesbridge Publishing. A boy and his mom get up to see the sun rise on the beach.

Rabe, Tish. *Clam I Am!: All About the Beach.* 48 pages. 2005. From the Cat in the Hat Learning Library. Random House Children's Books. Many sea creatures make guest appearances on the Fish Channel show.

Rey, H.A., and Margret Rey. *Curious George Goes to the Beach.* 32 pages. 1999. Houghton Mifflin Harcourt Trade & Reference Publishers. George feeds the seagulls at the beach but they fly away with something valuable.

Rockwell, Anne. *At the Beach.* 24 pages. 1991. Simon & Schuster Children's Publishing. There are so many things to do at the beach, including build sand castles and have a picnic.

Roosa, Karen. *Beach Day.* 40 pages. 2001. Houghton Mifflin Harcourt Trade & Reference Publishers. A family's trip to the beach told in rhyming text.

Rosen, Michael. *Bear Flies High.* 32 pages. 2009. Bloomsbury Publishing. Bear and friends go to an amusement park at the beach.

Rosenberg, Liz. *Moonbathing.* 1996. Harcourt Publishing. Boys play at the beach at night.

Schertle, Alice. *All You Need for a Beach.* 32 pages. 2004. Houghton Mifflin Harcourt Trade & Reference Publishers. Everything you need for

a trip to the beach including a surprise ending to the story.

Sierra, Judy. *Ballyhoo Bay.* 40 pages. 2009. Simon & Schuster Children's Publishing. The beach is in danger of being developed with a big building but the community bands together to stop it.

Soman, David. *Ladybug Girl at the Beach.* 40 pages. 2010. Penguin Group. Lulu uses her alter ego Ladybug Girl to help conquer her fear of the ocean.

Stanley, Mandy. *At the Beach.* 12 pages. 2002. Kingfisher. Introduces words related to the beach.

Stewart, Sarah. *The Friend.* 48 pages. 2004. Farrar, Straus & Giroux. A little girl looked after by a housekeeper who knows that there's more to life than just cleaning and cooking and they take some time to walk on the beach.

Wallace, Nancy Elizabeth. *Shells! Shells! Shells!* 32 pages. 2007. Marshall Cavendish Corporation. A little wordy for reading, but has nice cut paper artwork and good photos of shells.

Walling, Sandy Seeley. *A Day at the Beach: A Seaside Counting Book from One to Ten.* 28 pages. 2003. Abernathy House Publishing. A counting book.

Watt, Melanie. *Scaredy Squirrel at the Beach.* 32 pages. 2008. Kids Can Press Limited. Scaredy Squirrel decides to build his own beach.

Wells, Rosemary. *Beach Day. B*ased on the characters from Rosemary Wells. All Aboard Reading Level 1. 32 pages. 2011. Penguin Group. Max and Ruby build sand castles at the beach.

Yektai, Niki. *Bears at the Beach.* Presents numbers ten to twenty using illustrations showing bear families at the beach.

Ziefert, Harriet. *Buzzy's Big Beach Book.* 40 pages. 2006. Blue Apple Books. Buzzy is scared of the ocean when he goes to the beach.

Moon and Space

Advance planning: To plan for this storytime, find a theme-related song to play during craft and snack times, like "Harvest Moon," by Neil Young. You will also want to select a poem, such as "The Star," by Ann Taylor and Jane Taylor (find it at www.poetry foundation.org), along with the books you plan to read. Decorate your space with any kind of space toys you might have, like rockets or spaceships. A model of the moon, or posters of the solar system and the moon. You could paint a large rocket on the side of a big cardboard box, cut out an opening for the children to look through and they could pretend to be in the rocket.

Introduction to theme: We live on a big place called planet Earth. The moon that we see up in the sky goes around Earth in a circle. Demonstrate this by having the children sit or stand in a circle with you standing in the center of the circle holding a large ball that represents the Earth. Have the children pass around a small ball that represents the moon. It takes about a month for the moon to go around the earth and while it's moving the sun's light on it makes us see different shapes and sizes of it and sometimes we can't see it at all. It looks very bright but it doesn't have any light of its own — it's the sun that shines its light on the moon. The moon is much smaller than Earth. No one lives there. The air there isn't breathable, there's no water and the temperature can be very cold in some places and very hot in others. More than 40 years ago the Apollo 11 spacecraft landed on the moon and astronauts walked on its surface. The craft that have gone up into space since then are called space shuttles and they look kind of like an airplane. They just recently stopped flying the shuttles and they took one to a museum in Washington. Today we'll read about the moon and space, play a moon and space game, make a rocket craft and eat a moon and space snack.

Song: Raffi's "Mister Sun" but changed to "Mr. Moon." Lyrics can be found at www.metro lyrics.com. Movements to go along with the song:

- Hold hands up fingers make round shape over head
- Wiggle fingers coming down
- Point to self
- Hide face behind hands
- Point to children
- Hands up round shape
- Wiggle down

Game: Rockets to the moon

Materials needed: Picture of the moon. Several rocket pictures. Advance preparation: A poster-sized picture of the moon, and several pictures of rockets printed on card stock (cut these into smaller pieces if necessary, so that one image is on each piece). At storytime: Place the poster-sized picture of the moon on the floor. Give each child a card with a picture of a rocket. Give each child a turn trying to fly the rockets to the surface of the moon. Repeat as often as time allows, and fun continues.

Alternative Games

Low gravity dance. Explain that on the moon there is less gravity or force pulling on us so that we feel like we weigh less and can move around in a different way (demonstrate). Play some space-age sounding music and encourage the children to move around as though in low gravity.

Let's go to the moon. Tell the children you're going to pack for a trip to the moon. Go around and ask each child what they would like to take. It can be anything at all. Write down their list and post it.

Space race. Have the children line up next to each other, single-file. Hand the first child a large ball, such as a soccer or playground ball, and tell him/her it's the moon. When you say, "Blast off!" he passes the ball overhead to the player behind him/her, who then passes the ball under his/her legs to the player behind him/her. The ball continues to be passed over and under to the back of the line. The last player then runs to the front of the line with the ball and starts the process over again. Play continues until every player has been to the front of the line and the line is back to its original lineup.

Craft: Space shuttle

Materials needed: White computer paper, empty paper towel rolls, black, red and orange tissue paper, tape, glue sticks. Advance preparation: Roll up the computer paper lengthwise around the empty paper towel rolls. and tape. Cut large rounded corner triangles of computer paper. Cut black tissue paper sheets in quarters, tear or cut orange and red tissue paper into strips. At storytime: Have the children tape or glue the large triangles to the rolled up paper to form the shuttle. Run some glue around the inside of one end of the paper towel roll and then crumple the black tissue paper into a ball and put it in there to form the nose. Tape or glue multiple strips of red and orange to the inside of the other end to look like flames.

Space shuttle pieces.

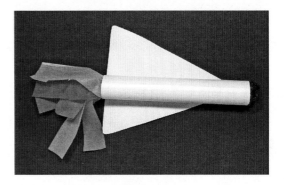

Space shuttle.

Alternative Crafts

Moon and stars mobile. Have moon and stars shapes pre-cut out of paper and holes punched. Let the children color the moon and stars and then tie yarn or string to the hole. Tie the other end to a dowel rod or paper towel roll with different lengths of string or yarn so that the shapes hang at different places.

Night sky scene. Give the children black or dark blue construction paper for the background and then white moon shapes and white crayons to attach and color in the stars.

Sky sponge painting. Cut sponges (or buy ready-made) into star, circle and crescent shapes. Let the children dip them into paint and stamp onto large pieces of construction paper.

Snack: Moon cupcake

Materials needed: Cupcakes, blue icing, fruit rollups or fruit by the foot, paper plates, plastic knives. Advance preparation: Color icing blue, cut crescent moon shapes from the Fruit Roll Ups or Fruit by the Foot. At storytime: Give each child a cupcake, a dol-

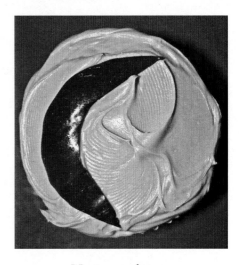

Moon cupcake.

lop of icing and a moon shape. Have them spread the icing on their cupcake and then place the crescent moon in the "sky."

Alternative Snacks

Moon phase Oreos. Give each child several Oreo sandwich cookies. Have them take the cookies apart and then carve different moon shapes into the filling.

Crescent moon cookie. Cut sugar cookies into crescent shape with cookie cutter.

Astronaut food. Serve pudding in Ziploc bags that you have inserted a small straw into (or cut off a corner) and explain that the astronauts eat food this way.

Space snacks. Get some actual dried food that astronauts would eat in space. Usually available at science centers.

Star fruit. Also called carambola, this fruit looks like a star.

SUGGESTED BOOKS

Alexander, Martha. *Maggie's Moon.* 24 pages. 1982. Dial. A little girl and her dog set out to capture the moon and bring it home with them.

Arnold, Tedd. *Green Wilma, Frog in Space.* 32 pages. 2009. Penguin Group. Green Wilma the frog gets taken accidentally by alien visitors.

Asch, Frank. *Happy Birthday Moon.* 32 pages. 2000. Aladdin. Bear loves the moon so much he wants to give him a birthday present.

Asch, Frank. *Moon Bear.* 32 pages. 1978. Atheneum. Worried that the moon is growing smaller each night, Bear decides to do something about it.

Asch, Frank. *Moongame.* 32 pages. 2000. Aladdin. Bear plays hide and seek with the moon.

Asch, Frank. *The Sun Is My Favorite Star.* 32 pages. 2008. Houghton Mifflin Harcourt. There's no star as wonderful as the sun.

Banks, Kate. *And If the Moon Could Talk.* 32 pages. 1998. Farrar, Straus and Giroux. What the moon might see and say if it could talk.

Barner, Bob. *Stars! Stars! Stars!* 32 pages. 2002. Chronicle Books. Simple rhyming text describes stars and planets.

Barton, Byron. *I Want to Be an Astronaut.* 32 pages. 1992. HarperCollins Publishers. It's fun to fly aboard the space shuttle.

Bell, Robert A. *My First Book of Space: Developed in Conjunction with NASA.* 48 pages. 1985. Simon & Schuster Books for Young Readers. An informative first book about our solar system.

Benjamin, Cynthia. *I Am an Astronaut.* 24 pages. 1996. Barron's Educational Series. Young twins visit the space museum and discover what it might be like to be part of the space program.

Branley, Franklyn M. *The Planets in Our Solar System.* 32 pages. 1998. HarperCollins Publishers. Introduces the planets in our solar system with full color illustrations.

Brett, Jan. *Hedgie Blasts Off.* 32 pages. 2006. Penguin Group. Hedgie wants to be an astronaut and travel into space.

Brown, Margaret Wise. *Goodnight Moon.* 32 pages. 1977. HarperCollins Publishers. Goodnight room, goodnight moon ... and all the things in it.

Carle, Eric. *Draw Me a Star.* 40 pages. 1992. Penguin Group. A young artist draws a star, and a sun, and more.

Carle, Eric *Papa, Please Get the Moon for Me.* 40 pages. 1991. Simon & Schuster Books for Young Readers. Monica wants to play with the moon, so her papa sets out to get it for her.

Carroll, James Christopher. *The Boy and the Moon.* 32 pages. 2010. Sleeping Bear Press. A young boy slips out of his house to celebrate the mystery and magic of the night.

Chorao, Kay. *Lemon Moon.* 32 pages. 1983. Holiday House. Grams has difficulty believing her grandchild who says that the moon grew stars and a cat ate the stars with a spoon.

Curtis, Carolyn. *I Took the Moon for a Walk.* 32 pages. 2004. Barefoot Books. A young boy goes exploring with his friend the moon.

Fowler, Allan. *So That's How the Moon Changes Shape.* 32 pages. 1992. Scholastic Library Publishing. A simple explanation of why the moon changes shape each month.

Gibbons, Gail. *The Moon Book.* 28 pages. 1998. Holiday House. Describes the moon and phases and discusses how we've observed and explored it.

Gibbons, Gail. *The Planets*. 32 pages. 2007. Holiday House. Basic information about each planet in our solar system.

Goldberg, Myla. *Catching the Moon*. 40 pages. 2007. Scholastic. An old woman wants to catch the man in the moon.

Graham, Ian. *My Book of Space*. 48 pages. 2001. Roaring Book Press. Join the crew and prepare to explore the galaxy.

Henkes, Kevin. *Kitten's First Full Moon*. 40 pages. 2004. HarperCollins Publishers. The moon is full and kitten is hungry.

Hort, Lenny. *How Many Stars in the Sky*. One night when Mama is away, Daddy and child look for a place to see the stars in the night sky.

Jeffers, Oliver. *The Way Back Home*. 32 pages. 2008. Penguin Group. A boy flies a plane into outer space.

Keats, Ezra Jack. *Regards to the Man in the Moon*. 40 pages. 2009. Penguin Group. With the help of his imagination, his parents and some junk, Louie and his friends travel through space.

Levitin, Sonia. *Who Owns the Moon?* 34 pages. 1973. Parnassus Press. When they run out of other things to argue about, three farmers argue about who owns the moon.

McNulty, Faith. *If You Decide to Go to the Moon*. 48 pages. 2005. Scholastic. If you decide to go to the moon, this book will tell you how to get there and what to do after you land.

Milbourne, Anna. *Mouse on the Moon*. 10 pages. 2002. Usborne Publishing Limited. Rhythmic language and look through holes for hiding and revealing pictures.

Mitton, Tony. *Roaring Rockets*. 24 pages. 2000. Kingfisher. A simple explanation of how rockets work, where they travel and what they do.

Moché, Dinah L. *If You Were an Astronaut*. 24 pages. 1999. Random House Children's Books. Describes the activities of the astronauts aboard the space shuttle.

Nelson, Nigel. *Looking into Space*. 13 pages. 1998. Reader's Digest Children's Publishing. A first look at the wonders of space.

Nicholls, Paul. *Blast Off to the Moon*. 12 pages. 2009. Penguin Group. Filled with facts about astronauts and space.

Olsen, Ib Spang. *The Boy in the Moon*. 30 pages. 1977. Parents Magazine Press. Seeing its reflection in water, the man in the moon thinks it's another moon and sends the boy in the moon to get it.

Preston, Edna Mitchell. *Squawk to the Moon, Little Goose*. 32 pages. 1985. Penguin Group. Little Goose disobeys her mother one night and almost gets swallowed by the fox.

Rabe, Tish. *There's No Place Like Space: All About Our Solar System*. 48 pages. 1999. Random House Children's Books. Dr. Seuss's Cat in the Hat introduces Sally and Dick to the planets, stars and moon.

Rey, H.A. *Curious George and the Rocket*. 20 pages. 2001. Houghton Mifflin Harcourt. George has an adventure where he becomes the first space monkey.

Rockwell, Anne. *Our Stars*. 24 pages. 2002. Houghton Mifflin Harcourt. A simple introduction to the stars, planets and outer space.

Schachner, Judith. *Skippyjon Jones Lost in Spice*. 32 pages. 2009. Penguin Group. Skippyjon knows that Mars is red because it's covered in red pepper.

Simon, Seymour. *Planets Around the Sun*. 32 pages. 2002. Chronicle Books. A simple introduction to the planets in our solar system.

Sweeney, Joan. *Me and My Place in Space*. 32 pages. 1999. Random House Children's Books. A young astronaut leads readers on a tour of the solar system.

Trapani, Iza. *Twinkle, Twinkle, Little Star*. 26 pages. 1998. Charlesbridge Publishing. A little girl wishes on a star.

Udry, Janice May and Sendak, Maurice. *The Moon Jumpers*. 32 pages. 1959. HarperCollins Publishers. As the sun grows tired, four children and a cat dance and play in the moonlit garden.

Wilkinson, Philip. *Spacebusters: The Race to the Moon*. 48 pages. 1998. DK Publishing. This is the story of the US trying to make sure man makes it to the moon by the end of the 1960's.

Wilson, Lynn. *What's Out There? A Book About Space*. 32 pages. 1993. Penguin Group. What's the sun made of? What causes night and day? Why does the moon change shape? All the answers and more in a simple introduction to the solar system.

Yaccarino, Dan. *Zoom! Zoom! Zoom! I'm Off to the Moon*. 40 pages. 1997. Scholastic Inc. Five Four Three Two One Blastoff I'm on my way to the moon.

Yoon, Salina. *What's in Space?* 10 pages. 2006. Penguin Group. Easy rhymes and slides that pull; this board book explains colors and what's outside the spaceship window.

Numbers

Advance planning: To plan for this storytime, find a theme-related song to play during craft and snack times, like "Ten Cookies," by Cookie Monster from *Sesame Street*. You will also want to select a poem, such as the classic "One, Two, Buckle My Shoe" (pretending to do the activities in the rhyme), along with the books you plan to read. Decorate your space with a poster of numbers 0–9, blocks with numbers on them, and any kinds of toys you can find with numbers, like fire trucks or police cars, for example.

Introduction to theme: Numbers are used for counting and measuring. Numbers can be used to label things, to put things in order. Do you know some numbers? Like zero? How about counting with me: 1-2-3-4-5-6-7-8-9-10. What are some ways we use numbers every day? How old are you? What time is it? What's your address? When your parents cook, do they use numbers? The temperature of the oven, the timer to tell how long to cook something, the spoons and measuring cups .. they all use numbers. Today we'll read about numbers, play a number game, make a number craft and eat a number snack.

Song: "Ten Little Numbers" to the tune of "Ten Little Indians":

> One little two little three little numbers
> Four little five little six little numbers
> Seven little eight little nine little numbers
> Ten little numbers
> Ten little nine little eight little numbers
> Seven little six little five little numbers
> Four little three little two little numbers
> One little number

Game: Bingo

Materials needed: Bingo cards with numbers one through five on them, something to use as markers, such as pennies. Advance preparation: Print bingo cards and call pieces. You can find bingo cards online at many different free websites. At storytime: Distribute bingo cards and markers. Call numbers from the call pieces that you made. Play until a card is filled.

Alternative Games

Musical numbered chairs. Make a row of chairs and place a piece of paper with a number from one to 10 on each chair. Give each child a number card with a number one to 10. Play music and when the music stops have each child find a chair with the corresponding number. Before the music starts again, have them exchange their number with someone else. No one is out, no chairs are removed.

Number blocks. Fill a pail with number blocks. Have the children stand in a line and count them, telling them to remember their number. Then have them find the matching number in the pail.

Number ball. Have the children sit on the floor in a circle. As they roll a ball from one to another, have each child call out a number. Start by counting. As they get to higher numbers, switch the game to random numbers and let them call out any number.

Count your pennies. Have a large container of some kind of object, such as pennies. Ask each child to count out a certain number of the objects, in quantities up to five.

Counting cups. Give each child a set of five paper cups, with the numbers one through five and the corresponding number of dots drawn on the outside of each cup. Then ask them to put in each cup the corresponding number of items that you've got spread out on the floor. Could be any items, such as pennies, cotton balls, etc.

Craft: Five fish in a bowl

Materials needed: Blue construction paper for bowls, several other construction paper colors for fish, scissors, glue sticks, crayons. Advance preparation: Cut out fish bowls and fish, enough for each child to have five fish. At storytime: Give each child five construction paper fish and a construction paper fishbowl that is large enough for them to glue the fish on. If desired, have them glue the fish bowl onto a background piece of paper, then glue the fish on the bowl. Have them number the fish one to five.

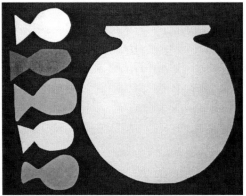

Five fish in a bowl pieces.

Alternative Crafts

Dot to dot. Find a simple dot to dot drawing on the internet or in a book. Have the children draw the lines to connect the dots and then color in the drawing.

Number caterpillar. Give each child 12 construction paper circles and a background sheet of paper. Have them glue the circles to the paper to look like a caterpillar. The first circle is the head and they should draw a face on it, complete with antennae. Then the second circle is number one, and each subsequent circle is numbered up to 10. The last circle is the tail end. Have them draw feet on each circle. When finished, count the numbered circles.

Five fish in a bowl.

Number animals. Either have the child draw a large number (any number) on a piece of construction paper or give them a cut out number to glue onto background paper. Then have them turn the number into some kind of animal by drawing with crayons.

Snack: Counting salad

Materials needed: Lettuce, carrots, celery, olives, cheese, dressing, forks, small plates. Advance

Counting salad.

preparation: Cut up the lettuce into bite sized leaves, the carrots into round slices, the celery into bite sized pieces, the olives slices, the cheese cubed. At storytime: Count out the parts of the salad as you prepare the plates: five lettuce leaves, four carrot slices, three celery slices, two olives, one cheese cube. Put a little dressing on it and serve.

Alternative Snacks

Number food. Find some cookies, gummies or other snacks that are shaped like numbers.

Counting snacks. Make a mixture of snack foods in numbered quantities, like five Chex cereal pieces, four pretzel sticks, three M&Ms, two raisins, one mini marshmallow and serve on small plates. You could also serve clementine oranges that are easy to peel. Encourage the children to count the number of segments in their orange as they take it apart and then eat it.

SUGGESTED BOOKS

Anno, Mitsumasa. *Anno's Counting Book.* 32 pages. 1986. HarperCollins Publishers. A counting book that shows the growth of a village.

Baker, Alan. *Gray Rabbit's 1, 2, 3.* 24 pages. 1999. Kingfisher. Gray Rabbit discovers numbers.

Baker, Alan. *Little Rabbits' First Number Book.* 32 pages. 2001. Kingfisher. Encourages children to learn to count.

Boynton, Sandra. *Fifteen Animals.* 24 pages. 2008. Workman Publishing Co. Counting 15 Bobs in one book.

Boynton, Sandra. *One Two Three!* 24 pages. 1993. Workman Publishing Co. Hippos, cats, pigs and cows lead readers from a quiet one to a loud ten and back again.

Bridwell, Norman. *Count on Clifford.* 32 pages. 1987. Scholastic. Everyone is invited to learn to count at Clifford's birthday party.

Brown, Margaret Wise. *Count to 10 with a Mouse.* 2012. Parragon Inc. Gentle illustrations help children get started counting.

Carle, Eric. *1, 2, 3 to the Zoo: A Counting Book.* 32 pages. 1998. Penguin Group. Animals riding on a train to the zoo help children learn to count.

Carle, Eric. *The Very Hungry Caterpillar.* 32 pages. 1981. Penguin Group. A hungry caterpillar eats his way through the days of the week.

Carpenter, Stephen. *Three Billy Goats Gruff.* 24 pages. 1998. HarperCollins Publishers. The three goat brothers outwit the terrible troll.

Crews, Donald. *10 Black Dots.* What can you do with 10 black dots? A counting book shows one can make a sun, two can make fox eyes, etc.

Dahl, Michael. *On the Launch Pad: A Counting Book About Rockets.* 24 pages. 2004. Picture Window Books. A countdown from twelve to one as a space shuttle awaits liftoff.

Ehlert, Lois. *Fish Eyes: A Book You Can Count On.* 40 pages. 1992. Houghton Mifflin Harcourt. Brightly colored fish give an introduction to counting.

Falconer, Ian. *Olivia Counts.* 12 pages. 2002. Atheneum Books for Young Readers. Olivia the piglet presents numbers 1–10.

Feelings, Muriel. *Moja Means One: A Swahili Counting Book.* 32 pages. 1976. Penguin Group. Numbers 1–10 in Swahili accompany pictures of African life.

Galdone, Paul. *The Three Bears.* 32 pages. 1985. Houghton Mifflin Harcourt. Once upon a time, there were three bears who lived in the woods until Goldilocks happened in.

Galdone, Paul. *The Three Little Kittens.* 40 pages. 2011. Houghton Mifflin Harcourt. Rhyme about the three little kittens who lost their mittens.

Giganti, Paul. *How Many Snails?* 32 pages. 1984. HarperCollins. A young child goes for a walk and wonders about the amount and variety of things along the way.

Gruetzke, Mary. *There Were Ten in the Bed.* 24 pages. 2005. Scholastic. Sing along and count down the puppies taking up space on the bed.

Hill, Eric. *Spot Can Count.* 24 pages. 2003. Penguin Group. Count with Spot in this lift the flap book.

Hoban, Tana. *Count and See.* 40 pages. 1972. Simon & Schuster Books for Young Readers. There are things to count all around you.

Hutchins, Pat. *The Doorbell Rang.* 24 pages. 1989. HarperCollins Publishers. Ma has made a dozen cookies, which should be enough, but the doorbell keeps ringing and more friends keep coming.

Johnston, Tony. *10 Fat Turkeys*. 32 pages. 2004. Scholastic. A silly rhyming story teaches counting backwards.

Katz, Karen. *Counting Kisses*. 32 pages. 2001. Margaret K. McElderry Books. Counting down from ten with each kiss helps baby get to sleep.

Kubler, Annie. *Ten Little Monkeys*. 16 pages. 2001. Child's Play Intl Ltd. Rhyme introduces readers to number skills.

Lionni, Leo. *Inch by Inch*. 32 pages. 1995. HarperCollins Publishers. An inchworm is proud of his ability to measure anything.

Litwin, Eric. *Pete the Cat and His Four Groovy Buttons*. 40 pages. 2012. HarperCollins Publishers. Count down with Pete as his shirt loses its buttons.

Martin, Bill, Jr., Michael Sampson and Lois Ehlert. *Chicka Chicka 1, 2, 3*. 40 pages. 2004. Simon & Schuster Books for Young Readers. One hundred and one numbers climb the apple tree.

Merriam, Eve. *12 Ways to Get to 1*. 40 pages. 1996. Aladdin. 1–2–3–4–5–6–7–8–9–10–12. What happened to 11?

Norman, Kim. *Ten on the Sled*. 24 pages. 2010. Sterling. All the animals are having fun speeding down the hill on the sled until they start falling off one by one.

Otoshi, Kathryn. *One*. 32 pages. 2008. KO Kids Books. Readers learn about numbers, counting and colors.

Otoshi, Kathryn. *Zero*. 32 pages. 2010. KO Kids Books. Zero is a big round number with a hole in her middle. She thinks she has no value.

Paparone, Pamela. *Five Little Ducks*. 32 pages. 2005. North-South Books. The ducklings go off to play and their numbers dwindle until their mother calls them all back.

Pinczes, Elinor J. *Inchworm and a Half*. What's a fraction? Several worms use their varying lengths to measure vegetables in the garden.

Scarry, Richard. *Richard Scarry's Best Counting Book Ever*. 44 pages. 2010. Sterling. Willy Bunny has learned to count and so will the children who read this book.

Schachner, Judith. *Skippyjon Jones 1-2-3*. 12 pages. 2008. Penguin Group. The Siamese cat who thinks he's a Chihuahua can count!

Seibert, Patricia. *The Three Pigs*. 32 pages. 2002. School Specialty Publishing. Each little pig is confident that his house is the strongest.

Seuss, Dr. *One Fish Two Fish Red Fish Blue Fish*. 63 pages. 1960. Random House Children's Books. Not just about numbers but introduces children to rhyming riddles.

Seuss, Dr. *Ten Apples Up on Top*. 58 pages. 1961. Random House Children's Books. A lion, a dog and a tiger are having a contest to see how many apples they can balance on their heads.

Tudor, Tasha. *1 Is One*. 48 pages. 2000. Simon & Schuster Books for Young Readers. Rhyming verse and pictures introduce numbers one to twenty.

Walsh, Ellen Stoll. *Mouse Count*. 32 pages. 1995. Houghton Mifflin Harcourt. Counting forward and backward in a suspenseful story.

Wells, Rosemary. *Max Counts His Chickens*. 32 pages. 2007. Penguin Group. The Easter Bunny hides the contents of their Easter baskets, so Max and Ruby go on a hunt and count as they find their marshmallow chicks.

Wise, William. *10 Sly Piranhas: A Counting Story in Reverse*. 32 pages. 2004. Penguin Group. Ten piranhas are swimming in a river, but one by one they disappear.

Ziefert, Harriett. *A Dozen Ducklings Lost and Found: A Counting Story*. 32 pages. 2003. Houghton Mifflin Harcourt. A mother duck wants to show off her ducklings but suddenly realizes that some of them are missing.

Monkeys

Advance planning: To plan for this storytime, find a theme-related song to play during craft and snack times, like "No More Monkeys Jumping on the Bed," by Baby Genius. You will also want to select a poem, such as "Monkey Me (Children)," by C.J. Heck (find it at www.authorsden.com), along with the books you plan to read. Decorate your space with stuffed monkeys, posters of monkeys, palm trees, jungle sounds, a pith helmet, green streamers to look like jungle vines.

Introduction to theme: Monkeys are kinds of animals called primates. There are very small monkeys, barely bigger than my hand, and there are very large monkeys that are bigger than I am. There are lots of different kinds of primates; some that you might know are Chimpanzees or Gorillas. Have you been to the zoo? Did you see a monkey or primate there? Which kind? Today we'll read about monkeys, play a monkey game, make a monkey mask craft and eat a jungle snack.

Song: "Going to the Zoo," by Raffi, which can be found at www.metrolyrics.com.

Game: Monkey in the middle

Materials needed: beach ball or playground ball. Advance preparation: None. At storytime: Have the children stand in a circle an arm's length apart and start with you in the middle of the circle as the "monkey." The object of the game is for the children to pass the ball by gently tossing it around the circle with letting the monkey in the middle get it. If the monkey intercepts the ball, the person who was passing it becomes the next monkey.

Alternative Games

Monkey see, monkey do. Everyone stand. Make movements with parts of your body and encourage the children to imitate what you do. You could raise your arms (one at a time or both), lift your feet (one at a time or both), turn around in a circle, put your hands on your hips, wave, put your hands on your head, and tap your toes. Let the children initiate movements and have everyone copy them, one at a time.

Paper plate monkey mask pieces.

Monkey sounds. Make a sound like a monkey. Let each child take a turn making a monkey sound and then encourage them all to do it at once.

Barrel of monkeys. If you can get a bunch of Barrels of Monkeys, dump them out on the tablecloth and let the children try to hook as many together as they can.

Craft: Paper plate monkey mask

Materials needed: Large paper plates, brown crayons, black crayons, light and black colored construction paper, scissors, glue sticks, craft sticks, hot glue gun. Advance preparation: Cut ear, eye and muzzle shapes from the light colored and black construction paper. Hot glue the craft sticks to the back of the paper plates as holders. At storytime: Have the children color the big paper plates brown. Glue light ear pieces to black ear piece. Draw a happy face on the muzzle to look like nostrils and a mouth. Then glue the eyes, ears and muzzle to the paper plate. It would be fun for everyone to hold up their monkey masks when they're finished and make monkey sounds.

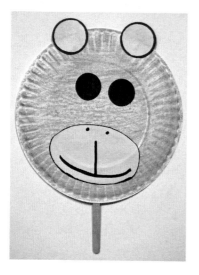

Paper plate monkey mask.

Alternative Crafts

Swinging monkey. Cut two construction paper circles to make a monkey body and head and tape or glue them together. Cut a chenille stem in half to make monkey arms. Staple one end of each chenille stem to the monkey body (curl end to hold to staple) and curl the other end around a straw. Twirl the monkey on the straw.

Monkey puppet on a stick. Have four dark brown circle shapes, one large for face and two small for ears. Glue the large circle to a craft stick and the two small circles to the large circle. Have a tan circle smaller than the face to glue on as the muzzle. Use crayons to draw the mouth, nose and eyes.

Monkey paper bag puppet. Use brown paper lunch bags for the puppets and glue on large brown circle for face, smaller tan circle for muzzle and two even smaller brown circles for ears. Add additional circles or use crayons to draw eyes and nose. Draw mouth.

Snack: Jungle mix

Materials needed: Something for individual servings like small paper plates, cups, Ziploc bags or bowls, large spoon, large bowl, spoons, animal crackers, dried banana chips, nuts, shredded coconut, chocolate chips, and other dried fruits and nuts of your choice. Advance preparation: None. At story-time: One by one, pour each ingredient into the large bowl while explaining that it is jungle mix — some foods that monkeys might like to eat, and some that are found in the jungle where the monkeys live and the animal crackers represent many of the animals found in the jungle. Spoon a portion into individual servings and serve with a spoon.

Jungle mix.

Alternative Snacks

Monkey bread. Ingredients for one tube pan (12 servings): ½ cup granulated sugar; 1 teaspoon cinnamon; 2 cans (16.3 oz. each) large size refrigerated buttermilk biscuits; 1 cup firmly packed brown sugar; ¾ cup butter or margarine, melted. Directions: (1) Heat oven to 350°F. Lightly grease 12-cup fluted tube pan with shortening or cooking spray. In large storage plastic food bag, mix granulated sugar and cinnamon. (2) Separate dough into 16 biscuits; cut each into quarters. Shake in bag to coat. Arrange in pan. In small bowl, mix brown sugar and butter; pour over biscuit pieces. (3) Bake 28 to 32 minutes or until golden brown and no longer doughy in center. Cool in pan 10 minutes. Turn upside down onto serving plate; pull apart to serve. Serve warm.

Bananas on a stick. Peel bananas and cut in half, so that each child has a half. Have them put the banana on a Popsicle stick and place some chocolate sprinkles on a paper plate for each child to roll the banana in before eating. Could also dip in melted chocolate. This works better if the bananas are placed on the sticks and frozen in advance.

Monkey cupcakes. Ice cupcake in chocolate. Add large vanilla wafer for muzzle, two mini vanilla wafers for ears. Use chocolate chips or chocolate candies for eyes and nose and licorice string for mouth.

SUGGESTED BOOKS

Alborough, Jez. *Hug*. 32 pages. 2009. Candlewick Press. Expressive Animals tell a story that's a tribute to love and belonging.

Andreae, Giles. *The Chimpanzees of Happytown*. 32 pages. 2006. Scholastic. The Chimpanzees of Drabsville are unhappy until a traveler comes along and plants a tree that makes the whole town blossom.

Aylesworth, Jim. *Naughty Monkeys*. 32 pages. 2006. Penguin Group. Rhyming text about 26 little monkeys looking after themselves.

Beard, Alex. *Monkey See, Monkey Draw*. 48 pages. 2011. Abrams. The monkeys are playing ball when their ball goes into a scary cave. Will they be able to overcome their fear and retrieve the ball? Not only do they go in, but in the cave they find artwork and they learn to make art too.

Blackford, Andy. *The Hungry Little Monkey*. 24 pages. 2011. Crabtree Publishing Company. A monkey can't figure out how to open the banana he wants to eat and needs help from other animals.

Browne, Anthony. *Little Beauty*. 32 pages. 2008. Candlewick Press. Once there was a gorilla who had everything he needed, except a friend.

Carter, Abby. *Maggie's Monkeys*. 32 pages. 2009. Candlewick Press. A family of monkeys has moved into the refrigerator. At least that's what Maggie says.

Christelow, Eileen. *Five Little Monkeys Bake a Birthday Cake*. 28 pages. 2005. Houghton Mifflin Harcourt Trade & Reference Publishers. The five little monkeys get up early to bake Mama a birthday cake.

Christelow, Eileen. *Five Little Monkeys Jumping on the Bed*. 32 pages. 1989. Houghton Mifflin Harcourt Trade & Reference Publishers. Right after saying goodnight, the monkeys start getting into trouble.

Christelow, Eileen. *Five Little Monkeys Sitting in a Tree*. 32 pages. 1991. Houghton Mifflin Harcourt Trade & Reference Publishers. Teaching numbers 1 through 5 through the monkeys' antics.

Donaldson, Julia. *Night Monkey Day Monkey*. 32 pages. 2008. Egmont Books Limited. Night Monkey and Day Monkey switch places to see what the other's life is like.

Dorling Kindersley. *Monkeys*. 32 pages. 2012. DK Publishing Inc. A DK Reader with photos and illustrations.

Durant, Alan. *I Love You Little Monkey*. 32 pages. 2006. Simon & Schuster Children's Publishing. Little Monkey tries to get Big Monkey to play, but there are chores to be done.

Fox, Mem. *Two Little Monkeys*. 32 pages. 2012. Simon & Schuster Children's Publishing. Two clever monkeys try to outwit a clever prowler.

Gibbons, Gail. *Gorillas*. 32 pages. 2012. Holiday House. Feeding habits, how they raise their young, their habitat and why so many live in zoos.

Gravett, Emily. *Monkey and Me*. 32 pages. 2008. Simon & Schuster Children's Publishing. A little girl and her toy monkey like to imitate other animals. Can you guess what animals they are?

Howe, James. *The Day the New Teacher Went Bananas*. 32 pages. 1987. Penguin Group. The new teacher turns out to be a gorilla.

Kaufman, Susanne. *I Love Monkey*. 36 pages. 2010. Compendium Publishing. Monkey keeps trying to be someone else, but ultimately realizes that it's best to be loved for who you are.

Koller, Jackie French. *One Monkey Too Many*. 32 pages. 2003. Houghton Mifflin Harcourt Trade & Reference Publishers. There is always one monkey too many with every thing the monkeys want to play with, starting with a bicycle.

Lucas, David. *Peanut*. 32 pages. 2008. Candlewick Press. A tiny monkey is afraid of everything until he becomes friends with a beetle.

MacLennan, Cathy. *Monkey Monkey Monkey*. 32 pages. 2009. Boxer Books, Limited. Little Monkey explores the jungle looking for monkey-monkey-monkey nuts.

Marcus, Oscar S. *Oscar: the Big Adventures of a Little Sock Monkey*. 32 pages. 2006. HarperCollins Publishers. Oscar goes on an adventure to help his friend Susie.

McGrory, Anik. *Quick Slow Mango*. 32 pages. 2011. Bloomsbury Publishing. A story about mangoes and silly monkeys.

Monroe, Chris. *Monkey with a Tool Belt*. 32 pages. 2007. Lerner Publishing Company. The monkey is captured but gets free using his tool belt.

Monroe, Chris. *Monkey with a Tool Belt and the Noisy Problem*. 32 pages. 2009. Lerner Publishing Company. Monkey is awakened by noises and after putting on his tool belt tries to figure out what the noises are.

O'Malley, Donough. *Monkey See, Monkey Do*. 32 pages. 2008. Lincoln, Frances Limited. The professor can't decide who should fly the rocket — the robot or the monkey.

Rathmann, Peggy. *Good Night Gorilla*. 40 pages. 2000. Penguin Group. The zookeeper doesn't realize the gorilla is following him on his night time rounds, letting out all the animals as they go.

Rex, Michael. *Furious George Goes Bananas*. 32 pages. 2010. Penguin Group. A parody of Curious George.

Rey, H.A., and Margret Rey. *Curious George*. There are many Curious George books. Any one of them could be used for this storytime theme.

Sanders-Wells, Linda. *Maggie's Monkeys*. 32 pages. 2009. Candlewick Press. Maggie's imagination has a family of monkeys moving into the refrigerator and her family goes along with the idea.

Schaefer, Carole Lexa. *Big Little Monkey*. 32 pages. 2008. Candlewick Press. Little Monkey gets up early and wants to play but everyone else is still sleeping or isn't the right playmate.

Sierra, Judy. *What Time Is It Mr. Crocodile?* 32 pages. 2007. Houghton Mifflin Harcourt Trade & Reference Publishers. A crocodile is outwitted by mischievous monkeys.

Slack, Michael H. *Monkey Truck*. 32 pages. 2011. Henry, Holt & Co. A monkey truck has fun and frolic looking for jungle bungles.

Slobodkina, Esphyr. *Caps for Sale*. 48 pages. 1987. HarperCollins Publishers. A peddler tries to outwit a band of mischievous monkeys.

Taylor, Barbara. *Apes and Monkeys*. 48 pages. 2007. Kingfisher. Learn about the lives of apes and monkeys.

Vere, Ed. *Banana!* 32 pages. 2010. Holt, Henry & Company. Two monkeys fighting over a banana have to learn to share.

Ward, Jennifer. *There Was an Old Monkey Who Swallowed a Frog*. 40 pages. 2010. Marshall Cavendish. A jungle rendition of the familiar song.

Watson, Richard Jesse. *The Boy Who Went Ape*. 40 pages. 2008. Scholastic. A misbehaving boy changes places with a chimp during a school field trip to the zoo.

Williams, Suzanne. *Ten Naughty Little Monkeys*. 32 pages. 2007. HarperCollins Publishers. One by one the monkeys do silly things in this rhyming text.

Trains

Advance planning: To plan for this storytime, find a theme-related song to play during craft and snack times, like "I've Been Working on the Railroad," by John Denver. You will also want to select a poem, such as "Steam Train," by Graeme King (find it at www.king-poetry.com), along with the books you plan to read. Decorate your space with a Brio train set or electric trains, pictures and posters of trains, an engineer's hat or whistle, overalls and bandana.

Introduction to theme: Have you ever seen a train? Ridden a train? Maybe at the zoo? Then you'll know that a train is a form of transportation where the cars are attached to each other and they move along a track pulled by an engine or locomotive. Most locomotives now are powered by diesel fuel, which is like the gas we use to run our cars, but in the past some used water that they heated to make steam. Who is the conductor? What are some of the things he says? (All aboard, tickets please, next stop). In cities there are trains that move on tracks that are attached to overhead wires and they are powered by electricity. Have you ever seen or ridden the Metro Link train? It's electric. What sounds do you think of when you see a train? Chugga, chugga. Or maybe toot toot? Can you make some train sounds with me? Chugga, chugga. Toot toot. Today we'll read about trains, play a train game, make a train craft and eat a train snack.

Song: "Down by the Station." Lyrics can be found at www.kidsongs.com.

Game: Let's be a choo choo train

Materials needed: None. Advance preparation: None. At storytime: Everybody line up behind you, putting hands on hips of person in front and go around walking in a shuffling manner slowly like a train, making train sounds, like chugga chugga with an occasional whistle Woo Woo.

Alternative Games

Train blocks. Empty out a large container of wooden blocks and show the children how they can make a train from the blocks. Then let them build their own trains.

Chair train. Line up chairs to look like a train, or alternately seat the children on the floor as though they're train passengers. You be the engineer and tell the children you're going on an adventure on a train. Animatedly describe the journey by talking about how the train moves, the sounds it makes, the scenery and decide where you're going and what will happen when you get there. You should plan the basics of the story in advance but let the children help with talking about what they see out the windows and making the train sounds and the speed and movement of the train.

Train stick puppet pieces.

Chugga, chugga, toot, toot. Duck, duck, goose game but with the children saying chugga, chugga, chugga until they reach the person they want to tag and then they say toot, toot.

Conductor says. Play like Simon says but saying conductor says instead. Try to include some train-related things, like train sounds or movement.

Coal toss. Make a big cardboard box look like a train engine. Let the children take turns tossing in black bean bags pretending they're coal to fuel the steam engine.

Craft: Train stick puppets

Materials needed: Blue, green, red, black, white construction paper, glue sticks, craft sticks. Advance preparation: Cut train-shaped backgrounds from white, blue rectangles, green squares, red triangles, black circles. At storytime: Glue shapes to background, then glue background to craft stick.

Alternative Crafts

Train scene. Cut construction paper shapes and glue to a background piece of construction paper to make a train scene. Could draw the tracks, add people and animals, trees, the sun.

Train stick puppet.

Toilet paper roll train. Paint toilet paper rolls in primary colors. Cut black circles from construction paper for wheels and punch a hole in the center of the wheel. Punch four holes in the toilet paper roll to attach the wheels using pipe cleaners as axles going through the roll and through the black circles and then folding over to hold. Tape a painted half toilet paper roll that's had the bottom cut to fit the curve of the other roll to one end to look like the cabin part of the engine.

Snack: Graham cracker train

Make a train from food. Rectangular graham cracker, half of graham cracker for square, marshmallow wheels, chocolate triangle for cowcatcher. Materials needed: Graham crackers, paper plates, marshmallows, chocolate bars. Advance preparation: Break some graham crackers in half to make square, cut chocolate bars into triangles.

At storytime: Give each child one whole graham cracker, one half graham cracker, two marshmallows and one triangular piece of chocolate bar. Have the children place shapes on plate to make train.

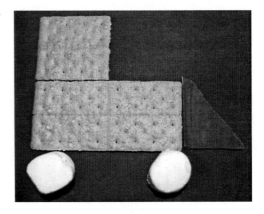

Graham cracker train.

Alternative Snacks

Swiss cake roll train. Use one whole chocolate Swiss cake roll for train engine body, add a half roll for the cab. Use gummy Life Savers for the wheels and a peanut butter cup (the mini unwrapped kind) for the smokestack. Can do this either standing up or it would be easier and use fewer candies if you lie it on its side.

Train cars. Square and rectangle crackers to make train engine and cars and carrot slices or cheese circles for the wheels.

Train cookies. Use a train-shaped cookie cutter to cut peanut butter and jelly or cheese sandwiches.

SUGGESTED BOOKS

Asch, Frank. *Short Train, Long Train*. 32 pages. 1992. Scholastic. Illustrations and brief text showing opposites.

Awdry, W. *Happy Birthday Thomas*. 32 pages. 1990. Random House Children's Books. Thomas thinks his friends have forgotten his birthday.

Awdry, W. *Wave Hello to Thomas*. 14 pages. 1993. Random House Books for Young Readers. A lift the flap book where children can tour with Thomas through the countryside.

Barkan, Joanne. *Locomotive*. 12 pages. 1992. Little Simon. A board book that introduces trains.

Barton, Byron. *Trains Board Book*. 34 pages. 1998. Harper Festival. Introduces young readers to the excitement of trains.

Barton, Chris. *Shark Vs. Train*. 40 pages. 2010. Little Brown Books for Young Readers. Shark and Train face off in multiple competitions.

Bee, William. *And the Train Goes...* 32 pages. 2007. Candlewick Press. A look at life on a train with sound words and surprises.

Berenstain, Jan, and Mike Berenstain. *The Berenstain Bears: All Aboard*. 32 pages. 2010. An I Can Read Book 1. HarperCollins Publishers. With the Berenstain Bear family on a steam train trip through Bear Country. Mama and Papa enjoy the scenery and the cubs want to learn about the train.

Blathwayt, Benedict. *Faster, Faster Little Red Train*. 25 pages. 2000. Random House. The Little Red Train must save the day when the train to Pebblecombe has broken down.

Boynton, Sandra. *Dog Train: A Wild Ride on the Rock and Roll Side*. 64 pages. 2005. Workman Publishing Company. A collection of songs. Features a bit of each song's lyric in a story. One of the stories is about dogs on a train.

Brown, Margaret. *Two Little Trains*. 32 pages. 2003. HarperCollins Publishers. Two little trains are heading west. One is shiny and new, the other old. Do they have anything in common?

Bunting, Eve. *Train to Somewhere*. 32 pages. 2000.

Houghton Mifflin Harcourt. Marianne travels west in the 1800's on the Orphan Train.

Burningham, John. *Hey Get Off Our Train*. 48 pages. 1994. Random House Children's Books. A boy sees environmental dangers as he takes a dream train trip around the world.

Burton, Virginia Lee. *Choo Choo: The Story of a Little Engine Who Ran Away*. 48 pages. 1988. Houghton Mifflin Harcourt. The adventures of a beautiful little train who decided to run away from her boring duties.

Chin, Oliver. *Timmy and Tammy's Train of Thought*. 32 pages. 2007. Immedium. Timmy and Tammy love trains so their parents treat them to a special train ride.

Crampton, Gertrude. *Tootle*. 24 pages. 2001. Golden Books. Tootle and the other little engines attend school to learn whistle blowing, puffing, screeching to a halt and the other skills necessary to be a locomotive.

Crews, Donald. *Freight Trains*. 26 pages. 1996. HarperCollins Publishers. The journey of a colorful train.

Crews, Donald. *Inside Freight Trains*. 12 pages. 2001. Greenwillow Books. In a sliding door board book children can see what's inside the freight train cars.

Crews, Donald. *Short Cut*. 32 pages. 1996. Greenwillow Books. The children know the freight train could come any time, but one night they decide to take a short cut on the train tracks anyway.

Ehrlich, Amy. *The Everyday Train*. 32 pages. 1977. Penguin Group. A little girl loves to watch the freight train pass her house.

Fleischman, Paul. *Time Train*. 32 pages. 1994. HarperCollins Publishers. On a class trip to Dinosaur National Monument, a class is taken back to prehistoric times.

Gibbons, Gail. *Trains*. 32 pages. 1988. Holiday House. Straightforward information about trains.

Gruney, John Steven. *Dinosaur Train*. 32 pages. 2002. HarperCollins Publishers. Jesse gets on board a mysterious dinosaur filled train that steams into his backyard one night at bedtime.

Harding, Deborah. *All Aboard Trains*. 32 pages. 1989. Penguin Group. All different kinds of trains with easy to read facts and realistic illustrations.

Highet, Alistair. *The Yellow Train*. 40 pages. 2001. The Creative Company. A young boy goes on a secret midnight ride on a train with his grandfather.

Ichikawa, Satomi. *My Little Train*. 40 pages. 2010. Penguin Group. The little train toots along taking his passengers wherever they want to go.

Lenski, Lois. *The Little Train*. 56 pages. 2000. Random House Children's Books. Engineer Small drives his train from Tinytown to the city and back.

Lewis, Kevin. *Chugga-Chugga Choo-Choo*. 32 pages. 2001. Hyperion. What works from dawn to dusk without a break? A very busy steam engine.

London, Jonathan. *A Train Goes Clickety Clack*. 32 pages. 2007. Henry Holt and Co. Trains are fast and sleek and make wonderful sounds.

McMullan, Kate. *I'm Fast*. 40 pages. 2012. Balzer & Bray. Can a freight train beat a speedy little race car to Chicago?

McNamara, Margaret. *The Whistle on the Train*. 16 pages. 2008. Hyperion Books for Children. A train version of the Wheels on the Bus.

McPhail, David M. *The Train*. 32 pages. 1990. Little, Brown and Company. When Matthew lets his baby brother drive the train, he crashes it.

Mitton, Tony. *Terrific Trains*. 24 pages. 2000. Kingfisher. Big trains, small trains, old trains, new trains.

Peet, Bill. *The Caboose Who Got Loose*. 48 pages. 1980. Houghton Mifflin Harcourt. Katy Caboose is tired of being last.

Piper, Watt. *The Little Engine That Could*. 48 pages. 2005. Penguin Group. The classic story of the determined little engine that wanted to save the day.

Potter, Marian. *The Little Red Caboose*. 24 pages. 2000. Golden Books. The original "choo-choo" book.

Rey, H.A., Margret Rey and Martha Weston. *Curious George Takes a Train*. 24 pages. 2010. Houghton Mifflin Harcourt Publishers. Curious George gets into some trouble when he heads to the train station to take a trip with the Man in the Yellow Hat.

Rockwell, Anne. *Trains*. 24 pages. 1993. Penguin Group. Trains of all kinds in simple text and illustrations.

Shields, Amy. *National Geographic Readers: Trains*. 32 pages. 2011. National Geographic Children's Books. A Level 1 Reader in which children will learn about all different kinds of trains.

Siebert, Diane. *Train Song*. 32 pages. 1993. HarperCollins Publishers. Listen to the sounds of the train as it goes past cities and towns, forests and fields.

Sobel, June. *The Goodnight Train*. 32 pages. 2006. Houghton Mifflin Harcourt. The Goodnight Train is full of coal and leaving town.

Steele, Michael Anthony. *Chuggington: The Chugger Championship*. 24 pages. 2011. Scholastic. Wilson and Koko both want to win, but when Wilson breaks down, will Koko help or race to the finish line?

Sturges, Philemon. *I Love Trains*. 28 pages. 2006. HarperCollins Publishers. A boy expresses his love of trains.

Wickberg, Susan. *Hey Mr. Choo-Choo, Where Are You Going?* 32 pages. 2008. Penguin Group. This little train is really going places, written in rhythmic verse.

August

Cats

Advance planning: To plan for this storytime, find a theme-related song to play during craft and snack times, like "Don't Put Your Cat in the Washing Machine," by Bruce Fite. You will also want to select a poem, such as "The Cat of Many Colors" which can be found at www.childfun.com in the cat and kitten activity theme. For the reading of this poem, make simple outline heads of paper cats (print on computer) in these colors: white, purple, red, orange, blue, green, yellow, black and hold each one up at the appropriate time in the reading of the poem asking the children to say the color out loud Be sure to also consider which books you will read. Decorate your space with stuffed cats, a poster of cat pictures. cat dishes and toys. You could make a cat faced balloon by drawing on the face and adding construction paper ears and whiskers.

Introduction to theme: Cats are small, furry mammals that have been around people for over 9,500 years. Cats have been our pets for hundreds and hundreds of years. They are currently the most popular pet in the world. They are fast and flexible, have claws that they can take in or out, sharp teeth and a natural talent for hunting. They need food, water and exercise, just like you do. They need to go to the doctor sometimes, also just like you. A long, long time ago, cats ran wild and had to hunt for their own food. Today the cats we keep as pets in our homes eat dry or canned food that we can buy at the store.

When cats are happy, do they purr or growl? (purr) The hair on a cat is called _____? (fur) Do you think cats like to have a bath? (no) A baby cat is called a _____. (kitten) Today we'll read about cats, play a cat game, make a cat craft and have a snack that looks like something cats might like to eat.

Song: "I Know A Kitty" — sung to "Bingo" tune. Lyrics can be found at www.perfect lypreschool.com.

Game: Copy cat game

Be the cat and act out simple cat moves. Have the children be copy cats, and act out all the same moves. Materials needed: None. Advance preparation: None.

At storytime: Act out these and/or other typical cat activities: licking a paw; washing your face with a paw; stretching; purring; scratching behind the ears; pouncing; taking a cat nap.

Alternative Games

Famous cats. Find and print from the Internet pictures of famous cats. Show each picture to the children and see if they know who it is. Suggestions: The Cat in the Hat, Sylvester, Garfield, Tom from Tom and Jerry, The Cheshire Cat, The Aristocats, Puss in Boots, Pink Panther, Felix the Cat, Mr. Bigglesworth, Morris.

Balancing act game. Practice balancing things on your heads like the Cat in the Hat. Use paper plates, cups, straws and count who could get the most on their head.

Mother cat, may I? Play this like the traditional "Mother, may I?" game. You are the Mother Cat and have the children stand in a line facing you, but at least ten feet away. You call to one child and tell her to take a certain number of steps toward you. Before the child can move she must remember to say "Mother cat, may I?" Then mother cat answers one "meow" for yes, and two "meows" for no. If the child doesn't ask the question, or follow the correct "meow" response, she can't move. Play until one child reaches mother cat.

Hunting for mice. Place small construction paper cutouts of mice all around the children's area. Have the children act like cats and go around finding the mice.

Craft: Paper bag cat puppet

Materials needed: Brown paper bags, pink, black and yellow construction paper, scissors, glue sticks. Advance preparation: Cut brown larger, pink smaller triangular paper ears, thin black paper whiskers, yellow circles, smaller black circles for eyes, pink triangle nose and pink tongue. At storytime: Fold the bottom flap into a triangular shape to make the cat's face. Glue the ears together, then onto the face. Add whiskers, nose, two piece eyes and tongue under flap.

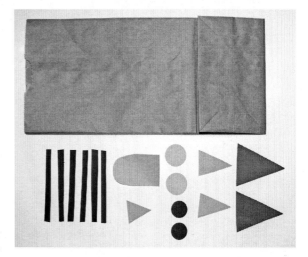

Paper bag cat puppet pieces.

Alternative Crafts

Doorhangers. Make doorhangers with the Fish on one side — Come Back Later! and the Cat in the Hat on the other — Do Come In! Remind them how the Fish was trying to get the Cat in the Hat to leave in the book.

Cats in hats! Take white paper bags and glue strips of red across to make them look like Cat in the Hat hats.

Paper plate cat face. Add construction paper ears and whiskers, eyes, mouth and nose to a paper plate. Could cut out the eyes to use as a mask.

Cat bookmark. Start with a square of paper. Fold in two cor-

Paper bag cat puppet.

ners. Glue a cut out cat face to the folded down corners. Draw a face on the cat. This is used as a bookmark by placing the folded over corner on the corner of a book page.

Snack: Cheese cubes and Goldfish crackers
Materials needed: Cheese blocks and Goldfish crackers, cups or paper plates.

Advance preparation: Cut the cheese into small cubes. At storytime: Pass small cups or plates of a few cheese cubes and some Goldfish crackers, explaining that sometimes cats might like to eat cheese and fish.

Alternative Snacks

Cat cupcake. Decorate cupcakes with icing, small candies to make a face, short pieces of licorice lace to make whiskers.

Cat cookies. Decorate round sugar cookies with candy corn ears, M & M eyes and mouth and licorice string whiskers.

Cheese cubes and goldfish crackers.

Suggested Books

Braun, Sebastian. *Meeow and the Blue Table*. 32 pages. 2012. Boxer Books. Meeow is ready to play.

Brown, Linda. *Cats*. 34 pages. 2011. CreateSpace. Whimsical book that explores numbers and sizes.

Burchall, Mark. *Copy Cat*. 32 pages. 2011. Child's Play International Limited. Cat imitates everything Dog does and it annoys him, but he misses Cat when he decides to play alone.

Carle, Eric. *Have You Seen My Cat?* 28 pages. 1997. Simon & Schuster Children's Publishing. An around the world tour with a little boy who is looking for his cat.

Cowley, Joy. *Mr. Wishy-Washy*. 18 pages. 2003. Penguin Group. Mr. Wishy-Washy wants everything clean, even the cat.

Czekaj, Jef. *Cat Secrets*. 32 pages. 2011. HarperCollins Publishers. A book that promises to tell cat secrets, but only if you are a cat.

Dodd, Emma. *I Don't Want a Cool Cat*. 32 pages. 2010. Little, Brown Books for Young Readers. Emma wants a cat and knows that there are many to choose from so it's hard to find just the right one.

Ehlert, Lois. *Feathers for Lunch*. 36 pages. 1996. Houghton Mifflin Harcourt Trade & Reference Publishers. A cat tries to catch birds for lunch.

Ehlert, Lois. *Top Cat*. 32 pages. 2001. Houghton Mifflin Harcourt Trade & Reference Publishers. Top Cat rules the house and doesn't take kindly to the new intruder.

Flack, Marjorie. *Angus and the Cat*. 32 pages. 1997. Square Fish. Angus the terrier has to share his home with the new cat.

Gag, Wanda. *Millions of Cats*. 32 pages. 2006. Penguin Group. Tells the story of an old couple and how they came to have just one cat.

Ganeri, Anita. *Cats and Kittens*. 24 pages. 2011. QEB Publishing. Simple text and illustrations about cats and kittens.

Gorbachev, Valeri. *The Best Cat*. 32 pages. 2010. Candlewick Press. When Bootsy plays with a ball of yarn, Jeff sees a clown. When Bootsy dances, Jeff sees a ballerina.

Graham-Barber, Lynda. *KokoCat, Inside and Out*. 24 pages. 2012. The Gryphon Press. One day Koko sees an open door and a chance to escape.

Grant, Joan. *Cat and Fish*. 32 pages. 2005. Simply Read Books. Cat and Fish come from different worlds, but they meet in the park one night and like each other.

Henkes, Kevin. *Kitten's First Full Moon*. 40 pages. 2004. HarperCollins Publishers. The moon is full and kitten is hungry.

Herman, Gail. *Otto the Cat*. 48 pages. 1995. Penguin Group. This Rebus book is about Otto, a funny cat.

Inkpen, Mick. *Rollo and Ruff and the Little Fluffy Bird*. 32 pages. 2012. Hodder & Stoughton, Ltd. A cat and mouse tale about helping others out.

Karlin, Nurit. *The Fat Cat Sat on the Mat*. 64 pages.

2006. Barnes & Noble. Simple rhymes for beginning readers that start with rat trying to get the fat cat off the mat.

Keats, Ezra Jack. *Hi Cat.* 40 pages. 1999. Penguin Group. Archie says hi to a cat and then it follows him, making a mess of his activities.

Keats, Ezra Jack. *Pet Show.* 40 pages. 2001. Penguin Group. Archie wants to enter his cat in the pet show but can't find him.

Kellogg, Steven. *A Rose for Pinkerton.* 32 pages. 2002. Penguin Group. Pinkerton the Great Dane gets a kitten named Rose.

Krasnesky, Thad. *That Cat Can't Stay.* 32 pages. 2010. Flashlight Press. Dad keeps objecting to all the cats that his family wants to bring home, but they keep coming.

LeGuin, Ursula. *Cat Dreams.* 32 pages. 2009. Scholastic. Climb into a cat's dreamland.

Litwin, Eric. *Pete the Cat: I Love My White Shoes.* 40 pages. 2010. HarperCollins Publishers. Pete's shoes change colors as he walks in different things going down the street.

Litwin, Eric. *Pete the Cat and His Four Groovy Buttons.* 40 pages. 2012. HarperCollins Publishers. Teaches children not to sweat the small stuff. Buttons pop off.

Martin, Bill, Jr., Michael Sampson and Laura J. Bryant. *Kitty Cat, Kitty Cat, Are You Waking Up?* 24 pages. 2008. Marshall Cavendish Corporation. Will Kitty Cat make it to school on time? She has so many things to do before she gets ready to leave.

Marzollo, Jean. *Pretend You're a Cat.* 32 pages. 1997. Penguin Group. Rhyming verses ask the reader to purr like a cat, scratch like a dog, leap like a squirrel...

Myron, Vicki. *Dewey: There's a Cat in the Library.* 40 pages. 2009. Little, Brown Books for Young Readers. The librarian finds a kitten and decides he will be the library's cat.

Neye, Emily. *All About Cats and Kittens.* 32 pages. 1999. Penguin Group. Tells everything you want to know about cats.

Nodset, Joan L. *Come Back, Cat.* 40 pages. 2008. HarperCollins Publishers. A story about a persistent little girl and a capricious cat.

Numeroff, Laura Joffe. *If You Give a Cat a Cupcake.* 32 pages. 2008. HarperCollins Publishers. One of the circular stories that starts with giving a cat a cupcake, which makes him want

something else, etc. until it comes back around to the cupcake again.

O'Hair, Margaret. *My Kitten.* 32 pages. 2011. Amazon Children's Publishing. A kitten is lots of fun.

Page, Gail. *How to Be a Good Cat.* 32 pages. 2011. Bloomsbury Publishing. Cat helps Bobo the dog take care of the naughty kitten.

Potter, Beatrix. *The Tale of Tom Kitten.* 64 pages. 2002. Penguin Group. Once upon a time there were three little kittens, Mitten, Tom and Moppet.

Rylant, Cynthia. *Brownie and Pearl Make Good.* 24 pages. 2012. Beach Lane Books. Brownie and Pearl make a mistake, then make it all better.

Schachner, Judith. *Skippyjon Jones.* 32 pages. 2005. Penguin Group. Skippyjon Jones is a Siamese cat who would rather be a Chihuahua.

Schwartz, Viviane. *There Are Cats in This Book.* 32 pages. 2008. Candlewick Press. Lift the flaps directly engaging the reader in this cat book.

Schwartz, Viviane. *There Are No Cats in This Book.* 32 pages. 2010. Candlewick Press. Flaps, pop-ups and other surprises in this book that the cats have escaped from.

Scotton, Rob. *Splat the Cat.* 40 pages. 2008. HarperCollins Publishers. Splat is worried about making friends at school.

Seuss, Dr. *The Cat in the Hat.* 72 pages. 1957. Random House Children's Books. The Cat comes to play, bringing trouble.

Spinelli, Eileen. *Hero Cat.* 32 pages. 2006. Marshall Cavendish Corporation. Mama Cat looks for a safe place to have her kittens.

Talbott, Hudson. *It's All About Me-Ow.* 32 pages. 2012. Penguin Group. A book about cats.

Tillman, Nancy. *Tumford the Terrible.* 32 pages. 2011. Feiwel and Friends. Tumford the cat isn't really terrible, he just has a way of finding mischief.

Van Fleet, Matthew. *Cat.* 20 pages. 2009. Simon & Schuster. Photos showcase many varieties of cats.

Willems, Mo. *Cat the Cat, Who Is That?* 32 pages. 2010. HarperCollins Publishers. Cat the Cat introduces the reader to her friends.

Yolen, Jane. *How Do Dinosaurs Love Their Cats?* 6 pages. 2010. Scholastic. A short board book that answers the question, "how does a dinosaur care for its kitty?"

School

Advance planning: To plan for this storytime, find a theme-related song to play during craft and snack times, like "The First Day of School," by Timmy Wells. You will also want to select a poem, such as "What to Remember in School," by Ken Nesbitt (find it at www.poetryteachers.com), along with the books you plan to read. Decorate your space with apples, bells, books, pictures of schools, playgrounds, school buses, children, teachers.

Introduction to theme: Summer vacation is coming to an end, and children who are old enough will be headed back to school, or some to school for the very first time. Maybe some of you have older brothers and sisters who have already started school again this year, or possibly you will get to go to school too. Do you know what happens at school? Children come together in a room called a classroom, where there's a grown up called a teacher, to learn. They read books, learn arithmetic, play on the playground, learn to create art, sing and play music — many of the same things we do at storytime. Usually when children first start going to school it's just for a few hours each day and as they get older their school day gets longer. Do any of you go to school? Do you have brothers or sisters who go to school? Have you been inside a school? What did you think? Today we'll read some books about school, play a game that you might play on the playground at school, paint like you might in school and eat a snack that you might find in school.

Song: "I Like to Go to School" which can be found at www.the-preschool-professor.com.

Game: Hopscotch

Materials needed: Masking tape, numbers and the word SCHOOL printed on computer paper. Advance preparation: Tape a hopscotch board layout on the floor and the numbers in each box. Tape the word SCHOOL in the final square. At storytime: Show the children how to jump from square to square to get to school, calling out the numbers as you jump. Encourage them to jump through the squares and call out the numbers. Where there's one number, they jump on one foot, where there are two, they jump with both feet.

Alternative Games

Teacher says. Play like Simon says but using the words "teacher says." Here are some ideas for what to say (sometimes say "teacher says" in front of the words, sometimes don't — but no one is out if they don't do it right — just remind them that they only have to do it when you say "teacher says"): clap your hands; hop on one foot; jump up and down; flap your arms; Laugh; roar like a lion; touch your toes; take a step forward; raise your hand; quack like a duck; turn around in a circle; take a step backward; sit down (if you end with this one with teacher says, you'll be ready to go on to the next activity).

Musical circles. Place some hula hoops or tape down some circle shapes on the floor. Talk about circles. Play music and have the children move around the room. Stop the music and direct them to move into one of the circles on the floor, start the music again, repeat. Could do with other shapes too, like squares and triangles and then vary where the children should stop when the music stops.

Rhythm mimic. Sit in a circle and choose a rhythmic pattern, like two hand claps.

Go around the circle and have each child imitate the pattern until it comes back to you. Then do another pattern. Patterns: two hand claps, one pat on the floor, one hand clap, two pats on the floor, three pats on knees. You could also clap out their names.

Conga line. Start Latin sounding music and have the children line up behind you, single file, each with hands on the hips of person in front of him/her. Move around the room to the music.

Roll the ball. Have the children sit in a circle and start by holding a large playground ball and saying something that you think you would like about going to school. Then roll the ball to a child and ask that child to say something he/she thinks he/she would like about school. You can offer suggestions, such as storytime, or snack time, or making crafts if the child seems unsure of what kind of activity might take place at school.

What's my name? Write each child's name on an index card and place all the cards in a line on the floor or attach to small chairs if available. Play music and have the children walk around the name cards while the music plays. When the music stops, have them find the card with their name and sit in the chair or stand by the card. Move the cards around and start the music again and repeat.

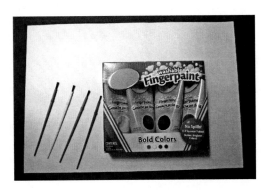

Craft: Painted school house

Materials needed: Large white paper, washable finger paints, paper plates, brushes. Advance preparation: None. At storytime: Paint a school using washable finger paints on paper with brushes. Talk about shapes and show examples of squares and triangles. Show them how to paint a big square, a little square and a triangle to make the school building, then let them paint how they want. If you can, give everyone some kind

Painted school house pieces.

of magnet that they can use to put their artwork up on their refrigerator at home since once they go to school there will be a lot of artwork coming home. You could buy a kit at a craft store to make your own, or buy stick on magnets and wooden shapes. Or print a schoolhouse picture on cardstock and attach stick on magnets to back. Or have making the magnet as your craft (see alternate craft below).

Alternative Crafts

Schoolhouse paper craft. Make a schoolhouse from two six-inch squares and two three-inch squares and a bell. You will need red construction paper squares and triangles and yellow construction paper bells plus construction paper background sheet in white or off white. You'll also need crayons and glue sticks. Cut six-inch red construction paper squares for the schoolhouse building and

Painted school house.

the roof (cut roof squares in half to make triangles). Cut three-inch red construction paper squares for the bell tower and bell tower roof (cut roof squares in half to make triangles). Cut yellow bells. At storytime talk about the shapes with the children — squares and triangles. Show them how a square cut in half diagonally makes a triangle. Then have them glue their pieces together onto the off white background sheet to make the schoolhouse. Show them the sample and then:

Start at the top — glue down the bell tower roof triangle. Then glue the bell tower square. Then glue down the schoolhouse roof triangle so that it partially covers the bell tower square. Draw in an outline for the bell in the bell tower and glue down the bell. Draw in the windows and the doors and another triangle inside the roof triangle, if desired.

If time, could draw additional things on the background sheet, like children, trees, playground equipment, fence, etc.

Made by _____ magnet. Using three-inch flat wooden stars, five inches of decorative ribbon about one-inch wide, craft paint, glitter glue pens, markers and stick on magnets, have the parent help the child write his/her name on the star along with "made by" and then let the child decorate the star with glitter glue. In advance, hot glue two pieces of ribbon to the bottom of the star to look like an award.

Pencil or crayon holder. Make a pencil holder from an empty juice or other can, covering with construction paper and decorating with crayons and/or stickers.

School collage. Cut from magazines or print from the Internet pictures of some activities that take place at school, like reading books, creating art, eating lunch and snacks, playing with toys, playing on the playground, etc. Let the children create a collage by gluing some of these pictures to a paper plate or a piece of paper.

ABC bookmark. Make black cardstock rectangular bookmarks and then let the children write ABC in white crayon on one side and their names on the other side.

Apple paper plate. Cut a notch out of a red paper plate (or have the children paint or color white paper plates red) so that it has an apple shape. Let the children attach a green stem.

Foam pencil case. Each child will need one sheet of foam 12 × 17.5 inches. Fold the foam sheet at 6.5 inches, then 13 inches, then the last section will be 4.5 inches. Punch holes in the sides up to the 13-inch folds. At storytime have the children lace up the sides with a 48-inch piece of yarn and then fold over the top. Have at least one pencil for each child to put in the case to take home.

Snack: Mini caramel apples

Materials needed: apples, melon baller, lollipop sticks, dipping caramel, sprinkles, small paper plates or bowls. Advance preparation: Scoop mini balls out of apples and place on lollipop sticks. Dip in lemon or sugar water to keep from turning brown. At storytime: Place a mini apple on stick on a paper plate or bowl with a spoonful of dipping caramel and a spoonful of sprinkles. Have the children dip their apples in the caramel and then in the sprinkles. Explain that you're having apples because apples are a traditional gift to take to teachers.

Mini caramel apples.

Alternative Snacks

Blackboard cookie and apple slices. You will need chocolate covered graham cracker cookies, white icing that dries hard, apples, small paper plates. Draw the letters A B C on the cookies in the white icing. Let dry. Slice apples. At storytime place a cookie and a few apple slices on a paper plate. Explain that the cookies look like blackboards that teachers write on and that often in old days students would bring apples as gifts for their teachers so apples have become something that is associated with teachers.

Alphabet or number cookies. Use letter or number cookie cutters to cut cookie dough.

Apple-shaped sandwiches. Cut bread with an apple-shaped cookie cutter.

Apple cupcake. Ice cupcakes with red icing or sprinkle with red sprinkles. Add a half pretzel stick as the stem and a few mint leaves.

SUGGESTED BOOKS

Ahlberg, Allan. *Starting School.* 28 pages. 1990. Turtleback Books. Introduces the activities of students just starting school.

Altaker-Mount, Marni. *My First Day of School.* 24 pages. 2006. Trafford Publishing. Colorful illustrations of early school days.

Andrews, Lisa. *Milton the Mouse Starts School.* 28 pages. 2011. Tate Publishing. Milton's first day of school.

Asher, Penny. *My First Day of School.* 32 pages. 2006. Change Is Strange. Charles describes his first day of school and how nervous he was.

Baer, Edith. *This Is the Way We Go to School.* 32 pages. 1992. Scholastic. Rhymed couplets in this informed international tale.

Bayer, Jane. *A My Name Is Alice.* 32 pages. 1992. Turtleback Books. A parade of animals sell their wares in this alphabet ditty.

Berenstain, Stan, and Jan Berenstain. *The Berenstain Bears Go to School.* 32 pages. 1978. Random House Children's Books. Sister Bear needs to conquer her fear of starting school.

Berry, Joy. *I Love Preschool.* 20 pages. 2010. Joy Berry Enterprises. Shows all the activities preschoolers do.

Blake, Stephanie. *I Don't Want to Go to School.* 32 pages. 2009. Random House. Simon the rabbit doesn't want go to school, but by the time his mother comes to get him he doesn't want to go home.

Bridwell, Norman. *Clifford's First School Day.* 32 pages. 1999. Scholastic. As a puppy, Clifford goes to school with Emily Elizabeth and gets into mischief.

Brown, Marc. *D.W.'s Guide to Preschool.* 32 pages. 2006. Little Brown Books for Young Readers. Arthur's little sister D.W. stars in this guide to preschool.

Capucilli, Alyssa Satin. *Biscuit Goes to School.* 32 pages. 2003. HarperCollins Publishers. A dog follows the bus to school, meets the teacher and takes part in class activities.

Carlson, Nancy. *Look Out Kindergarten, Here I Come!* 32 pages. 2009. Baker & Taylor. Henry the mouse is apprehensive about school but has a good time.

Codell, Esme Raji. *It's Time for Preschool.* 40 pages. 2012. HarperCollins. Illustrates the range of activities children will enjoy during a typical day.

Cohen, Miriam. *Will I Have a Friend?* 32 pages. 1989. Aladdin. Jim's anxiety on his first day of school lessens when he makes a new friend.

Cousins, Lucy. *Maisy Goes to Preschool.* 32 pages. 2010. Maisy is confident about going to preschool.

Cousins, Lucy. *Maisy Goes to School.* 16 pages. 2008. Candlewick Press. A lift the flap book about starting school.

Crews, Donald. *School Bus.* 32 pages. 1984. HarperCollins Publishers. What is large, bright yellow and filled with students? A school bus!

Cutbill, Andy. *First Week at Cow School.* 32 pages. 2011. HarperCollins Publishers. Starting school is full of fun but Daisy can't hoof paint or swat flies like the other cows.

Davis, Katie. *Kindergarten Rocks!* 32 pages. 2008. Houghton Mifflin Harcourt. Dexter knows everything there is to know about kindergarten and isn't worried about it, but his dog is very nervous.

Edwards, Pamela Duncan. *Dinosaur Starts School.* 32 pages. 2009. Albert Whitman and Company. Dinosaur worries about the first day of school but a classmate helps reassure him.

Ewart, Franzesca. *Starting School*. 24 pages. 2006. Parragon Inc. Sadie and Sam are excited about starting school.

Fisher, Valorie. *Everything I Need to Know Before I'm Five*. 40 pages. 2011. Random House. Learn lots of concepts such as letters and numbers.

Goodman, Joan Elizabeth. *Bernard Goes to School*. 32 pages. 2001. Boyds Mill Press. Until he makes a new friend, Bernard the elephant doesn't want to stay at preschool his first day.

Gutman, Anne. *Penelope at School*. 10 pages. 2005. Bodley Head. From mixing the paint to feeding the fish Penelope wants to try everything at school.

Hains, Harriet. *My New School*. 24 pages. 1992. DK Publishing. Lucy and Max have new experiences on their first day of school.

Haley, Amanda. *3-2-1 School Is Fun!* 24 pages. 2009. Scholastic Library Publishing. Follow along as the children share the fun they're having at preschool.

Hallinan, P.K. *My First Day of School*. 24 pages. 2002. Ideals Publications. On the first day of school a child finds out about all the things that go on there.

Hallinan, P.K. *That's What a Friend Is*. 24 pages. 2002. Ideals Publications. Describes friendship in rhymed text and illustrations.

Heine, Helme. *Friends*. 32 pages. 1997. Aladdin. Three friends discover there are times when it's not possible to all be together.

Herman, Emmi S. *My First Day of School*. 24 pages. 1992. Learning Horizons. A series of stories and rhymes.

Hest, Amy. *Off to School, Baby Duck!* 32 pages. 2007. Candlewick Press. It's the first day of school and Baby Duck's stomach is all jitters.

Hill, Eric. *Spot Goes to School*. 24 pages. 2008. Penguin Books. Spot spends his first day at playschool having fun.

Hills, Tad. *How Rocket Learned to Read*. 40 pages. 2010. Random House. Rocket the dog learns from a little yellow bird.

Hunter, Rebecca. *My First Day of School*. 24 pages. 2004. Evans Brothers. Exploring a memorable event in a child's life.

Iwamura, Kazuo. *Seven Little Mice Go to School*. 32 pages. 2011. North South Books. Mother is worried — how will she get her seven little mice to school?

Janowitz, Marilyn. *We Love School*. 24 pages. 2007. North South Books. Simple rhymes and illustrations describe what kittens like about going to school.

Johnson, Jacquitta. *My First Day of School*. 16 pages. 2007. Outskirts Press. A great tool for reading to someone going off to school for the first time.

Kuklin, Susan. *Going to My Nursery School*. 40 pages. 1990. Simon & Schuster Books for Young Readers. A realistic look at a New York City Nursery School.

Mayer, Mercer. *The Best Teacher Ever*. 24 pages. 2008. HarperCollins Publishers. Little Critter has the best teacher around.

Mayer, Mercer. *First Day of School*. 20 pages. 2009. HarperCollins Publishers. Little Critter is nervous about starting school.

Mayer, Mercer. *Little Critter's This Is My School*. 32 pages. 1990. Western Pub. Co. A Golden Easy Reader Level 2. Describes Little Critter's first day of school.

Murkoff, Heidi. *What to Expect at Preschool*. 24 pages. 2003. HarperCollins. Explains what happens at a typical day at preschool.

Numeroff, Laura Joffe. *If You Take a Mouse to School*. 32 pages. 2002. HarperCollins Publishers. If you take a mouse to school, he'll ask for your lunch box. When you give him your lunch box, he'll want a sandwich to go in it. A story that begins and ends with taking a mouse to school.

Packard, Mary. *Little Wolf Goes to School*. 24 pages. 2012. Little Wolf doesn't know what will happen tomorrow on his first day of school.

Parish, Herman. *Amelia Bedelia's First Day of School*. 32 pages. 2009. HarperCollins. A literal-minded little girl's first day of school is confusing.

Patterson, Bettina. *I Go to Preschool*. 12 pages. 1996. Scholastic. Little Bear discovers the fun of preschool in this lift the flap book.

Penn, Audrey. *The Kissing Hand*. 32 pages. 2006. Tanglewood Press. Chester Raccoon seeks love and reassurance from his mother on his first day of school.

Poydar, Nancy. *First Day, Hooray!* 32 pages. 2000. Holiday House. Ivy is excited about tomorrow, which is the first day of school.

Prelutsky, Jack. *What a Day It Was at School*. 32 pages. 2009. Baker & Taylor. A collection of poetry about school.

Rey, Margret, and H.A. Rey. *Curious George's First Day of School* 24 pages. 2005. Houghton Mifflin Harcourt. It's the first day of school and Curious George has been invited to be a special class helper.

Riddell, Edwina. *My First Day at Preschool*. 32 pages. 1992. Barron's Educational Series. A typical day at preschool.

Rockwell, Anne. *My Preschool*. 32 pages. 2008. Henry Holt. A warm look at a day in the life of a preschooler.

Rockwell, Anne. *Welcome to Kindergarten*. 32 pages. 2004. Walker & Company. A boy visits the classroom where he will attend kindergarten the following fall.

Rockwell, Harlow. *My Nursery School*. 32 pages. 1990. HarperCollins Publishers. A child discusses what goes on during a day at her nursery school.

Rosenberry, Vera. *Vera's First Day of School*. 32 pages. 2003. Henry Holt & Co. Vera can't wait until she starts school, but the first day doesn't go as she anticipated.

Rosenthal, Amy Krouse. *Cookies: Bite Size Life Lessons*. 40 pages. 2006. HarperCollins Publishers. These cookies taste good but also have something good to say.

Rosenthal, Amy Krouse *Sugar Cookies: Sweet Little Lessons on Love*. 40 pages. 2009. HarperCollins. Baking cookies teaches many lessons about life and love.

Scarry, Richard. *Great Big Schoolhouse*. 72 pages. 2008. Sterling. Richard Scarry's warm friendly and comforting classroom.

Schachner, Judith. *Skippyjon Jones Class Action*. 32 pages. 2011. Dutton. A Siamese cat who would rather be a Chihuahua wants to go to dog obedience school.

Schaefer, Lola M. *Mittens at School*. 32 pages. 2012. HarperCollins. Mittens the curious kitten explores the classroom while the students are away.

Senisi. *Hurray for Pre-K!* 32 pages. 2000. HarperCollins Publishers. Introduces preschoolers to the fun and adventure of the first few days of school.

Shannon, David. *David Goes to School*. 32 pages. 1999. Scholastic. David gets into a lot of trouble at school.

Skarmeas, Nancy J. *My First Day of School*. 32 pages. 2010. Ideals Publications. Daniel liked preschool but he's not sure he wants to go to kindergarten.

Slate, Joseph. *Miss Bindergarten Gets Ready for Kindergarten*. 40 pages. 2001. Penguin Group. Miss Bindergarten is hard at work getting the classroom ready for her students.

Slegers, Liesbet. *Kevin Goes to School*. 30 pages. 2009. Clavis Publishing. Kevin is reluctant to go to school but has a good time.

Strauss, Linda Leopold. *Preschool Day Hooray!* 24 pages. 2010. Scholastic. Rhyming text and illustrations describe activities at school.

Sturges, Philemon. *I Love School!* 32 pages. 2006. HarperCollins Publishers. What's your favorite part of the school day?

Tanner, Suzy-Jane. *Tinyflock Nursery School*. 24 pages. 2004. HarperCollins. Little lamb Baabaara is frightened of school at first, until she gets settled.

Thompson, Lauren. *Mouse Loves School*. 24 pages. 2011. Simon & Schuster. Learn to recognize words and begin to read.

Thompson, Lauren. *Mouse's First Day of School*. 34 pages. 2010. Little Simon. A board book that features Mouse going to school and discovering new things.

Vulliamy, Clara. *Starting School*. 32 pages. 2011. Trafalgar Square Books. A delightful story about the first day of school.

Weiss, Leatie. *My Teacher Sleeps in School*. 32 pages. 1985. Puffin. The speculations of young children about how and where their teacher lives.

Wells, Rosemary. *McDuff Goes to School*. 32 pages. 2005. Hyperion Books. McDuff and his neighbor are enrolled in obedience school but McDuff seems to have forgotten his lessons.

Wells, Rosemary. *Timothy Goes to School*. 32 pages. 2000. Puffin. Timothy is very excited about starting school, until he meets Claude.

Wing, Natasha. *The Night Before Kindergarten*. 16 pages. 2011. Penguin Group. A whole bunch of kids are excited about starting kindergarten.

Wing, Natasha. *The Night Before Preschool*. 32 pages. 2011. Penguin Group. Rhyming text based on The Night Before Christmas.

Wright, Michael. *Jake Starts School*. 48 pages. 2010. Square Fish. Jake is frightened and holds on to his parents until the end of the day when he finally lets go.

Yolen, Jane. *How Do Dinosaurs Go to School*. 32 pages. 2007. HarperCollins. Everyone's favorite dinosaurs are going to school.

Zelinsky, Paul O. *The Wheels on the Bus*. 16 pages. 1990. Dutton Juvenile. The classic rhyme brought to life in this lift the flap book.

Circus

Advance planning: To plan for this storytime, find a theme-related song to play during craft and snack times, like "Circus Music," by The Hit Crew. You will also want to select a poem, such as "Hey There, Hoopla," by C.J. Dennis (find it at www.middlemiss.org), along with the books you plan to read. Decorate your space with a clown wig, stuffed animals that might be found at the circus, like an elephant, tiger or lion. Play circus music as everyone arrives.

Introduction to theme: Have you ever been to the circus? A circus is a traveling group of performers and animals. There are usually funny clowns, some elephants and horses, maybe a lion or tiger or two, some acrobats and gymnasts, could be trapeze artists who fly through the air... They perform in an auditorium, or under a big tent, sometimes in ring-shaped areas. The man in charge of the performance is called the Ringmaster and he announces the different performers. What's your favorite thing to see or do at the circus?

Today we'll read about the circus, play some circus games, make a clown craft and have a snack that looks like a clown.

Song: "I Am Going to the Circus" to the tune of "I've Been Working on the Railroad":

> I am going to the circus
> So much fun for me
> I am going to the circus
> There's a clown just wait and see.
> We might see some horses dancing
> Some elephants there too
> Won't you come and be there with us
> The circus is for you!

Game: Three-ring circus

Materials needed: Three hula hoops or one hula hoop and masking tape, one dozen filled water or soda bottles, three or more paper plates, a short piece of rope or masking tape, poster board, picture of clown printed large from computer, three stuffed cats like lions or tigers, something to decorate hula hoop that looks like flames (either crepe paper streamers, flames printed from the computer or tissue paper). Advance preparation: You will make four stations — three with hoops and one with the clown poster. Place hoops on floor or make circles with masking tape. Cut the inside of the paper plates to make rings. Place the filled water or soda bottles in hoop one. Place the rope in hoop two. Decorate the third hoop with "flames" and place the stuffed cats inside of it. Make clown poster for the fourth station. How: Ring One — ring toss: Place a dozen filled water or soda bottles to use for a ring toss game. Make rings out of paper plates. Ring Two — walk the tightrope: Place a rope on the ground (or use masking tape to make a line through the hoop) and have the kids follow you walking over it, using exaggerated movements and holding your arms out at your sides. Ring Three — big cats leap through flames: decorate the hula hoop to look like it has flames on it. Have three stuffed tigers or lions for the children to toss through it. Clown station — have the children strike different clown poses and faces. At storytime: Could divide the children into three or four groups with parents to help so that they don't have to wait as long for their turns with the four activities. Then have them take turns doing the ring toss, walking the tightrope, the big cat ring toss, and posing as a clown.

Alternative Games

Feed the elephant. Make a large poster of an elephant with a large mouth. Cut an opening for the mouth and let the children throw peanuts or circus peanuts at it, trying to get them into the mouth in order to feed the elephant.

Pose like a clown. Make a poster board clown head with the face cut out that the kids can pose behind to look like a clown.

Circus movement. Have some circus like movement games, like three legged races, carrying peanuts or circus peanuts in spoons, holding balls between their knees.

Paper plate clown stick puppet pieces.

Craft: Paper plate clown stick puppet

Materials needed: Small paper plates, crayons, craft sticks, several colors of tissue paper, glue sticks, google eyes, red pom poms. Advance preparation: Use hot glue gun to glue craft sticks to paper plates. Cut several colors of tissue paper into 2-inch squares. At storytime: Have children crumple tissue paper squares and glue to outside rim of plate as clown hair. Glue google eyes and pom pom nose. Draw smile and rosy cheeks with crayons. Turn plate over and do the same except draw frown.

Paper plate clown stick puppet.

Alternative Crafts

Clown bag. Decorate a brown or white paper bag with facial features cut from construction paper and crayons and/or markers to look like a clown.

Circus animal masks. Make animals like lions and bears from paper plates.

Snack: Clown cupcake

Materials needed: Cupcakes, icing, large marshmallows, small marshmallows, mini Jujubes or small gumdrops, food marker, Bugles chips, red candy for nose like Skittles or M&Ms, paper plates, plastic knives. Advance preparation: Bake cupcakes. Mark eyes on side of large marshmallow with food marker. At storytime: Give each child a cupcake on a plate with a plastic knife and a dollop of frosting. After frosting the cupcake, they will put a large

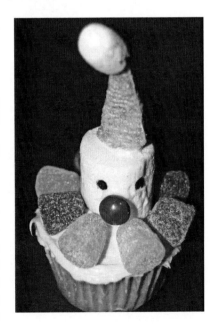

Clown cupcake.

marshmallow on top (flat side down), surround it with Jujubes to be the clown's collar (larger end outside), stick the red candy on the side of the large marshmallow with some icing, sit the bugle on top of the large marshmallow, put the little marshmallow on top of the bugle.

Alternative Snacks

Circus snacks. Have typical foods that one might find at the circus, like popcorn or cotton candy.

Clown ice cream. Use sugar ice cream cones upside down with a small scoop of ice cream to look like a clown. Decorate the face with candies.

SUGGESTED BOOKS

Argent, Kerry. *India the Showstopper*. 32 pages. 2008. Allen & Unwin Pty, Limited. India the circus elephant does not want to learn new tricks.

Beccia, Carlyn. *Who Put the B in the Ballyhoo?* 32 pages. 2007. Houghton Mifflin Harcourt. The historical truth behind circuses.

Bond, Michael. *Paddington Bear at the Circus*. 40 pages. 2000. HarperFestival. Paddington rushes off to save the man on the trapeze, turning the circus upside down.

Bottomley, Jane. *Today I Am... a Clown*. 1989. Ideals Publications. A family trip to the circus is exciting for a little girl who's dressed in her clown costume.

Bridwell, Norman. *Clifford at the Circus*. 32 pages. 2010. Scholastic. The circus is in town, but everything is going wrong.

Clements, Andrew. *Circus Family Dog*. 32 pages. 2008. Houghton Mifflin Harcourt Trade & Reference Publishers. Grumps the circus dog is content to do his one trick until a new dog shows up and threatens to steal the show.

Deneux, Xavier. *My Circus*. 18 pages. 2010. Walker Children's. Introduces the reader to the wonders of the circus.

Downs, Mike. *You See a Circus: I See*. 32 pages. 2006. Charlesbridge Publishing. When a young acrobat shows everyone around the circus tent, all is not the way it seems.

Ehlert, Lois. *Circus*. 40 pages. 1992. HarperCollins Publishers. Simple text and cut paper illustrations with many unusual animals in this extraordinary circus.

Falconer, Ian. *Olivia Saves the Circus*. 44 pages. 2001. Simon & Schuster Children's Publishing. Olivia embellishes her story of going to the circus over the summer when it's her turn to talk about her summer vacation upon returning to school.

Fleishman, Paul. *Sidewalk Circus*. 32 pages. 2007. Candlewick Press. A wordless book that shows the Garibaldi Circus coming to town.

Gottfried, Maya. *Last Night I Dreamed a Circus*. 32 pages. 2003. Knopf Books for Young Readers. The narrator dreams herself right into the circus acts.

Halsey, Megan. *Circus 1-2-3*. 32 pages. 2000. HarperCollins Publishers. Count from one to ten with acrobats and clowns.

Hill, Eric. *Spot Goes to the Circus*. 20 pages. 1994. Penguin Group. Spot goes behind the scenes at the circus to find his ball.

Hoff, Syd. *Oliver*. 64 pages. 2006. Sterling. Oliver the elephant arrives at the circus ready for work.

Hruby, Patrick. *ABC Is for Circus*. 56 pages. 2010. Ammo Books. Celebrates the colorful and festive world of the circus through each letter of the alphabet.

Hunt, Julie. *Precious Little*. 32 pages. 2011. Allen & Unwin Pty, Limited. Precious Little wants to be a circus performer.

Johnson, Crockett. *Harold's Circus*. 64 pages. 1981. HarperCollins Publishers. Harold and his purple crayon first draw a tightrope and then more circus antics ensue.

Knight, Hilary. *The Circus Is Coming*. 56 pages. 2007. Random House Children's Books. See the sensational sights of the circus parade.

Lindgren, Astrid. *Pippi Goes to the Circus*. 32 pages. 2000. Penguin Group. Pippi joins in when she goes to the circus.

Lobel, Anita. *Animal Antics A to Z*. 32 pages. 2005. HarperCollins Publishers. From alligators to zebras, the animals in this book will keep you amused with their antics.

Lopshire, Robert. *Put Me in the Zoo*. 72 pages. 1960. Random House Children's Books. A polka dot leopard tries to convince two children that he belongs in the zoo, but ultimately it's decided that he really belongs at the circus.

McGuirk, Leslie. *Tucker Over the Top*. 40 pages. 2000. Penguin Group. Tucker the terrier goes to the circus where he's recruited to perform a daredevil act.

Munro, Roxie. *Circus*. 24 pages. 2006. Chronicle Books. Lift the flap book where there's always a lot to do and see at the circus.

Murphy, Stuart. *Circus Shapes*. 40 pages. 1997. HarperCollins Publishers. Shapes presented in the context of the circus.

Parker, Emma. *At the Circus*. 20 pages. 2010. Second Edition. What fun there will be under the big top!

Priceman, Marjorie. *Emeline at the Circus*. 40 pages. 2001. Random House Children's Books. While Emeline's teacher is talking to the class about going to the circus, Emeline has already joined the troupe.

Rex, Adam. *Tree Ring Circus*. 32 pages. 2006. Houghton Mifflin Harcourt Trade & Reference Publishers. A tree becomes home to so many animals it's like a circus.

Rey, H.A. *Curious George Circus Act*. 16 pages. 2008. Houghton Mifflin Harcourt Trade & Reference Publishers. Curious George learns acrobatic circus skills after delivering a pizza to a troupe.

Rey, H.A. *See the Circus*. 22 pages. 1988. Houghton Mifflin Harcourt. Readers are quizzed in verse on characters and events at the circus.

Sampson, Mary Beth, and Michael R. Sampson. *Star of the Circus*. 32 pages. 1997. Holt, Henry & Co. Who is the star of the circus? Is it Mar-velous Mouse? Cannonball Cat? Or another character entirely?

Sendak, Jack, and Maurice Sendak. *Circus Girl*. 32 pages. 2002. HarperCollins Publishers. The story of the little circus girl Flora.

Seuss, Dr. *If I Ran the Circus*. 64 pages. 1956. Random House Children's Books. Young Morris McGurk lets his imagination run wild with his Circus McGurkus.

Slate, Joseph. *Miss Bindergarten Plans a Circus with Kindergarten*. 40 pages. 2005. Penguin Group. A rhyming book about Miss Bindergarten and her class and their plans for a circus.

Slobodkina, Esphyr. *Circus Caps for Sale*. 48 pages. 2002. HarperCollins Publishers. Another story about the cap salesman but this one involves an elephant.

Spier, Peter. *Peter Spier's Circus*. 48 pages. 1995. Random House Children's Books. Great illustrations in this celebration of life under the big top at the circus.

Stone, Tanya. *Sandy's Circus: A Story About Alexander Calder*. 40 pages. 2008. Penguin Group. Alexander Calder created wire sculptures. This is the story of his wire sculpture circus.

Van Dusen, Chris. *The Circus Ship*. 40 pages. 2009. Candlewick Press. The circus ship runs aground in a storm.

Wiseman, B. *Morris and Boris at the Circus*. 64 pages. 1990. HarperCollins Publishers. Morris the Moose has never been to the circus, so his friend Boris takes him there.

Wright, Johanna. *The Secret Circus*. 32 pages. 2009. Roaring Book Press. A Parisian circus so small that only the mice know where to find it.

Alphabet

Advance planning: To plan for this storytime, find a theme-related song to play during craft and snack times, like "Funk Alphabet," by Let's Start Smart. You will also want to select a poem, such as "Nonsense Alphabet," by Edward Lear which can be found at www.nonsenselit.org. This poem is long so it might be better to break it up into segments and read them periodically after a game or the craft or snack. Be sure to also consider which books you will read. Decorate your space with a magnetic board with alphabet magnet letters, or a large printout of the alphabet.

Introduction to theme: The alphabet is a family of letters that go together in a certain order. Do you know what a letter is? (show letter stencils or sponges). When letters are part of words, they have to be in a certain order too, but different from the way they are in the alphabet. Do you know which letter is the first letter in the alphabet? (show A) How about the last letter of the alphabet? (show Z) Which letter is the first letter of your name? (ask each child to say) What is your favorite letter of the alphabet? Why? Today we'll read about the letters of the alphabet, play a letter game, make an alphabet craft and eat a snack where we make letters out of food.

Song: "The Alphabet Song":

A, B, C, D, E, F, G,
H, I, J, K, L, M, N, O, P,
Q, R, S,
T, U, V,
W, X, Y, and Z
Now I know my ABC's,
Next time won't you sing with me?

Chicka chicka boom boom coconut tree pieces.

Chicka chicka boom boom coconut tree.

Game: The missing letter

Materials needed: Metal board, magnetic letters. Advance preparation: None. At storytime: Place three letters on the board. Have the children say the letters out loud. Then have the children close their eyes. Remove one of the letters. Have the children open their eyes and see if anyone can tell you which letter is missing. Adjust the number of letters to the age and recognition ability of the children — more letters for older children, fewer for younger. Depending on the number of children and the quantity of letters that you have, you could also spell each child's name on the board to see if they recognize it.

Alternative Games

Funk alphabet song. Play the funk alphabet song and form a conga line and dance around the reading area.

Alphabet bingo. Make up or buy a set of alphabet bingo cards.

Capital and small. Have capital and small letters of the alphabet and play a matching game with the children to see if they can match the large letters to their smaller ones.

What word starts with? Have a set of letters, either magnetic and a metal board, or felt and a felt board. Place a letter on the board and say a word that starts with that letter. Ask the children if they can think of something else that starts with that letter.

Craft: Chicka, chicka, boom, boom coconut tree based on the book by Bill Martin.

Materials needed: Light blue, brown and green construction paper, glue sticks, small alphabet sticker sheets.

Advance preparation: Cut brown paper into palm tree trunk shape. Cut four tropical palm leaf shapes per child from green paper. Cut four circles per child from brown paper for coconuts. At storytime: Children form their own coconut tree like in the book *Chicka, Chicka, Boom, Boom*. Add letter stickers free form.

Alternative Crafts

Name that caterpillar. Cut construction paper circles (enough for each child to have circles to make their name). Have parents help the children write one letter of the child's name on each circle (or use sponge stamps and paint). Glue the circles on to background construction paper in the shape of a caterpillar, adding a head (draw a face on it) and a tail. Draw legs and antennae.

Rope trick. Using pieces of yarn, have the children form the letters of their names out of yarn and glue them down to a piece of paper.

Snack: ABC food

Materials needed: Foods that start with the first three letters of the alphabet—A, B, C. Like apples, bananas, carrots. Or any other foods that start with those letters. Paper plates. Advance preparation: Wash and cut whatever foods you are using. At storytime: Place one of each of the foods on a paper plate. You could tease them a bit when asking about foods that start with the different letters, such as "do you think we will have cauliflower? Cabbage? Cucumber?" Then you could have cookies as your C food, and could draw the letters on the cookie if you like.

ABC food.

Alternative Snacks

Alphabet crackers. Using icing that hardens, draw the letters ABC on chocolate covered graham crackers.

Name your food. Small pretzels, block of cheese, large paper plates. Cut cheese into small cubes. Show the children how the pretzels can be broken to make different shapes to attach to the cheese cubes to form letters. Have the parents write the child's name on paper so that they can have something to copy.

SUGGESTED BOOKS

Anno, Mitsumasa. *Anno's Alphabet: An Adventure in Imagination*. 64 pages. 1988. HarperCollins Children's Books. Each letter of the alphabet accompanies a picture puzzle of an object that begins with that letter.

Baker, Keith. *L M N O Peas*. 40 pages. 2010. Beach Lane Books. Roll through the alphabet with some busy little peas.

Bar-el, Dan. *Alphabetter*. 32 pages. 2006. Orca Book Publishers USA. Each page has a child whose name begins with that letter of the al- phabet, but he's missing something that starts with the next letter.

Bourke, Linda. *Eye Spy: Mysterious Alphabet*. 64 pages. 1991. Chronicle Books. The reader is challenged in a guessing game trying to find the answer to the picture puzzles of each letter of the alphabet.

Brown, Margaret. *Goodnight Moon ABC*. 32 pages. 2010. HarperCollins Publishers. So many things can be found in the great green room.

Carlson, Nancy. *ABC I Like Me*. 32 pages. 1997. Penguin Group. The cheerful pig shows each positive trait illustrated by a letter of the alphabet.

Cleary, Brian P. *Peanut Butter and Jellyfishes: A Very Silly Alphabet Book.* 32 pages. 2006. Millbrook Press. Alphabet sentences presented in rhyme.

Cousins, Lusy. *Maisy's ABC.* 16 pages. 2008. Candlewick Press. Maisy parades through the alphabet.

Cronin, Doreen. *Click, Clack, Quackity-quack: An Alphabetical Adventure.* 24 pages. 2005. Simon & Schuster Children's Publishing. The cows are typing and you follow what they're typing one alphabet letter at a time.

Cushman, Doug. *The ABC Mystery.* 1993. HarperCollins Publishers. Crime doesn't pay readers learn in this romp through the alphabet.

Czekaj, Jef. *A Call for a New Alphabet.* 44 pages. 2011. Charlesbridge Publishing. X is tired of being underused and always being at the back of the alphabet.

Eastman, P.D. *The Alphabet Book.* 32 pages. 1974. Random House Children's Books. Entries from all letters of the alphabet, such as American Ants, Cow in Car, etc.

Ehlert, Lois. *Eating the Alphabet.* 40 pages. 1993. Houghton Mifflin Harcourt Trade. Teaches upper and lower case letters while showing lots of different fruits and vegetables.

Folsom, Michael. *Q Is for Duck: An Alphabet Guessing Game.* 64 pages. 2005. Houghton Mifflin Harcourt Trade. Try to guess how this new alphabet has the letters relating to these new things. Ducks quack, for example.

Frasier, Debra. *A Fabulous Fair Alphabet.* 40 pages. 2010. Simon & Schuster Children's Publishing. A visit to the fair showcases all the letters of the alphabet in things fair-related.

Geisert, Arthur. *Pigs from A to Z.* 64 pages. 1996. Houghton Mifflin Harcourt Trade. Seven piglets romp through a landscape of hidden letters while building a treehouse.

Inkpen, Mick. *Kipper's A to Z: An Alphabet Adventure.* 64 pages. 2005. Houghton Mifflin Harcourt Trade. Kipper and Arnold need to find something for each letter of the alphabet.

Jay, Alison. *ABC: A Child's First Alphabet Book.* 32 pages. 2005. Dutton's Children's Books. An introduction to the alphabet featuring ordinary objects.

Johnson, Stephen T. *Alphabet City.* 32 pages. 1992. Penguin Group. Realistic artwork shows how letters appear in all kinds of places.

Kalman, Maira. *What Pete Ate from A to Z: Where We Explore the English Alphabet (In Its Entirety) in Which a Certain Dog Devours a Myriad of Items Which He Should Not.* 48 pages. 2003. Penguin Group. Pete the dog eats his way through the alphabet.

Kaufman, Elliot. *Alphabet.* 60 pages. 2012. Abbeville Press. Each letter of the alphabet is represented by several different images.

Lionni, Leo. *Alphabet Tree.* 32 pages. 1990. Random House Children's Books. The letters in the alphabet tree must band together when the wind threatens to blow them out of it.

Lobel, Anita. *Animal Antics from A to Z.* 32 pages. 2005. HarperCollins Publishers. Animals form all 26 letters of the alphabet.

MacCuish, Al. *Operation Alphabet.* 64 pages. 2011. Thames & Hudson. Charming old fashioned book about Charlie learning the importance of letters.

MacDonald, Suse. *A Was Once an Apple Pie.* 32 pages. 2005. Scholastic. Edward Lear's alphabet poem in a picture book.

Martin, Bill, Jr., John Archambault and Lois Ehlert. *Chicka Chicka Boom Boom.* 40 pages. 1989. Simon & Schuster Children's Books. Here the letters of the alphabet are like actors, and while it showcases the alphabet, it does it more like they're characters.

Miller, Jane. *Farm Alphabet Book.* 32 pages. 1987. Scholastic. Photos of farm animals and objects that begin with the letters of the alphabet.

Mills, Liz. *My First Alphabet Book.* 12 pages. 2006. Scholastic. Touch and feel—a multisensory way to learn the alphabet.

Munari, Bruno. *ABC.* 48 pages. 1960. World Publishing Co. Beginning with Ant on an Apple, simple text introduces the alphabet.

O'Connor, Jane. *Fancy Nancy's Favorite Fancy Words.* 32 pages. 2008. HarperCollins Publishers. A helpful A to Z guide.

Pallotta, Jerry. *The Butterfly Alphabet Book.* 32 pages. 1999. Charlesbridge Publishing. A colorful selection of butterflies with names starting from A to Z.

Pallotta, Jerry. *The Underwater Alphabet Book.* 32 pages. 1991. Charlesbridge Publishing. Going through the alphabet showing all kinds of tropical creatures.

Rosenthal, Amy Krouse. *Al Pha's Bet.* 32 pages. 2011. Penguin Group. Turns the ABCs inside out.

Segal, Robin. *ABC in NYC.* 32 pages. 2006. Murray Hill Books. An alphabet book takes you on a tour of New York City.

Sendak, Maurice. *Alligators All Around: An Alphabet.* 32 pages. 1991. HarperCollins Publishers. All the letters starting with an Alligator Jamboree.

Seuss, Dr. *Dr. Seuss's ABC.* 72 pages. 1963. Random House Children's Books. Zany drawings and nonsensical verse help to teach children the alphabet.

Shannon, George. *Tomorrow's Alphabet.* 56 pages. 1996. HarperCollins Publishers. An alphabet book with a twist. A is the seed which becomes tomorrow's apple, for example.

Sierra, Judy. *The Sleepy Little Alphabet.* 40 pages. 2009. Alfred A. Knopf. Bedtime in Alphabet Town and the little letters all have something they need before going to sleep.

Slate, Joseph. *Miss Bindergarten Takes a Field Trip with Kindergarten.* 40 pages. 2004. Penguin Group. The class goes to all sorts of places, talking about shapes as well as reinforcing letters of the alphabet.

Sobel, June. *Shiver Me Letters A Pirate ABC.* 32 pages. 2006. Houghton Mifflin Harcourt. Animal pirates harmonize in this book.

Thurlby, Paul. *Paul Thurlby's Alphabet.* 64 pages. 2011. Candlewick Press. An alphabet where the shape of each letter is memorable.

Trasler, Janee. *Caveman ABC Story.* 32 pages. 2011. Sterling Children's Books. Adventures of a caveman and a squirrel from A to Z.

Van Allsburg, Chris. *The Z Was Zapped: A Play in Twenty-Six Acts.* 56 pages. 1987. Houghton Mifflin Harcourt Trade. Each letter performs in its own weird little way.

Wells, Rosemary. *Max's ABC.* 32 pages. 2006. Penguin Group. Max and Ruby the bunnies illustrate Max's escapades that start with each letter of the alphabet.

Wood, Audrey. *Alphabet Adventure.* 40 pages. 2001. Scholastic. All the letters of the alphabet are preparing for an exciting adventure, like going to school, or solving a mystery.

Wood, Audrey. *Alphabet Rescue.* 40 pages. 2006. Scholastic. The little letters build a fire truck and save the day.

September

Apples and Johnny Appleseed

Advance planning: To plan for this storytime, find a theme-related song to play during craft and snack times, like "Johnny Appleseed," as sung by Bing Crosby. You will also want to select a poem, such as "Five Apples in a Bucket" (find it at www.teachingfirst. net/Poems/Apples.htm). Have a pie tin with a crust colored (beige) cloth or napkin lining it along with five red apples to use to illustrate this poem. You could also read "Apple Magic," by Margaret Hillart (also at www.teachingfirst.net/Poems/Apples.htm). Recite this poem while slicing an apple crossways to show the star. Be sure to also consider which books you will read. Decorate your space with a basket or bowl of apples and a poster of an apple tree.

Introduction to theme: Have you ever eaten an apple? What's your favorite way to eat apples? Applesauce? Apple pie? Many years ago, apples were not the common fruit that they are today. John Chapman, known as Johnny Appleseed, was born September 26, 1774 and died in the spring of 1845. He was an American pioneer nurseryman who introduced apple trees to large parts of Ohio, Indiana and Illinois by bringing apple seeds with him as he traveled the land. He carried everything he needed to live outdoors while he wandered the land, including a cooking pot that he wore on his head while he walked (bring a pot and put it on your head to demonstrate). Today we'll read about apples and Johnny Appleseed, play some apple games, make an apple craft and eat a special apple snack that's sure to make you smile.

Song: "I Like to Eat Apples and Bananas." Lyrics can be found at www.metrolyrics.com.

Alternative Song

A-P-P-L-E (to be sung to tune of B-I-N-G-O) by Meish Goldish, lyrics can be found at www.canteach.ca/elementary.

Game: Put the seeds in the apple

Paint a big red apple shape on the side of a cardboard box. Cut several holes in it or just leave the top open. To make a black bean bag, cut two 4.5-inch squares from black felt, sew the squares together around three sides and half of the fourth side, insert the least expensive dried beans (like black eyed peas) you can find, pin the opening and then sew it shut. At storytime: Let the children throw black bean bag "seeds" through the holes or in the top of the box.

Alternative Games

Count the apples. Have a large basket full of apples, ideally different colors and varieties. Take them out one at a time and tell the children what kind of apple each one is. Ask the children to tell you what color the apple is. Then when all of the apples are out, put them back into the basket, asking the children to count out loud as you place each one in.

Teacher says. Explain to the children that apples are a traditional gift for teachers and so you're going to pretend to be the teacher and they are going to do everything the teacher says. Play like Simon says. Explain that if the teacher doesn't say to do it, they don't have to do it. Make a list of actions, like stand on your toes, wave your hand, walk around in a circle. Any kind of activity where they can move but still remain in place.

Find the apples. Red, green and yellow construction paper. Red, green and yellow buckets. Cut lots of apple shapes from the construction paper. At storytime, hide different color construction paper apples around the room (red, green and yellow). Have a basket or plastic bucket for each color apple. Each child is asked to find one apple of each color and put it in the correct basket.

Who took the apple? "Who took the apple from the apple tree?" Chant and clap as you pass an apple from child to child with the children sitting in a circle on the floor. Group chant: Who took the apple from the apple tree? "Johnny" took the apple from the apple tree! Child: Who me? Group: Yes you! Child: Couldn't be! Group: Then who? Group: "(Next child's name)" took the apple from the apple tree (child then passes the apple to the next child and play continues until all have had a turn).

Apple measuring. Take the paper apples that you used for the find the apples game and use them to measure the height of the children. Have large butcher or craft paper sheets for each child to lie down on and have the parent mark the top of the child's head and the bottom of their feet. Then have child and parent use paper apples to measure how many apples tall each child is.

Apple bean bag toss. Make apple-shaped bean bags from red felt with green leaves. Have the children take turns tossing the apple bean bags into a pie tin or basket from a set distance away that you've marked on the floor with a piece of masking tape. You might place the tin or basket under the poster of the apple tree, if you made one for decoration.

Apple hop. Cut large apple shapes from yellow, green and red construction paper. Tape the apple shapes to the floor. Play music and have the children jump from one apple to another.

Craft: Paper apple

Materials needed: Red and green construction paper, fiberfill, twine or ribbon, small twigs, white glue or glue sticks, paper plates and cotton swabs if using white glue. Advance preparation: Cut red paper into apple shapes, about four to five inches tall — two per craft. Cut green paper into long joined leaf shape — one per craft. Cut twine or ribbon into nine-inch lengths. At storytime: Place white glue in paper plates with swabs. Pull small piece of fiberfill for each child to place between the two pieces of red apple paper, then glue the edges together, inserting the twig at the top. Tie twine around twig, then glue long leaf around the twig.

Alternative Crafts

Apple magnet. Red sheet foam, green sheet foam, google eyes, foam glue, paper plates and cotton swabs for glue, strip or roll of self-stick magnets. Cut all shapes and magnet squares. At storytime, pour some foam glue into paper plates for children to dip swabs and glue pieces together. Glue stem, leaf and worm to apple. Glue eye to worm. Peel paper off magnet strip and attach to back.

Apple prints. Cut apples in half. Stick a fork in the apple (so children's hands don't get paint-covered) and let children dip apple in paint and make prints on paper. Use different paint colors like red, yellow and green.

Snack: Apple smiles

Materials needed: Red apples, knife, caramel sundae topping or dip, mini marshmallows, plastic knives, paper plates. Advance preparation: Slice apples and rinse in a sugar water solution to keep them from getting brown. At storytime: Give each child two apple slices on a paper plate, a plastic knife, a dollop of caramel for them to spread on their apples and four mini marshmallows to place between the slices to look like teeth. Let the children assemble and then eat their apple smiles.

Alternative Snacks

Wormy apple. Cut apples in half sideways and hollow out the core. carve a little ditch from one side to the center and place a gummy worm in it.

Apple muffins, apple tarts, apple pie, any kind of baked good made from apples.

SUGGESTED BOOKS

Aliki. *The Story of Johnny Appleseed.* 32 pages. 1963. Simon & Schuster. Tells the story of Johnny Ap-

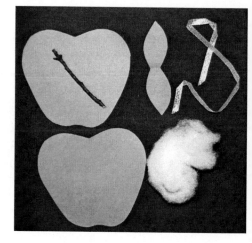

Paper apple pieces.

Paper apple.

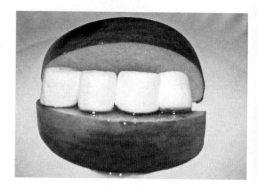

Apple smiles.

pleseed as he gave seeds and planted trees for the pioneers. Also describes his relationship with Indians and efforts to make peace between the settlers and the Indians.

Berry, Lynn. *Ducking for Apples.* 32 pages. 2010. Henry Holt & Co. The five little ducks see some great apples on the tree, but can they reach them?

Demuth, Patricia B. *Johnny Appleseed.* All Aboard Reading Learn to Read 1. 32 pages. 1996. Penguin Group Inc. Tells the story of John Chapman, also known as Johnny Appleseed, who traveled west to plant apple trees.

Dragonwagon, Crescent. *Alligator Arrived with Apples: A Potluck Alphabet Feast.* 40 pages. 1992. Simon & Schuster. Alliterative description of the guests and menu of a Thanksgiving feast.

Esbaum, Jill. *Apples for Everyone.* 16 pages. 2009. Baker & Taylor. Beautiful photography showing apples on the trees, in baskets and made into delicious foods.

Farmer, Jacqueline. *Apples.* 48 pages. 2007. Charlesbridge Publishing. A trip to an apple orchard explains how seeds and seedlings turn into apples. Includes recipes, trivia and fun facts.

Gibbons, Gail. *Apples.* 32 pages. 2000. Holiday House. Everything to know about apples, starting with pollination and ending with picking the fruit from the trees.

Gibbons, Gail. *The Seasons of Arnold's Apple Tree.* 28 pages. 1984. Harcourt Brace. Shows an apple tree as it changes each season.

Gravett, Emily. *Orange Pear Apple Bear.* 32 pages. 2007. Simon & Schuster Children's Publishing. Very simple picture book that contains only 5 different words, 4 of which are in the title.

Hall, Zoe. *The Apple Pie Tree.* 32 pages. 1996. Scholastic. Two sisters watch an apple tree change season to season.

Harrison, David L. *Johnny Appleseed: My Story.* 48 pages. 2001. A Step Into Reading Book Step 3. Random House Children's Books. Told from Johnny Appleseed's perspective, the story of how he headed west planting apple seeds.

Herman, Emmi S. *We All Fall for Apples.* A Scholastic Reader Level 1. 32 pages. 2006. Scholastic. A family and friends go to an apple farm where they pick apples and go on a hayride. The next day they make jam and bread out of their apples.

Hollub, Joan. *Apple Countdown.* 32 pages. 2009. Albert Whitney and Co. A class takes a field trip to an apple farm in this counting book.

Hopkinson, Deborah. *Apples to Oregon.* 40 pages. 2004. Simon & Schuster Children's Publishing. The mostly true story of a family's getting their fruit trees to Oregon during pioneer days.

Hutchings, Amy. *Picking Apples and Pumpkins.* 32 pages. 1994. Scholastic Inc. Going on a hayride and picking apples and pumpkins. Read just the first part until they get to the pumpkins.

Jeunesse, Gallimar. *Fruit.* 1989. Editions Gallamard. Use for the photos of apples and how they grow. Just read the beginning where it shows apples.

Kellogg, Steven. *Johnny Appleseed.* 48 pages. 2008. HarperCollins Publishers. Johnny Appleseed cleared the land and planted orchards of apple trees for the settlers he knew would be coming to the west.

Kurtz, Jane. *Johnny Appleseed.* 32 pages. 2004. Simon Spotlight. A Ready to Read Step 1 book that tells the story of Johnny Appleseed.

Lindbergh, Reeve. *Johnny Appleseed: A Poem.* 32 pages. 1993. Little, Brown Books for Young Readers. Rhymed text and illustrations describing the life of John Chapman, otherwise known as Johnny Appleseed.

Lipson, Eden Ross. *Applesauce Season.* 28 pages. 2009. Roaring Brook Press. A family makes applesauce with many different types of apples.

MacDonald, Suse. *A Was Once an Apple Pie.* 32 pages. 2005. Scholastic. Edward Lear's fun to say alphabet rhyme in a picture book.

McNamara, Margaret. *Apples A to Z.* 40 pages. 2012. Scholastic. An ABC book all about apples.

Murray, Allison. *Apple Pie ABC.* 32 pages. 2011. Hyperion Press. A little dog does everything in the alphabet to get some apple pie, but will he get a piece?

Olsen, Madeline. *Johnny Appleseed.* Hello Reader Level 1. 29 pages. 2001. Scholastic. Short easy story introducing Johnny Appleseed.

Parish, Herman. *Amelia Bedelia's First Apple Pie.* 32 pages. 2010. HarperCollins Publishers. The young Amelia Bedelia bakes her first apple pie with her grandmother.

Rockwell, Anne. *Apples and Pumpkins.* 24 pages. 2011. Aladdin. Right before Halloween a family visits a farm to pick apples and pumpkins.

Saunders-Smith, Gail. *From Blossom to Fruit.* 24 pages. 2000. Coughlan Publishing. Photos and text describing the growth of apples from blossom to fruit.

Seuss, Dr. *Ten Apples Up on Top*. 58 pages. 1998. Random House. A rhyming, counting story about animals carrying 10 apples on their heads.

Shepherd, Jodie. *Johnny Appleseed*. 32 pages. 2010. Scholastic Inc. The story of how Johnny Appleseed grew from a young man who loved the outdoors to a man who spread apple trees across the country.

Snyder, Inez. *Apples*. 24 pages. 2004. Children's Press. Basic information about how apples grow and are harvested.

Thompson, Lauren. *The Apple Pie That Papa Baked*. 32 pages. 2007. Simon & Schuster Children's Publishing. The story begins with the pie baked, but takes us back to the beginning with the gathering of the apples, then all the steps involved in a gentle rhythmic text.

Watts, Barrie. *Apple Tree*. 23 pages. 1986. A & C Black Limited. Describes how an apple grows from a blossom to fruit. It might be best to read the main sentence on each page to give a good basic description of how apples grow on trees.

Winget, Susan. *Tucker's Apple-Dandy Day*. 40 pages. 2006. HarperCollins Publishers. Tucker promises he'll bring home some apples, but he forgets.

Yolen, Jane. *Johnny Appleseed*. 32 pages. 2008. HarperCollins Publishers. Lovely paintings highlight the telling of facts and the legendary life of John Chapman.

Zoo

Advance planning: To plan for this storytime, find a theme-related song to play during craft and snack times, like "Going to the Zoo," by Raffi. You will also want to select a poem, such as "Zoo Fun," by Beverly Qualheim (find it at http://www.scrapbook.com/poems/doc/6413/110.html), along with the books you plan to read. Decorate your space with stuffed animals you might find in the zoo and a pith helmet that looks like a zoo keeper's hat.

Introduction to theme: Zoos are places where we can go see many animals that we might not be able to see around our neighborhoods, or towns, or even in our country. We can see the animals in places that look like where they live, in water or on rocks or in trees. Have you ever been to the zoo? What animals did you see? What's your favorite animal to visit at the zoo? Today we'll read about animals at the zoo, play a zoo game, make a zoo animal craft and eat a snack that looks like a zoo animal.

Song: "Going to the Zoo." Lyrics can be found at www.metrolyrics.com.

Game: Animal sounds

Materials needed: Recorded animal sounds on a CD, CD player. Advance preparation: Record animal sounds from the www.findsounds.com, make a list of the animals. Suggested animals: polar bear; lion; hippo; flamingo; zebra; snake; elephant; leopard; peacock; walrus; chimpanzee; seal; penguin; macaw; children. At storytime: Play the disk of animal sounds and ask the children what animals make those sounds.

Alternative Games

Where would you find it? Show pictures of different animals—some you find at the zoo, some at home—ask the children which place you'd find each animal.

To the tune of "If You're Happy": "If you want to be a monkey jump up high" (jump). Repeat with: bird—flap your wings; elephant—swing your trunk; lion—roar out loud;

giraffe—stand up tall; snake—slither slow; seal—clap your flippers; penguin—waddle walk.

Tail of the snake. Line up, single file, hands on the shoulders or waist of the child in front of you. The child in front then tries to tag the last one in line without the line falling apart.

What I saw at the zoo. Go around and let each child finish the sentence: "At the zoo I saw a ..."

Zoo-fari. Make up pictures of zoo animals and place them all around the storytime area. Send the children to hunt for the animals and bring them back to the zoo. Have a poster with a picture of a zoo and the word zoo on it for the children to place the animals.

Animal antics. Play some jungle music and have everyone act out different animals.

Zebra paper bag puppet pieces.

Craft: Zebra paper bag puppet

Materials needed: White paper bags, black and white construction paper, large google eyes, glue sticks. Advance preparation: Cut black triangles, white ears, black ear inserts, black nostrils, white muzzle, black forelock, black face stripes. At storytime: Have children glue black ear inserts onto white ears. Then glue ears onto white paper bag along with black face stripes, black body triangles, muzzle, nostrils and forelock. Add google eyes.

Alternative Crafts

Zoo collage. Gather *National Geographic, Zoobooks* or *Zoo Today* magazines. Let the children cut out pictures of animals from the magazines and glue them onto a background piece of paper in a collage.

Zebra paper bag puppet.

Brown or polar bear. If you're going to read the book *Brown Bear, Brown Bear, What Do You See?* or *Polar Bear, Polar Bear, What Do You Hear?* have the children make a stick puppet of each animal (copy pictures from the book and have the children cut around and glue them to popsicle sticks) then when they see their animal in the story they should stand up and make their animal's sound.

Snack: Tiger cupcake

Materials needed: Yellow or orange cupcakes, chocolate icing, Cheerios or other loop cereal, chocolate chips, brown M&Ms, miniature marshmallows. Advance preparation: Bake cupcakes. At

Tiger cupcake.

storytime: Decorate the cupcakes with icing as stripes, two chocolate chips as eyes, two Cheerios or other loop cereal as ears, one brown M & M or chocolate chip as nose, two miniature marshmallows as teeth.

Alternative Snacks

Animals in cages. Give each child half of a large graham cracker, so that it's square, and let them spread either marshmallow crème or peanut butter on it. Then let them place an animal cracker on top and several strips of licorice string on top of the animal cracker so that it looks like the animal is in a cage.

Tiger muffins. Make carrot muffins, decorate with raisins to look like tiger stripes.

Zebra cupcakes. Make white cupcakes, decorate with black licorice pieces as stripes and chocolate chips for eyes.

Animal sandwich. Use animal-shaped cookie cutters (a variety) to cut animal shapes from bread. Offer different spreads, like peanut butter, jelly, cream cheese, or cut pieces of cheese to match the animal shapes.

Animal crackers.

SUGGESTED BOOKS

Aliki. *My Visit to the Zoo*. 40 pages. 1999. Harper-Collins Publishers. See animals in their natural habitat as well as the zoo.

Amery, Heather. *What's Happening at the Zoo?* 16 pages. 1993. EDC Publishing. Detailed illustrations provide lots of things to talk about.

Beaton, Clare. *How Loud Is a Lion?* 24 pages. 2002. Barefoot Books. Felt, beads, braids and sequins are used to make the animals in this book.

Bleiman, Andrew. *Zooborns*. 160 pages. 2010. Simon & Schuster. Not a story book, but a collection of cute photos of new born animals at the zoo. Would be fun to show some of the photos.

Bostrom, Kathleen Long. *The View at the Zoo*. 32 pages. 2011. Ideals Publications. Who has the more interesting view? The zookeeper, the animals or the zoo guests?

Brennan, John. *Zoo Day*. 32 pages. 1989. Lerner Publishing Group. What goes on at an Australian zoo.

Bruna, Dick. *Miffy at the Zoo*. 24 pages. 2004. Big Tent Entertainment. Readers learn the names of different animals that Miffy visits at the zoo.

Bruna, Dick. *What's at the Zoo, Miffy?* 16 pages. 2004. Big Tent Entertainment. Miffy visits the zoo and readers are invited to guess what animals she sees by the questions that are asked.

Carle, Eric. *1, 2, 3 to the Zoo*. 32 pages. 1982. Penguin Group. Each car on the train has one more animal than the last. A counting book.

Degman, Lori. *1 Zany Zoo*. 32 pages. 2010. Simon & Schuster Children's Publishing. A counting book involving zoo animals and a zookeeper doing silly things.

Duffy, Carol Ann. *Moon Zoo*. 32 pages. 2011. Macmillan Publishers Limited. A special zoo on the moon where animals do strange things.

Ellis, Andy. *When Lulu Went to the Zoo*. 32 pages. 2010. Lerner Publishing Group. Lulu sneaks the animals at the zoo to her house.

Florian, Douglas. *At the Zoo*. 32 pages. 1992. HarperCollins Publishers. First time zoo visitors get a glimpse of who lives there.

Fore, S.J. *Read to Tiger*. 32 pages. 2010. Penguin Group Inc. A little boy is trying to read but the tiger wants to play.

Fox, Mem. *Zoo-Looking*. 32 pages. 1996. Mondo Publishing. A father and daughter visit the zoo and not only do they look at the animals, but the animals look at them too.

Garland, Michael. *Last Night at the Zoo*. 32 pages. 2003. Boyds Mill Press. Animals at the zoo plan a wild night on the town.

Gibbons, Gail. *Zoo*. 32 pages. 1991. HarperCollins Publishers. Provides a behind the scenes look at what happens at the zoo.

Hall, Michael. *My Heart Is Like a Zoo*. 32 pages. 2009. Harper Collins. Meet the 20 animals all made of heart shapes.

Hatkoff, Craig. *Leo the Snow Leopard*. 40 pages. 2010. Scholastic. Leo the cub was rescued and brought to the Bronx Zoo.

Howe, James. *The Day the Teacher Went Bananas*. 32

pages. 1992. Penguin Group. A class's new teacher must return to the zoo, as he is a gorilla.

Jarman, Julia. *Class Two at the Zoo*. 32 pages. 2007. Lerner Publishing Group. While the children are on their zoo field trip, they don't notice the anaconda that's gotten loose and is following them.

Jay, Alison. *Welcome to the Zoo*. 32 pages. 2008. Penguin Group. Search and find small details while visiting animals at the zoo.

Lopshire, Robert. *Put Me in the Zoo*. 72 pages. 1960. Random House Children's Books. Spot, a leopard, tries to convince two children that he belongs in the zoo, as he has some extraordinary talents.

Martin, Bill, Jr., and Eric Carle. *Brown Bear, Brown Bear, What Do You See?* 32 pages. 1992. Henry Holt & Co. Rhyme and repetition meeting a new animal on every page.

Martin, Bill, Jr. and Eric Carle. *Polar Bear, Polar Bear, What Do You Hear?* 28 pages. 1991. Henry Holt & Co. Children love to make the sounds of the zoo animals that they meet in this book.

McDonnell, Flora. *Splash!* 32 pages. 1999. Candlewick. When the jungle animals are hot, the baby elephant has a good solution.

McKee, David. *Zebra's Hiccups*. 32 pages. 2009. Andersen. Zebra must listen to the other animals to cure his hiccups or risk losing his stripes.

Munari, Bruno. *Bruno Munari's Zoo*. 48 pages. 2005. Chronicle Books. Artist Munari's book features animals at the zoo with retro text and bright, bold artwork.

Palecek, Libuse. *Brave as a Tiger*. 32 pages. 1995. North-South Books. After the other tigers make fun of him, a young tiger shows he can be brave when he needs to be.

Parramon, J.M. *My First Visit to the Zoo*. 32 pages. 1990. Barron's Education Series. Children visiting the zoo see lots of animals and also learn about how the zoo functions.

Paxton, Tom. *Going to the Zoo*. 40 pages. 1996. Harper Collins Publishers. Tom Paxton's classic song about going to the zoo comes to life. Includes the music and lyrics.

Pfister, Marcus. *Charlie at the Zoo*. 32 pages. 2007. North-South Books Inc. Charlie the Duck visits the zoo.

Rathmann, Peggy. *Goodnight Gorilla*. 34 pages. 1996. Penguin Group Inc. The gorilla follows the zookeeper as he makes his rounds at night, letting all the animals out and they follow the zookeeper home.

Rey, Margret, H.A. Rey and Alan J. Shalleck. *Curious George Visits the Zoo*. 32 pages. 1985. Houghton Mifflin Harcourt Trade and Reference. Curious George visits the zoo and takes some bananas from the zookeeper.

Rose, Deborah Lee. *Birthday Zoo*. 24 pages. 2006. Whitman, Albert & Company. A rhyming book with a child celebrating his birthday with zoo animals.

Rowan, James P. *I Can Be a Zookeeper*. 29 pages. 1985. Scholastic Library. Explores the world of people who work with animals in zoos.

Scheer, Ruth. *Giraffe at the Zoo*. 26 pages. 2000. Scheer Delight Publishing. A giraffe is trying to reach greener grass and thinks up a plan.

Schofield, Louise. *The Zoo Room*. 32 pages. 2005. Simply Read Books. A birthday party with zoo animals.

Seuss, Dr. *If I Ran the Zoo*. 64 pages. 1995. Random House Children's Books. Young Gerald McGrew thinks up many different animals for the zoo in this rhyming book.

Seuss, Dr. *On Beyond Zebra*. 64 pages. 1980. Random House Children's Books. Starts the alphabet after Z in this rhyming book.

Sierra, Judy. *There's a Zoo in Room 22*. 40 pages. 2004. Houghton Mifflin Harcourt. Miss Darling's class has 26 pets, one for every letter of the alphabet.

Sierra, Judy. *Wild About Books*. 40 pages. 2004. Random House Children's Books. Rhyming story about animals at the zoo and their love of reading.

Sierra, Judy. *ZooZical*. 40 pages. 2011. Alfred A. Knopf. In the winter when they're bored, some zoo animals decide to stage a musical production they call a zoozical.

Simon, Paul. *At the Zoo*. 32 pages. 1992. Harper-Collins Publishers. A musical romp through the zoo.

Stead, Erin. *A Sick Day for Amos McGee*. 32 pages. 2010. Roaring Brook Press. The zookeeper is ill and must stay home so the animals visit him instead.

Vaughan, Kathryn Mademann. *My Day at the Zoo*. 2004. Chaser Media. Singalong, readalong picture book with CD. Simple text with music takes a multi-cultural journey.

Wilson, Karma. *Animal Strike at the Zoo*. 32 pages. 2006. Harper Collins. The zoo animals go on strike.

Wilson, Karma. *Never Ever Shout in a Zoo*. 32 pages. 2004. Little, Brown Books for Young Readers. Rhyming text depicting the chaos caused by shouting at the zoo.

Dinosaurs

Advance planning: To plan for this storytime, find a theme-related song to play during craft and snack times, like "Walk the Dinosaur," by Was (Not Was). You will also want to select a poem, such as "Tricera-Flops," by Marilyn Singer (find it in *Dizzy Dinosaurs: Silly Dinosaur Poems*, by Lee Bennett Hopkins), along with the books you plan to read. Decorate your space with green streamers or live plants, jungle sounds background music, stuffed dinosaurs or posters.

Introduction to theme: Dinosaurs roamed the earth a long long time ago, millions of years ago. There were over 500 different kinds of dinosaurs. Some of them were really big, bigger than a house, but there were also some that were very small, about the size of a chicken. Some could swim, some could fly. They became extinct, which means there aren't any of them alive anymore, and no one knows exactly why, although it's thought that an asteroid may have hit Earth. Today we'll read about dinosaurs, play a dinosaur game, make a dinosaur craft and have a snack that even looks like a dinosaur.

Song: "I'd Like to Be a Giant, Fearsome Dinosaur," to the tune of "I Wish I Were An Oscar Meyer Weiner":

> Oh I'd like to be a giant, fearsome dinosaur,
> That is what I'd truly like to be-e-e.
> For if I were a giant, fearsome dinosaur
> Everyone would run away from me.

Game: What time is it, Ms. T. Rex?

Materials needed: None. Advance preparation: None. At storytime: You are the T. Rex and stand with your back turned to the children about 5 yards from them. Lead the children in calling out, "What time is it, Ms. T. Rex?" and you turn to face them and shout out a time, for example two o'clock. The children then take two steps toward you. They take the same amount of steps toward you as the amount of hours in the time. For example, two o'clock = two steps, six o'clock = six steps, etc. After each set of steps, you turn your back to them again for them to yell "what time is it Ms. T. Rex?" (You look at them only when you shout the time at the group. When they get close to you the next time they yell "What's the time, Ms. T. Rex?" you will say "DINNER TIME!" and run after them pretending to catch them before they get back to the start line.

Alternative Games

Dinosaur foot print musical chairs. Print from computer and copy or cut from construction paper dinosaur foot prints. Place one of these per child on the floor in a circle or a line. Play music like Everybody Walk the Dinosaur and have the children start walking around the foot prints. Stop the music and everyone should stand on a foot print. Start the music again and take away a foot print. When you stop the music everyone needs to be standing on a foot print (they can share a foot print with someone else) or at least touching someone who's touching a foot print. Repeat and take away another foot print. Do this until the group is all crowded together very tightly. You could then pretend to be a T. Rex and say that you have captured all the little dinosaurs.

Dinosaur concentration. Make a set of dinosaur picture cards, with two of each kind of dinosaur that are similar but not exactly the same. Hold up one picture to the children and tell them what kind of dinosaur it is. Then hold up another and ask if it's the same kind of dinosaur or different. Sometimes it will be and sometimes it won't. If it's not the same kind, tell them what kind the other one is.

Dinosaur dance. After reading *Dinosaurumpus*, ask the children to imagine how dinosaurs moved. Play Walk the Dinosaur and have the children dance like dinosaurs might.

Dinosaur length. Have an eighty foot-long piece of yarn. Give one end to one child and add children to its length until you've reached the other end. Once it's fully stretched out explain that that was the length of an average Apatosaurus.

Paper plate dinosaur pieces.

Craft: Paper plate dinosaur

Materials needed: Paper plates, scissors, crayons or markers, brass brads or stapler. Advance preparation: Cut neck, tail and leg pieces from paper plates. Cut tail piece first from plate rim, then neck. Round the head. Cut the two legs from the middle of the paper plate. Punch holes if using brads. At storytime: Have children color all paper plate pieces, then assemble using brads (or staple them together).

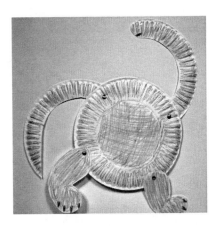

Paper plate dinosaur.

Alternative Crafts

Shape-o-saurus. Make several different shapes, like an oval for the body, triangles for the spikes on the back, a circle for the head, rectangles for the neck and the legs and tail and let the children pick out the shapes they want to use and glue together. Decorate with crayons.

Stained glass dinosaur. Cut small pieces of tissue paper. Let children stick the pieces of tissue paper onto clear contact paper. Put another piece of contact paper on top to seal and then cut in the shape of a dinosaur (have a template). Punch a hole in the top, attach string or yarn and hang.

What hatched? Have large white egg-shaped pieces of paper cut in half. Let the children glue the halves down to a piece of paper and draw the dinosaur that hatched from their egg.

Snack: Chocolate pudding with dinosaur fruit snack

Materials needed: Chocolate pudding in cups, dinosaur fruit snacks, spoons. Advance preparation: Bury some dino-

Chocolate pudding with dinosaur fruit snacks.

saur fruit snacks in each pudding cup. At storytime: Hand each child a pudding cup and a spoon.

Alternative Snacks

Dinosaur cookies. Use a dinosaur-shaped cookie cutter to make cookies ahead of time. Let children ice and decorate.

Dinosaur fruit snacks.

SUGGESTED BOOKS

Many of the older books refer to Brontosaurus, which is now called Apatosaurus by most paleontologists.

Aliki. *Digging Up Dinosaurs.* 32 pages. 1988. HarperCollins Publishers. Briefly introduces dinosaurs whose skeletons are found in museums.

Aliki. *Dinosaur Bones.* 32 pages. 1990. HarperCollins Publishers. Discusses how scientists get information from fossils.

Aliki. *Fossils Tell of Long Ago.* 32 pages. 1999. Houghton Mifflin Harcourt. Explains how fossils are formed and what they tell us about the past.

Aliki. *My Visit to the Dinosaurs.* 32 pages. 1985. HarperCollins Publishers. A visit to a museum provides a little boy with an introduction to dinosaurs.

Bakker, Robert T. *Dino Babies.* 24 pages. 2010. Random House Children's Books. Explores whether or not dinosaurs were good parents.

Barton, Byron. *Bones, Bones, Dinosaur Bones.* 32 pages. 1990. HarperCollins Publishers. A cast of characters looks for, finds and assembles some dinosaur bones.

Barton, Byron. *Dinosaurs, Dinosaurs.* 40 pages. 1993. HarperCollins Publishers. A colorful view of how it was when dinosaurs were around a long time ago.

Bauer, Marion Dane. *Dinosaur Thunder.* 32 pages. 2012. Scholastic. Brannon is scared by thunder, but once it's compared to dinosaurs, it helps him to get over his fear.

Berenstain, Michael. *The Biggest Dinosaurs.* 24 pages. 1990. Random House Children's Books. Describes what is known about some of the biggest dinosaurs.

Blumenthal, Nancy. *Count-a-Saurus.* 24 pages. 1993. Scholastic. Numbered groups of dinosaurs.

Bright, Paul. *Crunch Crunch Dinosaur Lunch.* 32 pages. 2010. Good Books. A big brother dinosaur ultimately looks after his little sister dinosaur.

Broach, Elise. *When Dinosaurs Came with Everything.* 40 pages. 2007. Simon & Schuster Children's Publishing. What happens when you're given a free dinosaur with everything you buy?

Carrick, Carol. *Big Old Bones.* 32 pages. 1992. Houghton Mifflin. Professor Potts puts together some big old bones in different ways until he's satisfied that he's found a dinosaur that once ruled the earth.

Carrick, Carol. *Patrick's Dinosaurs.* 32 pages. 1985. Houghton Mifflin Harcourt. When his older brother talks about dinosaurs, Patrick is afraid until he finds out that they no longer exist.

Carrick, Carol. *What Happened to Patrick's Dinosaurs?* 32 pages. 1988. Houghton Mifflin Harcourt. Fascinated by dinosaurs, Patrick invents an imaginary explanation for why they became extinct.

Chewning, Randy. *You Can Name 100 Dinosaurs and Other Prehistoric Animals.* 14 pages. 1994. Scholastic. Depicts 100 of the most popular dinosaurs.

DK Publishing. *Dinosaurs.* 14 pages. 2007. DK Publishing. Photographic pop ups with detailed images of dinosaurs.

Donnelly, Lisa. *Dinosaur Day.* 32 pages. 1987. Scholastic. Crazy about dinosaurs, a boy and his dog imagine they see them everywhere.

Eastman, David. *I Can Read About Prehistoric Animals.* 1997. San Val. Tells about the animals and how they lived.

Eastman, David. *Story of Dinosaurs.* 32 pages. 1989. Troll Communications. A brief introduction to dinosaurs and how they lived.

Faulkner, Keith. *David Dreaming of Dinosaurs.* 16 pages. 1992. W.J. Fantasy. David is crazy about dinosaurs and loves to go to the museum.

Freedman, Clare. *Dinosaurs Love Underpants.* 32 pages. 2009. Simon & Schuster Children's Publishing. Explains why dinosaurs disappeared in a funny way involving underpants.

Gibbons, Gail. *Dinosaurs*. 32 pages. 2008. Holiday House. Simple text and illustrations introduce young readers to dinosaurs.

Greathouse, Carol. *The Dinosaur Tamer*. 32 pages. 2009. Penguin Group. Brings together dinosaurs and cowboys.

Harrison, Carol. *Dinosaurs Everywhere*. 40 pages. 1998. Scholastic. Realistic illustrations showing how dinosaurs lived.

Hearne, Diane Dawson. *Dad's Dinosaur Day*. 32 pages. 1999. Simon & Schuster Children's Publishing. Dad has become a dinosaur, allowing his son to have a day of adventure.

Hoff, Syd. *Danny and the Dinosaur*. 64 pages. 1993. HarperCollins Publishers. Danny's out and about with his dinosaur.

Jablonsky, Alice. *Discover Dinosaurs*. 16 pages. 1994. Part of the Comes to Life book series.

Joyce, William. *Dinosaur Bob and His Adventures with the Family Lazardo*. 48 pages. 1995. HarperCollins Publishers. While vacationing in Africa, the Lazardo family finds and brings back a dinosaur.

Kelly, Milner Halls. *Hatchlings: Life Size Baby Dinosaurs*. 24 pages. 2012. Running Press Book Publishers. Shows actual size pictures of real baby dinosaurs within the pages of the book.

Kulka, Joe. *Vacation's Over! Return of the Dinosaurs*. 32 pages. 2010. Lerner Publishing Group. The dinosaurs aren't extinct, they were just away on vacation!

Mansell, Dom. *If Dinosaurs Came to Town*. 1998. Demco Media. Imagines what it would be like to meet up with dinosaurs today.

Marzollo, Jean. *I'm Tyrannosaurus! A Book of Dinosaur Rhymes*. 30 pages. 1993. Scholastic. Dinosaurs describe their characteristics in rhyme.

Mitton, Tony. *Dinosaurumpus*. 32 pages. 2009. Scholastic. Rhymes and illustrations of dinosaurs dancing to the dinosaur beat.

Mosley, Francis. *The Dinosaur Eggs*. 32 pages. 1989. Children's Press Choice. A lonely couple wishing for children hatches three dinosaur eggs and raises them.

Most, Bernard. *How Big Were the Dinosaurs?* 38 pages. 1995. Houghton Mifflin Harcourt Trade & Reference Publishers. Describes the size of different kinds of dinosaurs by comparing them to well-known things.

Most, Bernard. *If the Dinosaurs Came Back*. 32 pages. 1984. Houghton Mifflin Harcourt. A young boy wishes for the dinosaurs to come back and imagines how useful they would be.

Most, Bernard. *Whatever Happened to the Di-nosaurs?* 40 pages. 1987. Houghton Mifflin Harcourt. A humorous speculation on what really happened to the dinosaurs.

Noonan, Joe. *Dinosaur Dance*. 16 pages. 1994. Sundance/Newbridge Educational Publishing. A fanciful look at dinosaur dancing styles.

Pallotta, Jerry. *The Dinosaur Alphabet Book*. 32 pages. 1990. Charlesbridge Publishing. Pictures and descriptions of a whole alphabet of dinosaurs.

Parish, Peggy. *Dinosaur Time*. 32 pages. 1983. HarperCollins Publishers. Words and pictures help children learn about eleven dinosaur species.

Pfister, Marcus. *Dazzle the Dinosaur*. 12 pages. 2009. North-South Books. With his beautiful shiny spines, Dazzle is the most spectacular dinosaur ever.

Plourde, Lynn. *Dino Pets*. 32 pages. 2007. Penguin Group. A dinosaur fan goes to the dinosaur store to get a pet.

Pringle, Laurence. *Dinosaurs Strange and Wonderful*. 30 pages. 2004. Scholastic. Describes different kinds of dinosaurs and how paleontologists study them.

Pulver, Robin. *Mrs. Toggle and the Dinosaur*. 32 pages. 1995. Aladdin. Mrs. Toggle's new student is a dinosaur.

Rowe, Erna. *Giant Dinosaurs*. 29 pages. 2000. Scholastic. Discusses the size, diet and habitat of some of the largest dinosaurs.

Schnetzler, Patty. *Ten Little Dinosaurs*. 32 pages. 1996. Accord Publishing, Limited. Rhyming verse describes the antics of ten different kinds of dinosaur.

Schwartz, Henry. *How I Captured a Dinosaur*. 32 pages. 1996. Silver Burdett. Liz finds a living Albertosaurus on a camping trip and brings it home with her.

Shea, Bob. *Dinosaur vs. Bedtime*. 40 pages. 2008. Hyperion Books for Children. What happens when Dinosaur faces the biggest challenge of all? Bedtime.

Shea, Bob. *Dinosaur vs. the Library*. 40 pages. 2011. Hyperion Books for Children. How will Dinosaur's roaring go over at the library?

Sis, Peter. *Dinosaur!* 28 pages. 2005. HarperCollins Publishers. While taking a bath, a young boy is joined by all sorts of dinosaurs. A wordless book.

Smith, Stu. *Dinosaur Hide and Seek*. 20 pages. 2004. HarperCollins Publishers. A lift the flap book where you help the baby dino find all his friends.

Stickland, Paul. *Dinosaur Roar!* 12 pages. 1997. Penguin Group. Dinosaurs of all shapes and sizes roar through this book of opposites.

Stickland, Paul. *Dinosaur Stomp!* 14 pages. 2001. Penguin Group. A colorful collection of dinosaurs heads off for a dinosaur dance in the swamp.

Stickland, Paul. *Dinosaurs Galore!* 12 pages. 2010. Sterling Publishing Company Inc. A pop-up book featuring the Dinosaur Roar family.

Stickland, Paul. *Ten Terrible Dinosaurs.* 48 pages. 2000. Penguin Group. Rhyming text in this dinosaur counting book.

Surgal, Jon. *Have You Seen My Dinosaur?* 48 pages. 2010. Random House Children's Books. Rhyming story from the Dr. Seuss library about a boy's missing dinosaur.

Taback, Simms. *Dinosaurs: A Giant Fold-Out Book.* 20 pages. 2012. Blue Apple Books. Asks "who am I?" and then gives clues as you unfold the pages to show different dinosaurs.

Waddell, Martin. *The Super Hungry Dinosaur.* 32 pages. 2009. Penguin Group. Kids will be rooting for Hal to save his parents and his dog from the super hungry dinosaur.

Whybrow, Ian. *Harry and the Bucketful of Dinosaurs.* 32 pages. 2010. Random House Children's Books. Harry finds some toy dinosaurs in the attic and takes them around to play but accidentally leaves them on the train.

Wing, Natasha. *How to Raise a Dinosaur.* 24 pages. 2010. Running Press Book Publishers. Who knew that dinosaurs would make good pets?

Worth, Bonnie. *Oh Say Can You Say Di-No-Saur?* 48 pages. 1999. Random House Children's Books. From the Dr. Seuss library, a lot of facts about dinosaurs.

Yolen, Jane. *How Do Dinosaurs Clean Their Rooms?* 12 pages. 2004. Scholastic. A board book where dinosaurs learn to pick up their toys.

Yolen, Jane. *How Do Dinosaurs Say Good Night?* 40 pages. 2000. Scholastic. Ten sleepy dinosaurs are naughty at bedtime.

Yolen, Jane. *How Do Dinosaurs Say I Love You?* 40 pages. 2009. Scholastic. Dinosaurs are reminded that they're loved, even if they're naughty.

Autumn Leaves

Advance planning: To plan for this storytime, find a theme-related song to play during craft and snack times, like "Autumn Leaves," by Nat King Cole. You will also want to select a poem, such as "How the Leaves Came Down," by *Susan Coolidge* (find it at www.levelwise.org), along with the books you plan to read. Decorate your space with colorful leaves, a poster of a tree with colorful leaves, a bale of straw, pumpkins.

Introduction to theme: Do you know why leaves turn color in the fall? Inside leaves are little packages of color in green, yellow and orange. In the summer, the green packages are very busy. The green packages in the leaves catch sunlight and turn it into sugar. This sugar is the food for the tree. As Autumn approaches and the weather gets colder the tree gets ready for winter. The water tubes inside the leaves close up and no more water can get into the leaf! Without water, the green disappears and the yellow and orange colors in the leaf can be seen. Sometimes sugar gets caught inside the leaf and that causes the leaves to turn red or purple. Once the water stops and the leaves stop making sugar they begin to die. The green dies first, then the yellow and orange parts die too. When all the color parts are dead the leaves are brown and usually they're dry and crunchy. There are some trees whose leaves don't change color or lose their leaves — those are called evergreens. They hold on to the water inside them and stay alive and green all year. Today we'll read about Autumn leaves, play an Autumn game, make an Autumn leaf craft and have a snack that looks like a tree.

Song: "I Love Autumn," to the tune of "London Bridge Is Falling Down":

Leaves are falling from the trees, from the trees, from the trees
Leaves are falling from the trees, yellow, brown and red.
Falling, falling from above, from above, from above
Falling, falling from above, one landed on my head.
Take and rake and pile them up, pile them up, pile them up
Take and rake and pile them up, I love autumn.

Game: Pass the leaves, please

Materials needed: Paper plates, chopsticks or spoons, small Autumn-related objects like leaves, acorns, cranberries, other nuts like walnuts. Advance preparation: None. At storytime: Place four to six of these items on the paper plate in front of you and give everyone else a paper plate and a set of chopsticks or a spoon. Pass each item one at a time to the child next to you as fast as possible and have all the children pass each one along to the next until they're all back on your plate.

Alternative Games

Leaf toss. Need leaves and a bucket, child's rake if possible. Make a pile of leaves next to a bucket. See if the children can toss the leaves one by one into the bucket. Have them try holding each leaf higher or lower to see if it makes it easier or harder to get the leaves in. If you have a child's rake you could bring that in and let them have a turn raking the pile of leaves after they toss them.

Fall harvest bingo. Print up bingo cards with a fall theme. Use acorns as markers.

Leaves blowing. Give each child a leaf and a straw and line the children up and have them use the straws to blow the leaves across the room.

Craft: Autumn leaves wreath

Materials needed: Lots of leaves (either real or silk), circle wreath shape cut from large paper plate or construction paper in any color, glue sticks, yarn, scissors. Advance preparation: Cut circular wreath shapes from paper plate or any color construction paper; cut lengths of yarn roughly 16 inches long. At storytime: Give each child a circle wreath shape and leaves. Have them glue down leaves all around the circle. Tie a length of yarn to it so that they can hang on their door.

Autumn leaves wreath pieces.

Autumn leaves wreath.

Alternative Crafts

Sponge paint with leaf shapes. Either cut some leaf shapes (use real leaves as patterns) out of sponges or buy some. Put acrylic paint in large paper plates and let the children dip the sponges and stamp them on large pieces of plain paper.

Foliage friends. Have lots of leaves (either real or silk), background construction paper in any color (or multiple colors for choice), glue sticks or liquid glue, paper plates and cotton swabs, crayons or markers. Let children choose leaves to create their own character people from them. Glue down a leaf and then draw arms and legs and a head.

Rubbings with leaves. Collect fall leaves of all shapes and sizes. Place several leaves vein side up on a piece of white paper. Lay another sheet of plain white paper over the leaves. Peel the paper off some crayons. Use the side of the crayon and gently rub on the top sheet of the paper. Leaf shapes and their veins should appear.

Autumn placemat. Have the children stick leaves onto rectangles of clear contact paper. Cover with another piece of contact paper. Trim if necessary. Could tape around edge with colored masking or duct tape if desired.

Leaf ornaments. Place a colorful leaf in between two pieces of clear contact paper. Trim around the leaf. Punch a hole in the end near the stem and attach a piece of yarn or string to hang. Could do several leaves this way and make a mobile or just do one as a decoration.

Snack: Pretzel tree

Materials needed: Pretzel rods, paper plates, pretzel sticks, colored candies such as M&Ms or Skittles in fall colors such as orange, red, yellow. Advance preparation: None. At storytime: Show sample tree made of one pretzel rod trunk, several pretzel stick branches, and multiple candies placed around the branches as leaves. Give each child one pretzel rod, twelve pretzel sticks and twelve candies.

Alternative Snack

Leaf-shaped cookies. Make cookies using a leaf-shaped cookie cutter beforehand and let the children decorate them with fall colored icings and candies.

Pretzel tree.

SUGGESTED BOOKS

Berger, Carin. *The Little Yellow Leaf.* 40 pages. 2008. HarperCollins Publishers. A little yellow leaf that does not want to let go of its tree.

Bridwell, Norman. *Clifford's First Autumn.* 32 pages. 1997. Scholastic. Clifford the Small Red Puppy is introduced to Autumn as the seasons change and leaves fall.

Bullard, Lisa. *Leaves Fall Down: Learning About Autumn Leaves.* 24 pages. 2010. Picture Window Books. Discover why leaves change color

and feel the appeal of jumping into a big pile of leaves.

Buscaglia, Leo. *The Fall of Freddie the Leaf.* 32 pages. 1982. SLACK. Illustrating the delicate balance between life and death, the story of leaves that change with the seasons.

Colandro, Lucille. *There Was an Old Lady Who Swallowed Some Leaves.* 32 pages. 2010. Scholastic. A fall twist of the classic song.

Davis, L.J. *A Simple Brown Leaf.* 32 pages. 2004. Abovo Publishing. The story of a leaf who thinks that life is over when he falls from the tree but a squirrel finds another use for him.

dePaola, Tomie. *Four Friends in Autumn*. 32 pages. 2004. Simon & Schuster Children's Publishing. A beautiful fall day for the friends to come together to share friendship and food.

Dorman, Helen. *Okomi Plays in the Leaves*. 24 pages. 2003. Dawn Publications. Leaves are falling and Okomi gathers them and tosses them in the air.

Ehlert, Lois. *Leaf Man*. 40 pages. 2005. Houghton Mifflin Harcourt Trade & Reference Publishers. A journey with a man made of leaves.

Ehlert, Lois. *Red Leaf, Yellow Leaf*. 40 pages. 2010. Houghton Mifflin Harcourt Trade & Reference Publishers. Watercolor collage that shows the life of a tree.

Emerson, Carl. *The Autumn Leaf*. 32 pages. 2008. Picture Window Books. Only one leaf is left on the tree in the park. Will it fall too?

Emmett, Jonathan. *Leaf Trouble*. 32 pages. 2009. Scholastic. The squirrels are afraid when the leaves start falling from their trees.

Ferguson, Sarah. *Little Red's Autumn Adventure*. 40 pages. 2009. Simon & Schuster Children's Publishing. Little Red and her friends help mice who have lost their way.

Gerber, Carol. *Leaf Jumpers*. 32 pages. 2006. Charlesbridge Publishing. Rhyming text describes different kinds of leaves.

Glaser, Linda. *It's Fall!* 32 pages. 2001. Lerner Publishing Group. Paper sculpture illustrations showing the beauty of fall.

Good, Elaine W. *Fall Is Here! I Love It!* 32 pages. 1994. Good Books. Children learn about fall through the eyes of a country child.

Hawk, Fran. *Count Down to Fall*. 32 pages. 2009. Sylvan Dell Publishing. A counting book with the scenes all set in the fall.

Kelley, Marty. *Fall Is Not Easy*. 30 pages. 1998. Zino Press Children's Books. A rhyming story of a tree that's struggling to change its seasons for fall.

King, Stephen Michael. *Leaf*. 64 pages. 2008. Roaring Brook Press. A little boy who is afraid of getting his hair cut ends up with a plant growing from his head.

Metzger, Steve. *We're Going on a Leaf Hunt*. 32 pages. 2008. Scholastic. The traditional "going on a bear hunt" is turned into an Autumn leaf hunt.

Metzger, Steve. *When the Leaf Blew In*. 32 pages. 2009. Scholastic. Simple, repetitive text and silly illustrations that describe how one leaf turned a whole barnyard upside down.

Nidey, Kelly. *When Autumn Falls*. 32 pages. 2006. Whitman, Albert & Company. Beautiful cut paper artwork in a simple text book about Autumn.

Oelschlager, Vanita. *Ivan's Great Fall: Poetry for Summer and Autumn from Great Poets and Writers of the Past*. 44 pages. 2009. VanitaBooks. When a young boy is reluctant to leave summer behind he is introduced to the poetry of great authors who write about the seasons. A resource for poems about summer and fall.

O'Malley, Kevin. *Lucky Leaf*. 32 pages. 2007. Walker & Company. For children who would prefer staying inside and playing video games but whose parents want them to go play outside.

Polacco, Patricia. *For the Love of Autumn*. 40 pages. 2008. Penguin Group. Autumn is a kitten, beloved by the classroom teacher, who disappears in a storm but is found again.

Pragoff, Fiona. *Autumn*. 18 pages. 1993. Simon & Schuster Children's Publishing. Describes different aspects of autumn.

Raczka, Bob. *Who Loves the Fall*. 32 pages. 2007. Whitman, Albert & Company. Simple text and colorful paintings acknowledge that it can be hard to see summer end but there's much to look forward to in the fall.

Rawlinson, Julia. *Fletcher and the Falling Leaves*. 32 pages. 2008. HarperCollins Publishers. Fletcher's tree is losing its leaves and Fletcher is worried about it.

Robbins, Ken. *Autumn Leaves*. 40 pages. 1998. Scholastic. Examines the different kind of leaves and explains why they change color in Autumn.

Saunders-Smith, Gail. *Autumn Leaves*. 32 pages. 1997. Capstone Press. Different types and colors of leaves in the fall.

Schuette, Sarah L. *Let's Look at Fall*. 32 pages. 2007. Capstone Press. Describes what animals do and what happens to plants in the fall.

Spinelli, Eileen. *I Know It's Autumn*. 32 pages. 2004. HarperCollins Publishers. The many beautiful things about fall.

Stein, David Ezra. *Leaves*. 32 pages. 2007. Penguin Group. A young bear's first autumn and the falling leaves surprise him.

Thompson, Lauren. *Mouse's First Fall*. 32 pages. 2006. Simon & Schuster Children's Publishing. Mouse goes out to play in the colorful leaves of fall.

Wallace, Nancy Elizabeth. *Leaves Leaves Leaves*. 40 pages. 2007. Marshall Cavendish Corporation. Mama and Buddy Bear stroll through the seasons and look at their favorite trees.

Wells, Rosemary. *Ruby's Falling Leaves*. 24 pages. 2007. Penguin Group. Ruby makes a leaf collection book and Max makes a big pile of leaves.

Wiley, Thom. *The Leaves on the Trees*. 24 pages. 2011. Scholastic. Based on the song "The Wheels on the Bus" but about leaves on the trees falling down.

Yoon, Salina. *Leaves, Leaves*. 12 pages. 2008. Penguin Group. A stroll through the woods on a crisp autumn day.

October

Music

Advance planning: To plan for this storytime, find a theme-related song to play during craft and snack times, like "Crazy Horse," by John Trudell, "Danse Macabre," by Saint-Saëns, "Peer Gynt Suite No. 1," by Grieg, or "Bach Toccata and Fugue in D Minor." You'll also need the "Hokey Pokey" for the game. You will want to select a poem, such as "My Puppy Plays Piano," by Kenn Nesbitt (find it at www.poetry4kids.com), along with the books you plan to read. Decorate your space with musical instruments, posters of musical instruments and have some music playing as the children arrive.

Introduction to theme: Music is a kind of art where sound is used as the way the art is expressed. Think of the sounds like painters think of paint. Sometimes instruments are used to make music; sometimes our voices can make music — when we sing. We hear music all the time — in stores, on television, on the radio ... there are so many kinds of music. Today we'll make some of our own music plus listen to some different kinds. But first let's read some books including some that were written by some famous musicians. Today we'll read about music, play a musical game, make a musical craft and eat a musical snack.

Song: "I Am a Fine Musician" which can be found at www.songsforteaching.com.

Game: Hokey pokey. Lyrics for the song can be found at www.scoutsongs.com, or write them down after listening to a recording.

    Materials needed: Recording of "Hokey Pokey" on CD, CD player. Advance preparation: None. At storytime: Ask if everyone has heard the song before. If not, be prepared to show the moves and have the children practice them. Play the "Hokey Pokey" music and do the dance.

Alternative Games

    Cooperative musical chairs. Play like normal musical chairs except no one is ever out. They must sit together on the chairs, or in someone's lap, or just be touching someone who's in a chair.

    Mood music. Music can be used to deliver a message or it can make us feel a certain way. I have several pieces of music to play today and I'd like you to think about how the music makes you feel. Play "Crazy Horse," by John Trudell, "Danse Macabre," by Saint-Saëns, "Peer Gynt Suite No. 1," by Grieg, "Bach Toccata and Fugue in D Minor." Music also makes us want to move — to dance. Play another piece of dancing music, like something disco like "Y.M.C.A.," by Disco Fever.

Rhythm game. Sit in a circle and begin by choosing a simple rhythmic pattern like two beats of the tambourine or three beats that each child must imitate in turn until it comes back to you.

Craft: Tambourine

Materials needed: Heavy duty paper plates, hole punch, string, jingle bells, crayons. Advance preparation: Using a hole punch, make four holes around the plates, spacing them equally. Cut string in six-inch lengths, enough for each child to have four pieces. At storytime: Slip each jingle bell on a piece of string, slide it to the middle and tie a knot. Tie jingle bells to the holes. Decorate the tambourine with crayons. Shake to play.

Tambourine pieces.

Alternative Crafts

Comb buzzer. Need pocket comb and tissue paper. Fold a piece of tissue paper over the tooth edge of a comb. To play, hum through the tissue paper.

Guitar. Need empty shoe box, rubber bands, ruler or stick. Remove the cover from the box. Stretch the rubber bands around the box. Attach the ruler or stick to the back of the box on one end to act as the arm of the guitar. To play, strum or pluck the rubber bands.

Hand Bells. Two paper towel rolls, hole punch, four jingle bells, string or yarn. Punch a hole in each end of the paper towel rolls. Tie two jingle bells to each side of the paper towel rolls by running string or yarn through the holes and carefully tying off. Shake to play.

Attach crepe paper streamers to an empty paper towel roll or paper plate and use to move while dancing to music.

Snack: Drum cupcake

Materials needed: Cupcakes, two different colors of icing, pretzel sticks, paper plates, plastic knives. Advance preparation: Bake cupcakes. Buy two different colors of icing, or buy white icing

Tambourine.

and tint it two different colors. At storytime: Give each child a cupcake on a paper plate, a plastic knife, two different colors of icing and about six to eight pretzel sticks. Have them peel the paper liner off the cupcake and put one color of icing on the top and the other on the sides. Break pretzel sticks in half then place them around the sides in a V pattern to look like a drum. Save two pretzel sticks to use as drumsticks.

Drum cupcake.

Alternative Snacks

Cookie notes. Make cookies in the shape of a musical note by cutting a small round cookie or making a little dough ball and a long thin rectangle. Or make round cookies and use food markers to draw musical notes on the cookies.

Cracker notes. Spread any shape cracker with cream cheese and create musical notes out of pretzel sticks and grape halves.

Musical snacks. Bugles salty snacks, ready straight out of the box.

Chicken drummers. Chicken wing pieces that look like miniature drumsticks.

SUGGESTED BOOKS

Ackerman, Karen. *Song and Dance Man.* 32 pages. 2003. Random House Children's Books. Grandpa relives his vaudeville days.

Aliki. *Ah, Music!* 48 pages. 2005. HarperCollins Publishers. Surveys the history and components of music.

Brown, Marc. *Hand Rhymes.* 32 pages. 1993. Penguin Group. A collection of finger plays to accompany nursery rhymes.

Brown, Margaret Wise. *The Indoor Noisy Book.* 48 pages. 1976. HarperCollins Publishers. A little dog with a cold stays inside and listens to the sounds inside the house.

Carle, Eric. *I See a Song.* 32 pages. 1996. Scholastic Inc. When a violin plays, a world of shapes and colors comes to life.

Carlson, Nancy. *Loudmouth George and the Cornet.* 32 pages. 1997. Lerner Publishing Group. George's cornet playing is too much for both his family and the band.

Collins, Judy. *Over the Rainbow.* 26 pages. 2010. Charlesbridge Publishing Group. The introductory verse to the famous song beautifully illustrated.

Crews, Donald. *Parade.* 32 pages. 1986. Harper-Collins Publishers. Illustrations and text showing all the aspects of a parade.

Cronin, Doreen. *Dooby Dooby Moo.* 40 pages. 2009. Atheneum Books for Young Readers. Duck and his friends pool their talents so they can win a trampoline in a talent show but have to keep it all secret from the farmer.

Dylan, Bob. *Forever Young.* 40 pages. 2008. Atheneum Books for Young Readers. The lyrics of the song colorfully illustrated.

Falconer, Ian. *Olivia Forms a Band.* 50 pages. 2009. Atheneum Books for Young Readers. Olivia decides her family needs to form a band when they go to watch fireworks.

Galdone, Paul. *Cat Goes Fiddle-I-Fee.* 48 pages. 1988. Houghton Mifflin Harcourt. An old English rhyme that introduces children to their favorite animals.

Gauch, Patricia. *Dance, Tanya.* 32 pages. 1996. Penguin Group. Tanya loves to dance more than anything but her mother thinks she's too small to take lessons.

Griffith, Helen V. *Georgia Music.* 24 pages. 1990. HarperCollins Publishers. A young girl makes her sick grandfather laugh by bringing back the music they shared.

Grimm, The Brothers. *The Bremen Town Musicians.* 32 pages. 1997. North-South Books. Four animals join together in a band, foil some criminals and find a home.

Harper, Wilhelmina. *The Gunniwolf.* 32 pages.

2003. Penguin Group. Accentuates the importance of following instructions from adults when a child goes into the woods and meets up with the gunniwolf but fortunately she sings the gunniwolf to sleep.

Hayes, Ann. *Meet the Orchestra*. 32 pages. 1991. Voyager Books. Describes the features, sounds and role of each family of instruments in the orchestra.

Isadora, Rachel. *Ben's Trumpet*. 40 pages. 1991. HarperCollins Children's Books. Ben wants to play the trumpet but has only an imaginary instrument until one day when he meets a real musician.

Johnston, Tony. *Grandpa's Song*. 32 pages. 1996. Penguin Group Inc. When a young girl's grandfather becomes forgetful she helps him by singing their favorite song.

Keats, Ezra Jack. *Apt. 3*. 32 pages. 1999. Puffin. Two brothers try to determine who is playing the harmonica in their apartment building one rainy day.

Keats, Ezra Jack. *Whistle for Willie*. 32 pages. 1977. Penguin Group. Peter wishes he could learn to whistle for his dog.

Komaiko, Leah. *I Like the Music*. 32 pages. 1989. HarperCollins Publishers. Grandma says the symphony's the place to go but the little girl doesn't want to; she's happy with the music she hears in her everyday life.

Kovalski, Mary Ann. *Jingle Bells*. 39 pages. 1998. Fitzhenry & Whiteside, Limited. A grandmother and her grandchildren sing the song while taking a carriage ride through New York's Central Park.

Kovalski, Mary Ann. *The Wheels on the Bus*. 32 pages. 1990. Kids Can Press, Limited. An adaptation of the traditional song.

Liebman, Dan. *I Want to Be a Musician*. 24 pages. 2003. Firefly Books. Photos and easy to read text describe the job of a musician.

Martin, Bill, Jr., John Archambault and Ted Rand. *Barn Dance!* 32 pages. 1998. Henry Hold & Co. A boy feels drawn to the barn where he hears the fiddler and the sounds of people dancing.

McCloskey, Robert. *Lentil*. 62 pages. 1978. Penguin Group. Lentil can't sing but wants to make music so he gets a harmonica and plays it everywhere, even the bathtub.

McLerran, Alice. *Dreamsong*. 32 pages. 1992. HarperCollins Publishers. A boy named Pavel is haunted by a song he hears only in his dreams.

Moss, Lloyd. *Zin! Zin! Zin! A Violin*. 32 pages.

1995. Simon & Schuster Books for Young Readers. When this book begins the trombone is playing by itself. But soon all the other instruments join in.

Pinkney, Brian. *Max Found Two Sticks*. 40 pages. 1997. Aladdin. Max picks up twigs and begins to drum to everything he hears around him, ultimately meeting up with a marching band.

Raschka, Chris. *Charlie Parker Played Be Bop*. 32 pages. 1997. Scholastic. Introduces the famous saxophone player and his be bop style.

Rowe, Julian and Perham, Molly. *Making Sounds*. 32 pages. 1993. Scholastic Library Publishing. Describes in simple words how sounds are made and how they travel.

Ryder, Joanne. *Dance by the Light of the Moon*. 40 pages. 2007. Hyperion Books for Children. Farm animals dance by the light of the moon, based on the chorus of Buffalo Gals.

Ryder, Joanne. *Dancers in the Garden*. 32 pages. 1992. Sierra Club Books for Young Children. Follows the activities of a hummingbird in the garden on a sunny day.

Salzmann, Mary Elizabeth. *What in the World Is a Clarinet?* Musical Instrument Series. 24 pages. 2012. ABDO Publishing Company. Explains what the clarinet is, how to play it and shows children learning to play.

Salzmann, Mary Elizabeth. *What in the World Is a Flute?* Musical Instrument Series. 24 pages. 2012. ABDO Publishing Company. Explains what the flute is, how to play it and shows children learning to play.

Salzmann, Mary Elizabeth. *What in the World Is a Violin?* Musical Instrument Series. 24 pages. 2012. ABDO Publishing Company. Explains what the violin is, how to play it and shows children learning to play.

Saul, Carol. *Peter's Song*. 40 pages. 1994. Aladdin. When everyone in the barnyard is too busy to listen to young Peter Pig's song he leaves and finds a friendly frog who will listen.

Sedaka, Neil. *Waking Up Is Hard to Do*. 26 pages. 2010. Charlesbridge Publishing.. The hit song colorfully illustrated.

Sewell, Marcia. *Animal Song*. 28 pages. 1988. Little, Brown & Company. Illustrated rhythmic verses catalogue a variety of animals and their activities.

Spier, Peter. *Crash! Bang! Boom!* 24 pages. 1990. Random House Children's Books. Pictures of various objects or actions that make sounds.

Stringer, Lauren. *When Stravinsky Met Nijinsky*. 29 pages. 2013. Harcourt Children's Books. The story of what happened when the composer met the dancer and they combined their talents and produced the Rite of Spring.

Waddell, Martin. *The Happy Hedgehog Band. 32 pages.* 1994. Candlewick Press. A band of animals makes joyful noise in the forest.

Ward, Jennifer. *There Was an Old Monkey Who Swallowed a Frog.* 30 pages. 2010. Marshall Cavendish Corp. A variation on the traditional cumulative rhyming song that takes place in a jungle.

Williams, Vera B. *Music, Music for Everyone.* 32 pages. 1988. HarperCollins Publishers. Rosa organizes her friends into the Oak Street Band to earn money to help her family.

Yarrow, Peter. *Puff, the Magic Dragon.* 24 pages. 2007. Sterling. The famous song, where Puff and his friend Jackie Paper frolic together in the land of Honalee.

Bears

Advance planning: To plan for this storytime, find a theme-related song to play during craft and snack times, like "Teddy Bear's Picnic," by Anne Murray. You will also want to select a poem, such as "Grin and Bear It," by an unknown author (find it at www.dawlishteddybears.co.uk/Pages/TeddyBearPoems.aspx*)*, along with the books you plan to read. Decorate your space with stuffed bears and a jar of honey. Tell the children the week before to bring their own teddy bears if they have one.

Introduction to theme: Teddy bears are soft stuffed toys and everyone probably has seen many of them. Hold some up. Do you know why they're called Teddy Bears? The name comes from former president Theodore Roosevelt, whose nickname was Teddy. Over a hundred years ago someone made a stuffed bear and asked the president's permission to call it Teddy's bear. There are many kinds of bears and perhaps you've seen some of them at the zoo. There are Polar Bears, Grizzly Bears, Black Bears, Brown Bears. What color is a Polar Bear? (white). Do you know what a baby bear is called? (cub). Today we'll read about bears, play some bear games, make a bear craft and eat a snack that looks like a bear.

Song: "The Bear Went Over the Mountain." Lyrics can be found at www.dltk-kids.com. Here are the motions to go with the lyrics: make one arm wrist up in an inverted v to look like a mountain and walk your opposite hand's fingers up one side; hold walking fingers at top; walk fingers down other side.

Game: Bear hunt

Materials needed: The story below, to read aloud. Advance preparation: Read the story through a few times to familiarize yourself with it ahead of time. At storytime: Get the children to stand and follow you as you walk around the room pretending to go through the obstacles described in the story. Tell them this story as you walk:

We're going on a bear hunt. We're going to catch a big one. We're not scared. First there's a big grassy field. Can't go over it. Can't go under it. Gotta go through it. Through the tall grass we go; swishy swashy swishy swashy swishy swashy (making noises by rubbing your hands together). We're going on a bear hunt. We're going to catch a big one. We're not scared. Now we're coming to a river. Can't go over it. Can't go under it. Gotta go through it. Let's swim; swimmy swimmy swimmy swimmy swimmy swimmy (making swimming motions with your arms). We're going on a bear hunt. We're going to catch a big one. We're not scared. Oh no look at the mud. Can't go over it. Can't go under it. Gotta go through it. Squelch squelch squelch squelch squelch squelch (walk like your feet are sticking in the mud). We're going on a bear hunt. We're going to catch a big one. We're not scared. Ooh here's a cave. Let's go in (bend over like you're inside a cave). Gosh it's dark in here. Do you see anything? (put your hand up to your eyes like you're trying to see) Can you feel anything? (put your arms out in front like you're trying to feel around). I feel something. It feels big. And furry. Let me turn on my flashlight (make a click and pretend you're holding a flashlight). Yikes! It's a bear! (jump back and pretend to be scared) Quick let's get out of the cave! Hurry back through the mud (squelch squelch squelch squelch squelch squelch making the foot motions again). Let's get across that river (swimmy swimmy swimmy swimmy swimmy swimmy making the arm motions again). Back through the field (swishy swashy swishy swashy swishy swashy making the hand noises again). Let's go back into the house, up the stairs and hide under the covers (pretend to do those things). Whew! I think we're safe. Aw, we weren't scared, were we?

Alternative Games

Musical bears. If everyone has a bear (or if you have extras or enough for everyone to have one to hold) set up chairs in a line as for musical chairs but the children must put their bears on the chairs when the music stops. No one is out — they can put their bears together on other chairs as you remove the chairs. Eventually the bears should be all piled up on top of each other.

Bear search. Either print from the computer or cut out some bear shapes on paper and hide them around your storytime area. Tell the children to go around and find one bear and bring it back to you.

Feed the bear. Paint or glue a computer printed bear face on the side of a box with the mouth large enough to fit bean bags through. Cut a hole where the bear's mouth is and let the children toss bean bags through it to feed the bear. Be sure to warn the children that it's not safe to feed a wild bear.

Teddy bear introductions. If the children brought their own teddy bears let them take turns introducing them.

Teddy bear picnic. Set up a tablecloth on the floor along with small dishes and either have some pretend food or do your snack as part of this.

Craft: Styrofoam cup polar bear

Materials needed: Styrofoam cups, white construction paper, black construction paper, google eyes, gluestick, white cotton flat makeup applicators, black permanent marker. Advance preparation: Cut two circles (two small and one larger) of white paper to be the bear's face and ears. Cut a muzzle from a flat cotton makeup applicator and draw the mouth on it with black permanent marker. Cut two more white circles for paws and one small black circle or rounded

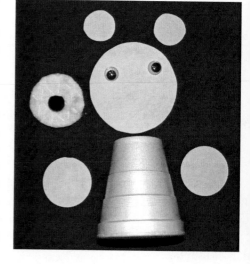

Styrofoam cup polar bear pieces.

triangle for the nose. Mark lines on paws to look like claws. At storytime: Glue the muzzle and the ears to the larger piece of white paper. Glue nose to muzzle piece. Add google eyes or draw eyes. Glue face to Styrofoam cup. Add two more circles to cup sides as paws.

Alternative Crafts

Brown paper bag bear puppet. Cut ears from brown construction paper and eyes from black construction paper. Glue on the ears and eyes. Draw on a mouth with crayon or marker.

Teddy bear ears. Cut a long strip of poster board, long enough to go around a child's head. Give the children two medium-sized white poster board circles for the ears. Tape or staple the ears to the headband. Glue a brown circle smaller than the white ones inside the white ones. Staple the band to fit the child's head.

Styrofoam cup polar bear.

Bear face masks. Made from large paper plate.

Lacing card bear. Print cardstock bears on computer, punch holes around outside edge, cut yarn piece and cover one end of the yarn with a small piece of masking tape to make it easier to get through the holes. At storytime children color bears with crayons and run lace around the outside.

Snack: Bear cookie

Materials needed: Cookie dough, small paper plates, icing, chocolate chips. Advance preparation: Make cookies using one larger piece of dough and two small ones set next to it to be the bear ears. Use a small biscuit cutter for the large circle and the plastic top of a soda bottle for the ears. Alternately, you can use a bear cookie cutter. At storytime: Place

Bear cookie.

a bear cookie on each child's plate, give them a dollop of icing and enough chocolate chips to make eyes, nose and mouth. White icing could make a polar bear. Chocolate icing could make a brown bear, a grizzly bear or a teddy bear.

Alternative Snacks

Bear sandwiches. Cut bread with a bear cookie cutter. Give the children cream cheese to spread on it to look like polar bears and then raisins for the eyes.

Teddies. Teddy graham cookies or crackers. Teddy gummy bears.

Polar bear treats. Rice cake spread with cream cheese for polar bear face with banana slices as ears, an Oreo as the muzzle and raisins as the eyes.

Bear hiking snack. Trail mix made from raisins, chocolate chips, sunflower seeds and Cheerios cereal.

SUGGESTED BOOKS

Asch, Frank. *Happy Birthday, Moon.* 32 pages. 2000. Aladdin. A little bear wants to give the moon a birthday present.

Asch, Frank. *Mooncake.* 32 pages. 2000. Aladdin. Bear builds a rocket to go to the moon so he can taste it.

Asch, Frank. *Moongame.* 32 pages. 2000. Aladdin. Bear plays hide and seek with the moon.

Becker, Bonnie. *A Bedtime for Bear.* 48 pages. 2010. Candlewick. Bear likes everything just so when he goes to sleep, and Mouse is a bit annoying.

Becker, Bonnie. *A Visitor for Bear.* 56 pages. 2008. Candlewick. Bear is quite sure he doesn't like visitors, but Mouse is persistent.

Brett, Jan. *The Three Snow Bears.* 32 pages. 2007. Putnam Juvenile. A retelling of *Goldielocks and the Three Bears* set in an Inuit village.

Brown, Peter. *Children Make Terrible Pets.* 40 pages. 2010. Little, Brown Books for Young Readers. The story of a young bear and her favorite pet boy.

Brown, Peter. *You Will Be My Friend.* 40 pages. 2011. Little, Brown Books for Young Readers. Today's the day Lucy is going to make a friend.

Degen, Bruce. *Jamberry.* 32 pages. 1985. HarperCollins. A young boy and a friendly bear romp through a berry world.

Doodler, Todd H. *Bear in Underwear.* 40 pages. 2010. Blue Apple Books. Bear finds a backpack full of underwear.

Douglass, Barbara. *Good as New.* 1982. Lothrop, Lee & Shepard Books. Grady's cousin treats Grady's teddy bear very badly.

Dunrea, Olivier. *Old Bear and His Cub.* 32 pages. 2010. Philomel. Old Bear loves Little Cub.

Flack, Marjorie. *Ask Mr. Bear.* 1932. Macmillan. 32 pages. 1971. Aladdin. Danny is trying to find the perfect birthday gift for his mother and it is suggested that he ask Mr. Bear.

Fleming, Denise. *Time to Sleep.* 32 pages. 2001. Henry Holt and Co. The animals that need to hibernate try to postpone it, just like children who don't want to go to bed.

Foley, Greg. *Don't Worry Bear.* 32 pages. 2008. Penguin Group. Bear worries about his friend Caterpillar.

Foley, Greg. *Good Luck Bear.* 32 pages. 2009. Penguin Group. Bear and Mouse are looking for luck.

Foley, Greg. *Thank You Bear.* 32 pages. 2007. Penguin Group. A simple story of friendship about Bear getting a gift for Mouse.

Freeman, Don. *Bearymore.* 1976. Viking Press. How will Bearymore come up with a new act for the circus when he has to sleep all winter?

Freeman, Don. *Corduroy.* 32 pages. 1976. Penguin Group. Corduroy is a teddy bear on the shelf at the store awaiting someone to take him home.

Freeman, Don. *Corduroy Lost and Found.* 32 pages. 2006. Penguin Group. Corduroy wanders off in search of a birthday present for Lisa.

Freeman, Don. *A Pocket for Corduroy.* 32 pages. 1980. Penguin Group. Corduroy's overalls need a pocket.

Galdone, Joanna C. [retold by]. *The Little Girl and the Big Bear.* 40 pages. 1980. Houghton Mifflin Harcourt Publishers. A retelling of a traditional tale of a little girl held captive by a bear.

Galdone, Paul. *The Three Bears.* 40 pages. 2011. Houghton Mifflin Harcourt. The story of the little girl who enters the bears' home when they're not there.

Garcia, Jerry. *The Teddy Bears' Picnic.* 34 pages. 1998. HarperCollins Publishers. A collection of singing, dancing teddy bears.

Gill, Shelley. *Alaska's Three Bears.* 32 pages. 1997. Sasquatch Books. A Polar Bear, a Black Bear and a Grizzly Bear travel together to find perfect homes.

Henkes, Kevin. *Old Bear.* 32 pages. 2008. HarperCollins Publishers. Explore the four seasons with Old Bear.

Julvert, Maria Angels. *The Fascinating World of Bears.* 31 pages. 1995. Barron's Educational Series. Describes different types of bears, their habits and diets and hibernation.

Kennedy, Jimmy. *The Teddy Bears' Picnic.* 32 pages. 1997. Turtleback Books. An illustrated version of the song about teddy bears who picnic without their owners.

Klassen, Jon. *I Want My Hat Back.* 40 pages. 2011. Candlewick Press. The bear's hat is gone and he wants it back. He asks every animal he sees if they've seen it. They all say no, some more elaborately than others.

Lindgren, Barbro. *Sam's Teddy Bear.* 32 pages. 1982. HarperCollins Publishers. A dog rescues toddler Sam's beloved teddy bear.

Martin, Bill, Jr., and Eric Carle. *Brown Bear, Brown Bear, What Do You See?* 32 pages. 1992. Henry Holt & Co. Brown Bear sees many different animals. A good opportunity to make animal sounds.

McCloskey, Robert. *Blueberries for Sal.* 64 pages. 1948. Penguin Group. Sal and her mother find themselves sharing a berry patch with a bear and her cub.

McPhail, David. *The Bear's Toothache.* 31 pages. 1988. Turtleback Books. How can a little boy help a bear with a toothache?

McPhail, David. *Emma's Pet.* 24 pages. 1993. Turtleback Books. Emma's search for a soft, cuddly pet has a surprise ending.

McPhail, David. *Lost.* 32 pages. 1993. Little, Brown Books for Young Readers. A boy befriends a lost bear.

McPhail, David. *Teddy Bear.* 32 pages. 2005. San Val. The story of a friend who is lost and found and lost and found again.

Murphy, Jill. *Peace at Last.* 32 pages. 1992. Turtleback Books. Mr. Bear spends the night searching for enough peace and quiet to sleep.

Rosen, Michael. *We're Going on a Bear Hunt.* 40 pages. 2009. Margaret K. McElderry Books. Going on a bear hunt. We're not scared! The story takes the reader through all kinds of noisy places to find the bear and then back home again.

Schoenherr, John. *Bear.* 32 pages. 1991. Penguin Group. Searching for his mother, a young bear finds his own independence.

Stevens, Janet. *Tops & Bottoms.* 40 pages. 1995. Houghton Mifflin Harcourt. Hare turns his bad luck around by making a deal with the rich and lazy bear.

Underwood, Deborah. *The Loud Book.* 32 pages. 2011. Houghton Mifflin Harcourt. A variety of loud sounds are explored.

Wilson, Karma. *Bear Feels Scared.* 40 pages. 2008. Margaret K. McElderry Books. Bear is out lost and scared until his friends find him and bring him home.

Wilson, Karma. *Bear Snores On.* 40 pages. 2002. Margaret K. McElderry Books. The animals have been gathering in Bear's cave and having fun while he slept.

Wilson, Karma. *Bear Wants More.* 40 pages. 2003. Margaret K. McElderry Books. Bear finds some roots to eat but wants more. He finds berries, but wants more.

Wilson, Karma. *Bear's New Friend.* 40 pages. 2006. Margaret K. McElderry Books. Bear is going to the swimming hole but must first find his friends.

Wood, Don, and Audrey Wood. *The Little Mouse, the Red Ripe Strawberry and the Big Hungry Bear.* 32 pages. 1989. Child's Play International. The mouse is worried that the bear is going to eat his strawberry.

Young, Ruth. *Golden Bear.* 32 pages. 1994. San Val. Rhymed couplets portray the friendship between a child and his life-sized teddy bear.

Naughtiness

Advance planning: To plan for this storytime, find a theme-related song to play during craft and snack times, like "You Can't Say Psbpsbpsb on the Radio," by Barry Louis Polisar. You will also want to select a poem, such as "Happy Hats" (find it at www.preschooleducation.com), along with the books you plan to read. Decorate your space with stuffed monkeys (think Curious George or the monkeys in the Caps for Sale book), blankets and pillows (because naughty children don't want to go to bed), or towels (naughty children don't want to take baths) and candy (naughty children want to eat lots of candy).

Introduction to theme: Do you know what it means to be naughty? Have you ever disobeyed your parents or not done something they told you to do? Have you ever been naughty? Have you ever been mischievous? Do you know what that means? Have you caused trouble? Or gotten into trouble for something you did? All children are probably naughty once in a while and that's ok as long as it's not too serious or dangerous. Today we'll read about naughty behavior, play a naughty game, make a naughty craft and eat a naughty snack.

Song: "Don't Put Your Finger Up Your Nose," by Barry Louis Polisar which can be found at www.metrolyrics.com.

Game: Yes means no and no means yes

Materials needed: None. Advance preparation: None. At storytime: We're going to be naughty today and play yes means no and no means yes. I'm going to ask questions and if your answer is yes, I want you to shake your head no (demonstrate) and say "yes" but if your answer is no I want you to nod your head yes and say "no." This is harder than it sounds. Sample questions: Do you like cupcakes? Is it cold outside? Did you wear a jacket today? Do you have a dog? Do you like cookies? Did you eat breakfast this morning? Can you ride a bicycle? Have we read some books today? Have you ever seen a dinosaur? Did someone bring you to storytime today? Would you like to go to the moon? Do you have a cat? Have you ever ridden a bus? Is it raining? Is this your favorite storytime?

Alternative Games

50 cents. Show how much 50 cents is in different coin combinations (like the 50 cents from Caps for Sale). Have a 50 cent piece, two quarters, five dimes, ten nickels, 50 pennies.

Musical feelings. Play a variety of musical styles and ask the children to act out how the music makes them feel. Are they happy? Sad? Angry? Mischievous? Naughty? Scared?

Naughty monkey caps pieces.

Craft: Naughty monkey caps

Materials needed: Cotton caps, fabric markers. Advance preparation: None. At storytime: Give each child a cap and explain that they are like the caps in the book *Caps for Sale.* They can decorate them however they like, but you might show them some pictures from the book.

Alternative Crafts

Monkeys in trees. Cut out tree shapes from brown construction paper and brown circles to make monkeys. Glue trees to background paper. Glue two circles to make each monkey. Use markers to make three dots on monkey face for eyes and mouth. Add arms, legs and tail.

Naughty faces. Give each child paper and either crayons or paint and brushes and encourage them to create a face or self portrait of a mischievous or naughty child. Alternately they could draw a naughty or mischievous pet.

Snack: Cup of worms

Materials needed: Clear plastic cups, plastic spoons, chocolate pudding, gummy worms. Cocoa powder or crushed chocolate wafer cookie to place on top to look like dirt if desired. Advance preparation: Make pudding in a large container. At storytime: Spoon some pudding

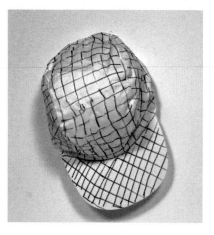

Naughty monkey caps.

into each clear plastic cup and top with crushed cookies or cocoa powder and a gummy worm. Tell the children that mud and worms are a delicious dish for someone who has been naughty, but since you're sure they're never naughty you will give them chocolate pudding and gummy worms.

Alternative Snacks

Naughty veggie faces. Give each child a rice cake, a dollop of cream cheese and some fruits and vegetables like green pepper strips, sliced olives, banana slices and encourage them to create a face on the rice cake by spreading the cream cheese and topping with the fruits and vegetables.

Naughty fruit faces. Make a face with fruits and/or vegetables on a paper plate using an apple slice for the mouth, banana slices for hair, grape halves for eyes, raisins for eyebrows, and carrot piece for nose.

Cup of mud and worms.

SUGGESTED BOOKS

Allard, Harry G., Jr. *Miss Nelson Is Missing.* 32 pages. 1977. Houghton Mifflin Harcourt. The kids in Miss Nelson's classroom try to take advantage of her absence until a substitute teacher takes charge.

Amery, Heather. *Naughty Sheep.* 16 pages. 2004. EDC Publishing. An Usborne farmyard tale.

Ashman, Linda. *M Is for Mischief: An A to Z of Naughty Children.* 32 pages. 2008. Penguin Group. Clever cautionary poems, raucously illustrated.

Aylesworth, Jim. *Naughty Little Monkeys.* 32 pages. 2006. Penguin Group. What happens when you leave twenty six little monkeys home alone?

Ayto, Russell. *Ella and the Naughty Lion.* 26 pages. 1996. Houghton Mifflin Harcourt. When Ella's mother comes home with the new baby, a lion slips in the door.

Barroux, Gilles. *Emily and Alex: Naughty and Nice.* 32 pages. 2010. Blue Apple Books. Emily and Alex are twins who are as different as night and day.

Beardsley, Martin. *Five Naughty Kittens.* 24 pages. 2005. Sea to Sea Publications. A rhyming, counting book that shows the naughty kittens as they disappear and then reappear.

Bonwill, Ann. *Naughty Toes.* 32 pages. 2011. Tiger Tales. Chloe and Belinda are sisters, but they couldn't be more different.

Brown, Peter. *Children Make Terrible Pets.* 40 pages. 2010. Little Brown Books for Young Readers. A young bear brings home a child to be her pet, even though her mother warns her that children make terrible pets.

Castle, Caroline. *Naughty.* 32 pages. 2001. Random House Children's Books. A wide awake toddler refuses to go to sleep.

Gardner, Wendy. *Naughty Naught Keifer.* 32 pages. 2002. Hyperion Books for Children. Naughty pets can't stop misbehaving.

Gosney, Joy. *Naughty Parents.* 32 pages. 2000. Lerner Publishing Group. A young child knows she has to keep an eye on her parents during their visit to the park.

Hargreaves, Roger. *Little Miss Naughty.* 32 pages. 1998. San Val. Mr. Small finds just the right person to teach Miss Naughty a lesson.

Harris, Robie H. *The Day Leo Said I Hate You!* 40 pages. 2008. Little, Brown & Co. A family book about what it feels like to hear and say those words.

Jensen, Derrick. *Mischief in the Forest.* 40 pages. 2010. PM Press. Grandma Johnson lived alone in the forest and spent her time knitting until she discovered one day that her yarn was gone. Mischievous animals had taken the yarn and so Grandma discovers she has neighbors and she's not alone.

Koller, Jackie French. *Peter Spit a Seed at Sue.* 32 pages. 2008. Penguin Group. Four friends turn a boring summer day into a rollicking seed spitting adventure.

Long, Ethan. *Have You Been Naughty or Nice?* 32 pages. 2009. Little, Brown Books for Young Readers. The duck excitedly awaits a visit from Santa but eats all of Santa's snacks and ends up on the naughty list.

McCloud, Carol. *Have You Filled a Bucket Today?* 32 pages. 2007. Nelson Publishing and Marketing. A heartwarming book that encourages positive behavior.

McPhail, David. *Pigs Aplenty, Pigs Galore.* 32 pages. 1993. Penguin Group. Pigs invade a house and have a party.

Oates, Joyce Carol. *Naughty Cherie.* 32 pages. 2008. HarperCollins Publishers. Naughty Cherie is the cutest kitten in the litter and also the naughtiest.

Rathmann, Peggy. *Goodnight Gorilla.* 34 pages. 1996. Penguin Group. The naughty gorilla takes the zookeeper's keys so that the animals can sleep inside instead of in the zoo.

Reid, Camilla. *The Littlest Dinosaur and the Naughty Rock.* 32 pages. 2010. Bloomsbury. The Littlest Dinosaur is in a bad mood.

Rey, H.A., and Margret Rey. *Curious George.* 64 pages. 1973. Houghton Mifflin Harcourt. Curious George's curiosity always gets him into trouble. This is the original story but there are many others.

Ross, Tony. *Naughty Nigel.* 32 pages. 2009. Andersen Press, Limited. Nigel pretends to be deaf so that he can play tricks on his parents.

Scarry, Richard. *Naughty Bunny.* 24 pages. 1989. Random House Children's Books. The little bunny is naughty when he spills his cereal and when he doesn't play nicely with his friend.

Shannon, David. *Alice the Fairy.* 40 pages. 2004. Scholastic. Alice is only a temporary fairy but she's using her powers to be mischievous.

Shannon, David. *David Gets in Trouble.* 32 pages. 2002. Scholastic. When David gets in trouble, he always says it's not his fault.

Shannon, David. *David Goes to School.* 32 pages. 1999. Scholastic. David is naughty in school.

Shannon, David. *Good Boy, Fergus!* 40 pages. 2006. Scholastic. Fergus the dog is always getting into trouble.

Shannon, David. *No, David!* 32 pages. 1998. Scholastic. A young boy is shown doing many naughty things.

Slobodkina, Esphyr. *Caps for Sale.* 32 pages. 2008. HarperCollins Publishers. Mischievous monkeys steal a peddler's caps while he's sleeping.

Sperring, Mark. *Captain Buckleboots on the Naughty Step.* 32 pages. 2011. Barron's Educational Series. Most of the time Sam is a good boy, but sometimes he is naughty. For punishment he has to sit on the bottom step.

Stein, David Ezra. *Interrupting Chicken.* 40 pages. 2010. Candlewick Press. A little chicken has a naughty habit of interrupting bedtime stories.

Sterling Publishing. *Naughty Kitten: A Touch and Feel Adventure.* 16 pages. 2005. Sterling Publishing. Kipper the kitten is getting into some naughty adventures.

Ward, Nick. *Nicest Naughty Fairy.* 24 pages. 2010. Idea & Design Works,. The naughty fairy has gone too far and the villagers are demanding some changes.

Willems, Mo. *Don't Let the Pigeon Drive the Bus.* 40 pages. 2003. Hyperion Books for Children. A pigeon volunteers when a bus driver takes a break.

Willems, Mo. *Don't Let the Pigeon Stay Up Late.* 40 pages. 2006. Hyperion Books for Children. The pigeon doesn't want to go to bed.

Willems, Mo. *Leonardo, the Terrible Monster.* 48 pages. 2005. Hyperion Books for Children. Leonardo is actually terrible at being a monster until he meets a nervous little boy.

Williams, Suzanne. *Ten Naughty Little Monkeys.* 32 pages. 2007. HarperCollins Publishers. Ten little monkeys jumping on the bed.

Pumpkins

Advance planning: To plan for this storytime, find a theme-related song to play during craft and snack times, like "Pumpkin Patch," by David Hall. You will also want to select a poem, such as "One Day I Found Two Pumpkin Seeds" (find it at www.dHK-holidays.com/pumpkinpoem1.htm), along with the books you plan to read. Decorate your space with pumpkins, hay bales and fall leaves.

Introduction to theme: A pumpkin is a kind of squash that's usually planted in July so that it will be ready in October for Halloween and then Thanksgiving. Pumpkins are grown from seeds and the seeds themselves are sometimes eaten as a snack. Pumpkins are usually orange and have creases on the outside shells. Have you ever seen pumpkins out in a field? Did you get a pumpkin this year? What holidays do you think of when you think about pumpkins? Did you have a Jack O'Lantern at Halloween? What about pumpkin pie for Thanksgiving?? To get the part of the pumpkin that we make into pie, the inside with all the goop and seeds has to be scraped out, then it's cooked and just the inside of the shell is scooped out to be blended with eggs, milk and spices and then put into pie pastry and baked. Do you like pumpkin pie? Have you had it with whipped cream? Today we'll read about pumpkins, play some games with pumpkins, make a pumpkin craft and eat a snack that looks like a pumpkin.

Fingerplay: "5 Little Pumpkins," which can be found at www.dltk-teach.com. Hold up five fingers, and then bend them down one at a time as the verse progresses. When you get to the wind, sway hand through the air and clap when the light goes out. And put your hands behind your back as the pumpkins run.

Game: Pumpkin tic-tac-toe

Materials needed: Bean bags, tic tac toe board with three pumpkins in a row printed or drawn on it. Advance preparation: Make bean bags. Prepare tic tac toe board. At storytime: Let the children take turns trying to throw the bean bags onto the pumpkins in order to get tic tac toe.

Alternative Games

Pumpkin ring toss. Have six or more small pumpkins and set up in a square. Cut some rings from paper plates or cardboard big enough to go over the pumpkins.

Pumpkin bowling. Set up several small pumpkins and try to knock down like bowling with a ball like a basketball or soccer ball. You might want to cover the floor for this area with newspaper, as it could get messy.

Pumpkin golf. Carve a face on a pumpkin with the mouth extra large. Build a cardboard ramp about one to two feet wide from the ground to the pumpkin's mouth. Tape the ramp to the floor. Have a small golf club and golf ball and let each child try to gently hit the ball up the ramp and into the pumpkin's mouth.

Craft: Tissue paper pumpkin

Materials needed: Orange tissue paper, chenille stem, fiberfill, pencils, possibly small treats or candies. Advance preparation: Cut two six-inch squares of orange tissue paper for each. At storytime: Place the two squares of tissue paper flat. Put a little fiberfill on top. Add some candies or treats if desired. Fold up the tissue paper around the fiberfill and treats and make it round. Wrap the chenille stem around the top, secure it and then wrap each end around the pencil to twirl like a stem.

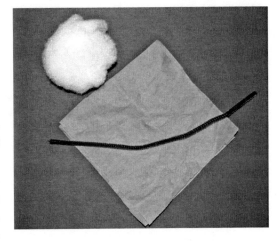

Tissue paper pumpkin pieces.

Alternative Crafts

Construction paper pumpkin. Cut orange pieces of construction paper into one-inch wide strips (each strip will be 1" × 12"). Then, shorten some of the strips so that you have (1) 6", (2) 8", (2) 10", and (2) 12" long pieces. Gather the strips of paper together (with the ends flush) and place the smallest one in the middle. Order them by size so that the largest strip is on the outside. Secure with a paper clip until you've added the other pieces of paper, then staple. Line up the opposite ends so that they are together like the top. Cut a brown strip of paper ¼" by 3" long for the stem. To make it curl, wrap the paper around a pencil. Cut out two leaf shapes from green paper. Add the stem, leaves, and a piece of string to the paper clip at the top then staple it all together.

Tissue paper pumpkin.

Pumpkin pie play dough. Ingredients: 2 cups flour; 1 cup salt; 4 teaspoons cream of tartar; 3 teaspoons pumpkin-pie spice; 2 cups water; 2 tablespoons vegetable oil; red and yellow food coloring. Combine all ingredients in a large pot. Stir on low heat until mixture starts forming a ball and will pull away from the sides. Let cool.

Snack: Pumpkin cookie

Materials needed: Sugar cookie dough, pumpkin or circle cookie cutter, orange icing, plastic knives, paper plates. Advance preparation: Bake pumpkin shapes or round cookies. If using round cookie cutter, add a little piece to look like a stem before baking. At storytime: Place a cookie and a dollop of orange icing on each child's plate along with a plastic knife. Have them ice the cookie making some vertical marks with their knife to look more like a pumpkin.

Alternative Snacks

Pumpkin cupcake. Yellow cake mix, canned pumpkin, pumpkin pie spice, orange frosting, green Twizzlers licorice. If desired could also use orange crystals. Bake cupcakes adding ¾ can pumpkin and 2 teaspoons pumpkin pie spice. Place a cupcake, a dollop of orange icing and a 1-inch piece of green Twizzler on each plate. Have the children ice the cupcake and insert the licorice to look like a stem. Add crystals if desired.

Pumpkin treats: pumpkin pie and whipped cream, pumpkin seeds or pumpkin bread.

Pumpkin cookie.

Suggested Books:

Cooper, Helen. *Pumpkin Soup.* 32 pages. 2011. Farrar, Straus & Giroux. Animal friends in the woods squabble over making pumpkin soup.

Cox, Judy. *Pick a Pumpkin, Mrs. Millie.* 32 pages. 2009. Amazon Children's Publishing. Silly Mrs. Millie takes her class to pick pumpkins for their harvest party.

Esbaum, Jill. *Seed, Sprout, Pumpkin, Pie.* 16 pages. 2009. National Geographic Society. Photographs show the progression of pumpkin from seed to plant to pumpkin to pie.

Farmer, Jacqueline. *Pumpkins.* 32 pages. 2004. Charlesbridge Publishing. Lots of fun facts about pumpkins.

Fleming, Denise. *Pumpkin Eye.* 32 pages. 2005. Square Fish. The moon lights the way for trick or treaters on Halloween.

Fridell, Ron. *Life Cycle of a Pumpkin.* 32 pages. 2009. Heinemann. An in depth view of the life cycle of a pumpkin.

Friesen, Helen Lepp. *Growing a Pumpkin.* 16 pages. 2008. Perfection Learning. Describes what happens when pumpkins grow.

Gibbons, Gail. *The Pumpkin Book.* 32 pages. 2000. Holiday House. Describes growing a pumpkin, history, carving and other uses.

Hall, Zoe. *It's Pumpkin Time!* 40 pages. 1999. Scholastic Paperbacks. A brother and sister get an early start on Halloween by planting a pumpkin patch.

Harris, Calvin. *Pumpkin Harvest.* 32 pages. 2007. Coughlan Publishing. Discusses the growth, harvesting and marketing of pumpkins in the fall with little text and many pictures.

Herman, R.A. *The Littlest Pumpkin.* 32 pages. 2011. Scholastic. The little pumpkin dreams of being the center of attention on Halloween.

Hills, Tad. *Duck and Goose Find a Pumpkin.* 22 pages. 2011. Random House Children's Books. A board book featuring friends Duck and Goose in their search for their own pumpkin.

Horowitz, Dave. *The Ugly Pumpkin.* 40 pages. 2008. Puffin. The ugly pumpkin has waited all October for someone to take him home but no one wants him.

Johnston, Tony. *The Vanishing Pumpkin.* 32 pages. 1996. Puffin. A very old woman and a very old man go to the pumpkin patch to find a pumpkin to make a pie but discover that their pumpkin has been taken.

Kann, Victoria. *Pinkalicious and the Pink Pumpkin.* 16 pages. 2011. Harper Festival. Pinkalicious is on a search to find a pink pumpkin in this lift the flap book.

Koontz, Robin Michal. *Pick a Perfect Pumpkin: Learning about Pumpkin Harvests.* 24 pages. 2010. Coughlan Publishing. Basic scientific information about pumpkins.

Kroll, Steven. *The Biggest Pumpkin Ever.* 32 pages. 2007. Cartwheel Books. Once there were two mice who fell in love with the same pumpkin.

Levenson, George. *The Pumpkin Circle, the Story of a Garden.* 40 pages. 2002. Random House Children's Books. From pumpkin seed to jack o'lantern and back to seeds again.

Lewis, Kevin. *Runaway Pumpkin.* 32 pages. 2003. Scholastic. Kids try to roll a big pumpkin down a hill to their farm but it gets away from them.

Mortimer, Anne. *Pumpkin Cat.* 24 pages. 2011. HarperCollins Children's Books. Cat and Mouse work together in the garden to grow pumpkins.

Moulton, Mark Kimball. *Miss Fiona's Stupendous Pumpkin Pies.* 32 pages. 2011. Ideals. Everyone loves Miss Fiona's pumpkin pies.

Moulton, Mark Kimball. *The Very Best Pumpkin.* 32 pages. 2010. Simon & Schuster. Peter knows about caring for pumpkins and when he finds a lonely one he looks after it. By autumn it's grown well and when someone else wants it, what will Peter do?

Nelson, Robin. *Pumpkins.* 23 pages. 2008. Lerner Publishing Group. A close up view of the life of a pumpkin.

Peterson, Mary. *Piggies in the Pumpkin Patch.* 28 pages. 2010. Charlesbridge Publishing. Mama pig naps among the pumpkins but the mischievous piggies go on a romp.

Pfeffer, Wendy. *From Seed to Pumpkin.* 40 pages. 2004. HarperCollins Publishers. Explains the stages of development of a pumpkin in simple terms.

Ray, Mary Lyn. *Pumpkins: A Story for a Field.* 32 pages. 1996. Sandpiper. A man loved a field enough to try to save it from development.

Robbins, Ken. *Pumpkins.* 32 pages. 2007. Square Fish. Describes the growing cycle of a pumpkin.

Rockwell, Anne. *Apples and Pumpkins.* 24 pages. 2011. Aladdin. A little girl spends a beautiful fall day picking apples and searching for the perfect pumpkin.

Rofe, Jennifer. *Piggies in the Pumpkin Patch.* 28 pages. 2010. Charlesbridge Publishing. Two piglets have a barnyard romp starting in the pumpkin patch.

Rynbach, Iris Van. *Five Little Pumpkins*. 24 pages. 1995. Boyds Mill Press. The familiar finger rhyme is illustrated here.

Serfozo, Mary. *Plumply, Dumply Pumpkin*. 32 pages. 2004. Aladdin. Peter's looking for the perfect pumpkin. See what happens when he finds it.

Silverman, Erica. *Big Pumpkin*. 32 pages. 1992. Simon & Schuster Books for Young Readers. Rhythmic text about a witch who longs for pumpkin pie.

Smath, Jerry. *I Like Pumpkins*. 32 pages. 2003. Cartwheel. A rhyming story about a little girl who loves pumpkins.

Thomas, Jan. *Pumpkin Trouble*. 40 pages. 2011. HarperCollins Publishers. Did that pumpkin just quack?

Titherington, Jeanne. *Pumpkin Pumpkin*. 24 pages. 1990. Greenwillow Books. Jamie plants a pumpkin seed in the spring, grows his pumpkin all summer, carves it on Halloween and saves seeds to plant again.

Tudor, Tasha. *Pumpkin Moonshine*. 40 pages. 2000. Simon & Schuster Books for Young Readers. A little girl has found the perfect pumpkin, but how will she get it home?

Walton, Rick. *Mrs. McMurphy's Pumpkin*. 32 pages. 2004. HarperFestival. One morning Mrs. McMurphy wakes up to find a large pumpkin by her door.

White, Linda. *Too Many Pumpkins*. 32 pages. 1997. Holiday House. What to do with all the pumpkins that grow when a pumpkin falls off a truck and sprouts plants in Rebecca Estelle's yard?

Art

Advance planning: To plan for this storytime, find a theme-related song to play during craft and snack times, like "Art Is Everywhere," by MGMT. You will also want to select a poem, such as "Paint Me a Picture," by Donna Caraig (find it at www.americangrandma.com/2011/08/09/art-show/), along with the books you plan to read. Decorate your space with art supplies like paints and brushes, an easel, crayons, a framed picture of something, a canvas, a palette, posters of famous artwork or artists.

Introduction to theme: Art can be a painting, a sculpture, a photograph. It's something that someone created using their skills and their imagination for others to enjoy experiencing, usually by looking at it. A person who makes art is called an artist. Have you ever made art? Have you painted? Drawn a picture? Then you're an artist too! Show the illustrations from a few books that have different kinds of art: paintings, drawings, paper collage. Today we'll read about art, play an art game, make a artistic craft and eat an artistic snack.

Song: "Pretty Paintings," to the tune of "Twinkle Twinkle Little Star":

Pretty paintings that we see
Some were made by you and me.
We are artists don't you know
When we paint or draw we show
That we can make lots of art
Let's stop singing and we'll start.

Game: Color dance

Materials needed: Colored construction paper, CD player, music that's good to move to. Advance preparation: None. At storytime: Place pieces of colored construction paper all over the floor. Start with each child standing on a piece of paper. Play music and have the children move through the space as the music plays. Stop the music and ask each child to stand on a piece of paper and then have them tell you what color their piece of paper is. You can vary the way they move, either dancing, or moving sideways, or backwards, crawling, hopping, holding hands, going fast, going slow, like a crab, etc.

Alternative Games

Choose your color. Place a variety of items in many different colors inside a hula hoop. Have the children walk around the hoop while you play music. When the music stops, direct one of the children to pick out an object of a particular color. Let them carry it until the game ends. Take turns until everyone is holding an object.

Color match. Get two sets of paint strips of the approximate number of children that come to storytime. Cut one of the strips apart and glue the colors to the flat, closed end of clothespins. At storytime, give each child a full paint strip and then have them search through the clothespins to find the colors that match and clip them to the paint strip. Could be done as a cooperative game by pairing two children together.

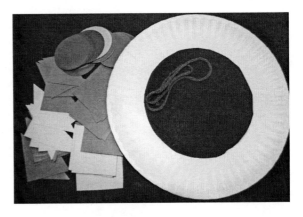

Picking up pom poms. Scatter a bunch of colored pom poms all over the floor. Give each child a plastic bucket or basket to carry. Sing the Paw Paw Patch song "Picking up pom poms put them in my basket" as the children go around and pick up the pom poms. Lyrics can be found at www.songsforteaching.com. Ask them to name the color of the pom pom as they pick it up. If you have tongs or tweezers available, you could let them use those to pick up the pom poms too.

Colors and shapes wreath pieces.

Crayon toss. Get an inflatable giant crayon and have the children stand in a circle and toss it back and forth to each other. You could also do the Limbo under the large crayon.

Bean bag toss. Draw or print from the computer a large painter's palette with colors of "paint" that match bean bags. Play a bean bag toss game with the children where they try to land a bean bag of a matching color on the palette's colors.

Craft: Colors and shapes wreath

Materials needed: Large paper plates, scissors, crayons, construction paper in several colors, glue sticks, yarn. Advance preparation: Cut the paper plates into wreaths, or ring shapes. Cut the construction paper into different shaped small pieces, like squares, triangles, circles. It's useful to have die cut punches for cutting shapes. Or you could cut the shapes to look like crayons. At

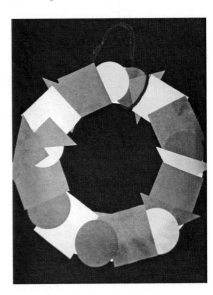

Colors and shapes wreath.

storytime: Have each parent tie a piece of yarn around the paper plate wreath to use as a hanger. Let the children have a variety of colors and shapes to glue onto the paper plate.

Alternative Crafts

Self stick collage. Provide a sheet of self stick paper, like Contact Paper, in either clear or any color and place it sticky side up. Let the children use small things, like sequins, pieces of tissue paper, die cut shapes to place on the sticky paper. If they cover the paper completely, nothing else will be needed. If you'd like to let them add glitter, cut another sheet of Contact Paper, this time definitely clear, and cover their collage. Trim around the edge if necessary.

Paper and fabric quilt. Provide a piece of cardboard or construction paper and 2-inch × 2-inch squares of fabric. Have the children glue the squares of fabric to the paper or cardboard.

Sculpture. Provide clay or play dough for the children to make into sculptures.

Burlap paintings. The artist Paul Klee sometimes painted on burlap. If you mix tempera paint with liquid glue it will work better to adhere to burlap. Give each child a small piece of burlap and let them paint on it with a brush.

Artist's palette fruits and vegetables.

Snack: Artist's palette fruits and vegetables

Materials needed: Bite-sized pieces of fruits and vegetables in a variety of colors, large platter, serving spoon and tongs, small plates, plastic forks. Advance preparation: Wash and cut the fruits and vegetables into bite-sized pieces. At storytime: Display the fruits and vegetables on a large platter to look like a painter's palette. Then pass the "palette" around and let the parents help the children choose the colors they'd like to try.

Alternative Snacks

Rainbow cupcakes. Make white cake batter, divide it into five or six small bowls and then add food coloring to make different colors. See Rainbow theme for complete specific instructions. Spoon each color in succession, starting with the darker colors, into paper cupcake holders. At storytime, have the children peel off the papers and examine all the colors in the cupcake. Top with white icing if desired.

Artist's palette cupcake. Top cupcakes with white icing and offer M&Ms or Skittles in many different colors to place around the top of the cupcake like an artist's palette. Could do the same idea but using round or oval-shaped sugar cookies.

Jell-O shapes. Make slightly thicker Jell-O in cake pans and cut into shapes with cookie cutters.

Rainbow Jell-O. Make several different flavors of Jell-O and when they have cooled slightly, layer them in clear plastic cups.

SUGGESTED BOOKS

Beaumont, Karen. *I Ain't Gonna Paint No More.* 32 pages. 2005. Houghton Mifflin Harcourt. A creative kid floods his world with color with the words flowing like the song "It Ain't Gonna Rain No More."

Bjork, Christina. *Linnea in Monet's Garden.* 56 pages. 1987. R & S Books. A little girl visits Monet's home in France.

Carle, Eric. *The Artist Who Painted a Blue Horse.* 32 pages. 2011. Penguin Group. The artist in this book paints the world just as he sees it.

Carle, Eric. *Draw Me a Star.* 40 pages. 1998. Penguin Group. An artist brings the world to life by drawing one thing at a time as requested.

Cohen, Miriam. *No Good in Art.* 40 pages. 1980. HarperCollins Publishers. A first grader is convinced he can't draw until he's given some encouragement.

dePaola, Tomie. *The Art Lesson.* 32 pages. 1997. Penguin Group. Young Tommy has learned to be creative at home, but is dismayed to find the art instruction at school more regimented.

dePaola, Tomie. *The Legend of the Indian Paintbrush.* 40 pages. 1996. Penguin Group. Little Gopher follows his destiny of becoming an artist for his people.

Eckler, Rebecca. *The Mischievous Mom at the Art Gallery.* 32 pages. 2010. Key Porter Books. A modern mother makes a point of always including her two children in her hectic life.

Falwell, Catherine. *David's Drawings.* 32 pages. 2001. Lee & Low Books. A shy child makes friends by drawing a picture of a tree with a group.

Hoban, Tana. *Colors Everywhere.* 32 pages. 1995. HarperCollins Publishers. A wordless book with color graphs that represent the proportions of the colors in each picture.

Hoban, Tana. *Is It Red? Is It Yellow? Is It Blue?* 32 pages. 1978. HarperCollins Publishers. Wordless book that teaches colors to very young children.

Hoban, Tana. *Red, Blue, Yellow Shoe.* 12 pages. 1986. HarperCollins Publishers. A board book with photographs of common objects with the color written on each page.

Hubbard, Patricia. *My Crayons Talk.* 32 pages. 1996. Henry Holt & Co. A story about talking crayons with colors and feelings explored.

Johnson, Crockett. *Harold and the Purple Crayon.* 64 pages. 1998. HarperCollins Publishers. Harold goes for a walk, drawing everything he needs as he goes.

Kesselman, Wendy. *Emma.* 32 pages. 1980. Knopf Doubleday Publishing Group. One day Emma bought paints and brushes and painted her village the way she remembered it.

Kunhardt, Edith. *Red Day, Green Day.* 32 pages. 1992. HarperCollins Publishers. Takes the reader through all the colors of the rainbow in the story about Andrew and his class when they have a day to learn about each color.

Laden, Nina. *When Pigasso Met Mootisse.* 40 pages. 1998. Chronicle Books. Pigasso and Mootisse live across the road from each other and do not get along.

Lionni, Leo. *Frederick.* 32 pages. 1973. Random House Children's Books. Frederick, the poet mouse, stores up something special for the winter.

Lionni, Leo. *Little Blue and Little Yellow.* 48 pages. 1995. HarperCollins Publishers. A little blue spot and a little yellow spot are best friends, and when they hug they turn green.

Lobel, Arnold. *The Great Blueness.* 32 pages. 1994. HarperCollins Publishers. A wizard discovers that each color that he invents has an emotional effect on people.

Markun, Patricia Maloney. *The Little Painter of Sabana Grande.* 32 pages. 1993. Bradbury Press. A young Panamanian artist paints the outside of his home because he has no paper.

McDonnell, Patrick. *Art.* 48 pages. 2006. Little Brown Books for Young Readers. A rhyming tribute to a young artist.

McMillan, Bruce. *Growing Colors.* 32 pages. 1998. HarperCollins Publishers. Photos of fruits and vegetables show the many colors found in nature.

Muhlberger, Richard. *What Makes a Monet a Monet?* 48 pages. 2002. Penguin Group. Useful for showing Monet paintings.

Munsch, Robert. *Purple, Green and Yellow.* 32 pages. 1992. Annick Press Ltd. Brigid loves markers and when she draws on herself with permanent ink she must find a solution to stay out of trouble.

Niepold, Mil. *Oooh! Picasso.* 48 pages. 2009. Random House Children's Books. Close ups of the everyday objects that Pablo Picasso transformed into sculptures.

O'Neal, Zibby. *Grandma Moses: Painter of Rural America.* 64 pages. 1987. Turtleback Books. Presents the simple life of the acclaimed artist.

Parker, Marjorie Blain. *Colorful Dreamer: The Story of Artist Henri Matisse.* 2012. Penguin Group.

More than a biography, an encouragement to never give up on your dreams.

Pinkwater, Daniel. *The Big Orange Splot*. 32 pages. 1977. Turtleback Books. When Mr. Plumbean's house gets splashed with orange paint he decides to make it a multi colored house.

Poulet, Virginia. *Blue Bug's Book of Colors*. 32 pages. 1994. Scholastic Library Publishing. Blue Bug discovers how colors mix to form different colors.

Reiss, John. *Shapes*. 32 pages. 1982. Simon & Schuster Children's Publishing. Introduces common shapes.

Rodrigue, George. *Why Is Blue Dog Blue?* 40 pages. 2002. Harry N. Abrams. Readers learn about colors and how artists use color.

Rogers, Alan. *Green Bear*. 16 pages. 1997. World Book. Green Bear changes the color of his house to match the seasons.

Rogers, Alan. *Red Rhino*. 16 pages. 2000. Cooper Square Publishing. Red Rhino has trouble finding his red balloon among all the red things he sees.

Rylant, Cynthia. *All I See*. 32 pages. 1994. Scholastic. A shy boy and a painter each paint what they see.

Scieszka, Jon. *Seen Art?* 48 pages. 2005. Penguin Group. Confusion abounds when a boy is looking for his friend Art but ends up at the Museum of Modern Art.

Venezia, Mike. *Mary Cassatt*. 32 pages. 1991. Scholastic Library Publishing. Examines the life and work of the American Impressionist.

Venezia, Mike. *Monet*. 32 pages. 1990. Scholastic Library Publishing. Traces the life of the artist and shows some of his paintings.

Venezia, Mike. *Van Gogh*. 32 pages. 1989. Scholastic Library Publishing. Briefly examines the life and work of the artist.

Walsh, Ellen Stoll. *Mouse Paint*. 32 pages. 1995. Houghton Mifflin Harcourt. Three white mice discover jars of paint.

Winter, Jeanette. *Josefina*. 36 pages. 1996. Houghton Mifflin Harcourt. A counting book inspired by Josefina Aguilar who makes clay figures.

Holiday — Halloween

Advance planning: To plan for this storytime, find a theme-related song to play during craft and snack times, like "Thriller," by Michael Jackson, "Purple People Eater," by Sheb Wooley, "Monster Mash," by Bobby "Boris" Pickett, or "I Want Candy," by The Strangeloves. You will also want to select a poem, such as "It's Halloween," by Jack Prelutsky (find it at www.thehalloweenday.com), along with the books you plan to read. Decorate your space with plastic jack o'lanterns, pumpkins, black cats, spiders and spider webs, bats, ghosts, caution tape. Wear a costume, earrings or a hat. Be sure to look for books earlier than usual, especially if you're using the library, as many books will be checked out and unavailable. Because it's a holiday, you will probably want to play several games.

Introduction to theme: Halloween is a holiday observed every year on October 31st. Traditionally it's a time for wearing costumes and going house to house trick or treating, having parties and carving Jack O'Lanterns out of pumpkins. Have you worn a costume on Halloween? Gone to a party? Trick or treated? Helped to carve a pumpkin? Today we'll read about Halloween, play a Halloween game, make a Halloween craft and eat a Halloween snack.

Song: "Pumpkin Pumpkin on the Ground," sung to the tune of "Twinkle Twinkle Little Star." Lyrics can be found at www.dltk-holidays.com.

Game: "Five Little Pumpkins" fingerplay
    Materials needed: None. Advance preparation: None. At storytime: Hold up hand with fingers splayed behind arm as gate.

Five little pumpkins sitting on a gate (rock hand back and forth)
The first one said, "Oh my it's getting late!" (put up index finger then hands to cheeks)
The second one said, "there are witches in the air,"
(put up two fingers then move hand about like flying)
The third one said, "But we don't care."
(put up three fingers then hands out in we don't care gesture)
The fourth one said, "Let's run and run and run." (put up four fingers then run in place)
The fifth one said, "Isn't Halloween fun?" (put up all five fingers)
Then Wooooo went the wind (move hand like you did for witches flying)
and Out went the lights (clap)
And five little pumpkins rolled out of sight. "(roll hands in front)

Alternative Games

Left and right pumpkin story. Materials needed: small plastic pumpkins (one for each child), items (candy, small toys or party favors). Advance preparation: Put items in pumpkins. At storytime: Have the children sit in a circle and give everyone a pumpkin. As you read the story, have them pass their pumpkin to the person seated next to them as the words left or right are spoken. At the end, they get to keep the pumpkin they're holding. It's not essential that each pumpkin have exactly the same items in them, but similar and equal in quantity. Read the story slowly and emphasize the left and right as you speak them.

On Halloween night, Susie left for trick or treating. Right away she ran into her friend Billy as she made a right turn at the corner. He was holding his trick or treat bag in his right hand. Billy suddenly realized he'd left part of his costume at home so he wanted to go back right away. To get home, he had to make a left turn at the corner, then a right turn at the next corner, two more right turns and then he was there. He went right in, only to find that his mom had left a note for him on the kitchen table. It said, "Dear Billy, if you get home right before I do, please take the dog out for a walk. I left his leash right by the door. Do it right away so he doesn't tinkle on the floor. Also, I left you a snack in the refrigerator. Love, Mom." Billy found his mask right where he'd left it and decided to wait until later to walk the dog. He went back to find his friends and they were right where he'd left them. They went trick or treating right away. Down one street, turning left, up another street, turning left again. Soon their bags were full of candy and they decided to go to Susie's house. Susie's mom had left some bottles of water right out on the counter since she knew they'd be thirsty after all that walking. Right away they drank down the water and then they left the kitchen to go into the family room to play Xbox. Billy could use his left hand as well as his right hand on the controller and he left Susie's house with his candy feeling very happy. Down the street, turning left, then right, then right and right again. This time he took the dog for a walk right away and then went back into the house, checked to see that his candy was left safely in a secret cabinet in the kitchen so his parents wouldn't eat it and then he went right to bed. What he didn't know was that his mom was right outside the door when he was hiding his candy so she was able to sneak a piece from the bag he'd left inside after Billy went to bed. And I can tell you right now, that I know all this because I am Billy's mom.

Eyeball relay. Supplies needed: spoons, two ping pong balls drawn on with marker to look like eyeballs Have the children form two lines. Give each one a spoon. Start one ping pong ball eyeball at front of each line and have them pass it down the line and back again without using hands to help. If it falls on the floor try to pick it up with the spoon.

Mummy wrap. Supplies needed: rolls of toilet paper. Divide the children into small groups, maybe three or four in each group, and give each group a roll of toilet paper. Start at same time and see which group can wrap the mummy in their group using the whole roll the fastest.

Eyeball toss. Supplies needed: lots of ping pong eyeballs, plastic pumpkins. Put plastic pumpkins together in a group. Give the children the ping pong eyeballs and have them try to toss or bounce the ping pong eyeballs into the pumpkins. Can number the pumpkins and the eyeballs to make it more difficult trying to get the correct number into the marked pumpkin.

Musical pumpkins. Cut pumpkin shapes from construction paper and arrange them on the floor; kids must move from pumpkin to pumpkin while music plays, just like in musical chairs. To keep kids from being excluded, allow them to share pumpkins as you remove a pumpkin for each round. By the end of the game, all the kids have to squeeze onto one spot.

Trick or treat. Have plastic pumpkins filled with candy, pencils, bookmarks or other small treats. The children will walk around your area and enlist parents or others to be the treaters. The children will need some type of bag or container if you're doing this. You could give them empty treat bags or make a treat bag as a craft.

Spider web. You will need a ball of black yarn. If you buy a skein you will need to wind it into a ball to play the game. Have the children stand in a circle. Start the game by gently tossing the ball of yarn across the circle to another child. That child holds on to a piece of the yarn and then throws the ball across to another child. Continue until all the children are holding onto the yarn and it makes a spider web.

Mummy walk. Tie two children's legs together with torn strips of muslin and make them walk together like mummies around cones.

Craft: Paper bag treat bag (do this craft if you plan to include Trick or Treating as a game)

Materials needed: White or brown paper lunch bags, black construction paper, scissors, glue sticks, black markers or crayons. Advance preparation: Cut spiders from black construction paper. Cut black circles and thin strips for legs. At storytime: Have the children

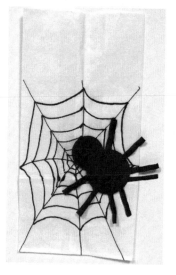

Left: **Paper bag treat bag pieces.** *Right:* **Paper bag treat bag.**

draw lines on their paper bag to make a spider web. Then glue the spider to the web. Accordion fold the legs for dimension.

Alternative Crafts

Tissue paper candy corn magnet. Print a large candy corn picture on card stock, or a rounded triangle with dividing lines. Cut small squares of orange, yellow and white tissue paper. Have the children crumple the tissue paper piece and glue them to the candy corn picture. Attach a magnet strip to the back.

Crepe paper streamer paper plate ghost. Large white paper plate with five two-foot lengths of white crepe paper streamer stapled or taped. Construction paper hands taped or stapled. Draw or cut paper from black construction paper eyes, nose and mouth. Draw with crayon around the eyes. Glue on to paper plate if using cut paper. Punch hole in top and put loop of yarn in it to hang.

Foam jack o'lantern magnet. Pumpkin-shaped orange foam sheets. Draw face with black permanent markers. Attach magnet strip to back.

Clothespin bats. Paint clothespins black using spray paint. Cut bat body and wing shapes from black construction paper. Glue bat bodies to clothespins and then bat wings to bat body. Could attach tiny google eyes if desired.

Snack: Popcorn witch hands

Materials needed: Plastic food handlers gloves, popcorn, candy corn, plastic spider rings, twist ties or yarn, large paper plates. Advance preparation: Make or buy popcorn. Cut eight-inch long pieces of yarn. At storytime: Give each child a glove, five pieces of candy corn, a spider ring, a tie and a plate full of popcorn. Have them put the candy corn into each finger of the glove. These are the "fingernails." Then fill each finger with popcorn and fill the rest of the hand with popcorn too. Tie it when full so it looks like a hand. Put the spider ring over the ring finger.

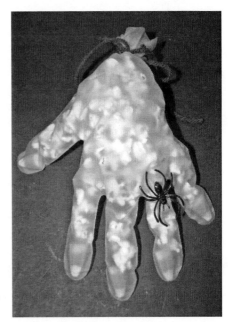

Popcorn witch hand.

Alternative Snacks

Jack o'lantern cookies. Sugar cookie dough, orange icing, brown M&Ms and/or chocolate chips. Bake cookies in pumpkin shape or just round shapes. If making round, use large biscuit cutter and add a little piece to look like a stem. Give each child a cookie on a paper plate along with a plastic knife, a dollop of orange icing three brown M&Ms and five chocolate chips. Cover in orange icing. Place two brown M&Ms as eyes, one as nose and several chocolate chips as mouth.

Ghost tootsie pop. Tootsie pops or any other lollipops, white tissues, black yarn, black markers. Place the white tissue over the Tootsie pop and tie so that it looks like a ghost. Use the marker to make three dots — two eyes and a mouth.

Jack o'lantern cake. Bake two bundt cakes. Slice a little off the bottoms of the cakes so that they can be placed bottom to bottom evenly on a plate. Cover in orange icing. "Draw" pumpkin lines with a knife. Decorate with icing triangle eyes, nose and typical jack o'lantern mouth. Place two waffle ice cream cones in middle (top one upside down) and cover with green icing to look like stem. Add green icing leaves around the stem.

Mummy treat cups. Cover small white cups with glued-on either white crepe paper streamers, white gauze or torn white cloth strips to look like a mummy. Add google eyes and a felt bow. The bow can be placed at the top to look like a girl's hair ribbon or at the bottom to look like a boy's bow tie. Fill the cups with snack foods like popcorn or candies.

SUGGESTED BOOKS

Accord Publishing Staff. *One Spooky Night: A Halloween Adventure.* 36 pages. 2011. Andrews McMeel Publishing. Die cuts and overlays add interest to this story about a little monster walking through the woods on Halloween.

Bourgeois, Paulette. *Franklin's Halloween.* 32 pages. 1996. Kids Can Press, Limited. Franklin the turtle is dressed up for Halloween and going to a party.

Brenner, Tom. *And Then Comes Halloween.* 32 pages. 2009. Candlewick Press. Rhythmic text leads us through the end of summer and fall until it's time for Halloween.

Bridwell, Norman. *Clifford and the Halloween Parade.* 28 pages. 1999. Scholastic Reader Level 1. Clifford and friends have a Halloween parade where they all dress up as firemen.

Bright, Robert. *Georgie.* 40 pages. 1944. Doubleday & Co. Georgie is the friendly ghost who lives in the Whittakers' attic.

Capucilli, Alyssa Satin. *Inside a House That Is Haunted a Rebus Read-Along Story.* 25 pages. 1998. Scholastic Inc. Cumulative rhyme in which everyone in a haunted house wakes up and startles each other, with pictures replacing the characters as they're introduced so that the children can read along with you.

Colandro, Lucille. *There Was an Old Lady Who Swallowed a Bat.* 32 pages. 2005. Scholastic. The familiar song with a Halloween theme.

Cushman, Doug. *Halloween Goodnight.* 32 pages. 2010. Holt, Henry & Company. How does everyone say goodnight to their little ones on Halloween?

Cuyler, Margery. *Skeleton Hiccups.* 32 pages. 2005. Simon & Schuster Children's Publishing. Skeleton has hiccups and Ghost figures out how to scare him to help get rid of them.

deGroat, Diane. *Trick or Treat, Smell My Feet.* 32 pages. 1999. HarperCollins Publishers. Gilbert is looking forward to Halloween at school until he discovers he took his little sister's ballerina costume.

Demas, Corinne. *Halloween Surprise.* 32 pages. 2011. Walker & Company. Lily tries on a lot of costumes before she finds the perfect one to surprise her father.

Dunrea, Olivier. *Ollie's Halloween.* 32 pages. 2010. Houghton Mifflin Harcourt Trade & Reference Publishers. Join the Goslings as they dress up for Halloween and have fun.

Engelbreit, Mary. *Queen of Halloween.* 24 pages. 2008. HarperCollins Children's Books. When friends go trick or treating they encourage each other to be brave and approach a scary house.

Fiorello, Frank. *Searching for the Perfect Pumpkin.* 40 pages. 1995. Pumpkin Patch Publishing. Two children and a black cat romp through a pumpkin patch.

Freeman, Don [based on the stories by]. *Corduroy's Best Halloween Ever.* 32 pages. 2001. Penguin Group. Corduroy plans a Halloween party for all his friends.

Gibbons, Gail. *Halloween Is.* 32 pages. 2003. Holiday House. Everything you want to know about Halloween.

Goeller, Dorothy. *Halloween.* 24 pages. 2010. Enslow Publishers. Learn all about the holiday.

Greene, Carol. *The 13 Days of Halloween.* 32 pages. 2009. Sourcebooks. A parody of the 12 Days of Christmas.

Hallinan, P.K. *Today Is Halloween.* 26 pages. 2008. Ideals Publications. Teaches safe Halloween behavior.

Hatch, Elizabeth. *Halloween Night.* 22 pages. 2005. Doubleday Book for Young Readers. A cumulative story about many different Halloween creatures and a jack o'lantern filled with treats (and a mouse).

Herman, R.A. *The Littlest Pumpkin.* 32 pages. 2001. Scholastic. The littlest pumpkin in the pumpkin patch dreams of being chosen for Halloween.

Krieb, Mr. *We're Off to Find the Witch's House.* 29 pages. 2005. Dutton Children's Books.

Wordplay and alliteration in this rhyming story of trick or treaters who want to be a little bit scared on Halloween.

Landau, Elaine. *What Is Halloween?* 24 pages. 2011. Enslow Publishers. Learn all about the traditions of Halloween.

Leuck, Laura. *One Witch.* 32 pages. 2005. Walker & Company. Count up and down again with the witch who visits all manner of ghoulish friends to get ingredients to make her gruesome stew.

Lewis, Kevin. *The Runaway Pumpkin.* 32 pages. 2008. Scholastic. Kids try to roll the gigantic pumpkin down the hill but it gets away from them.

Martin, Bill, Jr., Michael Sampson and Paul Meisel. *Trick or Treat?* 27 pages. 2002. Simon & Schuster Books for Young Readers. Trick or treat becomes stranger after neighbor Merlin plays a trick and everything is backwards.

Masurel, Claire. *Happy Halloween Emily!* 29 pages. 2002. Grosset & Dunlap. Emily the rabbit and her friends anticipate all the fun they'll have on Halloween.

Mortimer, Anne. *Pumpkin Cat.* 24 pages. 2011. HarperCollins Publishers. Cat and Mouse grow things (including pumpkins) in the garden and their friendship is the real story here.

Murray, Marjorie Dennis. *Halloween Night.* 40 pages. 2010. HarperCollins Publishers. A Halloween version of the Night Before Christmas.

Neitzel, Shirley. *Who Will I Be? A Halloween Rebus Story.* 30 pages. 2005. Greenwillow Books. After being invited to a party, a child has a hard time deciding what costume to wear. Pictures replace some of the words so that the children can read along out loud with you.

Numeroff, Laura Joffe. *Emily's Bunch.* 28 pages. 1978. Macmillan Publishing Co. Emily has a hard time coming up with a good Halloween costume, but amazes her older brother with her solution.

Parker, Toni Trent. *Sweets and Treats.* 14 pages. 2002. Cartwheel Books. A short book with photos of children dressed in different costumes.

Rey, Margret, and H.A. Rey. *Curious George Goes to a Costume Party.* 24 pages. 2001. Houghton Mifflin Harcourt Trade & Reference Publishers. Curious George accidentally stirs things up at his first Halloween costume party.

Rosenberry, Vera. *Vera's Halloween.* 29 pages. 2008. Henry Holt & Company. Vera gets lost and has some scary adventures before getting found by her father on a snowy Halloween.

Rylant, Cynthia. *Moonlight the Halloween Cat.* 32 pages. 2003. HarperCollins Publishers. A reassuring story about a cat that wanders about on Halloween.

Scotton, Rob. *Scaredy-Cat, Splat.* 40 pages. 2010. HarperCollins Publishers. Splat wants to be a scary cat but he's a scaredy-cat.

Shaw, Nancy. *Sheep Trick or Treat.* 32 pages. 1997. Houghton Mifflin Harcourt Trade & Reference Publishers. What will happen to the Sheep on their way home through the woods after trick or treating? There are wolves lurking in this book with rhyming text.

Silverman, Erica. *Big Pumpkin.* 1999. 32 pages. San Val. A witch grows a big pumpkin and wants to make it into a pie, but she can't lift it.

Slegers, Liesbet. *Happy Halloween!* 32 pages. 2011. Clavis Publishing. The whole family gets involved in preparing for Halloween.

Stutson, Caroline. *By the Light of the Halloween Moon.* 30 pages. 1993. Lothrop, Lee & Shepard Books. A host of Halloween spooks are drawn to the tapping of a little girl's toe. Could be a little scary for very young children, but the little girl prevails and the spooks end up dancing to her violin music.

Teague, Mark. *One Halloween Night.* 32 pages. 2005. Scholastic. The trouble for the group starts when a black cat crosses their path on the way home from school.

Thompson, Lauren. *Mouse's First Halloween.* 32 pages. 2000. Simon & Schuster Children's Publishing. Simple text and bold illustrations showing all the symbols of Fall and Halloween.

Trapani, Iza. *Haunted Halloween.* 28 pages. 2009. Charlesbridge Publishing. Count up and down again with the guests at Ghost's Halloween party.

White, Linda. *Too Many Pumpkins.* 32 pages. 1997. Holiday House. A woman who once had nothing to eat but pumpkins finds herself with a bumper crop.

Williams, Linda. *The Little Old Lady Who Was Not Afraid of Anything.* 32 pages. 1986. HarperCollins Publishers. A little old lady has a clever solution with what to do with the pants, shoes, etc. that are following her.

Wing, Natasha. *The Night Before Halloween.* 32 pages. 1999. Penguin Group. A take on the Night Before Christmas story.

November

Names

Advance planning: To plan for this storytime, find a theme-related song to play during craft and snack times, like "The Name Game," by Shirley Ellis. You will also want to select a poem, such as "Naming Things," by Arden Davidson (find it at www.kinderkorner.com/names.html), along with the books you plan to read. Decorate your space with alphabet blocks, name tags, children's names written on a poster.

Introduction to theme: When we're born, one of the most important things our parents do for us is give us a name. Usually we're given three names: a first name, a middle name and a last name. Most often everyone in a family shares the same last name, but everyone has a different first and middle name. Sometimes children are named after their parents or grandparents and called junior, or even given a number like the second or the third or the fourth. Some children have more than one middle name and some none at all. Our names are registered and put on a special piece of paper called a birth certificate. Most people keep the same first name all of their lives, but some people change them, and most women will change their last names to that of their husbands when they get married, although they don't have to, and not all women do. There's a famous quote by William Shakespeare about names "What's in a name? That which we call a rose by any other name would smell as sweet." Do you know what that means? Today we'll read about names, play a name game, make a name craft and eat a name snack.

Song: "_____, _____, what do you say?" (insert child's name, repeating whole verse for each child)

> "_____, _____, what do you say?"
> Raise your hand if you're here today! (child raises hand)
> Wave to your friends (child waves to group)
> And they'll wave to you (group waves to child)
> That is just what good friends do!

Game: Name ball

Materials needed: playground ball. Advance preparation: None. At storytime: Have the children stand in a circle. First child says his name and passes the ball to the child to his right or left. That child then says his/her name as he/she catches the ball. Continue around the circle until everyone's had a turn. Then reverse. At that point everyone should know each other's names so they can call out someone's name and toss the ball to them. If tossing and catching is too hard, they can roll to one another while seated. Could add having them say something about themselves when they catch the ball, like what they had for breakfast, or what they did over the weekend, or something they're going to do today.

Alternative Games

Alphabet blocks. Have some alphabet blocks or print letters on the computer. Make sure to have enough letters to spell everyone's name. Let each child and parent spell out the child's name with the blocks or printed letters.

Sign language. Get a book on sign language and let everyone try to learn how to spell their name using sign language.

Same letter. Ask each child to say the first letter of their name. Then ask them to name something that starts with that same letter. If time, you could ask for specific things, like a favorite food that starts with the same letter, or another friend whose name starts with the same letter, or a favorite activity.

ABC name. Sing the ABC song slowly and ask each child to jump up when they sing the first letter of their name. It might be a good idea to go around the circle first and ask each child to say his/her name and the first letter of his/her name. Could have the child pick out the letter from a set of magnetic letters or alphabet blocks.

Craft: Name caterpillar

Materials needed: Construction paper in multiple colors, gluesticks, crayons. Advance preparation: Cut circles from many colors of construction paper. At storytime: Have the children write the letters of their name on circles, then form a caterpillar with the circles and glue them to the background paper. Draw the antennae with crayon.

Alternative Crafts

Sponge letters. Let the children use sponge letters to make their name using white glue on background paper. Then have them sprinkle glitter on the glue letters. Or they could glue things to the letters, like some kind of dry pasta or macaroni.

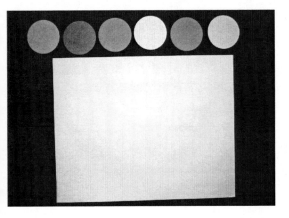 

Left: **Name caterpillar pieces.** *Right:* **Name caterpillar.**

Self portraits. Let children draw self-portraits and write their names.

Snack: Pretzel and cheese cube names

Materials needed: Small pretzel sticks, cubes of cheese, large paper plates. Advance preparation: Cut the cheese into cubes. At storytime: Have the child or parent write the child's name on the paper plate in capital block letters. Have the children copy the name in pretzel sticks and cheese cubes on the paper plate.

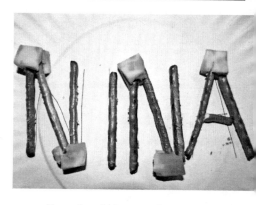

Pretzel and cheese cube names.

Alternative Snacks

Letter snacks. Find some kind of snack with letters, like cookies, gummies, and cereal. Let the children spell their names from the snack food.

Name fruits and vegetables. Choose some different kinds of food or fruits that start with the first letters of some of the children's names, or a food that starts with the first letter of your name.

SUGGESTED BOOKS

Allen, Constance. *My Name Is Big Bird*. 24 pages. 1999. Random House Children's Books. Big Bird talks about himself.

Allen, Constance. *My Name Is Elmo*. 24 pages. 1999. Random House Children's Books. Elmo talks about himself.

Archer, Peggy. *Name That Dog*. 32 pages. 2010. Dial. Twenty six poems, from A to Z, to help name your puppy.

Bayer, Jane. *A, My Name Is Alice*. 32 pages. 1992. Puffin. Meet characters with names that start with all the letters of the alphabet.

Beach, Judi K. *Names for Snow*. 40 pages. 2003. Hyperion. The Inuit language has many different words for snow, describing the kind of snow.

Bemelmans, Ludwig. *Madeline*. 48 pages. 1958. Penguin Group. The story of twelve little girls in two straight lines, the youngest one being Madeline.

Burke, Mary McManus. *A, My Name Is Andrew*. 40 pages. 2003. All About Kids Publishing. The book includes the entire alphabet and features a child's name starting with each letter.

Carlson, Nancy. *I Like Me*. 32 pages. 1990. Penguin Group. A pig proclaims that she likes a lot of things about herself and when she makes a mistake she tries again.

Choi, Yangsook. *The Name Jar*. 40 pages. 2003. Dragonfly Books. It's hard to be the new kid and even harder when no one can pronounce your name.

dePaola, Tomie. *Andy That's My Name*. Andy's friends construct different words from his name.

Dunklee, Annika. *My Name Is Elizabeth*. 24 pages. 2011. Kids Can Press, Limited. Elizabeth doesn't like it when people use nicknames instead of saying Elizabeth.

Dylan, Bob. *Man Gave Names to All the Animals*. 40 pages. 1999. Houghton Mifflin Harcourt. Based on a song, the story of how man named the animals of the world.

Falconer, Ian. *Olivia*. 40 pages. 2000. Atheneum Books for Young Readers. Olivia is a spunky little pig with a lot of enthusiasm.

Fosberry, Jennifer. *My Name Is Not Alexander*. 32 pages. 2011. Sourcebooks. Alexander discovers how great men become heroes.

Fosberry, Jennifer. *My Name Is Not Isabella*. 32 pages. 2010. Sourcebooks. Isabella is having an identity crisis.

Fox, Mem. *Whoever You Are*. 32 pages. 2006. Houghton Mifflin Harcourt. Despite the differences between people, there are similarities that bind us together.

Fox, Mem. *Wilfred Gordon McDonald Partridge*. 30 pages. 1989. Kane/Miller Book Publishers. A little boy tries to learn the meaning of memory so he can help an elderly friend find hers. He is drawn to her because she has four names, just like he does.

Freeman, Don. *Corduroy.* 32 pages. 1976. Penguin Group. The story of a small teddy bear named Corduroy.

Heilbroner, Joan. *Robert the Rose Horse.* 72 pages. 1962. Random House Children's Books. An allergy to roses causes trouble for this aptly named horse until one time his sneeze saves the day.

Henkes, Kevin. *Chrysanthemum.* 32 pages. 1996. HarperCollins Publishers. A perfect baby with a perfect name. Until she goes to school and the other children make fun of her name.

Johnson, Crockett. *Harold and the Purple Crayon.* 64 pages. 1998. HarperCollins Publishers. When Harold goes for a walk in the moonlight and realizes there's no moon, he simply draws one with his purple crayon. Thus begins quite an adventure of Harold's drawings.

Keats, Ezra Jack. *My Name Is Yoon.* 32 pages. 2003. Farrar, Straus & Giroux. Yoon's name means shining wisdom. She likes to write it in Korean, but her father tells her she must write it in English.

Long, Loren. *Otis.* 40 pages. 2009. Penguin Group. A little left behind tractor becomes a hero.

McKee, David. *Elmer.* 32 pages. 1989. Harper-Collins Publishers. Elmer the patchwork elephant tries to blend in with the herd, but it's impossible and he soon realizes he should just be himself.

Mosel, Arlene. *Tikki Tikki Tembo.* 32 pages. 1968. Henry Holt & Co. Recounts how the Chinese came to give their children short names.

O'Connor, Jane. *Fancy Nancy.* 32 pages. 2005. HarperCollins Publishers. Nancy likes everything fancy. Even though she's a very girly girl, she's also quite strong and independent and always has some kind of challenge to overcome.

Palatini, Margie. *Good as Goldie.* 22 pages. 2003. Scholastic. Goldie is a big girl with a new baby brother.

Rey, H.A., and Margret Rey. *Curious George.* 64 pages. 1973. Houghton Mifflin Harcourt. The first adventure tells the story of how George was caught in the jungle and brought back to the city. As always, George's curiosity gets him into mischief.

Root, Phyllis. *The Name Quilt.* 32 pages. 2003. Farrar, Straus & Giroux. Each night Sadie goes to sleep with Grandma's quilt with the names embroidered on it, until one day it gets blown away on the line.

Rosenthal, Amy Krouse. *Little Hoot.* 36 pages. 2008. Chronicle Books. Little Hoot is an owl that wants to go to bed at a reasonable time, but owls have to stay up late.

Rosenthal, Amy Krouse. *Little Pea.* 36 pages. 2005. Chronicle Books. If Little Pea doesn't eat all his sweets, there will be no vegetables for dessert!

Schachner, Judith. *Skippyjon Jones.* 32 pages. 2005. Penguin Group. A Siamese cat who thinks he's a Chihuahua.

Stead, Philip C. *A Sick Day for Amos McGee.* 32 pages. 2010. Roaring Book Press. When Amos McGee the zookeeper stays home sick, the animals come to visit him instead.

Viorst, Judith. *Alexander and the Terrible, Horrible, No Good, Very Bad Day.* 32 pages. 1987. Atheneum Books for Young Readers. Nothing goes right for Alexander this day.

Wells, Rosemary. *Yoko Writes Her Name.* 32 pages. 2008. Hyperion Books. Yoko is excited on the first day of school as she shows everyone how she writes her name. But some children make fun of her Japanese writing and until they learn to appreciate their cultural differences Yoko is unhappy at school.

Williams, Suzanne. *Mommy Doesn't Know My Name.* 48 pages. 1996. Sandpiper. Frustrated Hannah tries to get her mother to call her by her real name rather than pet names.

Wolfsgruber, Linda. *A Daisy Is a Daisy Is a Daisy (Except When It's a Girl's Name).* 32 pages. 2011. Groundwood Books. Girls' names in different languages with illustrations of the flowers that they are named after.

Yolen, Jane. *My Father Knows the Names of Things.* 32 pages. 2010. Simon & Schuster Books for Young Readers. The father in the story knows the names of the birds that sing, the clouds, the planets... and takes the time to share what he knows with his child.

Lions

Advance planning: To plan for this storytime, find a theme-related song to play during craft and snack times, like "The Lion Sleeps Tonight," by The Tokens. You will also want to select a poem, such as "It's Dark in Here," by Shel Silverstein (find it at www.shelsilversteinpoems.wordpress.com), along with the books you plan to read. Decorate your space with stuffed lions, green streamers or large tropical houseplants for jungle, pith helmet, binoculars (safari gear).

Introduction to theme: Lions are big cats. They're the second biggest cat. Can you guess what the biggest cat is? It's the tiger. Lions are mostly found in Africa. Male lions have the big bushy mane that makes them look very fierce. Lion babies are called cubs. Lions often say hello to each other by rubbing their foreheads together. They make many sounds, but the one we're probably most familiar with is the roar. Can you roar like a lion? Let's hear you! Today we'll read about lions, play a jungle animal game, make a lion craft and have a snack that looks like a lion.

Song: "I'm a Little Lion," to the tune of "I'm a Little Teapot":

> I'm a little lion, nice and brown
> I'm in the zoo right here in town.
> When I feel like talking I will roar
> It's very loud want to hear some more?
> ROAR! (let the children roar as loudly as they want)

Game: Loud as a lion

Materials needed: Cardstock, craft sticks, CD, CD player. Advance preparation: Print photos from computer on cardstock of jungle and/or zoo animals that make distinctive sounds, like: lion, elephant, zebra, chimpanzee, hippo, snake, crocodile, giraffe, parrot, flamingo, tiger, leopard. Glue these photos to craft sticks. Make enough for all the children, duplicating some if necessary. Find animal sounds on www.findsounds.com and make a recording. At storytime: Distribute the stick photos to the children. Play the CD recording of the different animals sounds and ask the child holding the animal of the sound to hold it up when the sound plays. Do a few times so they hear the sound and recognize it.

Alternative Games

Jungle boogie. You will need to create a CD with jungle songs on it and a CD player. At storytime play the CD and dance a "jungle boogie." If you make the paper plate maracas as craft, make them first and then the children can shake them while dancing.

Walk like a lion. Tape down a masking tape line across the room in a zig zag pattern. Have the children follow you walking on the lion and moving like a lion. Start slowly, stretching, plodding along, then move faster and as you see some prey, move fast and pounce on it, then slow down and stretch and end by relaxing and sitting in a regal lion pose and doing a cat paw face wash action.

Zoo animals musical chairs. Set up a line of chairs, alternating facing directions, one chair for each child. Tape a picture of a wild animal, such as a lion, tiger, gorilla, chimpanzee, etc. to each chair. Start some music, like The Lion Sleeps Tonight, and have the children walk around the chairs. Stop the music and have each child sit in a chair. Whatever chair they sit in, the next time you start the music, they become that animal and move around the room like that animal making the sounds the animal would make. Do this repeatedly so that everyone gets a chance to be different animals. This is not an exclusion kind of musical chairs — don't remove any chairs.

Craft: Paper plate lion

Materials needed: Large white paper plates, scissors, crayons, red pom poms, brown and black construction paper, google eyes, glue sticks. Advance preparation: Cut whiskers from black construction paper. Cut muzzle circles from brown construction paper. At storytime: Have children color the lion's mane around the edge of the paper plate. Have them snip around the edge to make the mane more dimensional. Glue red pom pom as nose, two brown paper circles as muzzle, two google eyes, and black paper whiskers. Draw muzzle with crayon.

Paper plate lion pieces.

Alternative Crafts

Lion crowns. Make cardboard, foam or paper crowns as the lion is the "king" of the jungle.

Jungle music. Make a paper plate maraca (decorate a paper plate, fold it in half, put a handful of dried beans inside and staple closed) and shake it when dancing the jungle boogie.

Lion paper plate mask. Cut out eyeholes in a large white paper plate. Punch holes around the outside of the plate and have the children loop short pieces of brown yarn through the holes. They could add a mouth, ears and nose with crayons.

Paper plate lion.

Snack: Lion cupcake

Materials needed: Yellow cupcakes, buttercream icing (it has a yellow tint) or white icing colored slightly yellow with food coloring gel, coconut, yellow candies like Skittles or M&Ms, pink or red candies like Skittles or M&Ms, chocolate chips or brown M&Ms, licorice laces (any color but black if you can find it). Paper plates, plastic knives. If preferred

Lion cupcake.

could use yellow gumdrop cut in half for muzzle and orange gumdrops (either whole or halves) around edge for mane instead of coconut. Advance preparation: Bake cupcakes. Cut licorice into half-inch pieces for whiskers. Toast coconut for five minutes at 350 degrees or until golden. At storytime: Place a cupcake, two yellow candies, a sprinkle of coconut, one red candy, two brown candies, four pieces of licorice and a dollop of icing on each paper plate. Make sample by icing the cupcake, placing some coconut around the edge for the mane, placing the yellow candies as the muzzle, the red as the nose, the brown as the eyes and the licorice as the whiskers.

Alternative Snacks

Lion cookies. Make cookies using a flower-shaped cookie cutter and turn them into lions by either drawing on a face using food markers or icing the mane with orange icing and making a face with candies such as chocolate chip eyes, M & M or Skittle nose and muzzle.

Animal crackers. See if the children can find lions in the animal crackers.

Animal fruit snacks. Try to find some zoo themed fruit snacks that have lions in them.

Lion in a cage. Pull out lions from animal crackers. Give each child a graham cracker square (half a graham cracker) and something to spread on it, like peanut butter, marshmallow creme or honey. Place the lion cracker on top of it and then place several cut pieces of licorice laces across to look like cage bars.

Lion crackers. Using a round cracker like a Ritz as the face, raisins for eyes, nose and mouth and half pretzel sticks for whiskers, make a lion face. Could spread cream cheese on it first before adding the facial features.

SUGGESTED BOOKS

Abercrombie, Barbara. *The Show and Tell Lion*. 32 pages. 2006. Simon & Schuster Children's Publishing. Matthew has nothing for show and tell until he invents a pet lion.

Axtell, David. *We're Going on a Lion Hunt*. 32 pages. 2007. Holt, Henry & Company. The familiar tale told with beautiful illustrations of children.

Burkett, Rand. *Mouse and Lion*. 32 pages. 2011. Scholastic. A retelling of the fable.

Cuyler, Margery. *We're Going on a Lion Hunt*. 32 pages. 2008. Marshall Cavendish Corporation. The familiar story of going on the hunt and catching a big one, but this time the quarry is a lion.

Fatio, Louise. *The Happy Lion*. 40 pages. 2004. Random House Children's Books. The lion at the French zoo is a favorite when visitors drop by, so one day he decides to return the favor and visit his visitors.

Fatio, Louise. *The Happy Lion Roars*. 40 pages. 2006. Random House Children's Books. The happy lion is lonely until he meets a beautiful lioness.

Foley, Greg. *Willoughby and the Lion*. 40 pages. 2009. HarperCollins Publishers. A little boy discovers a magical lion in his backyard but can he give him what he wishes for most of all? A friend?

Freeman, Don. *Dandelion: Story and Pictures*. 48 pages. 1977. Penguin Group. Dandelion is turned away from a party where he's not recognized because he's a bit overdressed for the occasion.

Kleven, Elisa. *The Lion and the Little Red Bird*. 32 pages. 1996. Penguin Group. A little bird learns why a lion's tail changes color every day.

Knudsen, Michelle. *Library Lion*. 48 pages. 2009. Candlewick Press. A beautifully illustrated story of a lion who comes to the library and learns to behave, but later when he roars out of necessity it's misunderstood.

Kraus, Robert. *Leo the Late Bloomer*. 32 pages. 1994. HarperCollins Publishers. When Leo can't seem to do anything right his mother explains that he's just a late bloomer.

McElligott, Matthew. *The Lion's Share*. 32 pages. 2009. Walker and Company. Math concepts of doubling and halving are introduced as the group of animals offers to bake cakes for the lion.

Morgan, Nicola. *Pride of Lions*. 30 pages. 1999. Fitzhenry & Whiteside, Limited. What happens when many different groups of animals get together?

Ossege, Kathie Martin. *The Lion, The Wind and Mariah*. 44 pages. 2007. Authorhouse. A little girl has a lion for a best friend and he teaches her about people's special gifts.

Pinkney, Jerry. *The Lion and the Mouse*. 40 pages. 2009. Little, Brown Books for Young Readers. Wordless with beautiful artwork retelling of the fable of the lion who is helped by the mouse and later returns the favor.

Steele, Cheryl. *Do Lions Wear Pajamas?* 28 pages. 2011. Tate Publishing and Enterprises. A series of questions about what goes on at the zoo at night.

Swordy, Gillian. *Reading Between the Lions*. 32 pages. 2010. Transworld Publishes Limited. After being picked on by a bully, Lionel goes to read between the stone lions in the garden.

Tierney, Fiona. *Lion's Lunch*. 32 pages. 2010. Scholastic. An interesting take on the traditional fable, but this time it's a little girl who is trying not to become the lion's lunch.

Waber, Bernard. *A Lion Named Shirley Williamson*. 40 pages. 2000. Houghton Mifflin Harcourt Trade & Reference Publishers. A rather long story of a lion who mistakenly was named Shirley Williamson. Much hilarity ensues.

Walsh, Melanie. *Do Lions Live on Lily Pads?* 32 pages. 2006. Houghton, Mifflin, Harcourt Trade & Reference Publishers. A silly book about where animals do and don't live.

Weeks, Sarah. *If I Were a Lion*. 40 pages. 2007. Simon & Schuster Children's Publishing. A rhyming story of an energetic child who sometimes gets into trouble.

Monsters and Strange Creatures

Advance planning: To plan for this storytime, find a theme-related song to play during craft and snack times, like "Monster Mash," by Bobby "Boris" Pickett. You will also want to select a poem, such as "It's Boring Being a Monster," by Richard Macwilliam (find it at www.behance.net/gallery/Its-Boring-Being-a-Monster/3342101), along with the books you plan to read. Decorate your space with crepe paper streamers, posters of strange creatures even some real life strange creatures like jellyfish or squids or octopuses and some stuffed toys if you have any that look strange like the monsters from *Where the Wild Things Are* or sea animals.

Introduction to theme: Monsters and other strange creatures like monsters aren't real but they're fun to imagine or read about. Sometimes they can be scary too, but try to remember that they're not real and maybe you won't find them so scary. Have you ever been afraid that there might be something hiding somewhere waiting to scare you? How did you deal with your fear? Today we'll read about some monsters and strange creatures, play a monster game, make a strange creature craft and eat a snack that looks pretty strange.

Song: "There's a Monster in My Closet," to the tune of "If You're Happy and You Know It." Lyrics can be found at www.perpetualpreschool.com.

Game: "Five Little Monsters" fingerplay

Materials needed: None. Advance preparation: None. At storytime: Have everyone stand up and hold up a hand.

Five little monsters looking for a meal (hold up five fingers)
One ate a rotten orange peel (pretend to pop these foods into mouth)
One ate a moldy piece of bread
One ate a glob of glue instead

One ate a bowl of bat wing jelly
One ate a tennis shoe, old and smelly
After their lunch, they gave a clap (clap hands)
Hung upside down (bend down from the waste and let hands hang)
and took a nap (snore loudly)

Alternative Games

Three legged creature. You'll need scarves or torn muslin pieces long enough to tie around legs, CD with monster music and CD player. At storytime, tie two children's legs together with a scarf, then have them walk and dance like monsters around the room while you play music like "Monster Mash."

Monster dash. This is a monster version of red light/green light. You be the monster first, and stand about 25 feet away from the children with your back to them. You might wear a monster mask, especially if that's your craft for today. You say "dash," and the children should creep up on you while your back is turned. Then quickly say "stop" and turn around. The children must freeze where they are as soon as they hear the word "stop." Continue saying "dash" and "stop." When a child is able to tag you he/she gets to be the monster in the next round of the game.

Eyeball relay race. Draw eyes (complete with iris, pupil and red squiggly tired eye lines) on ping pong balls. Have at least two lines of children, even numbers in each line. Give the child at the front of the line a spoon holding a ping pong ball eyeball, and each other child in line a spoon. Have each child walk to the other side of the room and back (it would be helpful to have a chair or a cone to mark the place for the children to walk around) and pass the eyeball to the next child in their line. When a child has taken his/her turn, he/she should sit down. The first line with everyone sitting down wins the relay. When everyone in the line is sitting down, you'll know that everyone has had a turn.

More monsters. Place a rope or mark a long line with masking tape on the floor. Start with one child on the line or the rope and have everyone say:

One little monster went out to play
Out on a little tightrope one day.
He (she) had such enormous fun,
He (she) called for another little monster to come.

Let the first child choose another child to join him (her) or you choose someone. Repeat the verse above reflecting the number of children, for example:

Two little monsters went out to play
Out on a little tightrope one day.
They had such enormous fun,
They called for another little monster to come.

Once all the children are on the line:

All the little monsters went out to play
Out on a little tightrope one day.
They had such enormous fun
Until the tightrope broke and they all fell down! (at that point all the children should fall down)

Mystery monster. Print a poster sized picture of one of the strange creatures that you showed a picture of earlier. Cut it into four or five pieces like a jigsaw puzzle. Put a piece of rolled up tape on the back of each piece. Place the pieces, one piece at a time, up on the wall, asking the children if they know what kind of monster creature it is. After you add a piece, ask again if they haven't guessed.

Craft: Monster collage

Materials needed: White, green, purple and orange construction paper, scissors, miscellaneous materials like foam stickers, wiggle eyes, ribbon, sequins, yarn, markers or crayons and glue. Advance preparation: Cut large circles and squares from different colors for monster face. Cut smaller circles and other shapes from the other colors for other monster facial features. Use white or black paper as background. At storytime: Have children choose a large circle or square for the face, then other shapes and materials to make monster faces. Could make several monster faces on one background sheet or could make a monster's whole body.

Monster collage pieces.

Alternative Crafts

Strange creature mask. Use large paper plates for the mask. Cut construction paper shapes as in monster collage to glue on to paper plate to make monster faces.

Strange creature puppet. Decorate paper bags of any color to look like strange creatures.

Snack: Fruit monster eyeballs

Materials needed: Dried apple rings, raisins, dried apricots or other dried fruit such as mangoes, small paper plates. Advance preparation: None. At storytime: Give each child two apple rings, two dried apricots and two raisins on a paper plate. Have them place the apricots on the apples and the raisins on the apricots so that they look like the eyeballs of a strange creature.

Monster collage.

Alternative Snacks

Marshmallow eyes. Two large marshmallows topped with Froot Loops.

Strange creature fingers. Have celery or carrot sticks, dab a bit of cream cheese at one end and apply a sliced almond to look like a fingernail.

Fruit monster eyeballs.

Monster cookie fingers or toes. Color cookie dough green. Shape cookies into finger or toe sized rolls, press a dark candy like a brown M & M into one end like a toenail or fingernail and bake.

SUGGESTED BOOKS

Baron, Alan. *The Red Fox Monster.* 24 pages. 1998. Candlewick Press. Is it really Red Fox hiding in the bushes or other animals dressed in his clothes?

Bissett, Josie. *Tickle Monster.* 36 pages. 2008. Compendium Publishing & Communications. The monster from Planet Tickle comes to tickle any child who follows along. Great for reading to a child who loves to be tickled.

Cuyler, Margery. *Monster Mess.* 40 pages. 2008. Margaret K. Elderry Books. A monster is ready to go to bed but discovers a mess that needs tidying.

deRubertis, Barbara. *Maxwell Moose's Mountain Monster.* 32 pages. 2011. Kane Press. Maxwell enjoys camping, but he's not sure whether or not he's alone in the mountains or if there's someone stalking him.

Diesen, Deborah. *Pout Pout Fish.* 32 pages. 2008. Farrar, Strauss & Giroux. The pout pout fish discovers that there's more to life than being glum.

Docherty, Thomas. *Big Scary Monster.* 40 pages. 2010. Candlewick Press. The monster will have to change his ways if he wants to keep his friends.

Emberley, Ed. *Bye-Bye, Big Bad Bullybug.* 32 pages. 2007. Little, Brown Books for Young Readers. Shows little bugs being bullied but they face up to the bully in the end.

Emberley, Ed. *Glad Monster, Sad Monster: A Book About Feelings.* 32 pages. 1997. Little, Brown Books for Young Readers. Cut outs show monster faces expressing many different kinds of feelings.

Emberley, Ed. *Go Away Big Green Monster!* 32 pages. 1993. Little, Brown Books for Young Readers. The book introduces the monster page by page with clever cut outs, and then the monster disappears page by page when told to go away.

Emberley, Rebecca. *If You're a Monster and You Know It.* 32 pages. 2010. Scholastic. A monster twist on the classic song.

Gackenbach, Dick. *Harry and the Terrible Whatzit.* 40 pages. 1979. Houghton Mifflin Harcourt Trade & Reference Publishers. Harry is brave enough to go into the basement to see why his mother hasn't returned when she went to get a jar of pickles.

Heller, Nicholas. *Goblins in Green.* 32 pages. 1999. Harper Trophy. Goblins from A to Z getting dressed.

Hicks, Barbara Jean. *Monsters Don't Eat Broccoli.* 40 pages. 2009. Alfred A. Knopf. Rhyming text that shows lots of things that monsters eat, including maybe some trees that resemble broccoli.

Hutchins, Pat. *Three-Star Billy.* 1994. Greenwillow Books. The monster Billy doesn't want to go to school and once there he behaves badly but because it's a school for monsters he still earns stars.

Hutchins, Pat. *The Very Worst Monster.* 32 pages. 1988. HarperCollins Publishers. Since the new baby monster arrived no one notices Hazel so she must do something.

Kasza, Keiko. *Grandpa Toad's Secrets.* 32 pages. 1998. Puffin. Little Toad learns from his grandpa the secrets to staying alive in the woods.

Landa, Norbert. *The Great Monster Hunt.* 32 pages. 2010. Good Books. Strange noises are coming from under Duck's bed.

Lionni, Leo. *A Color of His Own.* 32 pages. 1997. Random House Children's Books. A chameleon searching for his color finds a friend instead.

MacHale, D.J. *The Monster Princess.* 40 pages. 2010. Simon & Schuster Children's Publishing. Rhyming text about a monster who lives in a cave but wishes she could be a princess.

Mayer, Mercer. *Applelard & Liverwurst.* 34 pages. 1990. HarperCollins Publishers. The farm animals have a successful harvest led by a wayward rhinoceros.

Mayer, Mercer. *There Are Monsters Everywhere.* 32 pages. 2005. Penguin Group. The sequel to *There's a Nightmare in My Closet.*

Mayer, Mercer *There's a Nightmare in My Closet.* 32 pages. 1968. Penguin Group. About a child's fear of the dark and the monsters in his closet.

McCarty, Peter. *Jeremy Draws a Monster.* 40 pages. 2009. Holt, Henry & Company. Jeremy's monster is a tyrant and Jeremy tries to figure out how to get rid of him.

McCarty, Peter. *The Monster Returns.* 40 pages. 2012. Holt, Henry & Company. Jeremy gets help from the neighbors when the monster he drew threatens to return.

McElligot, Matthew. *Even Monsters Need Haircuts.* 40 pages. 2010. Walker & Company. A child runs a barber shop for strange creatures at night under a full moon.

Mosel, Arlene. *The Funny Little Woman.* 40 pages. 1993. Penguin Group. A little old lady is captured by creatures while chasing a dumpling.

Noble, Trinka Hakes. *The Day Jimmy's Boa Ate the Wash.* 32 pages. 1980. Penguin Group. A romp through a farm on a school field trip that's made exciting by a boa constrictor.

Noll, Amanda. *I Need My Monster.* 32 pages. 2009. Flashlight Press. When the monster that usually lives under a little boy's bed goes off fishing for a week, the little boy misses him so he tries to find a substitute monster.

Numeroff, Laura Joffe. *Laura Numeroff's Ten Step Guide to Living with Your Monster.* 32 pages. 2002. HarperCollins Publishers. A step by step guide for monster care.

Parrish, Peggy. *No More Monsters for Me.* 1981. 64 pages. 1987. HarperCollins Publishers. A Learn to Read book about a girl who brings home a monster that grows very large in her basement.

Pinkwater, Daniel. *Pickle Creature.* 21 pages. 1979. Atheneum. Conrad brings home a pickle creature instead of the jar of pickles he was asked to get at the store.

Rosenberg, Liz. *Monster Mama.* 32 pages. 1997. Puffin. Edward's mama is a monster, but it doesn't matter who your mama is, she will always come to help you.

Schnitzlein, Danny. *The Monster Who Ate My Peas.* 32 pages. 2001. Peachtree Publishers. A little boy agrees to give a monster various things in exchange for eating his peas until he makes an interesting discovery.

Sendak, Maurice. *Seven Little Monsters.* 1977. HarperCollins. A counting book that shows the mischievous side of the creatures from Where the Wild Things Are.

Sendak, Maurice. *Where the Wild Things Are.* 48 pages. 1963. HarperCollins. Max is naughty and gets sent to bed, but luckily for him there's a forest growing in there and it takes him away to find the wild things.

Smallman, Steve. *There's No Such Thing as Monsters!* 26 pages. 2009. Good Books. Brothers are afraid when they spend their first night apart in their own separate rooms.

Stein, David Ezra. *Monster Hug.* 40 pages. 2007. Penguin Group. Simple text and humorous illustrations play with size and perspective.

Stevenson, James. *What's Under My Bed?* 1983. Mulberry Books. Children are convinced there's something scary under their beds until their grandfather tells them what was under his bed when he was young.

Stone, Jon. *The Monster at the End of this Book.* 32 pages. 2004. Random House Children's Books. A Little Golden Book that has Grover from Sesame Street urging the reader not to turn the pages for fear of the monster at the end of the book.

Taylor, Sean. *When a Monster Is Born.* 40 pages. 2009. Roaring Book Press. There are two kinds of monsters: the in the forest kind or the under your bed kind. This circular story explores both kinds.

Weatherly, Lee. *The Scariest Monster in the World.* 32 pages. 2009. Boxer Books, Limited. The monster comes through the woods yelling at everyone to get out of his way. But then one day he needs help — will the others help him or be too afraid?

Willems, Mo. *Leonardo the Terrible Monster.* 44 pages. 2005. Hyperion Press. Leonardo is actually terrible at being a monster.

Willems, Mo. *Naked Mole Rat Gets Dressed.* 40 pages. 2009. Hyperion Book. Wilbur is the only mole rat who wears clothing, much to the annoyance of the other mole rats.

Wing, Natasha. *Go to Bed Monster!* 40 pages. 2007. Houghton Mifflin Harcourt Trade & Reference Publishers. The monster that Lucy creates by drawing him doesn't want to go to bed even though it's late and Lucy is tired.

Zade, Adam. *Who Is It?: Two Yellow Eyes Shining in the Dark.* 16 pages. 2012. Anzou Publishing. The reader might imagine all sorts of possibilities but in the end will find out that it's only a cat.

Zion, Gene. *Harry by the Sea.* 32 pages. 1976. HarperCollins. Harry is mistaken for a sea serpent when he gets covered by seaweed.

Turtles

Advance planning: To plan for this storytime, find a theme-related song to play during craft and snack times, like "The Little Turtle," by Burl Ives. You will also want to select a poem, such as "The Little Turtle," by Vachel Lindsay (find it at www.poetryfoundation.org), along with the books you plan to read. Decorate your space with stuffed turtles or posters of different kinds of turtles like pets or sea turtles in the ocean.

Introduction to theme: Turtles are a kind of animal called reptiles. Turtles have a very special body part that protects them called a shell. Have you ever seen a turtle or a picture of a turtle? They have two parts to their shells — the upper part and an underside. The shell is attached to the turtle's insides and he can't crawl out of it. Turtles have four short legs and they move very slowly. There are other names for certain types of turtles, like Terrapin and Tortoise. Some people like to keep turtles as pets. At the zoo you can see several different kinds of turtle — the great big tortoises that are usually outside all the way down to the tiny little swimming turtles in the water at the reptile house. Today we'll read about turtles, play a turtle game, make a turtle craft and eat a turtle snack.

Song: "I'm a Little Turtle," to the tune of "I'm a Little Teapot":

> I'm a little turtle
> Watch me go.
> I don't go fast
> I walk real slow.
> When I get too tired
> I take a rest.
> I pull in my head and legs
> and hide my best.

Game: Turtle race

Materials needed: Sheet of lined paper, coins to use as turtles (or use little plastic turtles if you have them available), and a die for rolling numbers. Advance preparation: Make the lined paper with a lane for each child's turtle and spaces to move the turtle as they roll the die. Draw Start at one end and Finish at the other end. At storytime: Each child places his coin or turtle at the starting line and they take turns rolling the die and moving their turtle the rolled number of spaces until someone crosses the finish line and wins. If you read *The Hare and the Tortoise* first, some of the players could be hares and some tortoises.

Alternative Games

Shell race. Mark off a four foot wide lane on the floor with masking tape. Have the children crawl two at a time down the lane with a chair pad or small pillow on their backs, pretending it's a turtle shell. The goal is to get to the end of the lane without losing their shell.

Turtle toss. Make a green bean bag that looks like a turtle. Take turns tossing the bean bag to each child while saying "Turtle, Turtle" and then ask the child to complete the thought by saying something they know or like about turtles.

Turtle hunt. Print pictures of turtles from the Internet or cut out of green construction paper and hide many of them around the storytime area. Tell the children they're going on a turtle hunt and ask them to bring back all the turtles that are hiding. Place a blue cloth or pan as a collection spot for the turtles that they find. Make sure you have placed enough of them for all the children to find several.

Craft: Green foam turtle

Materials needed: Green foam sheets, both light and dark, scissors, google eyes, glue sticks. Advance preparation: Cut large circles, four feet, head and tail from the dark green sheet foam, shell patches from the light green sheet foam for each turtle. At storytime: Have the children glue the shell patches to the top of the circle, and attach the head, feet and tail to the bottom around the edge. Glue google eyes to the head.

Alternative Crafts

Green bowl turtle. Turn small green paper or plastic bowl upside down. Staple four green construction paper legs, a green construction paper tail and a green construction paper head with google eyes glued to it to the rim of the bowl.

Paper plate turtle. Turn a white paper plate upside down. Staple four green construction paper legs, a green construction paper tail and a green construction paper head with google eyes glued to it to the rim of the plate. Tear pieces of green construction paper into small pieces and have the children glue those pieces to the back of the paper plate shell.

Rock turtles. Paint some large smooth flat rocks green. Have the children glue small green paper tail, head and feet to the underside of the rock and glue google eyes to the head. Glue the rock turtle to a larger circle of grey construction paper to look like the turtle is sitting on a rock.

Snack: Turtle cupcake

Materials needed: Cupcakes, green icing, Junior Mints, white hardening icing in a tube, green M&Ms or Skittles, paper plates, plastic knives. Advance preparation: Bake the cupcakes, color icing green, put two dots of white icing on each Junior Mints to look like eyes. At storytime: Give each child a cupcake, a dollop

Green foam turtle pieces.

Green foam turtle.

Turtle cupcake.

of icing, a knife, one Junior Mint and about five or six green candies. They will spread the icing, place the Junior Mint at one edge to look like the head and place the green candies around the top to look like the shell.

Alternative Snacks

Turtle cookies. Round sugar cookies that the children cover with green icing and place green Skittles or M&Ms on. Could use two chocolate chips or brown M&Ms for eyes.

Lettuce turtles. A round lettuce leaf on which you place some sliced olives to look like turtle shell spots. You could mention that this would be a snack that both looks like a turtle and turtles would like to eat.

Apple turtles. Quarter green apples and remove core, flattening it so that it can be placed skin side up on a plate and look like a turtle shell. Place six green grapes around it as legs, tail and head.

SUGGESTED BOOKS

Amery, Heather. *What's Happening at the Zoo*. 16 pages. 1984. EDC Publishing. Not really about turtles, but an amusing book that shows things going on at the zoo that stimulate conversation.

Armitage, Kimo. *Limu the Blue Turtle and his Hawaiian Garden*. 28 pages. 2004. Island Heritage Publishing. Limu meets a pink turtle and together they have a great adventure.

Bauer, Marian Dane. *A Mama for Owen*. 32 pages. 2007. Simon & Schuster Books for Young Readers. Owen the baby hippo befriends Mzee the tortoise after the tsunami that sweeps Owen's world away.

Berger, Melvin. *Look Out for Turtles*. 32 pages. 1996. Collins. Explains why turtles have survived for so long.

Bourgeois, Paulette. *Franklin in the Dark*. 32 pages. 1997. Demco Media. A turtle afraid of small dark places? Uh oh, what about his shell?

Bourgeois, Paulette. *Franklin Is Lost*. 32 pages. 1992. Kids Can Press, Ltd. Franklin's mother tells him never to go in the woods, but one day he's playing hide and seek and forgets what his mother told him.

Brennan, John. *Zoo Day*. 32 pages. 1989. Lerner Publishing Group. Animals in their Australian zoo and their keepers.

Brett, Jan. *Mossy*. 32 pages. 2012. Putnam Juvenile. Mossy is an amazing turtle with a garden growing on her shell. She misses her real home and finally the people around her realize how to get her back there but still keep her with them.

Brunelle, B.T. *Sunny's Ocean Adventure*. 64 pages. 2012. CreateSpace. A young turtle discovers the importance of balancing work and play.

Buckley, Richard. *The Foolish Tortoise (World of Eric Carle)*. 24 pages. 2009. Little Simon. Eric Carle's illustrations in this board book about a tortoise's journey of self-discovery.

Bunting, Eve. *Emma's Turtle*. 32 pages. 2007. Boyds Mill Press. The story of an adventurous pet turtle.

Carle, Eric. *1, 2, 3 to the Zoo*. 32 pages. 1982. Penguin Group. A counting book with animals on a train, each car with one more animal.

Carle, Eric. *The Rabbit and the Turtle*. 32 pages. 2008. Scholastic. Aesop's fable brought to life in the artwork of Eric Carle.

Chambers, Sally. *Tarquin's Shell*. 16 pages. 1998. Barron's Education Series. Tarquin is tired of his shell and his friends help him try on some other things to replace it.

Cyrus, Kurt. *The Voyage of Turtle Rex*. 40 pages. 2011. Harcourt Children's Books. The voyage of a sea turtle in a world of dinosaurs can be dangerous until she grows large.

Czekaj, Jef. *Hip & Hop, Don't Stop!* 40 pages. 2010. Hyperion Books. Hip is a turtle who raps slowly. Hop is a bunny who raps fast. When they compete in a rap contest this time neither slow nor fast wins the prize.

Davies, Nicola. *One Tiny Turtle: Read and Wonder*. 32 pages. 2005. Candlewick. The journey of the tiny, endangered loggerhead turtle.

Falwell, Cathryn. *Turtle Splash! Countdown at the Pond*. 32 pages. 2008. Greenwillow Books. One by one ten turtles splash into the pond.

Fontes, Justine. *How the Turtle Got Its Shell*. 24 pages. 2000. Golden Books. A Little Golden Book that gives many different stories from around the world to explain how the turtle got its shell.

Fridell, Ron. *Turtle*. 32 pages. 2009. Heinemann. An in depth look at the life cycle of turtles.

Gallimard, Jeunesse. *Turtles and Snails*. 24 pages. 1998. Scholastic Books. Not a lot of information but some plastic overlay pictures that show turtles and other animals that live in shells.

Gibbons, Gail. *Zoo*. 32 pages. 1991. HarperCollins Publishers. A behind the scenes look at a working day at the zoo.

Hatkoff, Isabella. *Owen & Mzee: The True Story of a Remarkable Friendship*. 40 pages. 2006. Scholastic Press. An orphaned baby hippo and a giant turtle's friendship touched the world.

Keats, Ezra Jack. *Over in the Meadow*. 32 pages. 1999. Puffin. In a lush meadow, one turtle digs, two fish swim, three bluebirds sing and so on.

Marlow, Layn. *Hurry Up and Slow Down*. 32 pages. 2009. Holiday House. Hare races through the day and tortoise can barely keep up. But at night it's hare who wants to slow down while reading books.

McDermott, Gerald. *Jabuti the Tortoise: A Trickster Tale from the Amazon*. 32 pages. 2005. Sandpiper. Sometimes Jabuti played mischievous tricks.

McGuinness, Elle. *Baby Turtle's Tale*. 26 pages. 2009. Accord Publishing. Baby Turtle hatches and realizes that he's a day late and all of his siblings have already headed out.

Murphy, Stuart J. *Seaweed Soup*. 40 pages. 2001. HarperCollins Publishers. It's slimy, green and gooey, and it's Turtle's favorite lunch.

Ormerod, Jan. *When We Went to the Zoo*. 40 pages. 1991. HarperCollins Publishers. A family goes on a tour of the zoo.

Simon, Paul. *At the Zoo*. 32 pages. 1991. Knopf Doubleday Publishing Group. A musical romp through the zoo.

Rey, Margret, H.A. Rey and Alan J. Shalleck. *Curious George Visits the Zoo*. 32 pages. 1985. Houghton Mifflin Harcourt. Curious George visits the zoo and manages to both make trouble and make up for it.

Seuss, Dr. *If I Ran the Zoo*. 64 pages. 1950. Random House Children's Books. Young Gerald McGrew thinks of all sorts of unusual animals he'd have in a zoo.

Seuss, Dr. *Yertle the Turtle and Other Stories*. 96 pages. 1958. Random House Children's Books. A lesson about power struggles.

Stevens, Janet. *The Tortoise and the Hare: an Aesop Fable*. 32 pages. 1995. Holiday House. The well known tale of slow and steady wins the race.

Yee, Tammy. *Baby Honu's Incredible Journey*. 32 pages. 1997. Island Heritage Publishing. Learn about the life of a baby sea turtle as he faces predators in this ocean adventure.

Ziefert, Harriet. *Where's the Turtle?* 14 pages. 1987. Carousel. A board book. After resting, swimming and eating, where does the turtle go? Life the flaps and find out.

Zoehfeld, Kathleen Weidner. *What Lives in a Shell?* 32 pages. 1994. Collins. For some animals a shell is a home.

Zollman, Pam. *A Turtle Hatchling Grows Up*. 24 pages. 2005. Scholastic Library Publishing. A turtle's life cycle from egg to adult.

Holiday — Thanksgiving

Advance planning: To plan for this storytime, find a theme-related song to play during craft and snack times, like "Be Our Guest" from *Beauty and the Beast*. You will also want to select a poem, such as "Thanksgiving Feasting," by Joanna Fuchs (find it at www.poems.greet2k.com), along with the books you plan to read. Decorate your space with cornucopias, stuffed turkeys, pumpkins, autumn leaves, straw bales, Indian corn — anything that makes you think of Autumn and Thanksgiving time.

Introduction to theme: In the United States, Thanksgiving Day is celebrated on the fourth Thursday in November. In Canada, Thanksgiving Day is celebrated on the second Monday in October. It's not celebrated in any other countries. Some other countries have harvest festivals or celebrations but North America is the only place where it's called Thanksgiving. The first Thanksgiving in the U.S. was a feast in 1621 shared by the Pilgrims (who had recently settled Plymouth Colony in what is now Massachusetts) and the Wampanoag

Indians, who shared their corn, squash, and wild turkeys. This first feast was not repeated until ten years later. Thanksgiving was declared a national holiday in 1863 by President Abraham Lincoln. Today we'll read about Thanksgiving, play a Thanksgiving game, make a Thanksgiving craft and eat a Thanksgiving snack.

Song: "If You're Thankful and You Know It," to the tune of "If You're Happy and You Know It":

> If you're thankful and you know it, clap your hands.
> If you're thankful and you know it, clap your hands.
> If you're thankful and you know it,
> Then your face will surely show it.
> If you're thankful and you know it, clap your hands.
> If you're thankful and you know it, stomp your feet.
> If you're thankful and you know it, stomp your feet.
> If you're thankful and you know it,
> Then your face will surely show it.
> If you're thankful and you know it, stomp your feet.
> If you're thankful and you know it, shout "I am!"
> If you're thankful and you know it, shout "I am!"
> If you're thankful and you know it,
> Then your face will surely show it.
> If you're thankful and you know it, shout "I am!"
> If you're thankful and you know it, do all three.
> If you're thankful and you know it, do all three.
> If you're thankful and you know it,
> Then your face will surely show it.
> If you're thankful and you know it, do all three.

Game: Thankerchief (Use this game to write the feathers for the group craft.)

Materials needed: Handkerchief, construction paper, marker. Advance preparation: Create a large construction paper turkey and many construction paper feathers. Glue the turkey body to a background sheet but leave the feathers for storytime. At storytime: Arrange the children and their parents in a circle. Pass a "thankerchief" (handkerchief) around the circle, as everyone recites this poem:

> Thankerchief, thankerchief, around you go —
> Where you'll stop, nobody knows.
> But when you do, someone must say,
> What they are thankful for this day.

The player holding the "thankerchief" when the poem ends, must say aloud, one thing for which they are thankful. This includes the parents. Write this on one of the large feathers on the turkey and enlist a parent's help to glue each one to the turkey. This continues until everyone has had their turn.

Alternative Games

Bowling for turkeys. You will need several 2 liter soda bottles, brown construction paper, feathers, playground balls. Cover 2 liter soda bottles with brown construction paper and add some feathers. At storytime set the bottles up as bowling pins and let the children bowl them over by rolling playground type balls at them.

What are you thankful for? You will need construction paper and pencils. Cut large number fours from construction paper. At storytime hand each child a number four and the parent a pencil. Have the parent ask their child what they're thankful "for." The parent writes it on the number four and then everyone takes a turn telling what they're thankful for. This could also be done without any numbers, just by going around to each child and asking.

Craft: Thanksgiving handprint poem

Materials needed: Light and dark brown, white, red, yellow and orange construction paper, pencils, scissors, glue sticks, google eyes, printed copies of poem on cardstock. Advance preparation: Print the poem which can be found at www.dltk-kids.com and a clip art turkey on white cardstock. Glue the white cardstock with poem on a background sheet of construction paper (brown, orange, yellow or red). Cut out light brown turkey bodies, orange or yellow beaks and red wattles. At storytime: Have the parent trace around the child's hand on the dark brown construction paper and together they cut it out. Glue the handprint to the blank side of the white cardstock with the poem on it. Glue the light brown turkey body on the handprint turkey, the beak, the wattle over the beak and the google eyes.

Thanksgiving handprint poem pieces.

Thanksgiving handprint poem.

Alternative Crafts

Turkey feather painting. Put acrylic paint of several colors in large paper plates. Provide several large feathers by each color and a large light colored piece of paper. Show the children that they can use both ends of a feather to paint — the feather and the quill.

Pine cone turkeys. Use a pine cone as the turkey body. Glue tissue paper cut to look like feathers or actual feathers stuck into the pine cone. Add google eyes and a triangle of orange felt for the beak.

Plastic cup turkey. Using red, orange, yellow or brown plastic drinking cups, turn the cup upside down to be the turkey body. Glue a large pom pom (red, yellow, orange, brown) to the bottom of the cup as the turkey's head and glue a small piece of red felt as the wattle, a triangular piece of orange felt for the beak, and google eyes. Add tissue paper, construction paper or real feathers to one side of the cup.

Indian corn painting. Use cardboard box lids in which to put acrylic paint. Let the children roll Indian corn cobs in the paint and then roll them on paper to see what kind of designs they can make.

Snack: Turkey cupcake

Materials needed: Cupcakes, chocolate icing, candy corn, Junior Mints, chocolate sprinkles, white decorator hardening icing, small paper plates, plastic knives. Advance preparation: Bake cupcakes. At storytime: Give each child a cupcake, a dollop of icing, eight candy corn, one Junior Mint and a plastic knife on a paper plate. Let them spread the icing over the top of the cupcake. Have them insert five of the candy corn point down around the back edge of the cupcake for the tail. Place the Junior Mint on the opposite side as the head, put two small dots of icing on the Junior Mint for the eyes, and one candy corn as the beak, sprinkle the area between the head and the tail with chocolate sprinkles, then place the last two candy corn next to the cupcake on the plate as the feet.

Turkey cupcake.

Alternative Snacks

Plastic glove turkey. Fill plastic gloves with popcorn, putting one piece of candy corn in the thumb for the turkey's beak.

Graham cracker turkey. Place half a cracker (a square) on a paper plate and use three one-fourth crackers (small rectangles) as three tail feathers. Use two pretzel sticks as legs plus two more pretzel sticks broken in half for additional toes. Place two raisins for eyes on the square cracker and a small triangular bit of orange cheese or orange starburst candy for the beak.

Apple turkey. Cut apples in half and core. Turn the apple skin side up to be the turkey body on a paper plate. Use fruit leather or fruit by the foot for the feathers and face.

Apple and bread turkey. Cut round piece of bread or use large round cracker for turkey body. Surround it with apple slices for the feathers. Add raisins for eyes and cheese for beak.

Suggested Books

Adams, Michelle Medlock. *What Is Thanksgiving?* 24 pages. 2009. Candy Cane Press. A board book that gives a lively introduction to the true meaning of Thanksgiving.

Anderson, Laurie Halse. *Thank You, Sarah: The Woman Who Saved Thanksgiving.* 40 pages. 2005. Simon & Schuster Children's Publishing. Sarah Hale started a letter writing campaign to make Thanksgiving a national holiday.

Arnosky, Jim. *I'm a Turkey.* 32 pages. 2009. Scholastic. A spoken word song filled with facts about turkeys.

Atwell, Debby. *The Thanksgiving Door.* 32 pages. 2006. Sandpiper. Thanksgiving is about opening your heart to others including strangers who become friends.

Bateman, Teresa. *Gus, the Pilgrim Turkey.* 32 pages. 2008. Whitman, Albert & Company. When

Gus the turkey finds out from his friends what happens on Thanksgiving, he makes a plan to get away.

Bridwell, Norman. *Clifford's Thanksgiving Visit.* 32 pages. 2010. Scholastic. Emily Elizabeth and her big red dog learn how much they have to be thankful for.

Brown, Marc. *Arthur's Thanksgiving.* 30 pages. 1984. Little Brown Books for Young Readers. Arthur is in charge of directing the school Thanksgiving play.

Bunting, Eve. *A Turkey for Thanksgiving.* 32 pages. 1995. Houghton Mifflin Harcourt Trade. The plot twist involves inviting the turkey for Thanksgiving rather than "having" him.

Child, L. Maria. *Over the River and Through the Woods: A New England Boy's Song About Thanksgiving Day.* The original text of the poem beautifully illustrated.

Dalgliesh, Alice. *The Thanksgiving Story.* 32 pages. 1978. Simon & Schuster. Tells the Pilgrim story from one family's point of view.

Davis, Nancy. *The First Thanksgiving.* 14 pages. 2010. Little Simon. A board book that explains the holiday in very simple terms.

dePaola, Tomie. *My First Thanksgiving.* 14 pages. 2008. Penguin Group. A board book that introduces Thanksgiving to very young children.

Dougherty, Brandi. *The Littlest Pilgrim.* 32 pages. 2008. Cartwheel Books. A Thanksgiving story celebrating the true meaning of friendship.

Friedman, Laurie B. *Thanksgiving Rules.* 32 pages. 2009. Lerner Publishing Group. Rhyming text that explains all that one needs to know about getting the most out of Thanksgiving.

Gibbons, Gail. *Thanksgiving Is...* 32 pages. 2005. Holiday House. Thanksgiving is turkey, cranberry sauce... and celebrating life's blessings.

Greene, Rhonda Gowler. *The Very First Thanksgiving Day.* 32 pages. 2006. Simon & Schuster Children's Publishing. Rhyming text story of two girls, one a Native American and the other a Pilgrim.

Gunderson, Jessica. *Thanksgiving Then and Now.* 24 pages. 2011. Picture Window Books. Explains how the first Thanksgiving differed from those of today.

Hall, Margaret. *Thanksgiving.* 24 pages. 2010. Rourke Publishing. Explains the basics of the Thanksgiving holiday.

Haugen, Brenda. *Thanksgiving.* 24 pages. 2003. Picture Window Books. Explains the story of the Pilgrims and their first Thanksgiving and how many Thanksgiving traditions started.

Hayward, Linda. *The First Thanksgiving.* 48 pages. 1990. Random House Children's Books. A Step 3 Learn to Read book that shows what it was like at the very first Pilgrim Thanksgiving.

Hennessey, B.G. *One Little Two Little Three Little Pilgrims.* 32 pages. 2001. Penguin Group. Ten Pilgrim children and ten Wampanoag children prepare for the Thanksgiving feast.

Jackson, Alison. *I Know an Old Lady Who Swallowed a Pie.* 32 pages. 2002. Penguin Group. Based on the classic song about the old woman and the fly.

Johnston, Tony. *10 Fat Turkeys.* 32 pages. 2004. Cartwheel. Silly rhyming story that teaches children to count backwards.

Levine, Abby. *This Is the Turkey.* 32 pages. 2003. Albert Whitman & Company. A takeoff on the poem The House That Jack Built but based on the Thanksgiving celebration.

Maccarone, Grace. *Turkey Day.* 32 pages. 2010. Scholastic. A rhyming learn to read book about how the turkeys get together and celebrate.

Markes, Julie. *Thanks for Thanksgiving.* 32 pages. 2008. HarperCollins Publishers. Where to begin to say thanks on Thanksgiving?

Mayer, Mercer. *Just So Thankful.* 24 pages. 2006. Harper Festival. The new kid has everything that Little Critter thinks he wants, but he soon realizes that he has what's really important.

Mayr, Diane. *Run, Turkey, Run!* 32 pages. 2009. Walker & Company. Can Turkey find a place to hide?

McDoogle, Farrah. *Olivia Talks Turkey.* 16 pages. 2011. Simon Spotlight. Olivia gets a pet turkey but her parents won't let her keep it.

Mcgovern, Ann. *The Pilgrims' First Thanksgiving.* 32 pages. 1993. Scholastic Paperbacks. Simple text introduces children to the struggles of the Pilgrims their first few years.

Melmed, Laura Krauss. *This First Thanksgiving Day: A Counting Story.* 32 pages. 2003. HarperCollins Publishers. Celebrates the first Thanksgiving Day with lively verse and vibrant illustrations.

Metzger, Steve. *Give Thanks for Each Day.* 24 pages. 2011. Scholastic. Shows children all the simple things they can be thankful for.

Milgrim, David. *Thank You, Thanksgiving.* 32 pages. 2003. Houghton Mifflin Harcourt Trade. A little girl is thankful for many things.

O'Connor, Jane. *Our Thanksgiving Banquet.* 24 pages. 2011. HarperCollins Publishers. Fancy

Nancy and her family celebrate Thanksgiving.

Pilkey, Dav. *'Twas the Night Before Thanksgiving.* 32 pages. 1990. Scholastic. A takeoff on the traditional poem that has a busload of children saving the Thanksgiving turkeys.

Rockwell, Anne F. *Thanksgiving Day.* 40 pages. 2002. HarperCollins Publishers. The class puts on the Thanksgiving play and everyone has a part and a reason to be thankful.

Ross, Katharine. *The Story of the Pilgrims.* 24 pages. 1995. Random House Books for Young Readers. From the dangerous ocean voyage to the first harsh winter to the delicious Thanksgiving feast, all the excitement and wonder of the Pilgrims' first year.

Rylant, Cynthia. *In November.* 32 pages. 2000. Harcourt Children's Books. The air grows cold, animals prepare for winter and people gather together to count their blessings.

Skarmeas, Nancy. *The Story of Thanksgiving.* 26 pages. 1999. Ideals Publications. A board book that gives a traditional story of Thanksgiving with a focus on thanking God for what we have.

Slater, Teddy. *The Best Thanksgiving Ever.* 32 pages. 2007. Scholastic. A rhyming story that describes how turkeys celebrate Thanksgiving.

Spinelli, Eileen. *The Perfect Thanksgiving.* 32 pages. 2003. Henry, Holt & Co. Two completely opposite families celebrate Thanksgiving.

Stone, Tanya Lee. *T Is for Turkey: A True Thanksgiving Story.* 24 pages. 2009. Penguin Group. The elementary school puts on a play showing the true Thanksgiving story.

Sutherland, Margaret. *Thanksgiving Is for Giving Thanks.* 24 pages. 2000. Penguin Group. Simple text about all the things that bring people together on the holiday.

Wing, Natasha. *The Night Before Thanksgiving.* 24 pages. 2001. Penguin Group. A takeoff on the Night Before Christmas poem that illustrates a family's preparations for Thanksgiving.

Yoon, Salina. *Five Silly Turkeys.* 10 pages. 2005. Penguin Group. A board book for counting.

Ziefert, Harriet. *What Is Thanksgiving? A Lift the Flap Book.* 16 pages. 1992. HarperCollins Publishers. Little Mouse helps her parents prepare for the Thanksgiving feast and in so doing learns about the holiday.

December

Africa

Advance planning: To plan for this storytime, find a theme-related song to play during craft and snack times, like "Nkosi Sikelel Africa" which is the South African National Anthem — it translates to "God Bless Africa" and there are five different African languages in the song by Ladysmith Black Mambazo. You will also want to select a poem, such as "Walking Through Africa" (a Zulu chant the children sing; find it at http://www.canteach. ca/elementary/africasong.html), along with the books you plan to read. Decorate your space with stuffed animals that might be found in Africa, like lions, elephants, zebras and giraffes and a map of the continent.

Introduction to theme: Bring a globe and show where Africa is located on it. Africa is the second largest continent in the world after Asia. It's such a long stretch of land that the weather can be very different in different parts, ranging from very hot in some places to extremely cold in others. A day for an African child is different depending on what country the child lives in and whether they live in the country or a city. Usually children start their days with chores and then go to school. Some children go to school far from home so they have to wake up early. Most children in Africa wear uniforms to school. Once at school children learn similar things to children here in the United States, like Reading, Writing, Math and other languages. They also have playtime. Soccer is a favorite sport. After school children go home and do chores, homework or play. Today we'll read about Africa, play a game that African children might play, make a craft that looks like a traditional African mask and have a snack that children in Nigeria, a country in Africa, might eat.

Song: "He's Got the Whole World in His Hands" which can be found at www.metro lyrics.com.

Game: Da ga game
   Materials needed: Hula hoop, masking tape or chalk. Advance preparation: Make tape or draw chalk circle on the floor, or could use hula hoop if just a few children. At storytime: This is a game from Ghana named after the boa constrictor. A group of children stands around a circle marked with a hula hoop, masking tape or chalk on the ground. You step inside the circle as the head of the snake and try to tag the players outside the circle. Kids

around the outside of the circle dance around it, trying to avoid the snake's touch but must stay within inches of the marked circle. Any child outside the circle who is touched by the snake must join hands with the snake and become part of it. Together, the two hold hands and move around the circle to tag others. Play continues with tagged kids joining the snake until only one person remains outside the circle, and that last person is the tail of the snake.

Alternative Games

Clap game. At storytime, tell the children to clap when you say something that's related to Africa. Caution them that you might say something that doesn't have to do with Africa and so they shouldn't clap. Some suggestions: zebras (clap); gorillas (clap); shoes, tacos, hippopotamuses (clap); Nile River (clap); Sahara Desert (clap); African masks (clap); the color blue, polar bears, socks, drums (clap); lions (clap); dung beetles (clap); rhinoceroses (clap); sinks, televisions, shields (clap); watches, computers, chimpanzees (clap); walruses, rocks (clap); pythons (clap); cheetahs (clap); spoon, balloon, monkeys (clap); elephants (clap); leopards (clap); chairs, hair, forks, tables, rainsticks (clap); giraffes (clap); grasslands (clap); jungles (clap)

Chigora danda. Use two poles like broomsticks and have two of the parents sit on the floor holding the pole ends with the poles parallel to each other. Have the children in a line and lead them stepping through the poles as the parents lift them slightly in a rhythmic movement. Have the parents alter the rhythm as the children step through the poles.

Galloping zebras. Children will stand in a circle pretending to be zebras. You stand in the middle and beat a drum using fast and slow rhythms and the other children gallop around to the beat of the drum.

African mask pieces.

Balancing. Some African people carry things on their heads. Offer the children the opportunity to balance bundles of blankets or clothes on their heads.

Craft: African mask

Materials needed: cardboard, crayons, scissors, glue sticks. Advance preparation: cut mask and facial feature shapes. At storytime: African masks are supposed to look like ghostly spirits, departed ancestors or other kinds of spiritual beings. Masks are often worn by performers in traditional dances. Show photo samples of masks found on the Internet. Today we're going to make some masks that we can decorate with crayons. You can make your mask look happy, sad, scary or any other way you'd like. Glue facial features to masks with glue sticks. Use crayons to decorate.

African mask.

Alternative Crafts

Drum. Small containers like oatmeal boxes, Pringles cans, coffee cans. Cover top with freezer or craft paper and secure with a large rubber band. Could cover sides with paper and secure with tape, then decorate the paper coverings with crayons or markers. Provide an opportunity for everyone to tap gently on their drums in rhythm.

Shekere. These musical instruments are usually made from gourds whose seeds rattle inside when they dry out. Shells are sometimes attached for decoration and they are used to accompany dancing. Use plastic jugs with lids, assorted dried beans, beads or shells and cording to decorate. Put a handful of beans inside the jug, put glue inside the lid and close it tightly. Tie a length of cord around the neck of the jug and attach some beads.

Snack: Shuku shuku cookie

Shuku shuku coconut ball cookies, a traditional sweet from Nigeria, an African country. Materials needed: Paper plates or napkins, Shuku Shuku cookies. Advance preparation: Bake Shuku Shuku cookies. Ingredients (makes 23 cookies): 1½ cups and 2 tablespoons flaked coconut; ⅓ cup and 1 tablespoon and 1 teaspoon superfine sugar (put regular granulated sugar into blender for about 10 seconds if you don't have superfine); 5 egg yolks; ¾ cup and 1 tablespoon self-rising flour (decrease flour by 2 teaspoons and add 1½ teaspoons baking powder and ½ teaspoon salt if you don't have self-rising flour). Instructions: Preheat the oven to 350 degrees. In a medium

Shuku shuku cookies.

bowl, mix together the coconut, sugar and egg yolks to form a stiff dough. Squeeze into 1-inch balls, and roll each ball in flour to coat. Press the flour into the ball. Place on a baking sheet, spacing about 2 inches apart. Bake for 20 minutes in the preheated oven, or until golden. Remove from baking sheet, place on wire rack to cool. At storytime: Serve one cookie on napkin or paper plate.

Alternative Snacks

Couscous is an African staple and easy to prepare.

Ginger cookies are commonly eaten in South Africa.

Plantains look similar to bananas but have a different taste. These must be cooked before eating.

Cassava root is a plant similar to the potato and can be cooked and eaten in much the same way.

Suggested Books

Aardema, Verna. *Bringing the Rain to Kapiti Plain: A Nandi Tale* 32 pages. 1990. Penguin Group. A rhyme telling how rain was brought to the Kapiti Plain.

Adlerman, Daniel. *Africa Calling, Nighttime Falling.* 32 pages. 2001. Charlesbridge Publishing. A young African-American girl imagines herself among animals in Africa.

Alakija, Polly. *Catch that Goat!* 40 pages. 2007. Barefoot Books. Ayoka is left in charge of the family goat but it disappears.

Atinuke. *Anna Hibiscus' Song.* 32 pages. 2011. EDC

Publishing. Anna wakes up so full of happiness she doesn't know what to do.

Axtell, David. *We're Going on a Lion Hunt.* 32 pages. 2007. Holt, Henry & Company. The traditional story of going on a bear hunt retold in an African setting.

Baker, Jeannie. *Mirror.* 48 pages. 2010. Candlewick Press. Side by side stories contrasting the lives of a family in a Western city with a family in an African village.

Base, Graeme. *Jungle Drums.* 40 pages. 2004. Abrams. The littlest warthog wants to play with the bigger ones.

Beake, Lesley. *Home Now.* 32 pages. 2007. Charlesbridge Publishing. A little girl remembers where she used to live but can't make sense of it until she sees an elephant in an elephant park.

Beard, Alex. *The Jungle Grapevine.* 48 pages. 2009. Abrams. A case of the misunderstanding game of "telephone" among the animals in an African Savannah.

Beard, Alex. *Monkey See, Monkey Draw.* 48 pages. 2011. Abrams. Monkey tale set in an African location where the monkeys that love to play games learn how to create artwork.

Brett, Jan. *Honey, Honey, Lion! A Story from Africa.* 32 pages. 2005. Penguin Group. The honeyguide bird and the African honey badger have always been partners in finding honey but one day have a disagreement about it.

Brett, Jan. *The Three Little Dassies.* 32 pages. 2010. Penguin Group. A retelling of the 3 Little Pigs story with an African flavor.

Cunnane, Kelly. *For You Are a Kenyan Child.* 40 pages. 2006. Simon & Schuster Children's Publishing. Description of the daily life of a Kenyan child.

Doner, Kim. *On a Road in Africa.* 46 pages. 2008. Ten Speed Press. An animal rescuer in Africa makes her daily journey.

Galvin, Laura Gates. *Kakuda the Giraffe.* 36 pages. 2004. Soundprints. An orphan giraffe is rescued by villagers in Zambia.

Graber, Janet. *Muktar and the Camels.* 32 pages. 2009. Holt, Henry & Co. Muktar lives in an orphanage and daydreams about his old life of taking care of camels.

Greenfield, Eloise. *Africa Dream.* 32 pages. 1992. Harper Collins Publishers. An African-American child dreams of an African village where she sees shops and animals and her grandfather welcomes her.

Grifalconi, Ann. *The Village That Vanished.* 40 pages. 2004. Penguin Group. A family must come up with a plan to hide from slave traders on the way to their village.

Isadora, Rachel. *At the Crossroads.* 32 pages. 1994. Harper Collins Publishers. Children in a South African village wait at the crossroads for their fathers to come home from working in the mines.

Joosse, Barbara M. *Papa Do You Love Me?* 36 pages. 2005. Chronicle Books. Set in an African Maasai village, tells the story of the bond between father and child.

Kessler, Cristina. *The Best Beekeeper of Lalibela.* 32 pages. 2006. Holiday House. A young girl in Ethiopia wants to make the best honey in the land.

Kimmel, Eric. *Anansi and the Moss Covered Rock.* 32 pages. 1988. Holiday House. Anansi the spider continues to trick all the animals until they teach him a lesson.

Krebs, Laurie. *We All Went on Safari: A Counting Journey Through Tanzania.* 32 pages. 2004. Barefoot Books. A counting journey through the grasslands of Tanzania.

Kroll, Virginia. *Masai and I.* 32 pages. 1997. Simon & Schuster Children's Publishing. A little girl learns of the African people called the Masai and imagines herself living among them.

McDermott, Gerald. *Anansi the Spider.* 48 pages. 1987. Holt, Henry & Company. Anansi the spider is rescued by his sons. Which one should he reward?

Milway, Katie Smith. *One Hen: How One Small Loan Made a Big Difference.* 32 pages. 2008. Kids Can Press, Limited. Tells the story of a boy from Ghana who turns a small loan into a thriving farm.

Njeng, Pierre Yves. *Vacation in the Village: A Story from West Africa.* 24 pages. 1999. Boyds Mill Press. A family goes to a small village from the big city.

Noble, Kate. *Bubble Gum.* 32 pages. 1999. Silver Seahorse Press. Beautiful paintings of Africa with the story of a young baboon.

Noble, Kate. *Oh Look It's a Nosserus.* 32 pages. 1993. Silver Seahorse Press. The story of a young rhino in a game park in Africa.

Paye, Won-Ldy and Lippert, Margaret H. *Head, Body, Legs.* 32 pages. 2005. Holt, Henry & Company. This traditional Liberian creation story illustrates the importance of cooperation.

Steig, William. *Dr. De Soto Goes to Africa.* 32 pages. 1994. Harper Collins Publishers. Dr. De Soto is asked to come to Africa to treat the teeth of an elephant.

Steptoe, John L. *Mufaro's Beautiful Daughters: An African Tale*. 32 pages. 1987. Harper Collins. The Cinderella story set in Africa.

Stewart, Dianne. *The Gift of the Sun: A Tale from South Africa*. 32 pages. 2007. Lincoln, Frances Limited. Thulani tires of milking his cow and so exchanges it for a goat. Then he trades the goat for another animal, etc. until he finds himself with only sunflower seeds. From these he makes his fortune.

Stojic, Manya. *Rain*. 32 pages. 2000. Random House Children's Books. Animals use their senses to tell when rain is coming to the African savannah.

Fish

Advance planning: To plan for this storytime, find a theme-related song to play during craft and snack times, like "Octopus's Garden," by Ringo Starr or Raffi. You will also want to select a poem, such as "Fish" (find it at www.teacher.scholastic.com/lessonrepro/lessonplans/profbooks/fishpoems.htm), along with the books you plan to read. Decorate your space with plastic fish, stuffed fish, fishing poles, posters, maybe a fish in a small bowl of water.

Introduction to theme: Fish are a kind of animal that live in water. They breathe with special parts of their bodies called gills. They usually have fins and tails that help them move through the water. Some fish eat plants, some eat bugs, and some big fish eat smaller fish. Have you ever seen a fish? Where did you see it? Does anyone have pet fish at home? Today we'll read about fish, play a fishing game, make a fish craft and have a snack that looks like fish swimming in the sea.

Song: "I'm a Little Fish," to the tune of "I'm a Little Teapot." Lyrics can be found at www.dltk-kids.com.

Game: Gone fishing (Fish for goldfish in the pond.)

Materials needed: Newspapers, regular tape, double sided tape, yarn or string, orange construction paper, blue plastic tablecloth or other blue cloth. Advance preparation: Roll up newspaper (one double page section folded and rolled up so it's the short side of the paper's width) and taped closed. This is the same rolled up newspaper as used in the Pig Storytime game to herd the balloon pigs. Attach an arm's length of string or yarn at one end by tying and taping then put a piece of double stick tape at the other end of the yarn. Cut out small simple fish shapes from orange construction paper to look like goldfish. At storytime: Place the fish randomly on the blue plastic tablecloth on the floor to look like water and let the children fish for a goldfish. Make sure everyone gets at least one fish and let them keep what they catch.

Alternative Games

Magnetic fishing. Make fishing poles out of dowel rods, string and paper clips. Attach magnetic strips to pieces of cardboard with individual letters on them. Let the kids fish for the letters in their name.

Little fish. Place a blue plastic tablecloth or blue tarp on the floor. You stand on it and call out:

I'm a little fish who came out to play
In a big blue pool of sea water one day

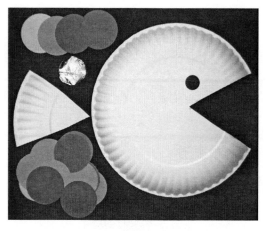

Paper plate fish pieces.

Paper plate fish.

Fish in the sea Jell-O.

I am having so much fun
That I'd like another fish to come
(call to a child by name to join you)

Then repeat with:

We're little fish who came out to play
In a big blue pool of sea water one day
We are having so much fun
That we'd like another fish to come
(call another child, and then repeat
until all the children are in the "water").

Once all the children are in the water, swim around a little before swimming back to the storytime area.

Craft: Paper plate fish

Materials needed: Large white paper plates, construction or tissue paper, glue sticks, stapler. Advance preparation: Cut a V-shape from a paper plate to make the mouth, staple the cut out piece to the back to make the tail. Cut or tear small pieces of tissue paper or cut circles from construction paper to use as scales. Cut one circle scale per child out of aluminum foil to be like the Rainbow Fish who ended up with only one shiny scale. Cut one small black circle for eye. At storytime: Have children glue paper pieces to fish as scales, glue black circle.

Alternative Crafts

Stained glass fish. Cut clear contact paper — two sheets cut in a square or rectangle, small pieces tissue paper in many colors, two pieces construction paper with fish shape cut out. Stick the tissue paper pieces down on one piece of contact paper. Cover with the other piece of contact paper. Enclose in the two cut out pieces of construction paper, gluing them together, so that the fish appears as if made of stained glass.

Tissue paper fish. Cut a fish shape out of card stock or cardboard. Cut small pieces of tissue paper in many different colors. Crumple them slightly and glue the crumpled pieces to the fish shape.

Snack: Fish in the sea Jell-O

Materials needed: Blue Jell-O (either as cups or large batch to ladle into cups), gummy fish (such as Swedish Fish, Nemo fruit snacks, shark fruit snacks), and spoons. Advance preparation: Make Jell-O. At storytime: Place a big spoonful of Jell-O in a clear plastic cup, drop in some of the fish fruit snacks, then cover with more blue Jell-O. Serve with a plastic spoon and tell the children there are some fish swimming in the ocean.

Alternative Snacks

Goldfish crackers or goldfish bread.

Fish cupcakes. Ice cupcakes and then stand up M&Ms on half of the cupcake top to look like fish scales. Place other candies as the eye and mouth.

Swedish fish candy.

SUGGESTED BOOKS

Asch, Frank. *Little Fish, Big Fish*. 1992. Scholastic. Asch uses fold out pages to help distinguish between large and small, long and short things.

Bennett, Kelly. *Not Norman: A Goldfish Story*. 32 pages. 2005. Candlewick Press. Norman the goldfish is not what the little boy had in mind for a pet. But when he tries to trade him for a different pet, things don't go as planned.

Blevins, Wiley. *Max Has a Pet Fish*. 32 pages. 2012. Penguin Group. Max is disappointed to find out that his pet fish can't dance.

Boyle, Alison. *1, 2,3,4,5 Once I Caught a Fish Alive*. 16 pages. 2000. David & Charles Children's Books. Jack gets nipped on the finger by a fish so he and his friends are determined to catch the fish that did it.

Bradman, Tony. *That's Not a Fish*. 24 pages. 1993. J.M. Dent & Sons. Dad promises to take Jack fishing and he is so delighted that he practices for a week beforehand.

Bright, Paul. *Fidgety Fish and Friends*. 24 pages. 2008. ME Media. A collection of rhymes.

Bryant, Jen. *Abe's Fish: A Boyhood Tale of Abraham Lincoln*. 40 pages. 2009. Sterling. Based on an actual incident that shows the president had a mischievous streak.

Bushell, Isobel. *Alexander and the Little Fish*. 1994. Barron's Education Series. Alexander Panda has fun at the beach and does a good deed.

Cannon, A.E. *Sophie's Fish*. 32 pages. 2012. Penguin Group. What naptime story would you read to a fish?

Carle, Eric. *Mister Seahorse*. 32 pages. 2004. Penguin Group. Introduces the reader to unusual daddies of the sea.

Cohen, Caron Lee. *How Many Fish?* 25 pages. 2000. HarperCollins Children's Books. There are six little fish. Along come six little feet. What will happen when they meet?

Cook, Bernadine. *The Little Fish That Got Away*. 64 pages. 2005. HarperCollins Publishers. A little boy fishes every day for a long time without catching anything until...

Cousins, Lucy. *Hooray for Fish*. 40 pages. 2010. Candlewick Press. Swim along with Fish and meet some of his friends.

Diesen, Deborah. *The Pout Pout Fish*. 32 pages. 2008. Farrar, Straus & Giroux. The Pout Pout fish discovers that being gloomy all the time isn't all that great.

Diesen, Deborah. *The Pout Pout Fish in the Big Big Dark*. 32 pages. 2010. Farrar, Straus & Giroux. Mr. Fish wants to help his friend Ms. Clam when she loses her pearl, but he's got a secret — he's afraid of the dark.

DiPuccio, Kelly. *Gilbert Goldfish Wants a Pet*. 32 pages. 2011. Penguin Group. Gilbert has everything he could want, except a pet.

Donaldson, Julia. *The Fish Who Cried Wolf*. 40 pages. 2008. Scholastic. A little fish comes late to school every day with a series of elaborate excuses.

Ehlert, Lois. *Fish Eyes: A Book You Can Count On*. 40 pages. 1990. Houghton Mifflin Harcourt Publishers. Counting and basic addition is introduced with colorful fish.

Galloway, Ruth. *Fidgety Fish*. 32 pages. 2001. ME Media. Tiddler the fish goes inside a deep dark cave.

Geist, Ken. *The Three Little Fish and the Big Bad Shark*. 32 pages. 2007. Scholastic. A spoof of the Three Little Pigs story.

Gilbertsen, Neal. *Little Red Snapperhood*. 32 pages. 2003. Graphic Arts Center Publishing Company. Once upon a maritime, begins this tale told in verse — a version of Little Red Riding Hood.

Gomi, Taro. *Where's the Fish?* 32 pages. 1986. HarperCollins Publishers. There's the fish! Where's the Fish? Repeated until the fish is home at last.

Grant, Joan. *Cat and Fish*. 32 pages. 2005. Simply Read Books. Cat and Fish come from different worlds but they meet in the park and become friends.

Grant, Joan. *Cat and Fish Go to See*. 32 pages. 2006. Simply Read Books. The unlikely pals of Cat and Fish go to see where waves come from.

Harris, Trudy. *Pattern Fish*. 40 pages. 2000. Millbrook Press. Rhyming prose and brightly colored cartoon fish show the world of patterns.

Heap, Sue. *Baby Bill and Little Lill*. 32 pages. 1999. Kingfisher. In search of a pet fishy, Little Lill and Baby Bill run down a hill to the sea.

Hendra, Sue. *Barry the Fish with Fingers*. 40 pages. 2010. Alfred A. Knopf. The fish thought they'd seen it all until they met Barry.

Hubbell, Patricia. *Papa Fish's Lullaby*. 32 pages. 2007. Cooper Square Publishing. A full day in an underwater world ends with Papa Fish singing his little one to sleep.

Lionni, Leo. *Fish Is Fish*. 32 pages. 1987. Random House Children's Books. A tadpole and minnow are friends but once the tadpole grows legs he explores a different world and returns to tell his fish friend about it.

Lionni, Leo. *Swimmy*. 32 pages. 1991. Random House Children's Books. The only survivor of a tuna attack works on a plan to disguise himself and his new friends.

MacDonald, Suse. *Sea Shapes*. 32 pages. 1998. Houghton Mifflin Harcourt Trade & Reference Publishers. Simple text encouraging readers to find different shapes in creatures of the sea.

Mayer, Mercer. *A Boy, a Dog, a Frog and a Friend*. 32 pages. 2003. Penguin Group. First came a boy, then his dog, then they found a frog and then a turtle. A wordless book to discuss.

Palmer, Helen. *A Fish Out of Water*. 64 pages. 1961. Random House Children's Books. From the Dr. Seuss library, a fish keeps outgrowing his containers.

Pfeffer, Wendy. *What's It Like to Be a Fish?* 32 pages. 1996. HarperCollins Publishers. How can fish live in water? Why don't they drown? Part of the Let's-Read-And-Find-Out Science Series that introduces young readers to fish.

Pfister, Marcus. *Rainbow Fish*. 32 pages. 1992. North-South Books. The message is that things are enjoyed more if shared.

Pfister, Marcus. *Rainbow Fish and the Whale*. 28 pages. 2011. North-South Books. Rainbow Fish makes a new friend.

Poydar, Nancy. *Fish School*. 32 pages. 2009. Holiday House. Charlie takes his goldfish on a school trip to the aquarium.

Scillian, Devin. *Memoirs of a Goldfish*. 32 pages. 2010. Sleeping Bear Press. The goldfish is quite put out when others come to visit and take up too much room.

Seuss, Dr. *One Fish Two Fish Red Fish Blue Fish*. 72 pages. 1960. Random House Children's Books. Easy rhyming words about lots of different creatures, but begins with the famous One Fish Two Fish Red Fish Blue Fish.

Sill, Cathryn P. *About Fish: A Guide for Children*. 40 pages. 2005. Peachtree Publishers. In easy to understand language, describes what fish are, how they swim, breathe and reproduce.

Turcios, Omar. *David, Fish & Penguins*. 36 pages. 2012. Cuento de Luz SL. David has his own magical world full of animals that surround him all the time.

Wood, Audrey. *Ten Little Fish*. 40 pages. 2004. Scholastic. A counting book about fish.

Wu, Norbert. *Fish Faces*. 32 pages. 1997. Holt, Henry & Company. Beautiful color photography of real sea creatures with simple rhyming text.

Yaccarino, Dan. *The Birthday Fish*. 40 pages. 2005. Holt, Henry & Company. The story of a little girl and her goldfish friend.

Sizes and Shapes

Advance planning: To plan for this storytime, find a theme-related song to play during craft and snack times, like "Learning Our Shapes," by Twin Sisters. You will also want to select a poem, such as "Shapes," by Shel Silverstein (find it in *A Light in the Attic*), along with the books you plan to read. Decorate your space with very large things and very small things, ideally of different shapes, like round balls or square boxes. Toy blocks would have many different shapes, perhaps different sizes.

Introduction to theme: Different shapes are all around us. There are circles, squares, triangles. Show examples of each. Can you think of something that's a circle shape? (cheerio, doughnut, button). What about a square? (window). And a triangle? (pizza slice). A rectangle is a square that's been squished. (towel, rug, door). Show example. An oval is a circle that's been squished. Show example. We know how things are different sizes, don't we? Some things are big. Some things are small. Show example of each. Is a mouse big or small? An elephant? Today we'll read about things big and small and different shapes, play a game that has to do with big and small and different shapes, make a craft with different sizes and shapes and eat a snack made of different shapes.

Song with Fingerplay: "Do You Know a Circle Shape?" to the tune of "Do You Know the Muffin Man?":

> Do you know a circle shape? (hands form circle)
> A circle shape, a circle shape
> Round and round and round it goes
> to make a circle shape.
> Do you know a triangle (hands form triangle)
> a triangle, a triangle
> Three pointy corners and three straight sides
> to make a triangle
> Do you know a rectangle (hands form rectangle)
> a rectangle, a rectangle
> Two long sides and two short sides
> make a rectangle.

or:

> Do you know what shape this is?
> What shape this is? What shape this is?
> Do you know what shape this is, I'm holding in my hand?

Note: Hold up a different shape each time and have your children yell out the shape.

Game: Shape twister

Materials needed: Construction paper, regular paper, scissors, music, two containers like small buckets or bowls. Advance preparation: Cut many different shapes (squares, circles, triangles, rectangles) from different colored construction paper. Write out the descriptions (like blue triangle or red square) or print from the computer small versions of the different colors of the shapes that you cut out and put those in the bucket. Write left hand, right hand, left foot and right foot on pieces of paper and put those in another bucket. At storytime: Tape the different construction paper shapes fairly close together on the floor (like a twister mat). Play background music if desired. Pick the shapes from the bucket one at a time along with a body part from the other bucket and call them out together, as in left hand on blue triangle, or right foot on yellow square. The children should then place their hands and feet on the shape. If the children are too young to know right and left, you could just use hand and foot and let them place either hand or foot on the shape. The game is about recognizing the shapes.

Alternative Games

Shape flannel board. Make shapes from felt to place on a flannelboard: squares, circles, triangles, rectangles and make them in at least two different sizes so there is a big one and a little one.

Shape bingo. Print cards from www.dltk-kids.com.

Shape throw. Divide a piece of poster board into eight sections (heart, square, circle, triangle, diamond, rectangle, oval, star). Have the children throw a bean bag at the poster board and then tell you what shape the bean bag landed on.

Musical shapes. Tape different shapes onto the floor. Have the children step from shape to shape as you play music. When the music stops have the children stop and yell out what shape they are standing on.

Shape sort. Bring out an assortment of boxes and ask the children to sort them by size, going from biggest to smallest.

Shapes in the circle. Give each child a small card, like an index card, with a shape on it, like square, rectangle, triangle, circle. Play some music and have them pass the cards around the circle. Stop the music and hold up one of the shapes and ask the children also holding that shape to wave it in the air. Repeat with the other shapes.

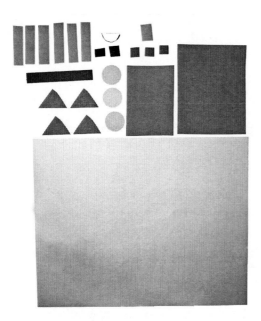

Construction paper robot pieces.

Shapes in a bag. Show the children three-dimensional examples of each shape (a cube, a sphere and a pyramid) and then place them in a bag that the children can't see through. Let each child feel the shape inside the bag and see if they can identify what shape it is.

Craft: Construction paper robot

Materials needed: Construction paper, scissors, gluesticks. Advance preparation: Cut lots of different sized squares from construction paper. If desired could cut other shapes like triangles, circles and rectangles. At storytime: Let the children glue different shapes to a background piece of construction paper to form a robot.

Alternative Crafts

Read the book *Mouse Shapes* and then have the children make their own images similar to the ones in the book using many different colorful shapes glued to a background piece of paper.

Square shapes puzzle. Cut pieces of stacked different colored construction paper into several different sized squares. Then mix the different colors up keeping one of each size shape piece together. Give each child a set of the shapes and a whole piece of construction paper and see if they can figure out how to glue them down to form back into one rectangle.

Rectangle xylophone. Give each child a

Construction paper robot.

number of different sized construction paper rectangles and have them glue them down in size order on a larger piece of construction paper to make a paper xylophone. If desired, you could give each child two large marshmallows and two bamboo skewers that they could make into mallets and then pretend to play their xylophone while you play actual xylophone music on a CD player.

Paper chain. Provide rectangular strips of construction paper and tape. Show the children how to make a paper chain by first forming a circle from the rectangle strip of paper and taping it closed, then adding the next strip by inserting the strip through the first closed circle. Each child could make their own chain or you could combine all of the chains they make into one long one and use it to decorate the story time area.

Shape mobile. Give each children a piece of paper printed from the computer with different shape outlines on it, such as square, triangle, circle, rectangle. Have them color in the shapes and cut them out, punch a hole in each shape and attach string or yarn then attach that to a paper towel tube to form a mobile.

Spilt milk. If you read the book *It Looked Like Spilt Milk*, this would be a good accompanying craft. Use dark blue construction paper and white paint and let the children draw their own shapes on the paper.

Snack: Bread and cheese shape house

Materials needed: Bread loaf, cheese slices, small paper plates, plastic knives. Advance preparation: Cut cheese slices in half diagonally, then cut rectangles for the door and square windows. At storytime: Use bread for the square house. Half a piece of sliced sandwich cheese for the roof (on its side as a triangle). A small rectangle of cheese for the door and small cheese squares for the windows. Place a piece of bread and the cheese slice parts on a paper plate. Have the children assemble their house by placing the triangle over the bread and the door and windows on the bread.

Alternative Snacks

Shape snacks. Pancakes make a good round snack. Waffles can be either round or square. Both can be eaten with the hands either plain or dipping in syrup or sprinkled with powdered sugar. English muffins are round. They can be topped with some tomato sauce and then different shapes cut from cheese,

Bread and cheese shape house.

such as squares and triangles can be placed on top to be like a pizza. Many crackers come in different shapes all in one box. Or cookies come in different shapes too.

SUGGESTED BOOKS

Aigner-Clark, Julie. *Baby Einstein: My First Book of Shapes*. 24 pages. 2007. Disney Press. A board book that introduces shapes.

Baker, Alan. *Brown Rabbit's Shape Book*. 24 pages. 1994. Kingfisher. Brown rabbit finds five balloons that take on all sorts of shapes.

Beaton, Clare. *How Big Is a Pig?* 24 pages. 1990. Barefoot Books. Learn about opposites and animals.

Bedford, David. *Big and Small*. 16 pages. 2006. Little Hare Books. Using flaps this book illustrates the concepts of big and small.

Blackstone, Stella. *Bear in a Square*. 24 pages. 2000. Barefoot Books. A bear roams through different settings of many different shapes.

Burns, Marilyn. *The Greedy Triangle*. 32 pages. 2008. Scholastic Paperbacks. Bored and dissatisfied, a triangle visits a shapeshifter and adds another angle to his shape. But he's greedy and keeps adding angles until he's completely transformed.

Burton, Virginia. *Katy and the Big Snow*. 40 pages. 1973. Houghton Mifflin Harcourt. Katy is a brave tractor who saves the town when she clears a very big snow.

Carle, Eric. *Draw Me a Star*. 40 pages. 1992. Penguin Group. A young artist brings a world to life one drawing at a time.

Cousins, Lucy. *Maisy Big Maisy Small*. 56 pages. 2007. Candlewick. Maisy demonstrates thick and thin, tall and short, young and old, wiggly and straight...

Cox, Tracey M. *Shaping Up the Year*. 24 pages. 2009. Guardian Angel Publishing. Each shape is associated with a holiday.

Curtis, Jamie Lee. *Big Words for Little People*. 40 pages. 2008. HarperCollins Publishers. Rhyming text teaches children some very important but very big words.

dePaola, Tomie. *The Cloud Book*. 32 pages. 1984. Holiday House. Introduces the ten most common types of cloud, their shapes and what they can tell about weather changes.

DK Publishing. *Are Eggs Square?* 21 pages. 2003. DK Publishing. On each page a question is posed with a strange shape. Turn the page to reveal the correct answer.

DK Publishing. *Are Elephants Tiny?* 21 pages. 2003. DK Publishing. Learn about sizes and animals too.

Dodd, Emma. *Big, Small, Little Red Ball*. 18 pages. 2001. Dutton Juvenile. Three animal friends follow a trail of opposites as they look for a favorite toy.

Eastman, P.D. *Big Dog Little Dog*. 48 pages. 2003. Random House Children's Books. A book about opposites, starting with a big dog and a little dog.

Emberley, Edward. *Go Away Big Green Monster*. 32 pages. 1993. Little, Brown Books for Young Readers. This die cut book creates a monster by showing a different part of it as each page is turned and another shape appears. Eventually though the child is given the power of making the monster disappear and conquering the fear of it.

Florian, Douglas. *A Pig Is Big*. 24 pages. 2000. Greenwillow Books. A big pink pig travels around town, taking a look at things that are big, bigger, biggest.

Frasier, Craig. *Lots of Dots*. 40 pages. 2010. Chronicle Books. A celebration of dots, or circles, in rhyme.

Geist, Ken. *The Three Little Fish and the Big Bad Shark*. 32 pages. 2007. Scholastic Inc. A retelling of the three little pigs story.

Gerth, Melanie. *My First Jumbo Book of Shapes*. 10 pages. 2004. Scholastic. With textures, pull tabs and moveable parts, this book teaches the concept of shapes.

Graves, Keith. *Chicken Big*. 40 pages. 2010. Chronicle Books. There's a gigantic chicken on this teensy farm.

Greene, Rhonda Gowler. *When a Line Bends...A Shape Begins*. 32 pages. 1997. Houghton Mifflin Harcourt. Rhymed text describes how shapes are made from simple lines.

Hall, Michael. *My Heart Is Like a Zoo*. 32 pages. 2009. Greenwillow Books. The drawings all have heart shapes in them and express many different feelings.

Harris, Nicholas. *How Big?* 30 pages. 2003. Cengage Gale. Facts, records and size comparisons of ordinary and extraordinary things.

Hill, Eric. *Spot Looks at Shapes*. 14 pages. 1986. Penguin Group. Spot the dog introduces many different shapes in this board book.

Hoban, Tana. *Circles, Triangles and Squares*. 32 pages. 1974. Simon & Schuster Children's Publishing. Black and white photographs give a first geometry lesson.

Hoban, Tana. *Cubes, Cones, Cylinders and Spheres*. 24 pages. 2000. Greenwillow Books. When you look at the photographs you realize these shapes are part of everyday life.

Hoban, Tana. *Is It Larger? Is It Smaller?* 32 pages. 1997. HarperCollins Publishers. An introduction to size relativity.

Hoban, Tana. *Shapes Shapes Shapes*. 32 pages. 1986. HarperCollins Publishers. Wherever you are there are shapes to discover.

Hoban, Tana. *So Many Circles, So Many Squares*. 40 pages. 1998. HarperCollins Publishers. After looking through this book you'll see so many more circles and squares everywhere.

Hutchins, Pat. *Titch*. 32 pages. 1993. Turtleback Books. Titch is little and everything he has is little. Mary and Pete are big and everything they have is big.

Leake, Diyan. *Circles*. 24 pages. 2005. Heinemann. Find circle shapes in the photographs.

Martin, Elena. *So Many Circles*. 32 pages. 2006.

Coughlan Publishing. Photos of circle shapes in many places and things.

McMullan, Kate. *I'm Big*. 40 pages. 2010. Balzer & Bray. The big lizard is lost and needs to find his herd.

Minters, Frances. *Too Big, Too Small, Just Right*. 40 pages. 2001. Harcourt Children's Books. A book about opposites, friendship and things in life that are just right.

Moncure, Jane Belk. *Word Bird's Shapes*. 32 pages. 2002. The Child's World. A young bird learns about shapes.

Murphy, Stuart J. *Circus Shapes*. 40 pages. 1997. HarperCollins Publishers. Shape recognition cloaked in a circus performance story.

Nilsen, Anna. *Sizes*. 20 pages. 2003. Miles Kelly Publishing. Split pages allow one to turn the page until the correct answer can be found.

Olson, Nathan. *Circles Around Town*. 32 pages. 2006. Coughlan Publishing. An introduction to simple shapes.

Paratore, Coleen. *26 Big Things Small Hands Do*. 32 pages. 2008. Free Spirit Publishing. The message is that anyone, no matter how big or how small, can make a difference in others' lives.

Pienkowski, Jan. *Shapes*. 16 pages. 1998. Little Simon. The author shows the shape and then the word and then incorporates it into a picture of an object.

Pienkowski, Jan. *Sizes*. 24 pages. 1991. Little Simon. Brief text and illustrations show the concepts of big and little.

Primavera, Elise. *Louise the Big Cheese: Divine Diva*. 40 pages. 2011. Simon & Schuster Children's Publishing. Louise dreams of being the big cheese, being in the limelight, lots of fuss, the red carpet.

Rand, Ann. *I Know a Lot of Things*. 40 pages. 2009. Chronicle Books. A celebration of new knowledge that children love to possess.

Rau, Dana Meachen. *Circles*. 24 pages. 2006. Cavendish, Marshall Corporation. Circles appear in many different places in these photos.

Reiss, John. *Shapes: A Book*. 32 pages. 1982. Simon & Schuster Children's Publishing. Introduces common shapes such as circles and squares.

Rubinger, Ami. *Big Cat, Small Cat*. 28 pages. 2009. Abbeville Kids. An interactive book about cats of all sizes.

Seuss, Dr. *The Shape of Me and Other Stuff*. 36 pages. 1973. Random House Children's Books. Rhyme and drawings introduce the shapes of many familiar objects.

Shaw, Charles G. *It Looked Like Spilt Milk*. 32 pages. 1988. HarperCollins Publishers. The white shape on the blue background changes on every page.

Thong, Roseanne. *Round Is a Mooncake: A Book of Shapes*. 40 pages. 2000. Chronicle Books. A little girl discovers round, square and rectangular things in her neighborhood.

Top That! Staff. *Sammy the Snake*. 18 pages. 2008. Top That Publishing. Follow the snake through the pages to learn all about shapes.

Van Laan, Nancy. *The Tiny Tiny Boy and the Big Big Cow*. 40 pages. 1993. Random House Children's Books. What should a tiny tiny boy do when a big big cow won't stand still for him to milk her?

Walsh, Ellen Stoll. *Mouse Shapes*. 40 pages. 2007. Houghton Mifflin Harcourt. The mice are discussing shapes and arranging them into recognizable images.

Whitman, Candace. *Lines That Wiggle*. 36 pages. 2009. Blue Apple Books. Follow the line that runs through the book and turns into all sorts of different things.

Willems, Mo. *Big Frog Can't Fit In*. 16 pages. 2009. Hyperion Books for Children. A pop up book with a frog so big that the book has a hard time holding her.

Winton, Ian. *My First Book of Shapes and Colors*. 18 pages. 1995. Little Simon. A board book with colorful illustrations of basic shapes and objects of those shapes.

Wood, Don and Audrey. *The Little Mouse, the Red Ripe Strawberry and the Big Hungry Bear*. 32 pages. 1989. Child's Play International. Little Mouse worries that the Big Bear will take his strawberry.

Pigs

Advance planning: To plan for this storytime, find a theme-related song to play during craft and snack times, like "Pig Power," by Kangaroo Kids or "Bein' a Pig," by Pig. You will also want to select a poem, such as "Pigs," by Charles Ghigna (find it at www.porkopolis.

org/library/pig-poetry/charles-ghigna/), along with the books you plan to read. Decorate your space with plastic or stuffed pigs, a toy barn, maybe a poster or photograph of a pig.

Introduction to theme: Pigs are animals with a long snout and four legs with hooves. They are often raised on farms for their meat, which is called pork and for leather. They will eat just about anything, but on farms are mostly fed corn or soybeans. They use their snouts to root around for food on the ground and to dig. Certain kinds of pigs are sometimes kept as pets. Today we'll read about some unusual pigs with lots of different personalities, we'll play some piggy games, make a pig craft and eat snack that looks like a pig.

Song: "The Big Pig Song" from Hooked on Phonics which can be found at www.learn ingphonics.blogspot.com/2010/10/big-pig-song.html. Repeat singing it softer and then louder, and then just the girls and then the boys, and then all together.

Fingerplay: "This Little Piggy"

Hold up hand with all five fingers extended.
This little piggy went to market (point to thumb and fold it down)
This little piggy stayed home (point to index finger and fold it down)
This little piggy ate roast beef (point to middle finger and fold it down)
This little piggy had none (point to ring finger and fold it down)
And this little piggy, this little piggy, went "Whee, whee, whee, all the way home!"
(point to little finger and wiggle it all around).

Game: Pig races/sheep herding

Materials needed: Pink balloons, permanent marker, pink curling ribbon, newspaper, rubber bands, hula hoop or masking tape. Advance preparation: Blow up large pink balloons. With a permanent marker make piggy faces and attach curly pink ribbon to one end of each pig. Roll up several sheets of newspaper and rubber band them to use as pig swatters. Have some extra balloons in case of popping. If using masking tape to mark the "barn" either make a circle, square or just mark an X on the floor. Otherwise place the hula hoop there. At storytime: Choose a starting point and an ending point. Get the group together and give everyone a newspaper swatter and a pig balloon. Tell the children that the pigs need to be herded through the field back to the barn. Let them bat at their balloons, trying to keep them up in the air, as you walk from one point to another and once all the balloons are there (you could mark the point with tape on the floor or by placing a hula hoop there) Make sure to have extra pink balloons just in case any pop.

Alternative Games

Hot pig. Played like hot potato but use a stuffed pig to toss around while sitting in a circle playing music. The child holding the pig when the music stops moves to the center of the circle. Have another stuffed pig for the circle inside the other circle. The first child will just toss the pig up in the air to himself, but then as each subsequent turn occurs, there will be a child from the outside circle added to the inside. Gradually the children will all come to the inside circle. The game ends when there is only child left on the outside (the remaining children will have to move around to pass the pig to each other as the inside circle gets bigger and the outside has fewer children in it.

Poor piggy. Have the children sit in a circle on the floor and pass around a stuffed pig while you play the pig themed song you chose. When you stop the music, the child holding the pig must say "oink, oink" in their best piggy voice. Keep the game going until most or all of the children have had a turn to oink.

House bean bag toss. Make three large cardboard boxes look like the straw house, the stick house and the brick house. Make black or grey (wolf) bean bags and also pink bean bags (pigs). Have the children take turns tossing the wolves and the pigs into the houses.

Craft: Pig paper bag puppet

Materials needed: Pink paper bags, dark and light pink, black and white construction paper, white chenille stem, glue sticks, pencils, tape. Advance preparation: Cut black circles and white circles (slightly larger than the black ones) for eyes; large dark pink circle for face; black oval for nose background, slightly smaller dark pink oval for nose and two smaller black circles for nostrils; dark pink triangular shapes for ears and light pink smaller trianglar shapes for insides of ears. At storytime: Glue big dark pink circle to bag bottom, glue black circles for eyes on top of white circles, then glue to big circle. Glue nostrils to pink nose and nose to black background, then to face. Glue insides of ears to ears and ears to top of face. Curl chenille stem using pencil and tape it to back of bag at opening or punch hole and attach to hole.

Pig paper bag puppet pieces.

Alternative Crafts

Three pigs' houses. Give each child a piece of paper that has three basic house shapes printed on it. Provide materials like the ones used by the Three Little Pigs in the story, such as straw, sticks (craft sticks or toothpicks) and bricks (small rectangles cut from red or brown construction paper. Put white glue in plates and provide cotton swabs to spread the glue on the house images so that the children can glue down the house materials. Alternately have one house on each piece of paper and let each child choose which house to "build."

Terra cotta pig pot. Paint small terra cotta pots pink. Cut sheet foam or felt shapes for ears and nose. Attach to pot along with google eyes and pink chenille stem for tail. Mark nostrils on nose with black permanent marker.

Pig paper bag puppet.

Paper plate pig. Either paint large and small paper plates pink, or buy pink plates. Glue small plate on top of large to look like head on body. Attach paper ears, nose, google eyes, and curly tail from chenille stem or curly ribbon. Could make using large paper plate and construction paper pig head shape.

Snack: Pig cupcake

Materials needed: Cupcakes, pink icing, large pink marshmallows (regular or heart-shaped), food marker, M&Ms or Skittles or chocolate chips, pink sprinkles, paper plates, plastic knives. Advance preparation: Bake cupcakes. If necessary color white icing pink. Put dots with food marker on flat side of one marshmallow per child for snout. Cut marshmallows in half and quickly sprinkle cut sides with pink sprinkles. These will be the ears. At storytime: Give each child a cupcake on a plate with a plastic knife. Add a dollop of pink icing, two cut and sprinkled marshmallows, one whole marshmallow, two matching M&Ms or Skittles or chocolate chips for eyes. Ice the cupcake; add the whole marshmallow for the nose, then the cut marshmallows for the ears and the other candies for the eyes.

Alternative Snacks

Pig cupcake.

Pig cookies. Big cookies and small cookies. Ice with pink icing, place small cookie on large cookie, two M & M for eyes, two for nostrils.

Ham and cheese pig. Get ham in rounds. Cut cheese slices into smaller rounds with a biscuit or cookie cutter. Place the cheese on the ham as the snout, then use two raisins for nostrils and two raisins for eyes.

Pigs in a blanket. Roll a triangle of refrigerated crescent roll dough around half a hot dog. Bake at 350 degrees for 12 to 14 minutes. Serve with ketchup and mustard if desired.

Pig Shapes. use a pig-shaped cookie cutter to cut pieces of cheese or bread.

SUGGESTED BOOKS

Amery, H. *Three Little Pigs*. 16 pages. 2003. EDC Publishing. Part of the First Stories Series for beginning readers has two levels of text.

Bedoyere, Camilla de la. *Pigs*. 32 pages. 2010. QEB Publishing. All the facts about daily life of pigs.

Black, Michael Ian. *A Pig Parade Is a Terrible Idea*. 40 pages. 2010. Simon & Schuster Books for Young Readers. Pigs hate to march, refuse to wear uniforms. There are all sorts of reasons why a pig parade is not a good idea.

Dunn, Judy. *The Little Pig*. 32 pages. 2001. Random House Books for Young Readers. Follows one little pig's life on a farm.

Emmett, Jonathan. *The Princess and the Pig*. 32 pages. 2011. Walker Childrens. There's been a mix up in the royal nursery and Priscilla the Princess has accidentally changed places with Pigmella, the farmer's new piglet.

Falconer, Ian. *Olivia*. 40 pages. 2000. Atheneum Books for Young Readers. Have fun with Olivia and all the things she does.

Falconer, Ian. *Olivia ... and the Missing Toy*. 42 pages. 2003. Atheneum Books for Young Readers. Olivia's favorite toy disappears and an all-out search ensues.

Falconer, Ian. *Olivia Forms a Band*. 50 pages. 2006.

Atheneum Books for Young Readers. How can there be fireworks without a band?

Falconer, Ian. *Olivia Goes to Venice*. 48 pages. 2010. Atheneum Books for Young Readers. Olivia goes to Venice on a family vacation.

Falconer, Ian. *Olivia Saves the Circus*. 44 pages. 2001. Atheneum Books for Young Readers. Olivia remembers her trip to the circus well. All the performers were sick so she had to do everything.

Geisert, Arthur. *Oink*. 32 pages. 1995. Sandpiper. Mama Pig and her piglets speak only one word in this book about Mama taking a nap and the piglets running off in search of adventure.

Gibbons, Gail. *Pigs*. 32 pages. 2000. Holiday House. Here are many interesting facts about pigs.

Hobbie, Holly. *Toot and Puddle*. 32 pages. 2010. Little, Brown Books for Young Readers. Toot and Puddle are good friends, but go their separate ways for a time.

King-Smith, Dick. *All Pigs Are Beautiful: Read and Wonder*. 32 pages. 2001. Candlewick. Stories about pigs mixed with facts.

Kissock, Heather. *Pigs*. 24 pages. 2011. Weigl Publishers. Part of the animals on the farm series.

Lobel, Arnold. *Odd Owls and Stout Pigs: A Book of*

Nonsense. A collection of rhyming stories featuring owls and pigs.

Macken, JoAnn Early. *Pigs.* 24 pages. 2009. Gareth Stevens Publishing. Part of the animals that live on the farm series.

Marshall, James. *Three Little Pigs.* 32 pages. 1996. Penguin Group. A not so traditional turn of events follows the three little pigs who've been turned out of their mother's house and have built their own houses.

McPhail, David *Pig Pig Meets the Lion.* 32 pages. 2012. Charlesbridge Publishing. A lion escapes from the zoo and comes to Pig Pig's house.

McPhail, David *Pig Pig Returns.* 32 pages. 2011. Charlesbridge Publishing. Pig Pig spends his summer vacation with relatives.

McPhail, David. *Pigs Aplenty, Pigs Galore.* 32 pages. 1996. Penguin Group. Pigs descend on the narrator's house.

Most, Bernard. *The Cow that Went OINK!* 40 pages. 2003. Sandpiper. A cow and a pig are laughed at because they're not like the other farm animals.

Munsch, Robert N. *Pigs.* 32 pages. 1992. Annick Press. Megan is told to feed the pigs but not to open the gate. So of course she opens the gate.

Numeroff, Laura Joffe. *If You Give a Pig a Pancake.* 32 pages. 2005. Harper Collins. If you give a pig a pancake, she'll want some syrup. If you give her some syrup, etc. etc. until it comes around again to giving the pig a pancake.

Numeroff, Laura Joffe. *If You Give a Pig a Party.* 32 pages. 2005. Harper Collins. If you give a pig a party, she'll want some balloons to decorate. If you give her some balloons, etc. etc. until it comes around to giving her a party.

Older, Jules. *Pig.* 32 pages. 2004. Charlesbridge Publishing. A lot of factual information presented in a chatty style.

Pichon, Liz. *The Three Horrid Little Pigs.* 32 pages. 2010. ME Media. The three little pigs are so horrid their own mother sends them away to build their own houses. The wolf, who's a builder, helps them.

Rosenthal, Amy Krouse. *Little Oink.* 36 pages. 2009. Chronicle Books. Little Oink likes to be neat, but his parents want him to behave like a pig.

Sattler, Jennifer. *Pig Kahuna.* 32 pages. 2011. Bloomsbury USA. Fergus and his little brother love collecting things that wash up on the beach.

Scieszka, Jon. *The True Story of Three Little Pigs.* 32 pages. 1996. Penguin Group. The wolf claims he was framed.

Spinelli, Eileen. *Princess Pig.* 40 pages. 2009. Random House Children's Books. Princesses can't do a lot of things and Pig re-thinks her desire to be a princess after all.

Teague, Mark. *Pigsty.* 32 pages. 2004. Scholastic. Wendell's mother can't get him to clean up his room.

Trivizas, Eugene. *The Three Little Wolves and the Big Bad Pig.* 32 pages. 1997. Margaret K. McElderry Books. A retelling in reverse of the story of the three little pigs with a happy surprise ending.

Twohy, Mike. *Poindexter Makes a Friend.* 32 pages. 2011. Simon & Schuster Books. How does a shy pig make friends?

Waddell, Martin. *The Pig in the Pond.* 32 pages. 1996. Candlewick. The pig takes a swim on a hot day, which throws the farm into an uproar.

Wiesner, David. *The Three Pigs.* 40 pages. 2001. Clarion Books. One by one the pigs exit the fairy tale and take off on their own adventures.

Willems, Mo. *Happy Pig Day.* 64 pages. 2011. Hyperion Books for Children. Piggie celebrates her favorite day of the year. But will Gerald be invited?

Willems, Mo. *I Am Going.* 64 pages. 2010. Hyperion Books for Children. Piggie ruins Gerald's day by telling him she's going.

Willems, Mo. *Pigs Make Me Sneeze.* 64 pages. 2009. Hyperion Books for Children. Elephant thinks Pig is making him sneeze, but he's just got a cold.

Willems, Mo. *There Is a Bird on Your Head.* 64 pages. 2007. Hyperion Books for Children. Gerald discovers there's something worse than having a bird on your head — having two birds on your head.

Willems, Mo. *We Are in a Book.* 64 pages. 2010. Hyperion Books for Children. Gerald and Piggie discover the joy of being read.

Wilsdon, Christina. *Pigs.* 48 pages. 2009. Gareth Stevens Publishing. Information and photographs about pigs.

Yamaguchi, Kristi. *Dream Big Little Pig!* 32 pages. 2011. Sourcebooks. Little Pig won't give up on her big dreams.

Yamaguchi, Kristi. *It's a Big World, Little Pig!* 32 pages. 2012. Sourcebooks. Poppy skates at a world competition even though it's scary to travel so far from home.

Yolen, Jane. *Pretty Princess Pig.* 24 pages. 2011. Little Simon. Princess Pig is getting ready for a party with her friends.

Holiday — Christmas

Advance planning: To plan for this storytime, find a theme-related song to play during craft and snack times, like "It's Beginning to Look a Lot Like Christmas," by Bing Crosby. You will also want to select a poem, such as "Dear Santa Claus," by Jennie D. Moore (find it at www.apples4theteacher.com), along with the books you plan to read. Decorate your space with green and red bows, decorated small Christmas trees, snow (quilt batting or fiber fill), lights.

Introduction to theme: Christmas is a holiday celebrated on December 25th to commemorate the birth of Jesus Christ. Christmas is an important part of the holiday season and we do lots of things to celebrate—can you name some? Give gifts, bake cookies, send cards, put up lights and decorations, go to church, have special meals, play holiday music. With whom do you celebrate the holidays? Do you have a Christmas tree? What's your favorite ornament? What's on top of your tree? Do you have a special holiday dinner? What will you eat? What's the best present you ever got for Christmas? What do you hope you'll get this year? Today we'll read about Christmas, play a holiday game, make a Christmas craft and eat a Christmas snack.

Song: Because it's a holiday, singing several songs throughout the storytime will make it more festive. Here are some popular ones that the parents will probably know so you won't need to make lyric posters for all of them: "Rudolph the Red-Nosed Reindeer," "We Wish You a Merry Christmas," "Jingle Bells," or "Santa Claus Is Coming to Town," all of which have lyrics on www.metrolyrics.com.

Game: Santa says

Materials needed: None. Advance preparation: None. At storytime: Have everyone stand up and do Simon says but saying Santa says. A few examples: Touch your toes; raise your left hand; put your hands on your shoulders; stand on your right foot; turn around; touch your nose; wave your arms; stand on your left foot; hop up and down; put your hands on your head; raise your right hand; put your hands on your waist; pat your tummy; clap your hands; put your hands behind your back.

Alternative Games

Santa bingo. Make holiday bingo sheets on the Internet at www.dltk-cards.com/bingo/. Pass around bingo sheets and pencils, markers or crayons to mark. Explain that you will call and show the item and if they have it anywhere on their sheet they should mark it with a big X. When someone gets five in a row in any direction (across, up and down or diagonally) they should call out SANTA and the game will end. (If it ends too soon go on to play full card).

Christmas tree tear. Children try to create Christmas trees out of green construction paper by tearing the paper behind their backs. They shouldn't look at their tree until it's finished. Then have everyone share the one they made.

Jingle bells. Place a handful of small jingle bells on a parachute, blanket or tablecloth with the children standing all around it. Have them pick it up by the edges and gently bounce it, trying to keep the bells on the blanket, while you sing the song "Jingle Bells."

Rudolph hokey pokey (wearing the who jing-tinglers craft, below)

Everyone stand up in a circle. Play the "Hokey Pokey" on CD player or sing it. Play the hokey pokey, but use reindeer body parts:

> You put your red nose in, you put your red nose out,
> You put your red nose in, and you shake it all about,
> You do the Rudolph Pokey and you turn yourself around,
> That's what it's all about. Hey!
> (continue with antlers, left hoof, right hoof, tail)

Craft: Who jing-tinglers

Materials needed: Cardboard, hole punch, scissors, thin red ribbon, jingle bells, red and green pony beads, a copy of *How the Grinch Stole Christmas*. Advance preparation: Cut a two by four-inch wide strip of cardboard and punch a hole in the middle of each short end and three holes along one of the long edges. Cut enough six-inch long pieces of ribbon for each child to have three pieces and one ten-inch long piece. At storytime: Read *How the Grinch Stole Christmas* before the following craft. Tie a pony bead to one end of each of three pieces of six-inch ribbon and slip a jingle bell over the fourth piece of ten-inch ribbon and tie a knot with it in the middle. Let the child decorate the cardboard with crayons. Tie the pony beads to the three holes in the long side of the cardboard and then use the piece of ribbon with the jingle bell on it to tie the ends of the cardboard together around the child's ankle. The jing-tingler will be worn during Rudolph hokey pokey.

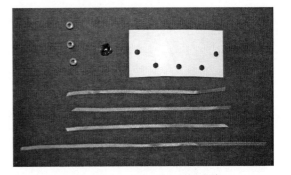

Who jing-tinglers pieces.

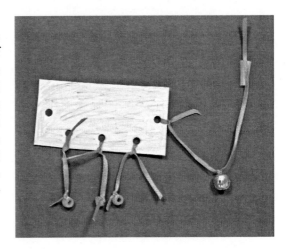

Who jing-tinglers.

Alternative Crafts

Santa face puppet. Use hot glue to attach craft sticks to small white paper plates. Give each child a paper plate on stick, six cotton balls, glue stick, red triangle paper hat, black and red crayons. Have them pull apart the cotton balls a little, then glue them around the bottom edge of the plate as Santa's beard. Glue the red paper triangle hat to the top, then draw his face with the red and black crayons.

Stocking lacing cards. Two red construction paper Christmas stockings with holes punched down one side and up the other, write name across top. Lace with white yarn down one side and up the other and tie off each end

White pipe cleaner snowflakes. Cut white pipe cleaners into some long pieces and some short pieces. Wind the long pieces around each other into an asterisk shape, then wind the short pieces around the ends to look like snowflakes.

Pipe cleaner candy cane ornament. Hand out one 5.5-inch white pipe cleaner and one red pipe cleaner and one strand of gold cord. Demonstrate the winding together of the pipe cleaners and then bending into candy cane shape. Tie loop of cord to hang.

Paper snowflake. Fold white paper circles in half then in half again, then once more so it looks like a cone. Cut shapes all around — triangles, squares, circles. Unfold.

Snack: Wreath cupcakes

Materials needed: Cupcakes, white icing, paper plates, plastic knives, green and red M&Ms or Skittles. Advance preparation: Bake cupcakes. At storytime: Hand each child a cupcake on a paper plate, a dollop of icing, eight green candies and two red candies. Have them place the green candies flat in a circle and the red candies on their sides at the bottom to look like a bow.

Wreath cupcake.

Alternative Snacks

Reindeer cupcakes. Chocolate icing, red candy for nose, brown candies for eyes, broken mini pretzels for antlers.

Tree cookies. Bake cookies in the shape of Christmas trees. At storytime let the children ice them with green icing and decorate with small candies to look like ornaments.

Rudolph cookies. Bake round sugar cookies but press into them small chocolate covered pretzels as the antlers, two brown M&Ms as eyes, and one red M & M as the nose.

Christmas tree cake. Bake a large rectangular cake and then cut it into the shape of a Christmas tree. Cover in green icing and decorate with candies and icing to look like ornaments and lights.

SUGGESTED BOOKS

On holidays with religious significance it's best to choose books to suit your audience.

Biedrzycki, David. *Santa Retires*. 32 pages. 2012. Charlesbridge Publishing. After an exhausting Christmas, Santa and Mrs. Claus head for Mistletoe Island to relax, and have so much fun that Santa decides to retire.

Black, Birdie. *Just Right for Christmas*. 32 pages. 2012. Candlewick Press. A king buys some red cloth to make a gift for his daughter and the leftover cloth doesn't go to waste.

Brett, Jan. *Home for Christmas*. 32 pages. 2011. Penguin Group. A troll runs away from home because he doesn't want to do his chores, but soon discovers that there's no place like home.

Brett, Jan. *The Mitten*. 32 pages. 1989. Penguin Group. The woodland animals find a mitten that a child dropped in the snow.

Brown, Michael. *Santa Mouse*. 18 pages. 1996.

Sandy Creek. Giving is the best gift of all in this story about a lonely mouse with a big imagination.

Buehner, Caralyn. *Snowmen at Christmas*. 32 pages. 2005. Penguin Group. It's Christmas Eve and people are all asleep, but the snowmen outside are stirring.

Carle, Eric. *Dream Snow*. 32 pages. 2000. Penguin Group. On December 24th, the old farmer wonders how Christmas can come when there's no snow.

Clark, Emma Chichester. *Merry Christmas to You, Blue Kangaroo*. 32 pages. 2004. Random House Children's Books. Lily has a present for Blue Kangaroo and he wishes he had a present for her.

Cousins, Lucy. *Merry Christmas Maisy!* 22 pages.

2012. Candlewick Press. Maisy is getting ready for Christmas.

Dewdney, Anna. *Llama Llama Holiday Drama*. 40 pages. 2010. Penguin Group. Llama doesn't like waiting for anything, especially Christmas.

Dicker, Katie. *Christmas*. 24 pages. 2012. Cherry-tree Books. Introduces the reader to many of the traditions surrounding Christmas.

Freedman, Claire. *On This Special Night*. 32 pages. 2009. Scholastic. An introduction to the Christmas Nativity story told from the perspective of a kitten in the barn.

Freeman, Don. *Corduroy's Christmas*. 16 pages. 1992. Penguin Group. A lift the flap book where you see all the things Corduroy does to get ready for Christmas.

Garland, Michael. *Oh, What a Christmas!* 40 pages. 2011. Scholastic. The sleigh harness breaks and Santa's reindeer fly off. Who will save Christmas?

Godfrey, Jan. *Ten Christmas Sheep: A Counting Story*. 28 pages. 2010. Pauline Books & Media. One by one, ten sheep join a shepherd boy on a starry night.

Hills, Tad. *Duck and Goose: It's Time for Christmas*. A board book featuring the adorable pair of Duck and Goose, who are supposed to be getting ready for Christmas but Goose would rather play.

Holabird, Katharine. *Angelina's Christmas*. 32 pages. 2006. Penguin Group. When Angelina sees old Mr. Bell alone at Christmas she wants to bring him some holiday cheer.

Horacek, Petr. *Suzy Goose and the Christmas Star*. 32 pages. 2009. Candlewick Press. Suzy wants to top her tree with a star from the sky.

Keane, Michael. *The Night Santa Got Lost: How NORAD saved Christmas*. 28 pages. 2012. Regnery Publishing. Santa sets out and NORAD is tracking him, but when Santa disappears from the radar screen, how will NORAD help him?

Keats, Ezra Jack. *Little Drummer Boy*. 32 pages. 2000. Penguin Group. An illustrated version of the Christmas carol about the little drummer boy and his offer to play for the baby Jesus.

Litwin, Eric. *Pete the Cat Saves Christmas*. 40 pages. 2012. HarperCollins Publishers. Santa falls ill and Christmas may have to be canceled unless Pete the Cat can save the day.

Milgrim, David. *Santa Duck*. 32 pages. 2010. Penguin Group. Nicholas Duck loves Christmas and is happy to put on the Santa hat he finds at his door, but he doesn't know what to do when his friends start giving him their Christmas lists.

Moore, Clement Clarke. *'Twas the Night Before Christmas*. 26 pages. 2009. Accord Publishing. The popular poem comes to life.

Moore, Tim. *Must Be Santa*. 32 pages. 2011. Random House Children's Books. The song that asks the question, "Who's got a beard that's long and white?" comes to life in this book.

Myron, Vicki. *Dewey's Christmas at the Library*. 40 pages. 2010. Little, Brown Books for Young Readers. Dewey the Cat longs to be part of the holiday fun and after a series of misadventures he finds the best way to be involved.

Numeroff, Laura. *If You Take a Mouse to the Movies*. 40 pages. 2000. HarperCollins Publishers. If you take the mouse to the movies, he'll want to do other things like decorating the Christmas tree, etc. which will lead him back to going to the movies eventually.

O'Connor, Jane. *Fancy Nancy Splendiferous Christmas*. 30 pages. 2009. HarperCollins Publishers. What could be fancier than Christmas?

Piper, Sophie. *The First Christmas*. 32 pages. 2008. Lion UK. A series of Bible stories.

Rey, H.A., Margret Rey and Mary O'Keefe Young. *Merry Christmas, Curious George*. 32 pages. 2012. Houghton Mifflin Harcourt. George goes with his friend to the tree farm to pick out their Christmas tree, and you can be sure that he's curious and there's trouble.

Rosenberg, Amye. *Is It Christmas Yet?* 24 pages. 1990. Random House Children's Books. Everyone is making preparations for Christmas, but Pinky Rabbit wants to know when it's going to be Christmas.

Scarry, Richard. *Richard Scarry's Best Christmas Book Ever*. 44 pages. 2010. Sterling. A series of stories showing how everyone in Busytown celebrates the holiday.

Schulz, Charles M. *Charlie Brown Christmas*. 48 pages. 2011. Running Press Book Publishers. The Peanuts gang learns the true meaning of Christmas.

Scotton, Rob. *Merry Christmas Splat*. 40 pages. 2009. HarperCollins Publishers. It's the night before Christmas, and Splat the Cat wonders if he's been good enough to get a really big present for Christmas.

Seuss, Dr. *How the Grinch Stole Christmas!* 64 pages. 1957. Random House Children's Books. The Grinch hates Christmas and wants to stop it from coming.

Shannon, David. *It's Christmas, David!* 32 pages. 2010. Scholastic. David is getting into all kinds of trouble before Christmas, from playing with ornaments to peeking at gifts.

Shea, Bob. *Dinosaur vs. Santa.* 40 pages. 2012. Hyperion. Dinosaur is getting ready for Santa by facing many challenges and trying not to be naughty.

Shields, Gillian. *Sam's Snowflake.* 32 pages. 2008. Macmillan UK. A warm tale about a little bear, a Christmas surprise and a special snowflake.

Smath, Jerry. *Merry Christmas: Storybook Collection.* 96 pages. 2007. Scholastic. Three stories are included in this collection.

Sturges, Philemon. *The Gift of Christmas.* 32 pages. 1995. North-South Books. Christmas brings many wonderful things, but the newborn infant is the greatest joy.

Thomson, Emma. *Dandelion's Christmas.* 32 pages. 2007. Hodder & Stoughton, Ltd. Dandelion has a lot to do to get ready for Christmas.

Van Allsburg. *The Polar Express.* 32 pages. 2009. Houghton Mifflin Harcourt. A young man tells the story of his childhood and how his belief in Santa Claus came to be.

Wells, Rosemary. *Max's Christmas.* 24 pages. 1986. Penguin Group. Max wants to stay up and see Santa Claus.

Williams, Margery. *Velveteen Rabbit.* 48 pages. 1996. Sterling. A stuffed rabbit's quest to become real.

Wilson, Karma. *Bear Stays Up for Christmas.* 40 pages. 2008. Margaret K. McElderry Books. Bear's friends are determined to see that Bear stays up for Christmas.

Yolen, Jane. *How Do Dinosaurs Say Merry Christmas?* 40 pages. 2012. Scholastic. From decorating the tree to wrapping presents, little dinosaurs love to celebrate Christmas.

Holiday — Hanukkah

Advance planning: To plan for this storytime, find a theme-related song to play during craft and snack times, like "I Had a Little Dreidel." You will also want to select a poem, such as "It's Hanukkah!" from Classroom Junior Website (find it at www.classroomjr.com), along with the books you plan to read. Decorate your space with a menorah and dreidels, sparkling hanging ribbons or a paper chain made of Stars of David in blue and silver, blue cloths.

Introduction to theme: Hanukkah is the Jewish Festival of Lights or Festival of Dedication. The Hebrew word *Hanukkah* means *dedication.* Hanukkah usually falls in the month of December, but occasionally can start in November because it follows the Hebrew lunar calendar instead of our regular calendar. It lasts eight days. The story of Hanukkah is that after three years of struggle, the Jews in Judea defeated the Syrian king Antiochus. The Jewish people held festivities in the Temple of Jerusalem and rededicated it. They found only one container of oil which they used to light their holy lamps. Miraculously, the oil lasted for eight days, which was the time it took to make more oil. They then proclaimed a festival. During Hanukkah, sometimes gifts are exchanged and contributions are made to the poor. Each evening, one additional candle is lit on the Hanukkah menorah at sundown. By the last night there are eight lighted candles. Today we'll read about Hanukkah, play a Hanukkah game, make a Hanukkah craft and eat a Hanukkah snack.

Song: "Oh Hanukkah" lyrics can be found at www.metrolyrics.com.

Game: Dance the hora

Materials needed: CD Player, CD with "Hava Nagila" or other Israeli folk music. Advance preparation: Record music. At storytime: Stand in a circle holding the hands of the people on either side of you. When the music starts, follow the circle as it rotates. Step to the left, passing your right foot behind your left. Then move the left foot beside the right foot. Step to the side again, passing your right foot in front of your left this time. Continue as the circle keeps spinning, adding a little hop to your steps as you go faster. Still holding on to the hands of those next to you, move toward the center of the circle and raise your hands in the air. Lower your hands and move backward. Repeat several times. Resume spinning around the circle.

Alternative Games

Dreidel. Materials needed: wooden dreidels, pennies. Before playing, sing "The Dreidel Song," which can be found at www.metrolyrics.com. Give each child five pennies. Before spinning the dreidel, each child places one of his pennies in the middle of the group. Take turns spinning the dreidel. Depending on which side the dreidel falls, the Hebrew letter that's face up will determine the action taken by the child whose turn it was to spin. Hay means take half, Gimel — take all, Nun — do nothing, Shin — put one in. After every Gimel, everyone puts another penny in. The game ends when someone is out of pennies or set your own time limit. If possible, have small dreidels to give each child one to take home.

Hanukkah latke. Print out bingo sheets on the Internet at www.dltk-cards.com/bingo/ with pictures of Hanukkah things and call it LATKE instead of bingo. Use pennies, crayons or markers to cover the spaces as they're called.

Find the gelt. Hide small round pieces of yellow or gold construction paper in the storytime area and tell the children that gelt (Yiddish for Hanukkah money) is a traditional gift for children on Hanukkah. If they find at least one piece of gelt they'll get to take home a piece of gelt at the end of the storytime. Provide gold foil covered chocolates for that.

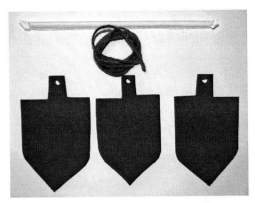

Dreidel mobile pieces.

Craft: Dreidel mobile

Materials needed: Blue sheet foam or blue construction paper, yarn, large straws, scissors, hole punch, tape. Advance preparation: Cut foam or construction paper into Dreidel shapes (three per mobile) and punch holes in the tops. At storytime: Have the children attach varying lengths of yarn to the shapes and hang them from the straw. Tape the yarn to the straw after tying to keep them on and keep spaced.

Alternative Crafts

Craft stick menorah. Have each child glue nine craft sticks as the candles and one as the base down to a piece

Dreidel mobile.

of paper and cut small bits of orange or yellow construction or tissue paper to the tops as the flames.

Buy Magic Scratch dreidels from party store or on the Internet.

Color the menorah. Print pictures of menorahs on the computer and copy. Let the children color them.

Craft stick Star of David. Use hot glue to glue together craft sticks in Star of David pattern. Let the children decorate them with markers, crayons, glue small gemstones or stickers on them. Hang from the top with a blue piece of yarn. You can also have the children glue craft sticks onto a piece of construction paper in the Star of David shape and then decorate.

Snack: Edible menorah

Materials needed: Large pretzel rods, celery and/or carrots, raisins, paper plates. Advance preparation: Cut celery and/or carrots into thin sticks. At storytime: Give each child a paper plate with one large pretzel rod, nine celery and/or carrot sticks and nine raisins. Have them lay the pretzel rod horizontally to form the menorah base, then the celery or carrot sticks vertically to represent the candles and the raisins at the tops of the sticks to be the flames. (You can also use marshmallows with pretzel sticks and raisins instead.)

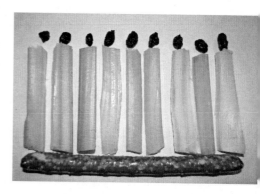

Edible menorah.

Alternative Snacks

Dreidels made of marshmallow, pretzel stick, Hershey's kisses, sprinkles and icing. Gently stick the pretzel into the marshmallow. Coat the marshmallow with icing and dip it in sprinkles on the sides and attach the Hershey's Kiss to the opposite side of the pretzel stick.

Dreidel-shaped cookies cut with cookie cutter. Let children decorate with icing and small candies.

Jelly doughnuts are often eaten on Hanukkah because they are usually fried in oil and they're called sufganiyot.

Latkes are often eaten on Hanukkah. They are basically potato pancakes made with shredded potatoes and matzo meal and fried in oil.

Chocolate gelt. The giving of gelt (Yiddish for Hanukkah money) is traditional on Hanukkah. It is easy to find chocolate coins wrapped in gold foil and these are often given as gelt nowadays.

Applesauce is often served with latkes. Could make homemade applesauce or buy it in small containers.

SUGGESTED BOOKS

On holidays with religious significance it's best to choose books to suit your audience.

Alko, Salina. *Daddy Christmas and Hanukkah Mama.* 32 pages. 2012. Knopf Books for Young Readers. A celebration of blended families.

Auerbach, Annie. *Eight Chanukah Lights.* 18 pages. 2004. Dalmatian Publishing Group. Count up from one to eight as lights appear on the menorah with each turning page.

Baum, Maxie. *I Have a Little Dreidel.* 32 pages. 2006. Scholastic. A retelling of the classic Hanukkah song.

Bullard, Lisa. *Caleb's Hanukkah.* 24 pages. 2012. Millbrook Pr Trade. Find out the different ways people celebrate Hanukkah.

Capucilli, Alyssa Satin. *Biscuit's Hanukkah.* 16 pages. 2005. HarperCollins Publishers. A board book where Biscuit the puppy makes a menorah.

Cooper, Alexandra. *Spin the Dreidel.* 14 pages. 2004. Little Simon. A dreidel attached to the book explains the dreidel game.

Da Costa, Deborah. *Hanukkah Moon.* 32 pages. 2007. Lerner Publishing Group. When Isobel is invited to Aunt Luisa's for Hanukkah, she's not sure what to expect.

Davis, Linda. *A Chanukah Story.* 24 pages. 2004. Feldheim Publishers. A book that prepares children for Chanukah, told in rhyme.

dePaola, Tomie. *My First Chanukah.* 12 pages. 1989. Penguin Group. A board book describing the traditional celebration of Chanukah.

Edwards, Michelle. *The Hanukkah Trike.* 24 pages. 2010. Whitman, Albert & Company. Gabi loved Hanukkah so much she named her new tricycle Hanukkah. On her first try at riding it she falls off but perseveres by remembering the story of Hanukkah.

Ehrlich, Amy. *The Story of Hanukkah.* 24 pages. 1989. Penguin Group. Picture book introduction to Hanukkah, the festival of lights.

Fishman, Cathy Goldberg. *On Hanukkah.* 40 pages. 2001. Aladdin. A family Hanukkah celebration.

Freeman, Don. *Happy Hanukkah, Corduroy!* 14 pages. 2009. Penguin Group. Celebrate the festival of lights with Corduroy the bear.

Gellman, Ellie. *It's Hanukkah.* 12 pages. 1985. Kar-Ben Publishing. During Hanukkah, Gila counts apples, chocolate coins and candles.

Gellman, Ellie. *Jeremy's Dreidel.* 32 pages. 2012. Kar-Ben Publishing. At the dreidel workshop, Jeremy's friends think he's molding a special code on his clay dreidel when he's making it for his father, who is blind.

Glaser, Linda. *The Borrowed Hanukkah Latkes.* 32 1997. Whitman, Albert & Company. A young girl finds a way to include her elderly neighbor in her family's holiday celebration.

Ho, Jannie. *Light the Menorah.* 12 pages. 2009. Penguin Group. Light the menorah with pull tabs and learn the story of Hanukkah.

Holub, Joan. *Light the Candles: a Hanukkah Lift the Flap Book.* 16 pages. 2000. Penguin Group.

Hanukkah is here and there are so many fun things to do.

Howland, Naomi. *Latkes, Latkes, Good to Eat.* 32 pages. 2004. Houghton Mifflin Harcourt. Sadie and her four little brothers are poor and are always hungry. But on Hanukkah, a magic frying pan appears. It then becomes a take on the Sorcerer's Apprentice when her little brothers misuse the pan.

Kaiser, Cecily. *On the First Night of Hanukkah.* 24 pages. 2007. Scholastic. A twist on the Twelve Days of Christmas song.

Katz, Karen. *Where Is Baby's Dreidel?* 14 pages. 2007. Little Simon. A board book with flaps to lift to find baby's dreidel.

Kimmelman, Leslie. *Hanukkah Lights, Hanukkah Nights.* 24 pages. 1999. HarperCollins Publishers. An extended family celebrates the eight nights of Hanukkah.

Kroll, Steven. *The Hanukkah Mice.* 37 pages. 2007. Cavendish, Marshall Corporation. The Mouse Family explores the dollhouse when the family is asleep and each night enjoys a special Hanukkah treat.

Kropf, Latifa Berry. *It's Hanukkah Time!* 24 pages. 2004. Kar-Ben Publishing. A preschool classroom prepares for a Hanukkah party.

Lanton, Sandy. *Lots of Latkes: A Hanukkah Story.* 32 pages. 2003. Kar-Ben Publishing. A board book with elderly characters who are invited to come eat latkes and each plans to bring something to go with them, but things go wrong so they all end up bringing more latkes.

Lister, Claire. *My First Hanukkah.* 32 pages. 2001. DK Publishing. A board book that presents the origins of the Festival of Lights.

Martin, David. *Hanukkah Lights.* 26 pages. 2009. Candlewick Press. Simple language and sweet illustrations in this board book bring the holiday to life.

Martinez, Debbie. *Celebrating Hanukkah: Eight Nights.* 16 pages. 1999. Creative Teaching Press. A Learn to Read book that explains the holiday in very simple terms.

Marx, David F. *Chanukah.* 32 pages. 2006. Scholastic Library Publishing. An early reader book that asks the reader if he celebrates the holiday and then goes on to give a brief history and description of it.

Melmed, Laura Krauss. *Eight Winter Nights: A Family Hanukkah Book.* 32 pages. 2010. Chronicle Books. A collection of poems.

Moorman, Margaret. *Light the Lights! A Story About Celebrating Hanukkah and Christmas.* 42 pages. 1999. Scholastic. Every year Emma and her family celebrate two holidays: Hanukkah and Christmas.

Newman, Leslea. *Eight Nights of Chanukah*. 24 pages. 2005. Harry N. Abrams. Incorporating the idea of the 12 Days of Christmas song into a Chanukah book.

Newman, Leslea. *Runaway Dreidel*. 32 pages. 2007. Square Fish. When a dreidel takes off through a boy's living room, readers are taken on a runaway adventure through city streets.

Novack, Danielle. *My Two Holidays: A Hanukkah and Christmas Story*. 32 pages. 2010. Scholastic. Celebrate two special holidays with one special family.

Oberman, Sheldon. *By the Hanukkah Light*. 32 pages. 2003. Boyds Mill Press. When the family gathers for Hanukkah, grandpa tells his own story of the holiday from World War II.

Randall, Ronne. *The Hanukkah Mice*. 20 pages. 2002. Chronicle Books. While searching for the Hanukkah lights, three mouse children and their mother discover different treasures each night.

Rauchwerger, Diane Levin. *Dinosaur on Hanukkah*. 24 pages. 2005. Lerner Publishing Group. A dinosaur comes to a young boy's house to help him celebrate Hanukkah.

Rosen, Michael J. *Chanukah Lights*. 16 pages. 2011. Candlewick Press. A Robert Sabuda pop up book that follows the Festival of Lights through place and time.

Rosenfeld, Dina. *A Chanukah Story for Night Number Three*. 30 pages. 2009. Hachai Publishing. A tall tale told in rhyme relates the story of a boy whose birthday occasionally falls on night three of Chanukah.

Roth, Susan L. *Hanukkah, Oh Hanukkah*. 24 pages. 2006. Penguin Group. A family of mice celebrates the eight days of Hanukkah.

Rouss, Sylvia A. *Sammy Spider's First Hanukkah*. 32 pages. 1993. Lerner Publishing Group. Sammy wants to participate in the Hanukkah festivities, but he's a spider and they spin webs, not dreidels.

Schotter, Roni. *Hanukkah*. 22 pages. 2003. Little, Brown Books for Young Readers. Describes the meaning and traditions of Hanukkah.

Silberg, Francis Barry. *The Story of Chanukah*. 26 pages. 2010. Ideals Publications. The real story of Chanukah.

Silverman, Erica. *The Hanukkah Hop!* 32 pages. 2011. Simon & Schuster Books for Young Readers. Lively text celebrating the Festival of Lights.

Sper, Emily. *Hanukkah: A Counting Book in English, Hebrew and Yiddish*. 28 pages. 2003. Scholastic. Die cut candles and artwork visually present the holiday of Hanukkah in this counting book.

Spinner, Stephanie. *It's a Miracle! A Hanukkah Storybook*. 48 pages. 2007. Aladdin. Every night of Hanukkah, Owen's grandmother tells a different bedtime story.

Springer, Sally. *Let's Make Latkes*. 12 pages. 1991. Kar-Ben Publishing. Pictures show how latke ingredients are bought, mixed, fried and eaten.

Trueit, Trudi Strain. *Hanukkah*. 32 pages. 2006. Scholastic Library Publishing. Simple text and many pictures describe the celebration of Hanukkah.

Yolen, Jane. *How Do Dinosaurs Say Happy Chanukah?* 40 pages. 2012. Scholastic. The dinosaurs romp through Chanukah with melting gelt and tumbling dreidels.

Yoon, Salina. *My First Menorah*. 20 pages. 2005. Little Simon. A board book with candle shaped pages that teaches about the eight days of Hanukkah.

Zalben, Jane Breskin. *Pearl's Eight Days of Chanukah: With a Story and Activity for Each Night*. 40 pages. 1998. Simon & Schuster Books for Young Readers. Pearl is looking forward to celebrating Chanukah with her family, but not with her cousins.

Ziefert, Harriet. *Hanukkah Haiku*. 32 pages. 2008. Blue Apple Books. Simple poetry that celebrates the eight nights of Hanukkah.

Zucker, Johnny. *Eight Candles to Light: A Chanukah Story*. 24 pages. 2002. Barron's Education Series. Describes a typical family celebration of the Festival of Lights.

Appendix A: Helpful Websites

www.allkidsnetwork.com • Crafts and games. Also has worksheets and puzzles.

www.alphabet-soup.net • Themed activities, recipes, songs and poems.

www.amazon.com • Mp3 files of songs that can be downloaded inexpensively and stored on computer in ITunes, where they can be made into monthly playlists that can be burned on disks or transferred to IPods.

www.americangrandma.com • Recipes, poetry, activities, stories and reading suggestions.

www.angelfire.com/az/alphabet/fingerplays.html • Themed snacks and crafts.

www.apples4theteacher.com • Crafts, games and poetry.

www.authorsden.com • Poetry. Search first for poetry, then childrens.

www.thebestkidsbooksite.com • Themed books and crafts.

www.birthdaypartyideas.com • Themed birthday party ideas that include decorations, activities, crafts and snacks.

www.bussongs.com • Kids' songs and nursery rhymes.

www.canteach.ca • Use the Elementary Resources tab and find recipes, poetry, games.

www.charlesghigna.blogspot.com • Poetry — use the poems for children tab.

www.childfun.com • Activities, games, crafts.

www.cleverkidsparty.com • Games, recipes, crafts.

www.creativecrafts4kids.com • Crafts.

www.dltk-cards.com/bingo/ • Bingo cards for many different themes.

www.dltk-holidays.com • Crafts, poetry. Also worksheets, cards, coloring pages.

www.dltk-kids.com • Crafts, songs, poetry. Also coloring pages and worksheets.

www.dltk-teach.com (Links to www.dltk-kids.com) • Crafts, songs, poetry.

www.dawlishteddybears.co.uk/Pages/TeddyBear Poems.aspx • Teddy bear poems.

www.easycupcakes.com • Cupcake decorating ideas.

www.ehow.com • A clearing house for other websites for games, activities, recipes.

www.english-for-students.com • Use the Nursery Rhymes tab.

www.everythingpreschool.com • Some themes' songs, crafts, activities.

www.famouspoetsandpoems.com • Poetry.

www.findsounds.com • Recorded sounds that can be downloaded and burned to disks to use in games and activities.

www.firstpalette.com • Crafts.

www.gigglepoetry.com • Poetry.

www.itunes.com (Links to www.apple.com/itunes) • Download the Itunes program in order to store Mp3 files of songs. The songs can be downloaded inexpensively and stored on computer, where they can be made into monthly playlists that can be burned on disks or transferred to iPods.

www.kidnkaboodle.net • Use the curriculum theme ideas. Songs, crafts, activities by theme.

www.kidsongs.com • The Kid's Tube tab has videos of kids' songs. Downloads tab has mp3 files available for sale. Listen to songs, view lyrics.

www.kinderart.com • Crafts.

www.kinderkorner.com • Poems, books, crafts, songs by theme.

www.kinderteacher.com • Teachers sitemap tab takes you to months of the year, leading to different themes. Also sales of flannel boards.

www.kingpoetry.com • Graeme King's poetry.

www.k12.hi.us/~shasincl/poems_ocean.html • Ocean poetry.

www.levelwise.org • Poetry.

www.lifeinaskillet.com • Recipes.

www.lyrics007.com • Song lyrics.

www.macaronisoup.com • Music and movement activities.

www.mamalisa.com • Songs and rhymes from around the world.

www.maxilyrics.com • Song lyrics.

www.metrolyrics.com • Song lyrics.

www.middlemiss.org/lit/authors/denniscj/book forkids/circus.hrml • The Circus poem.

www.mrsjonesroom.com • Songs, activities, games.

www.netpoets.com • Poetry.

www.nonsenselit.org • Silly poetry like Edward Lear's.

www.perfectlypreschool.com • Activities, games, songs and crafts.

www.perpetualpreschool.com • Songs, snacks, games, crafts by theme.

www.perrypubliclibrary.org • Book search.

www.poems.greet2k.com • Poetry.

www.poems.writers-network.com • Poetry. Search by poem or poet.

www.poetry4kids.com • Kenn Nesbitt's poetry.

www.poetryfoundation.org • Poetry.

www.the-preschool-professor.com • Activities, crafts, games, snacks, songs.

www.prekfun.com • Book suggestions, crafts, games, songs.

www.preschooleducation.com • Games, snacks, books, crafts.

www.preschoolrainbow.org • Activities, songs, fingerplays, crafts.

www.readinglady.com • Poetry.

www.richardmacwilliam.com • Poetry.

www.scoutsongs.com • Song lyrics.

www.scrapbook.com • Use the Resources tab to find poems and nursery rhymes.

www.shelsilversteinpoems.wordpress.com • Shel Silverstein poems.

www.songsforteaching.com • Song lyrics. Can also buy recordings and sheet music.

www.spoonful.com • Crafts, recipes, games

www.squidoo.com • Search poetry for links to sites.

www.teacher.scholastic.com • Use the Lesson Plan tab to search for themes, then in the themes find activities, crafts, books.

www.teachingfirst.net • A starting point for other websites with resources that include lesson plans with activities.

www.thehalloweenday.com • Halloween crafts, quotes, humor.

www.wonderworkshopsongs.com • Song lyrics.

www.wrensworld.com • Poems and games.

Appendix B: Storytime Template

Set the Scene Props: _____

_____

_____

_____

_____

Group Gathering (Group arrival song, name introductions, assembly of Friend):

_____

_____

_____

_____

Introduction to Theme: _____

_____

_____

_____

Book 1 (longest book): _____

Book 2 (short or non-fiction book about the theme): _____

Book 3 (medium length storybook): _____

Song or Fingerplay: _____

_____

_____

Game 1:_____

_____

_____

_____

_____

Poem or Book 4 (short book):_____

_____

Game 2:_____

_____

_____

_____

_____

Book 5 (short book):_____

Craft:_____

_____

_____

_____

_____

Theme-related song to play while assembling craft:_____

Snack:_____

_____

_____

_____

_____

Book 6 (read while children are eating their snack):_____

Closing:
    Cleanup, list of books from this week's theme, announce next week's theme, calendar, other announcements (upcoming events, discounts, suggestions for books to take home)

Suggested Reading

Chanko, Pamela. *101 Content-Building Fingerplays, Action Rhymes and Songs*. Scholastic. 2009. Fingerplays listed by circle time, concept and theme.

Charner, Kathy, ed. *The Giant Encyclopedia of Circle Time and Group Activities for Children 3 to 6*. Gryphon House, Inc. 1996. Content divided into major themes, then activities. In each activity there are instructions plus a list of related books.

Charner, Kathy, Maureen Murphy and Charlie Clark, eds. *The Giant Encyclopedia of Lesson Plans for Children 3 to 6*. Gryphon House, Inc. 2008. Divides content by overall theme, then subcategories. Suggested books, snack and song, along with a circle time activity. Provides a learning objective.

Cullum, Carolyn N. *The Storytime Sourcebook*. Neal-Schuman Publishers. 1990. Includes lists of books, films, crafts, activities and songs. It refers you to the original source to get instruction.

Emerson, Sally, compiler. *Nursery Rhyme Songbook*. Kingfisher Books. 1991. Words and music for baby games, action rhymes, favorite first songs, dancing games and lullabies.

Kladder, Jer. *Story Hour*. McFarland. 1995. Themed programs that have subcategories and include filmstrips, books, fingerplays, poetry, songs and some activities that include crafts.

Nichols, Judy. *Storytimes for Two-Year-Olds*. American Library Association. 1998. Program themes that include a list of books, a rhyme or fingerplay, a craft and a suggestion for parents to follow up at home.

Pica, Rae. *Great Games for Young Children*. Gryphon House, Inc. 2006. Group games for children that are non-competitive. Some can be done in a circle, some musical, some teach a concept, others are cooperative and some are to play outdoors.

Press, Judy. *The Little Hands Art Book*. Williamson Publishing. 1994. Art projects with instructions listed by material. Gives a list of materials needed, illustrated instruction and suggestions for additional creative fun.

Sadler, Linda. *101 Quick and Easy Party Ideas for Kids*. Creative Kids Products. 2005. Craft, game and treat ideas for children's parties that can be adapted for storytime. Photo of finished craft, supply list, advance preparation and instruction. Games list supplies needed, advance preparation, objective and instruction. Treats have a photo, give a supply list and instruction.

Schiller, Pam, and Kay Hastings. *The Complete Resource Book for Preschoolers*. Gryphon House, Inc. 1998. Divides information by theme, then subcategory offering learning centers with an activity that addresses a different skill. Reading suggestions and circle time ideas.

Sitarz, Paula Gaj. *More Picture Book Story Hours from Parties to Pets*. Libraries Unlimited, Inc. 1990. 22 additional themed storytime programs with fingerplays, book suggestions, poems and activities.

Sitarz, Paula Gaj. *Picture Book Story Hours from Birthdays to Bears*. Libraries Unlimited, Inc. 1987. Contains 22 themed storytime programs with general instruction as an introduction. For each theme there are suggestions for a fingerplay, poem and a list of books both to read aloud and to talk about, plus a song and a filmstrip.

Totten, Kathryn. *Storytime Crafts*. Alleyside Press. 1998. An introduction to storytime plus stories to tell, along with themed programs that include a book list, fingerplay, song and a craft.

Warner, Penny. *Kids' Party Games and Activities*. Meadowbrook Press. 1993. Offers instructions for games listed by age (2–5, 6–9 or 10–12) and then by traditional, contemporary, group, outings and entertainers. Basic instruction for each game with options.

Index